CAMBRIDGE STUDIES IN
ANGLO-SAXON ENGLAND

24

ÆLFRIC'S LETTER TO THE
MONKS OF EYNSHAM

CAMBRIDGE STUDIES IN ANGLO-SAXON ENGLAND

FOUNDING GENERAL EDITORS:
MICHAEL LAPIDGE AND SIMON KEYNES

CURRENT GENERAL EDITORS:
SIMON KEYNES AND ANDY ORCHARD

Volumes published

1. *Anglo-Saxon Crucifixion Iconography and the Art of the Monastic Revival* by BARBARA C. RAW
2. *The Cult of the Virgin Mary in Anglo-Saxon England* by MARY CLAYTON
3. *Religion and Literature in Western England, 600–800* by PATRICK SIMS-WILLIAMS
4. *Visible Song: Transitional Literacy in Old English Verse* by KATHERINE O'BRIEN O'KEEFFE
5. *The Metrical Grammar of* Beowulf by CALVIN B. KENDALL
6. *The Irish Tradition in Old English Literature* by CHARLES D. WRIGHT
7. *Anglo-Saxon Medicine* by M. L. CAMERON
8. *The Poetic Art of Aldhelm* by ANDY ORCHARD
9. *The Old English Lives of St Margaret* by MARY CLAYTON and HUGH MAGENNIS
10. *Biblical Commentaries from the Canterbury School of Theodore and Hadrian* by BERNHARD BISCHOFF and MICHAEL LAPIDGE
11. *Archbishop Theodore: Commemorative Studies on his Life and Influence* edited by MICHAEL LAPIDGE
12. *Interactions of Thought and Language in Old English Poetry* by PETER CLEMOES
13. *The Textuality of Old English Poetry* by CAROL BRAUN PASTERNACK
14. *The 'Laterculus Malalianus' and the School of Archbishop Theodore* by JANE STEVENSON
15. *The Text of the Old Testament in Anglo-Saxon England* by RICHARD MARSDEN
16. *Old English Biblical Verse* by PAUL G. REMLEY
17. *The Hymns of the Anglo-Saxon Church* by INGE B. MILFULL
18. *Scenes of Community in Old English Poetry* by HUGH MAGENNIS
19. *Two Old English Apocrypha and their Manuscript Source: 'The Gospel of Nichodemus' and 'The Avenging of the Saviour'* edited by J. E. CROSS
20. *The Composition of Old English Poetry* by H. MOMMA
21. *Trinity and Incarnation in Anglo-Saxon Art and Thought* by BARBARA C. RAW
22. *Heathen Gods in Old English Literature* by RICHARD NORTH
23. *Beowulf and Old Germanic Metre* by GEOFFREY RUSSOM

ÆLFRIC'S LETTER TO THE MONKS OF EYNSHAM

CHRISTOPHER A. JONES
Idaho State University

PUBLISHED BY THE PRESS SYNDICATE OF THE UNIVERSITY OF CAMBRIDGE
The Pitt Building, Trumpington Street, Cambridge CB2 1RP, United Kingdom

CAMBRIDGE UNIVERSITY PRESS
The Edinburgh Building, Cambridge, CB2 2RU, UK
40 West 20th Street, New York, NY 10011–4211, USA
10 Stamford Road, Oakleigh, Melbourne 3166, Australia

© Christopher A. Jones 1998

This book is in copyright. Subject to statutory exception and to the provisions of relevant collective licensing agreements, no reproduction of any part may take place without the written permission of Cambridge University Press.

First published 1998

Printed in the United Kingdom at the University Press, Cambridge

Typeset in Garamond 11/13 pt. [CE]

A catalogue record for this book is available from the British Library

Library of Congress cataloguing in publication data
Jones, Christopher A.
Ælfric's letter to the monks of Eynsham / Christopher A. Jones.
p. cm. – (Cambridge Studies in Anglo-Saxon England; 24)
Revision of a doctoral thesis, University of Toronto, 1995.
Includes bibliographical references and indexes.
ISBN 0 521 63011 8 (hardback)
1. Ælfric, Abbot of Eynsham – Correspondence. 2. Monastic and religious life – England – Eynsham – History – Middle Ages, 600–1500.
3. Latin letters, Medieval and modern – England – Eynsham – History and criticism.
4. Latin letters, Medieval and modern – England – Eynsham – Translations into English.
5. Abbots – England – Eynsham – Correspondence. 6. Eynsham Abbey (Eynsham, England) 7. Anglo Saxons – England – Eynsham. 8. Civilization, Anglo-Saxon.
I. Title. II Series.
PR1524.A64J66   1998
271′.102–dc21
[B]   97-39146   CIP

ISBN 0 521 63011 8 hardback

Contents

	Acknowledgements	page vi
	List of abbreviations	ix
1	The Eynsham 'letter' and the study of Ælfric	1
2	Structure and sources	18
3	The manuscript	71
4	Critical and editorial history	92
	Editorial principles	103
	Ælfric's *Letter to the Monks of Eynsham*: text and translation	110
	Commentary	150
	Appendix	229
	Bibliography	231
	Index of liturgical formae	241
	General index	245

Acknowledgements

The demands of research may sometimes tempt even the most willing student to echo, with new meaning, A. E. Housman's lament, 'The time lost, the tissues wasted, in doing anew the brainwork done before by others . . . are in our brief irreparable life disheartening to think of.' Preparation of this book has often meant recourse to less familiar disciplines wherein, as a virtual beginner, I depended heavily on the work of previous scholars. If today I can claim that such remedial 'brainwork' was not too often 'disheartening', it is because time and again, and oftener by luck than merit, the task has led to acquaintance with some truly delightful, generous people. I am glad for the opportunity here to acknowledge their contribution to this work and to own as mine whatever faults remain in it.

This book is an extensive revision of a doctoral thesis submitted at the University of Toronto in the summer of 1995. The topic came *de foris*, however, from Milton McC. Gatch of Union Theological Seminary, who would eventually do me the additional favour of acting as external examiner in the thesis defence. What is more, in suggesting the topic he effectively handed over a project that he had planned to undertake himself, and on which he had already profitably expended some effort. While I cannot hope to have finished the job as expertly as he would have, a determination that his generosity should not have cost the scholarly world too dearly has been both a goad and an inspiration.

But even a good topic and earnest intentions would not have come to much without the guidance of a supportive thesis committee. I doubt that there exists a more insightful and good-humoured supervisor than Roberta Frank, whose office door was always open and who, by her example, defined for me all the aptitudes required of an Anglo-Saxonist

Acknowledgements

and professional scholar. The thesis was co-directed by David Townsend, whose enviable knowledge of Latin and whose instincts as a translator, combined with a salutary wit, solved many a problem and helped put many more in proper perspective. On that most difficult of topics, medieval liturgy, I was fortunate to have as a guide Roger E. Reynolds, who criticized much of the thesis in draft and offered me materials from his own files of unpublished research. Antonette DiPaolo Healey brought to the role of advisor her characteristic enthusiasm, her eye for detail and, most memorably, her warm welcome any time my work took me to the offices of the *Dictionary of Old English*. There, as if the *Dictionary*'s collection of books and microfilms were not a sufficient lure, my visits were often doubly rewarded by the help of David McDougall and Ian McDougall, whose knowledge is, I am convinced, as inexhaustible as their generous willingness to share it.

On numerous specific questions, other teachers and fellow students at Toronto provided welcome help, especially Michael Allen, Don Chapman, Robert Deshman, E. Ruth Harvey, Andrew Hughes, Hartwig Meyer, Marc Ozon, David Pelteret and Georges Whalen. To include others who, during my schooling and since, have kindly responded to queries made in person, by post or electronic mail, I would also thank James E. Cross, Allen Frantzen, Scott Gwara, Joyce Hill, Lucia Kornexl, Ursula Lenker, John C. Pope and Greg Rose. I owe special debts to Mildred Budny, David Dumville, Simon Keynes, Hans Sauer and Patrick Wormald, who took the extra pains to send typescripts or photocopies of work as yet unpublished or otherwise unavailable to me. Finally, in the long course of transforming the thesis into a volume in this series, I have appreciated Michael Lapidge's scrupulous editorial advice and his unflagging encouragement whenever the process threatened to grind to a halt.

For their permission to re-edit Ælfric's text, I thank the Master and Fellows of Corpus Christi College, Cambridge, and, for their warm hospitality during my two-week visit to the Parker Library, Gil Cannell, Catherine Hall and Patricia Aske. Permission to print unique passages from Salisbury, Cathedral Library, 154, has been granted by the Dean and Chapter of Salisbury Cathedral. Preliminary work on that manuscript was done from microfilm seen on a visit to the very welcoming Hill Monastic Manuscript Library, and when fortune at last brought the opportunity to examine the book *in situ*, the librarian of Salisbury Cathedral, Suzanne Eward, graciously accommodated my visit. Additional microfilms were

Acknowledgements

provided by Corpus Christi College and Trinity College, Cambridge, and the Bibliothèque Municipale in Boulogne-sur-Mer. In North America, most of my research was conducted at the Library of the Pontifical Institute of Mediaeval Studies, Toronto, where I was assisted in every possible way by librarians Nancy Kovacs and Caroline Suma. More recently I have become absolutely dependent on the Interlibrary Loan offices at Idaho State University, where Nancy Anthony and Joan Juskie-Nellis routinely track down even my most obscure requests with amazing speed.

The research for this book would not have been possible without the financial support I received as a graduate student from the Connaught Foundation, the Centre for Medieval Studies, the Provincial Government of Ontario and, dearest of all, Massey College. A grant from the Faculty Research Committee at Idaho State University has at last enabled me to finish the project by generously funding a research trip to the United Kingdom.

The most personal acknowledgements usually come last in remarks such as these, perhaps because the formulas of gratitude are, for this group, least equal to the task. As the only expression of thanks even remotely adequate, then, the dedication of this book I offer to my brothers and, most of all, to my mother and father, who alone know how much its completion owes to their selflessness and encouragement, through moments both 'disheartening' and rewarding, down to this very day.

Abbreviations

AEOLO	*Amalarii episcopi opera liturgica omnia*, ed. Hanssens
AH	*Analecta hymnica medii aeui*, ed. Dreves *et al.*
AMS	*Antiphonale missarum sextuplex*, ed. Hesbert
ASE	*Anglo-Saxon England*
BaP	Bibliothek der angelsächsischen Prosa
BL	British Library
Brief(e)	Ælfric's pastoral letter(s), numbered as in *Hirtenbriefe*, ed. Fehr
CAO	*Corpus antiphonalium officii*, ed. Hesbert
CCCC	Cambridge, Corpus Christi College
CCCM	Corpus Christianorum, Continuatio Mediaevalis
CCM	Corpus Consuetudinum Monasticarum
CCSL	Corpus Christianorum, Series Latina
CH I	*The Homilies of the Anglo-Saxon Church*, vol. I, ed. Thorpe
CH II	*Ælfric's Catholic Homilies: The Second Series*, ed. Godden
CSASE	Cambridge Studies in Anglo-Saxon England
CUL	Cambridge University Library
DEC	*De ecclesiastica consuetudine*
DMA	*Dictionary of the Middle Ages*, ed. Strayer
DR	*Downside Review*
EC	*The Cartulary of the Abbey of Eynsham*, ed. Salter
EEMF	Early English Manuscripts in Facsimile
EETS	Early English Text Society
EHR	*English Historical Review*
HBS	Henry Bradshaw Society
Hughes	Hughes, *Medieval Manuscripts for Mass and Office*
Hymnar	Gneuss, *Hymnar und Hymnen im englischen Mittelalter*

List of abbreviations

IBA	*Institutio beati Amalarii de ecclesiasticis officiis*
Lect.discr.long.	*Lectiones a textu discrepantes longiores* (variants of Amalarius's *Liber officialis*), in AEOLO II, 545–65
Lib.off.	Amalarius of Metz, *Liber officialis*, in AEOLO II, 13–543
LME	Ælfric's *Letter to the Monks of Eynsham*
LS	Ælfric's *Lives of Saints*, ed. Skeat
Milfull	Milfull, *The Hymns of the Anglo-Saxon Church*
n.s.	new series
ODCC	*The Oxford Dictionary of the Christian Church*, ed. Cross and Livingstone
OR	*Ordo romanus / Ordines romani*, ed. Andrieu
o.s.	original series
PL	*Patrologia Latina*
PMLA	*Publications of the Modern Language Association of America*
PRG	*Le Pontifical romano-germanique*, ed. Vogel and Elze
R1	the *Retractatio prima* of Amalarius's *Liber officialis*
R1(Sa)	the version of *R1* in Salisbury, Cathedral Library, 154
RC	*Regularis concordia Anglicae nationis*, ed. Symons and Spath
RC (Fa)	*Regularis concordia* in London, BL, Cotton Faustina B. iii, 159r–198v (+ London, BL, Cotton Tiberius A. iii, 177r–v)
RC (Kornexl)	*Die Regularis Concordia und ihre altenglische Interlinearversion*, ed. Kornexl
RC (Symons)	*Regularis concordia Anglicae nationis monachorum sanctimonialiumque: The Monastic Agreement of the Monks and Nuns of the English Nation*, ed. and trans. Symons
RC (Ti)	*Regularis concordia* in London, BL, Cotton Tiberius A. iii, 3r–27v
Roper	Roper, *Medieval English Benedictine Liturgy*
RSB	*Benedicti regula*, ed. Hanslik
S	*Anglo-Saxon Charters*, ed. Sawyer
Sacr.Greg.	*Le Sacramentaire grégorien*, ed. Deshusses
SASH	Studies in Anglo-Saxon History
Schmidt	Schmidt, *Hebdomada Sancta*
SEEH	Studies in Early English History
s.s.	supplementary series
Tolhurst	Tolhurst, *An Introduction to the English Monastic Breviaries*
TUEP	Münchener Universitätsschriften, Texte und Untersuchungen zur englischen Philologie

1

The Eynsham 'letter' and the study of Ælfric

Even at the height of his literary activity, to the question 'What do you do?', Ælfric of Eynsham (c. 955–c. 1010) is easily imagined responding in words like those of his fictitious monastic novice in the Latin *Colloquy*, or classroom dialogue. Ælfric there has the boy say, when confronted with this question ('Quid habes operis?'): 'Professus sum monachus, et psallam omni die septem sinaxes cum fratribus, et occupatus sum lectionibus et cantu.'[1] Though the *Colloquy* then proceeds to describe the work of numerous other, secular professions, the schoolmaster eventually returns to the novice, this time to pose a different question: which of the occupations is best? The boy again answers in terms of which Ælfric himself doubtless approves: 'mihi uidetur seruitium Dei inter istas artes primatum tenere, sicut legitur in euangelio: "Primum querite regnum Dei et iustitiam eius, et hęc omnia adicientur uobis."'[2] Such assertions of primacy are of course commonplace in monastic literature, and the *Colloquy*, a school exercise, hardly presented its author an occasion to expound a nuanced theory of monkhood. The novice's words nevertheless remind us of an obvious yet often forgotten truth: to Ælfric, the 'greatest

---

[1] 'I am a professed monk, and every day I shall sing the seven liturgical hours with my brothers, and I keep busy with reading and chanting' (*Colloquy*, ed. Garmonsway, p. 19, lines 13–15).

[2] 'I think that the service of God holds chief place among these skills, as it says in the gospel: "Seek ye first the kingdom of God and his righteousness, and all these things will be added unto you" [cf. Matt. VI.33]' (*Colloquy*, ed. Garmonsway, p. 39, lines 213–16). On the centrality of monasticism in this dialogue, see E. R. Anderson, 'Social Idealism in Ælfric's "Colloquy"', *ASE* 3 (1974), 153–62, at pp. 158–9, and J. Ruffing, 'The Labor Structure of Ælfric's Colloquy', in *The Work of Work: Servitude, Slavery, and Labor in Medieval England*, ed. A. J. Frantzen and D. Moffat (Glasgow, 1994), pp. 55–70.

prose writer of the Anglo-Saxon period',[3] the role of author was inevitably subsumed into his vocation as a monk and mass-priest, whose chief occupation was to worship God in the liturgy and carry out other duties laid down by the *Rule* of St Benedict. The passing of centuries and fortunate survival of Ælfric's many Old English homilies have ironically reversed the hierarchy of occupations that he would have considered properly his. Recovery of this largely implicit context of Ælfric's 'authorship' is exceedingly hard, and not only because crucial evidence has been lost to the intervening centuries. The difficulty also inheres in the nature of medieval monasticism, with its bewilderingly complex rituals that both shaped and were shaped by modes of thought and piety often remote from modern understanding.

Though it remains one of the least studied of Ælfric's writings, his so-called *Letter to the Monks of Eynsham* preserves the most direct record of the daily and yearly patterns of prayer and work in which Ælfric, not unlike the Venerable Bede before him, spent most of his life. Despite this importance, the content of the 'letter' is quite forbidding, both in the sheer amount of its technical detail and manner of its presentation. Equally discouraging to modern readers, the subject at hand – monastic liturgy – seems to afford few opportunities to glimpse the interesting persona that Ælfric elsewhere conveys so strongly and that has elevated him, like Bede, King Alfred and Archbishop Wulfstan, to the very exclusive ranks of 'known' Anglo-Saxon authors. Yet, on close examination, the *LME* is a vital document, both as a rare witness to the life of a specific Anglo-Saxon monastery and as a significant item in Ælfric's canon, bearing many more hallmarks of his intelligence and characteristic concerns than might at first be apparent. The text has much to reveal about the author's use of sources and methods of composition, and perhaps, more subtly, about a changing sense of mission in the last stage of his career.[4] But the *LME* also shows the familiar Ælfric in a different light, for it reminds us that his 'authorial' occupations of reading, writing and tireless revision were crowded into a busy schedule dominated by the liturgy. Because of its content, the *Letter to the Monks of Eynsham* is today

---

[3] S. B. Greenfield and D. G. Calder, with M. Lapidge, *A New Critical History of Old English Literature* (New York, 1986), p. 75. The judgement is typical; cf. R. M. Hogg, 'Introduction', in *The Cambridge History of the English Language, Volume I: The Beginnings to 1066*, ed. R. M. Hogg (Cambridge, 1992), pp. 1–25, at 16.

[4] Adumbrated by Gatch, 'The Office', pp. 348–9 and 352–62.

viewed as a marginal text, when in fact the observances it describes – and the many more it does not – must be understood as an essential context of Ælfric's career. Given the importance, moreover, of monastic scriptoria to Anglo-Saxon literary culture, something like this context probably informs, by extension, the activity of a great many Old English and Anglo-Latin 'authors', and of the scribes who copied their works.

THE TITLE

The *Letter to the Monks of Eynsham* survives only in a single eleventh-century copy.[5] The text bears no title in the manuscript and begins directly with the greeting 'Ælfricus abbas Egneshamnensibus fratribus salutem in Christo.'[6] This prominent salutation and the similarly epistolary farewell (at *LME* 80) may explain the tendency, evidenced as early as the twelfth century, to identify the composition as a 'letter'. These framing devices aside, however, the substance of the work is an adaptation of the liturgical institutes known as the *Regularis concordia*, which were compiled in the early 970s by Ælfric's mentor, Æthelwold, bishop of Winchester.[7] Both Æthelwold's text and Ælfric's revision of it belong more properly to a class of documents known as monastic customaries or consuetudinaries – descriptions of specific liturgical and some extra-liturgical customs (*consuetudines*) by which a particular monastery put into practice the teachings of St Benedict's *Rule*.[8] Ælfric virtually defines the genre when, in his preface to the *LME*, he

---

[5] On the manuscript and its implications, see below, ch. 3.
[6] *LME* 1: 'Abbot Ælfric to the brothers of Eynsham: Greetings in Christ.' All references are to the section numbers of the present edition, which in turn correspond to the editorial divisions of *Aelfrici abbatis epistula*, ed. Nocent.
[7] On this text as a source, see below, pp. 19–58.
[8] Gatch, 'The Office', p. 347. Such detailed descriptions were necessary because the *Rule* covered only the essentials of monasticism and did not reflect the significant changes in the life and liturgy that took place in the centuries after Benedict's death (*c.* 550). On the evolution of the term *consuetudo* (or plural, *consuetudines*) in this technical sense, see the opening chapter of *Initia consuetudinis Benedictinae*, ed. K. Hallinger, CCM 1 (Siegburg, 1963), and E. Palazzo, *Histoire des livres liturgiques: Le Moyen Age: Des origines au xiiie siècle* (Paris, 1993), pp. 221–7. On extant Anglo-Saxon customaries, see Gneuss, 'Liturgical Books', p. 136. Apart from the *LME* and the *Regularis concordia* (and derivatives thereof), Gneuss's list includes only one other item, the post-Conquest and non-native *Decreta* or 'Monastic Constitutions' of Archbishop Lanfranc.

characterizes its contents as 'certain matters upon which our [Benedictine] *Rule* does not touch'.[9] The English title *Letter to the Monks of Eynsham* does not appear to have become standard until after the nineteenth-century *editio princeps* and pioneering articles by Mary Bateson.[10] Fearing that to rename the text now would only perpetuate a long history of confusion over the work, I have thought it best to retain the now-common title, one that is commended, at least, by a degree of familiarity.[11]

AUTHORSHIP

The identification of 'Ælfricus abbas', compiler of the *LME*, with the celebrated homilist of the same name has won wide acceptance, and the present book will, in its course, review numerous similarities among the *LME* and other Ælfrician works that place the attribution beyond serious doubt. The homilist's sermons and pastoral letters not only make occasional use of the same sources as the *LME* but draw on the same portions of these texts and adapt them in similar ways.[12] Slightly more disagreement has surrounded the validity of the *LME*-preface as evidence that Ælfric was abbot of Eynsham. Although he styled himself as 'abbot' in several contexts,[13] he never stated explicitly where he held the office, and at least one modern scholar has inferred that the 'tone' of the *LME* is not that of an abbot addressing his own community.[14] Against that argument, others have pointed out that in the preface Ælfric claims to be 'abiding' with his Eynsham audience ('uobiscum degens'), and that at the

---

[9] *LME* 1: 'aliqua quae regula nostra non tangit'.

[10] *Excerpta ex institutionibus*, ed. Bateson. Subsequent references to the text occur throughout her 'Rules for Monks' and 'A Worcester Cathedral Book'.

[11] The unfortunate critical history of the *LME* is discussed below, ch. 4. Gatch ('The Office', pp. 348–9) urges a renaming, calling it variously 'Ælfric's Customary for Eynsham' or simply 'the Eynsham Customary'. The latter suggestion, however, would invite confusion with another famous 'Eynsham Customary' of the fourteenth century, which has nothing to do with Ælfric's text; see *The Customary of the Benedictine Abbey of Eynsham in Oxfordshire*, ed. A. Gransden, CCM 2 (Siegburg, 1963).

[12] See, for example, commentary to *LME* 25–6, 29–30, 32–3 and 44.

[13] For example, in prefaces to the *Vita S. Æthelwoldi* and to the letters to Sigeweard and Sigefyrth, and in the Latin preface to the Old English letters to Archbishop Wulfstan (Briefe II–III). These are all now conveniently assembled in *Ælfric's Prefaces*, ed. Wilcox.

[14] Hohler, 'Some Service-Books', p. 73.

end of the customary he refers to the audience's continued obedience to him on certain matters ('obedienter mihi consensistis in hoc').[15] Given the latter evidence and the risks of any too-literal reading of the conventional epistolary frame, nothing in the *LME* refutes the traditional location of Ælfric's abbacy at Eynsham. Far more complex are the issues of the date of the text and the circumstances behind its composition.

THE FOUNDING OF EYNSHAM ABBEY AND DATE OF THE *LME*

The outlines of Ælfric's career are well known.[16] He must have been born around the middle of the tenth century and, to judge from the dialect of his vernacular writings, in the southwest of England. After an inadequate early education received from a local priest (recounted in the famous preface to his translation of Genesis), he became a monk of the Old Minster, Winchester, during Æthelwold's episcopacy (963–84). His literary career seems to have begun in earnest, however, with his transfer *c.* 987 to the abbey of Cernel (Cerne Abbas, Dorset), where during the next decade and a half he would compose his best-known works, including the two series of *Catholic Homilies*, a set of *Lives of Saints*, the *Grammar*, the *Colloquy*, the partial translation of Genesis and numerous additional Temporale homilies. Around the year 1005 he appears to have left Cernel to become abbot of Eynsham, where he remained until the end of his life, *c.* 1010. His works from this later period include the *Letter to Sigeweard* on the Old and New Testaments, four pastoral letters (two in Latin, two in Old English) to Archbishop Wulfstan, the *Vita S. Æthelwoldi* and further additions to and revisions of his previous series of homilies.

It is generally assumed that the *LME* was written in or near 1005, the supposed date of the foundation of Eynsham and Ælfric's appointment as its head.[17] The major external witness to these events is a charter (S 911)

---

[15] *LME* 80, noted by Gatch, 'The Office', p. 348, n. 28.
[16] Dietrich, 'Abt Ælfrik'; White, *Ælfric*; Dubois, *Ælfric*; Clemoes, 'Ælfric'; Hurt, *Ælfric*; and now also the introduction to *Ælfric's Prefaces*, ed. Wilcox. Recovering the facts of Ælfric's career has been closely linked to the establishment of his canon, for which see Clemoes, 'Chronology', and the introduction to Pope's *Supplementary Collection* I, 136–45.
[17] E.g., White, *Ælfric*, p. 63; *Hirtenbriefe*, ed. Fehr, p. xlvii; Clemoes, 'Chronology', p. 245; Hurt, *Ælfric*, p. 38; and Gordon, *Eynsham Abbey*, p. 37. The title page of

issued in the name of King Æthelred and dated 1005, confirming endowment of a monastery at Eynsham by Æthelmær.[18] This Æthelmær – known from another source as Æthelmær *se greata* ('the stout') – was the son of Æthelweard the Chronicler, ealdorman of the western shires in the closing decades of the tenth century.[19] Ælfric enjoyed the friendship and patronage of father and son. At their request he took up a number of translation projects and by their agency received his appointments both to Cernel and to Eynsham.[20] Æthelmær, who eventually succeeded his father as ealdorman of the western provinces,[21] founded or (as now seems more likely) refounded both monasteries, and S 911 states that he himself appointed the first abbot of Eynsham, presumably Ælfric (although the charter does not name the appointee).[22] It has been argued that the

---

Nocent's edition in the CCM gives the date 'post 1004' without explanation (likewise at CCM 7.1, 157: 'verfaßt nach 1004').

[18] The charter is witnessed by Archbishop Ælfric of Canterbury, who died on 16 November 1005. The earliest surviving manuscript is the copy preserved in the twelfth-century portion of the Eynsham cartulary (Oxford, Christ Church, Eynsham Cart.). For other manuscripts and editions of the charter, see *Anglo-Saxon Charters*, ed. Sawyer, p. 278 (= S 911), plus addenda and corrigenda to this entry by M. Gelling, *The Early Charters of the Thames Valley*, SEEH 7 (Leicester, 1979), 138–9 (no. 290).

[19] The epithet *se greata* ('the fat' or 'the stout') is given to Æthelmær in the Anglo-Saxon Chronicle, *s.a.* 1017, and attested in late medieval reflexes such as 'Ailmerus Grossus', 'Almari le Grete' and 'magni Almari' (see *EC* II, 68, 37 and 57). The family of Ealdorman Æthelweard has been much discussed; see the *Dictionary of National Biography*, ed. L. Stephen and S. Lee (Oxford, 1908–19), *s.v.* 'Ethelwerd'; *Anglo-Saxon Wills*, ed. Whitelock, pp. 144–5; Flower, 'The Script of the Exeter Book', pp. 87–9; *Anglo-Saxon Charters*, ed. Robertson, pp. 386–7; and *Chronicon Æthelweardi*, ed. Campbell, pp. xii–xvi. More recent and reliable are Keynes, *Diplomas*, pp. 192 and 209–10, and Yorke, 'Æthelmær'.

[20] For the impact of this friendship on Ælfric's works, see Gatch, *Preaching and Theology*, pp. 48–9.

[21] Æthelweard's last certain attestation of a charter occurs in 998, and he is assumed to have died in that year or shortly thereafter; see Keynes, *Diplomas*, p. 192, n. 139. Keynes rejects the basis of an alternate death-date of 1002 accepted by Whitelock (*Anglo-Saxon Wills*, p. 145), Robertson (*Anglo-Saxon Charters*, p. 387) and, with important implications for the chronolgy of Ælfric's career, Clemoes ('Chronology', p. 243). Æthelmær's presumed succession to his father's office is problematic; see Keynes, *Diplomas*, pp. 197–8, n. 163.

[22] 'abbatem sanctę monachorum congregationi preferre se uiuente instituit'. At the end of the charter (after the bounds and before the witness list), an Old English appendix, seemingly dictated by Æthelmær himself, repeats these terms: 'And <ic> wille þere

monastery at Cernel existed for some time prior to Æthelmær's endowment of 987 and had perhaps been founded by some member of his family before the death of King Edgar in 975.[23] The prehistory of Eynsham and the exact nature of what Æthelmær did there in 1005 may be similarly complex. The relevant portion of the charter S 911 clearly indicates that the king is confirming privileges to a monastery already established:

Quapropter ego Æthelredus . . . ueracibus litterarum apicibus insinuare curaui, quod Æthelmaro, uiro ualde fidelissimo michi quoque dilectissimo, impetrante, absolutissimum libertatis priuilegium constituo monasterio eius in honore sancti saluatoris, omniumque sanctorum suorum, iure dedicato, in loco celebri iuxta fluuium qui uocatur Tamis constituto, quod ab incolis regionis illius Egnesham nuncupatur uocabulo.[24]

The privilege mentions a monastery already built, staffed and dedicated to the Saviour and All Saints. The king's confirmation of the endowment and conferral of privileges would, by normal procedure, come as the last in a series of events including the dedication of the monastic church. The establishment of a new monastery was a process that might begin years before the official date recorded in document such as

> beo ofer hi ealdor þe þær nu is þa hwile þe his lif beo' (*EC* I, 19–28, at pp. 20 and 24). Note the implication that the appointment has already been made. There may also be a discrepancy between the terms of the Latin 'se uiuente' (referring to Æthelmær?) and the Old English, where 'þa hwile þe his lif beo' refers to the abbot. The inference that the unnamed abbot is Ælfric is wholly circumstantial, since the assertion that he witnessed the charter (e.g., White, *Ælfric*, p. 62; Hurt, *Ælfric*, p. 37) rests on a misreading of the name *Ælfsige* that occurs twice in the witness list; see *EC* I, 27, n. 2, and Keynes, *Diplomas*, p. 260.
>
> [23] Squibb, 'Foundation'. The Cernel charter (S 1217) states that Æthelmær's gift occurred a few years after the foundation of the abbey. Squibb's principal evidence that 'a few' equals twelve years or more lies in the finding of a very late (1440) enquiry that King Edgar donated a manor at Muston (Musterston) to one John, abbot of Cerne ('Foundation', p. 13). Yorke ('Æthelmær', p. 22) accepts this part of Squibb's argument and further suggests that the actual founder may have been some member of the previous generation of Æthelmær's family.
>
> [24] *EC* I, 20: 'Wherefore I, Æthelred . . . have taken care to record in truthful written testimony that, at the petition of Æthelmær, a man most loyal and dear to me, I am establishing an unconditional privilege of freedom for his monastery, duly dedicated to the honour of the holy Saviour and all his saints, located beside the river called Thames in a famous spot named Eynsham by the inhabitants of that region' (trans. mine; see also Gordon, *Eynsham Abbey*, pp. 10 and 15).

S 911.[25] The Eynsham charter continues, too, with a brief but crucial reference to the history of the property before it came into Æthelmær's possession: 'Quod quidem monasterium Æþelmarus ab Æþelweardo genero suo mutuando accepit, & pro illis triginta mansiunculis dedit triginta sex mansiones, tribus diuisas in locis . . . [here follows a list of the properties given in exchange for Eynsham].'[26] This statement indicates that a *monasterium* already existed at Eynsham while the land was held by Æthelmær's son-in-law. John Blair's study of the early history of the Thames Valley confirms that Eynsham was the site of a minster of considerable wealth and importance by the year 864, and very likely by 821.[27] Recent excavations at Eynsham have, moreover, confirmed Blair's reading of the documentary evidence by proving that Æthelmær built his monastery on the site of a major, much older minster.[28] Sadly, the condition of the site that passed into Æthelmær's hands cannot be known. The Eynsham *monasterium* might have been an abandoned ruin, but it might also have been a minster inhabited by

---

[25] Squibb, 'Foundation', p. 14.

[26] *EC* I, 20: 'Æthelmær received the monastery from his son-in-law, Æthelweard, through an exchange, and for those thirty *mansiunculae* [i.e., Eynsham and its lands] gave thirty-six *mansiones* divided over three locations . . .' The terms of the exchange that follow are translated and discussed by D. Hooke, *Worcestershire Anglo-Saxon Charter-Bounds*, SASH 2 (Woodbridge, 1990), 328–9; the Old English bounds are translated by Salter, *EC* I, 24–6, Gordon, *Eynsham Abbey*, pp. 24–5, and analysed in detail by G. B. Grundy, *Saxon Oxfordshire: Charters and Highways*, Oxfordshire Record Society 15 (Oxford, 1933), 33–6. For other lands that may have been part of the original endowment but are not mentioned in S 911, see *EC* I, viii. On the economic rationale of the original endowment, see Gordon, *Eynsham Abbey*, pp. 20–5 and 155–6.

[27] *Anglo-Saxon Oxfordshire*, p. 63: 'The first [documentary evidence] is the agreement of c. 821 by which the archbishop of Canterbury relinquished to King Coenwulf of Mercia . . . a 300-hide estate at *Iogneshomme*, almost certainly Eynsham . . . The second text [S 210], dated 864, is a grant by the Mercian king of five hides at Water Eaton, the grantee to pay 30s. "to Eynsham to that church" after one year, which looks very much like compensation for the dispersal of monastic lands.' On the prehistory of Eynsham, see also Blair's 'The Minsters on the Thames', in *The Cloister and the World: Essays in Medieval History in Honour of Barbara Harvey*, ed. J. Blair and B. Golding (Oxford, 1996), pp. 5–28.

[28] Blair, *Anglo-Saxon Oxfordshire*, pp. 114–16. Details of the excavations at Eynsham from 1989 to 1991 and of additional minor digs are summarized by D. R. M. Gaimster, S. Margeson, M. Hurley and B. S. Nenk in *Mediaeval Archaeology* 34 (1990), 207; 35 (1991), 180–3; 36 (1992), 257–8; and 38 (1994), 240–1.

secular clerks on whom Æthelmær imposed the reformed monastic life as a condition of their remaining in his new monastery. The presence in Æthelmær's foundation of clerks newly converted to the monastic life has even suggested to some a possible occasion for Ælfric's writing a document such as the *LME*.[29] In any event, it seems that the 'foundation' of Eynsham around 1005 was in effect a refoundation after the general pattern of the tenth-century reformers, who preferred, whenever possible, to revive the regular life in ancient minsters or at other sites, such as Æthelwold's Ely, venerated for their ties to a supposed golden age of Anglo-Saxon Christianity.[30]

The unknown status of the pre-existing *monasterium* or details of the transaction urge that the date of S 911 (1005) be accepted rather as a *terminus ante quem* for the refoundation of the monastery and beginning of Ælfric's abbacy. The chronological relation of the *LME* to these events, however, remains largely a separate issue. The date of the charter will not do as a *terminus post quem* for the drawing up of Ælfric's customary, since he and his community were already in residence before the drafting of the king's confirmation, either as restorers of an abandoned site or reformers of a previously secular minster. How much time passed between Æthelmær's acquisition of the estates and the drawing up of the charter is unknown, as are the ancestry and early fortunes of the younger Æthelweard who held the site previously.[31] It would be helpful to know how the

---

[29] Thus Gordon, *Eynsham Abbey*, p. 31, though Ælfric's text does not easily accommodate this hypothesis. Apart from the fact that the *LME* is not an introduction to the monastic life (see below, pp. 11 and 18), Ælfric devotes much attention to the secular liturgy wherever this replaces the monastic form (i.e., the Triduum and in Easter week). Arguably, this emphasis would better serve an audience of monks (relatively unfamiliar with the secular Office) than clerks; see commentary to *LME* 34 (at n. 181), 47 (at nn. 240 and 243–4) and 48 (at nn. 245–6, 248–50 and 254).

[30] Yorke ('Æthelmær', p. 20) implies that Æthelmær's act at Eynsham was a refoundation. On the nostalgia of the tenth-century reformers, see Wormald, 'Æthelwold and his Continental Counterparts', pp. 38–41.

[31] On the younger Æthelweard, see Flower, 'The Script', Keynes, *Diplomas*, pp. 192 and 209–10, and additional remarks by P. W. Conner, 'A Contextual Study of the Old English Exeter Book' (unpubl. PhD dissertation, Univ. of Maryland, 1975), pp. 29–37. The most recent biographical summary is by Keynes, 'Cnut's Earls', pp. 67–70. It is supposed that Æthelweard II married a daughter of Æthelmær named Æthelflæd (the granddaughter of the senior Ealdorman Æthelweard). Æthelmær's own son (also named Æthelweard) was put to death by Cnut in 1017, so his son-in-law (Æthelweard II) succeeded to the ealdordom of the western provinces, which he held

latter came to possess Eynsham and its *monasterium*, and whether or not he, too, was a fosterer of reformed monasticism, who might have allowed his father-in-law's new community to occupy the site before the transfer of estates was final. The obscurity of so many details cautions against the natural impulse to date the *LME* too narrowly on the basis of S 911. A *terminus ante quem non* for Ælfric's abbacy is at least given by the so-called private letter to Archbishop Wulfstan, who was elevated to the see of York (in plurality with Worcester) in 1002. In this letter Ælfric still styles himself *frater*,[32] so his promotion to the abbacy can be dated as narrowly as 1002 × 1005.

At two points the text of the *LME* itself may bear on the issue of date, though the possible inferences conflict. In the preface Ælfric claims that the 'recent' establishment of the monastery has occasioned his present labour ('quia nuper rogatu Æþelmæri ad monachicum habitum ordinati estis').[33] Standing prominently, as it does, at the head of the work, this remark probably accounts for the widespread association between the *LME* and the date of S 911. As already demonstrated, however, the establishment of a monastery (or whatever specific act is meant by *ad monachicum habitum ordinari*) cannot be simply equated with the issue of that charter. Once the date of S 911 is disallowed as a *terminus post quem*, Ælfric's adverb 'recently' retains value only as a very general indicator. A second internal clue at the end of the *LME* further complicates the matter: commending the Eynsham monks' practice of reading three lessons at the Office of Nocturns during the summer period (instead of the one required by Benedict's *Rule*), Ælfric notes affectionately that they have obeyed him in this matter 'for years now':

Volo etiam uos scire, fratres karissimi, ualde gratum mihi fore quod obedienter mihi consensistis in hoc, ut tres lectiones cum totidem responsoriis tota aestate ad nocturnas sicut hieme *iam preteritis annis* tenuimus.[34]

---

until he was outlawed in 1020 for conspiracy against Cnut. Æthelweard II's possession of a large estate in Oxfordshire, Eynsham, prompts Keynes to speculate ('Cnut's Earls', p. 68, n. 142; see also *Diplomas*, p. 212) that he might even be identified with Æthelweard the brother of Eadric Streona and, consequently, a member of a family in rivalry with Æthelmær's.

[32] *Hirtenbriefe*, ed. Fehr, pp. 222–7 (Brief 2a), at 222.
[33] *LME* 1: 'because you have recently been ordained to the monastic habit at Æthelmær's request'.
[34] *LME* 80: 'I also wish you to know, dearest brothers, how very pleased I am that you

The phrase *iam preteritis annis* suggests that Ælfric has been head of the community for some time. Given the indeterminate value of the adverb *nuper* ('recently') in the preface, this latter clue offers the only firm internal evidence for the date of the text relative to the beginning of Ælfric's tenure as abbot.[35] Unless the part of the customary containing the phrase *iam preteritis annis* (*LME* 80) was a later addition, Ælfric by his own account composed the document two or more years after his appointment. The shadow of doubt accordingly falls across the assumption that the customary must have been one of the first works Ælfric produced as abbot.[36] The *LME* is not an introduction to the monastic life, but an explanation of some of the finer points of the liturgy. The Eynsham monks could perhaps get by for a long time without such a document, especially with Ælfric present to guide by word and example. He may have committed this information to writing early on, as is often assumed, but it is equally possible that years passed between his arrival at Eynsham and the composition of the *LME*. An awareness, for example, that the end of his life was approaching might also have moved him to write down the kind of instructions he had been used to delivering orally and as needed.

Unfortunately, the assembled evidence weakens not one but two chronological mainstays (the date of Ælfric's transfer to Eynsham and the date of the *LME* itself) without providing any more satisfactory alternatives. One should, in any case, resist the assumption that the date of the *LME* necessarily corresponds to that of the charter, or that the writing of the *LME* must have immediately followed Ælfric's promotion. In the face

---

have obediently agreed with me on this matter: namely, that *for years now* we have retained three lessons and the same number of responsories at Nocturns for the whole summer period just as in winter' (emphasis added). On the grammatical difficulties of this passage, see the commentary to *LME* 80 and cf. the trans. by Gatch, 'The Office', p. 356, n. 49. Bateson also called attention to the key phrase *iam preteritis annis*, but in a different context; see her 'Rules for Monks', p. 702, n. 48.

[35] The implications of *LME* 80 have passed unnoticed, even though some scholars have allowed that Ælfric arrived at Eynsham before the often-cited date of 1005: e.g., *Excerpta ex institutionibus*, ed. Bateson, p. 174, White, *Ælfric*, pp. 61 and 63, Hurt, *Ælfric*, p. 37 and Dubois, *Ælfric*, p. 63. The assumption may also explain the date 'post 1004' in the CCM edition.

[36] E.g., White, *Ælfric*, p. 63. More significantly, the assumption appears to have influenced Fehr, much of whose relative chronology is taken over in the now-standard treatment by Clemoes ('Chronology', pp. 241 and 243); see below, p. 25, n. 26.

of so many uncertainties, the date of 1005, qualified by an cautious *circa*, will have to suffice.

In addition to providing an approximate date for the *LME*, S 911 has also encouraged speculation that the circumstances attending the establishment of Eynsham were unusual. If in some respects Æthelmær's refounding of Eynsham resembled his earlier activity at Cernel, in others the two occasions differed dramatically, for the Eynsham charter declares the ealdorman's intent to retire to his new foundation and spend the rest of his days there, 'acting as a father, living among [the monks] in community'.[37] This vow recurs in the Old English statement, apparently dictated by Æthelmær himself, just before the witness list.[38] The sort of retirement here proposed would not have been unusual for a wealthy, devout layman and offers the simplest explanation of Æthelmær's motives in establishing the monastery. Other sources hint, however, that the causes of his retirement may not have been so pious. To judge from the evidence of charter witness lists, Æthelmær had enjoyed the steady increase of King Æthelred's favour through the 990s and appears to have succeeded his father as ealdorman at some point after the latter's death *c*. 998.[39] But soon after the turn of the millennium, the witness lists indicate dramatic changes among the ranks of Æthelred's retainers. With the charters of 1005–6, the attestations of some of the king's closest associates disappear: Æthelmær, a kinsman and hitherto important advisor, retires suddenly to Eynsham; the *minister* Ordulf, uncle of the king, also retires, perhaps to his own family monastery at Tavistock.[40] The names of the important *ministri* Wulfgeat and Wulfheah also cease to appear, as does that of the latter's father, Ealdorman Ælfhelm of Northumbria: the grim annal for 1006 in the *Anglo-Saxon Chronicle* records the fates

---

[37] *EC* I, 20: 'ipse patris uice fungens uiuensque communiter inter eos'. Elsewhere (*ibid*. I, vii, n. 4) Salter remarks, 'Perhaps the words [*scil*. 'uiuens communiter inter eos'] only mean "sharing the property with them"'. Salter does not give reasons for questioning the literal sense of the Latin, but only refers to the corresponding Old English (see following note) with its added phrase *þære are mid him notian*.

[38] *EC* I, 24: '⁊ ic me sylf wille mid þære geferrædene gemænelice libban. ⁊ þære are mid him notian þa hwile þe min lif bið' ('And I myself will live in common with the convent and enjoy the possessions with them during my life' (trans. Salter, *EC* I, 27); cf. Gordon, *Eynsham Abbey*, p. 28).

[39] Keynes, *Diplomas*, pp. 188, 192–3 and 197–8, n. 163; also Yorke, 'Æthelmær', p. 19.

[40] Keynes, *Diplomas*, pp. 209–10.

of these three men.⁴¹ Considering who benefited from this apparent purge, Simon Keynes has argued that the upheavals at court may have been engineered by Eadric Streona, ealdorman of Mercia (1007–17) and son-in-law of the king.⁴²

In such circumstances, it is hard to quell the suspicion that Æthelmær's retirement was somehow related to events at court, and that the founding of Eynsham represents either the shrewd anticipation of troubles ahead or the response to a fall from favour already complete. In either case, Æthelmær's withdrawal from public life may not have been entirely voluntary, and the likelihood that his plans to establish a monastery at Eynsham far anticipated the year 1005 decreases accordingly. Political pressures would also account for the location of the house of his retirement at Eynsham rather than in the territories of his father's ealdormanry. If retirement were his only aim, presumably the family monastery at Cernel would have been a more convenient choice. But Æthelmær's enemies at court would doubtless want to distance him from the seat of his family's power: perhaps the Oxfordshire site was dictated as one condition of withdrawal with life and honour intact.⁴³ If the younger Æthelweard, moreover, also had family connections to powers ascendant in Mercia,⁴⁴ his role in the refounding of Eynsham would hardly be a disinterested one. His offer of the *monasterium* at Eynsham could be seen as a move to facilitate his father-in-law's safe departure from court or, less commendably, as a favour to the king or to Eadric Streona (possibly his brother) as they chose a suitable place of retirement for Æthelmær outside the western shires. Admittedly, such reconstructions of motive remain entirely conjectural; nothing about the tone of the Eynsham charter itself hints of strife between Æthelmær and his son-in-law, much less between Æthelmær and the king. But it may be naive to assume that the protests

---

⁴¹ *Ibid.*, pp. 210–11. See the *Chronicle*, *s.a.* 1006: 'In the same year Wulfgeat was deprived of all his property, and Wulfheah and Ufegeat were blinded and Ealdorman Ælfhelm killed' (*Anglo-Saxon Chronicle*, ed. and trans. Whitelock *et al.*, p. 87).

⁴² Keynes, *Diplomas*, pp. 212–14. According to the *Chronicle* (versions C, D and E), the year 1005 also saw an abatement of the Scandinavian attacks, perhaps related to the great famine reported in that year.

⁴³ Suggested by Yorke, 'Æthelmær', pp. 19–20. A different interpretation is offered by Campbell, who suggests that Eynsham may have been chosen in the hopes – vain, as time would soon prove – that areas so far inland would be safe from Scandinavian assault; see his 'England *c.* 991', p. 15.

⁴⁴ See above, n. 31.

of affection and pious motive in this highly conventional, public document tell the whole story.[45] If some controversy did attend Æthelmær's retirement to Eynsham and the job of drafting the charter fell to the royal writing office, the amiable tone of S 911 would suit the interests of a king eager not to appear arbitrary or treacherous in his dealings with a kinsman and once-close advisor.[46] Conversely, if the charter was drawn up in the Eynsham scriptorium, the monks would be no less eager to put a good face on events that had left them in the awkward position of benefiting from their patron's misfortune while acting as the enforcers of his virtual exile.[47]

Further considerations caution against taking the narrative portions of the charter at face value. Although Æthelmær's absence from the witness lists of charters after 1005 is consistent with a retirement from public life, no source explicitly confirms that he acted on the vow expressed in S 911. If he did, his retirement appears to have been only temporary: the *Anglo-Saxon Chronicle* records that an Ealdorman Æthelmær led the thegns of the western provinces to submit to Swein Forkbeard at Bath in 1013.[48] If this is indeed Æthelmær 'the stout', his re-emergence in these

---

[45] The king refers to Æthelmær as 'uiro ualde fidelissimo michi quoque dilectissimo', and Æthelmær to the monarch as 'minon leofan hlaforde Æþelrede cynge' (*EC* I, 20 and 24).

[46] Keynes makes a forceful case for a royal scriptorium as the principal agent in charter production in Æthelred's reign; see the third chapter of his *Diplomas* (esp. pp. 134–53). Consensus on the issue, however, does not appear to be forthcoming; Keynes (*ibid.*, pp. 14–28) offers a lucid survey of the history of the debate.

[47] The assumption of monastic origins for S 911 must underlie the curious speculation that Ælfric himself drafted that charter. I can trace this suggestion back no further than Dietrich ('Abt Ælfrik', p. 240) and White (*Ælfric*, pp. 60–1), though it has resurfaced as recently as 1991 (Campbell, 'England, *c.* 991', p. 14). If the assertion rests on a claim that the charter is composed 'in the clear, graceful Latin of Ælfric's other Latin works' (thus Hurt, *Ælfric*, p. 37), it has no merit, for S 911 departs little, if at all, from the pretentious style typical of tenth-century Anglo-Saxon charters. Any statement about the authorship of S 911 must also take into account the extensive verbatim parallels in another charter (S 792 = King Edgar to Thorney, dated 973, though probably a forgery), and the relation of both of these, in turn, to the proem of the *Regularis concordia*; see C. R. Hart, *The Early Charters of Eastern England*, SEEH 5 (Leicester, 1966), 176, n. 2, and also below, p. 45, n. 111. On a possible echo of S 911 in the *LME*, see the present commentary to *LME* 63 (at n. 298).

[48] 'Then King Swein turned from there [*scil.* London] to Wallingford, and so went across the Thames to Bath, where he stayed with his army. Then Ealdorman Æthelmær came

circumstances does little to thwart suspicions that his withdrawal in 1005 was not voluntary. The length of his retirement at Eynsham was at most seven to eight years.[49] If he did spend all eight intervening years at Eynsham, the impact of his presence on the community there can only be guessed. Even in the happiest circumstances, the presence of a powerful lay patron – especially one determined to act 'as a father' (*patris uice*) to the monks – could easily disrupt monastic discipline and subvert the abbot's authority. Conceivably, a retirement imposed from without would exacerbate whatever difficulties already inhered in the arrangement. The *LME* does not betray the existence of such tensions; indeed, it makes no mention of Æthelmær whatsoever, apart from the single reference to his role in the foundation, discussed above. Such reticence certainly accords with the practical nature of the work, since Æthelmær's presence would have little bearing on the liturgical customs that are the main business of the *LME*. But the fate of Æthelmær will be a context worth recalling when we eventually turn to consider Ælfric's handling of the *Regularis concordia* and its political implications.[50]

From this attempt to view the composition of the *LME* in its historical setting, more questions than answers have emerged. The combined data of S 911, the witness lists and the *Chronicle* do not tell a straightforward story, and the *LME* offers no explicit comment on contemporary events, however aware of them the monks must have been as they chanted their Offices. But an interpretation of Ælfric's customary as a deliberate response both to its sources and to the needs of its historical moment requires sensitivity to such backgrounds, however faint. The *LME* is the only complete English monastic customary extant from the period between the *Regularis concordia* and the *Monastic Constitutions* of Lanfranc (*c.* 1077), and the former, apparently conceived as a type of 'national customary', offers little perspective on any specific foundation. In the absence of significant comparanda, Ælfric's text frames a rare window on the life of a particular

there, and with him the western thegns, and all submitted to Swein, and they gave him hostages' (*Anglo-Saxon Chronicle*, ed. and trans. Whitelock *et al.*, p. 92).

[49] Though he might have re-entered secular life to assume, or resume, the office of ealdorman before 1013, his name does not return to the witness lists until that year; see Keynes, *Diplomas*, pp. 209–10, nn. 202–3. Our Æthelmær is to be distinguished from another prominent Æthelmær *minister* who attests frequently in the years 1005–9.

[50] On political concerns at the margins of the *LME*, see below, pp. 43–9.

Anglo-Saxon monastery whose customs, like those of any house, were determined in part by the circumstances of its foundation, the numbers and relative experience of its community and, especially, the plan of its buildings and church, down to the number and location of side altars or chapels.[51] The irony could hardly be greater, then, that so crucial a witness as the *LME* should emanate from a centre about which so little is otherwise known. From the time of the refoundation by Æthelmær *c.* 1005 until the Norman Conquest, the history of Eynsham Abbey is a virtual blank.[52] The 'abbot and entire community of Eynsham' turn up in the witness list of a minor St Alban's charter (S 1425), the original of which is datable to 1050 × 1052, and this attestation is the only evidence of the community's continued existence through the mid-eleventh century.[53] The early thirteenth-century *Magna uita* of St Hugh of Lincoln reports that the monks still resident at Eynsham in 1066 abandoned the site during the Norman invasion, but that Bishop Remigius of Dorchester, later of Lincoln (1067–93), refounded the monastery, which was thereafter a dependency of the see of Lincoln.[54] There appears to have

---

[51] Few will hazard an estimate of the size of a community for which records are so scarce, but see D. H. Farmer's conjectures about Ælfric's previous house, Cernel, in 'The Monastic Reform of the 10th Century and Cerne Abbas', in *The Cerne Abbey Millennium Lectures*, ed. Barker, pp. 1–10, at 6. Some implications of the *LME* for the layout of Eynsham Abbey receive passing notice in Spurrell's 'Architectural Interest', pp. 173–4.

[52] Salter's introduction to the *Eynsham Cartulary* (I, ix–xxxii) includes a detailed history of the abbey down to the Dissolution; see also his article in *The Victoria History of the County of Oxford*, ed. W. Page (London, 1907) II, 65–7, as well as E. Chambers, *Eynsham Under the Monks*, Oxfordshire Record Society 18 (Oxford, 1936), and Gordon's *Eynsham Abbey*.

[53] Edited among the *additamenta* to *Matthæi Parisiensis chronica maiora*, ed. H. R. Luard, 6 vols., Rolls Series 57 (London, 1872–82) VI, 29–30. A recently discovered transcript of the Old English original is discussed by S. Keynes, 'A Lost Cartulary of St Albans Abbey', *ASE* 22 (1993), 253–79, at pp. 266–7, and Blair, *Anglo-Saxon Oxfordshire*, pp. 107 and 138–40; see also Gordon, *Eynsham Abbey*, pp. 43–4. The Latin edition by J. M. Kemble (*Codex diplomaticus aeui Saxonici*, 6 vols. (London 1839–48) IV, no. 950) gives the erroneous reading *Hauuensis* for *Egneshamiensis*.

[54] *Magna uita sancti Hugonis: The Life of St Hugh of Lincoln*, ed. and trans. D. L. Douie and H. Farmer, 2 vols. (London, 1961–2) II, 39: 'Blessed bishop Remigius, who had founded the magnificent cathedral church of Lincoln shortly after the conquest, had refounded the ruined abbey [*scil.* Eynsham], from which the monks had fled out fear of the enemy.'

been no continuity betweeen the Anglo-Saxon and Norman refoundations, although Remigius must have restored Eynsham before 1086, for the Domesday Book records the estates of his refounded monastery. Between 1091 and 1093 the monks were transplanted to another refounded site at Stow in Lincolnshire, but Remigius's successor, Robert Bloet, transferred them back to Eynsham, where the community prospered from 1094 until the formal dissolution of the house on 4 December 1539.[55]

[55] *EC* I, ix–xii and xxxi. It is sometimes asserted that Stow was refounded by Bishop Eadnoth I of Dorchester (1006–16) *from* Eynsham; see J. W. F. Hill, *Medieval Lincoln* (Cambridge, 1948), p. 75, and Knowles, *Monastic Order*, pp. 66 and 721 (Table I). The sole evidence for this claim is the presence of certain pre-Conquest documents pertaining to Stow in the Eynsham Cartulary, but there is no definite link between Eynsham and Stow before Remigius's transplantation of 1091, on which see Gordon, *Eynsham Abbey*, p. 61.

2

Structure and sources

GENERIC FEATURES

Like most monastic customaries, Ælfric's Eynsham 'letter' assumes a great deal of prior knowledge on the reader's part. Indeed, as an abridgement of sources already dense and technical, the LME may well compound the interpretative challenges of the genre. Customaries also typically emphasize departures from everyday observance, so it is not surprising that Ælfric gives the most details about customs peculiar to special days or seasons but has comparatively little to say about normal routines. Recognition of these generic qualities should discourage some unrealistic expectations of the 'letter', such as the assumption that Ælfric is writing a kind of beginners' guide to the Benedictine life.[1] On the contrary, he is clearly addressing an audience with some experience of monastic liturgy and discipline. Even if, as he claims in the preface, his monks do not know the *Regularis concordia*,[2] they would require considerable knowledge of St Benedict's *Rule* and much else simply in order to make sense of the 'letter'. The commentary that follows the present edition aims to unpack Ælfric's tightly bundled instructions, to fill in the information that he assumes and to distinguish the unusual or problematic from the routine. The sheer amount of explanation needed to put us on more or less the same footing as Ælfric's intended readers is instructive.

---

[1] On the long confusion over the nature of Ælfric's customary and its relation to the *Regularis concordia*, see below, ch. 4. On customaries generally, see also above, p. 3, n. 8.

[2] This claim (at *LME* 1) is problematic; see below, nn. 48 and 53.

Structure and sources

Because study of the details tends, however, to lose sight of the larger organization and emphases of the *LME*, the present chapter surveys these features and the extent of their correlation to Ælfric's sources. The *LME* contains three major divisions: an epistolary preface (§ 1); the customary proper, based largely on the *Regularis concordia*, but with significant interpolations from the *Liber officialis* of Amalarius of Metz and other liturgical sources (§§ 2–69); and an extensive supplement that outlines the readings and responsories used in the Night Office (§§ 70–80).[3] This arrangement is straightforward enough; the real difficulties lie in the body of the second and third parts. There the context of many provisions, the rationale of their arrangement and the logic of transitions tend to fade in and out of view. Consultation of the fuller texts from which Ælfric was working is so necessary that study of the *LME* inevitably becomes, to a great extent, a study of its sources.

ÆLFRIC AND THE *REGULARIS CONCORDIA*

By its arrangement and frequent verbatim borrowings from the *Regularis concordia*, Ælfric's customary leaves little doubt that the *liber consuetudinum* cited in the preface[4] is the document drawn up by St Æthelwold and his fellow reform-minded bishops, abbots and abbesses and promulgated by King Edgar (957/9–975) in the early 970s.[5] The *LME* repeatedly reminds its readers of this textual dependence by introducing quotations or paraphrases of the *Concordia* with tags such as 'consuetudo: . . .' or

---

[3] The tripartite structure was pointed out by Gatch, 'The Office', pp. 348–9. These divisions are indicated in the manuscript by the use of coloured initials (the first letters of *LME* 1, 2 and 70) and rubrics ('Finiunt consuetudines' at the end of *LME* 69). The only other use of colours in the entire text is in *LME* 69, with the heading 'Oratio pro defuncto fratre' in red and a green initial in the prayer 'Satisfaciat'.

[4] *LME* 1: 'haec pauca de libro consuetudinum quem sanctus Aðelwoldus Wintoniensis episcopus . . . undique collegit ac monachis instituit obseruandum'.

[5] Arguments over the authorship of the *Concordia* (insofar as a composite text may be said to have an 'author') now strongly favour Æthelwold, based on the evidence of Ælfric's testimony at *LME* 1, the Latin style of certain parts of the *Concordia* and the emphases shared by both the proem to the *Concordia* and the Old English prose tract known as 'King Edgar's Establishment of the Monasteries'; see *RC* (Kornexl), pp. xxxi–l. More controversial are the date and circumstances of the Winchester council that led to the text (see *ibid.*, pp. xxiv–xxx) and the extent of its adoption as a national standard (see *ibid.*, pp. li–lvi).

'consuetudo docet . . .'⁶ These references serve a practical function, usually to signal a return to teaching based on the *Concordia* after an interpolation from another source. But they also call attention to 'the customary' as an authority, explicitly linked (in *LME* 1) to Æthelwold, Winchester and, by association, the entire reforming tradition. Much more than bibliographical citations, these references in the text indirectly elevate Ælfric's own credentials before his audience, whether within or beyond the walls of Eynsham.⁷

Modern scholarship has dealt at length with the cardinal events of the tenth-century reform or 'Benedictine revival', embracing the careers of Æthelwold, bishop of Winchester (963–84), Dunstan, archbishop of Canterbury (961–88) and Oswald, archbishop of York (972–92), as well as King Edgar's reign and restoration of the monasteries, the expulsion of the clerks and foundation of monastic cathedrals.⁸ This complex history cannot be rehearsed here, but some aspects of the reform and the contexts of the *Regularis concordia* demand review in as much as they bear immediately on the *LME*. Ælfric's choice of the *Concordia* as his principal source now seems obvious, given his close identification with the reform movement. Yet a careful look at what Ælfric did to this source suggests that his choice, if inevitable, was not altogether convenient. However strong the attraction of the *Concordia* as a badge of loyalty to Æthelwold and his contemporaries, on a less abstract level Ælfric seems to have

---

[6] There are fourteen such references. In addition to that in the preface (*LME* 1: 'libro consuetudinum'), see also *LME* 9, 26, 28–30, 33, 36–7, 40, 58, 60, 62 and 63. The *explicit*-phrase *Finiunt consuetudines* at *LME* 69 (*q.v.* in the commentary, at n. 319) separates the main portion of Ælfric's customary from his appended *ordo lectionum* and suggests that Ælfric perceived his own work as being fundamentally of the same genre as the *Regularis concordia*.

[7] On Ælfric's disclosure of sources as part of his self-definition within the reformed tradition, see Hill, 'Reform and Resistance'.

[8] Important treatments include Robinson, *The Times of Saint Dunstan*; F. Stenton, *Anglo-Saxon England*, 3rd ed. (Oxford, 1971), pp. 433–69, Knowles, *Monastic Order*, pp. 16–82; John, 'The King and the Monks'; Stafford, *Unification and Conquest*, pp. 180–200; and Wormald, 'Æthelwold and his Continental Counterparts'. On the *Concordia* and its function in the movement, see *RC* (Symons), pp. ix–xxviii (introduction), which also serves, with some alterations, as the introduction to the collaborative edition in CCM 7.1, 371–92. On all aspects of the *Concordia* and its backgrounds, see the introduction to *RC* (Kornexl) and summary in Kornexl, 'The *Regularis Concordia* and its Old English Gloss'.

Structure and sources

found working with the text rather challenging. All who know the *Concordia* can bear witness that it is hardly a lucid document. No less a modern expert than Dom David Knowles could admit that, quite apart from the text's often difficult Latinity, 'the whole, though at first glance logically planned, abounds in repetitions, dropped threads, and paragraphs which appear to have been inserted without reference to the sequence of ideas', and that 'it only yields all its information after careful and repeated inspection'.[9] In settling on this source Ælfric had to address linguistic and structural difficulties, to be sure, but also practical and ideological ones that rendered the *Concordia* less than ideal for the needs of a small monastery in the early eleventh century.

Ælfric's exemplar

A consideration of Ælfric's response to these challenges must first confront a more fundamental problem. Ælfric's copy of the *Regularis concordia* has not survived, and the obscure textual history of that source does not allow confident assumptions about the exact form of his exemplar.[10] The *Concordia* survives complete in only two manuscripts. London, BL, Cotton Faustina B. iii, 159r–198v (+ Cotton Tiberius A. iii, 177r–v),[11] and London, BL, Cotton Tiberius A. iii, 3r–27v, were both copied at Christ Church, Canterbury, in the mid-eleventh century. The latter is by far the higher-status production, preserving the *Regularis concordia* (with an interlinear Old English gloss) as part of a larger collection of reformed-monastic texts, including the *Regula S. Benedicti* and four Carolingian supplements to it commonly found in Anglo-Saxon manuscripts.[12] Each manuscript has served as the basis of at least one

---

[9] *Monastic Order*, p. 43. Kornexl's analysis suggests how the structure might have been more lucid to its intended audience than to modern readers; see *RC* (Kornexl), pp. lvii–lxxxiii.

[10] See Hill, 'The "Regularis Concordia"', updating *RC* (Symons), pp. liii–lviii. The most complete discussion of the manuscripts is that in *RC* (Kornexl), pp. xcvi–clv, and Kornexl, 'The *Regularis Concordia* and its Old English Gloss', pp. 104–11.

[11] For the foliation of the original manuscript, see Ker, *Catalogue*, item 155. On the theory that this copy was originally part of a 'booklet' of related material, see *RC* (Kornexl), pp. ci and cxii–cxvi.

[12] The portion of the manuscript containing the *Concordia* is variously dated to the middle or second half of the eleventh century; on the dates, see Ker, *Catalogue*, item 186 (s. xi^{med}); cf. *RC* (Symons), p. lv (s. xi^2). On the localization, see *RC* (Kornexl),

edition of the *Concordia*, and the disputed priority of one copy over the other has occasioned much debate.[13] A collation of the two extant witnesses *RC* (Fa) and (Ti) raises difficult questions about the relationship of either version to a putative archetype. Their discrepancies cannot be enumerated here,[14] but attempts to reconstruct a textual history that would fully explain the differences between the two manuscripts have met little success. Lucia Kornexl has offered the most plausible explanation by distinguishing Æthelwold's original draft of the text ('Urfassung' or 'Erstfassung') from later, presumably more polished stages.[15]

pp. cxxii–cxxiv. On the supplements to the *Regula S. Benedicti*, see Bateson, 'Rules for Monks', pp. 694–5, and H. Sauer, 'Die Ermahnung des Pseudo-Fulgentius zur Benediktregel und ihre altenglische Glossierung', *Anglia* 102 (1984), 419–25. Inclusion of the *Regularis concordia* in such a collection promoted a view of English monastic reform as a development of Carolingian precedents; see *RC* (Kornexl), pp. cxxxv–cxli, and R. Deshman, '*Benedictus Monarcha et Monachus*: Early Medieval Ruler Theology and the Anglo-Saxon Reform', *Frühmittelalterliche Studien* 22 (1988), 204–40.

[13] Cotton Faustina B. iii (= *RC* (Fa)) is the base manuscript of the Symons–Spath edition in CCM 7.3 (1984), 69–147. The most recent edition from Cotton Tiberius A. iii (= *RC* (Ti)), with its Old English gloss, is *RC* (Kornexl), pp. 1–149. Earlier editions based on *RC* (Ti) are *RC* (Symons) of 1953 (Latin only, with partial collations with *RC* (Fa)), and Logeman, 'De Consuetudine Monachorum' (Latin and Old English gloss).

[14] To list only the most significant: the order of the various sections of the proem is hopelessly confused in (Fa); instead of the list of chapter headings found in (Ti), (Fa) contains only the instructions, probably copied from an exemplar, 'hic inserenda sunt capitula'; (Ti) includes the rubric 'Explicuit liber' shortly *before* the actual end of the customary; in both (Ti) and (Fa) the presence of ch. 6, on the duties of the officer known as the *circa*, is awkwardly inserted between chapters on the order of the liturgy from Easter to Pentecost; (Fa) does not contain the so-called epilogue – the exemption of monasteries from the payment of a tax known as the heriot. These differences are summarized and discussed by *RC* (Symons), pp. lv–lvi; see also the introduction at CCM 7.1, 159–60, and *RC* (Kornexl), pp. cv–cviii and cxliii–cxlvii.

[15] *RC* (Kornexl), p. cxliv: 'The inadequacies of both texts raise the question of possible deficiencies in the original version of the *RC* . . . It appears . . . entirely plausible that . . . "perfect" copies were prepared later, while the first version of the rule, which was undoubtedly composed under the pressure of a deadline, was not yet complete and ordered in every respect. It would accordingly be a mistake to proceed from [the idea of] one, definitive original of the *RC* and to measure the later tradition (especially the two extant witnesses) according to the ideal of this supposedly authoritative version of the text. Perhaps we ought to conceive of the archetype of the *RC* as a collection of individual chapters, not yet bound together, the "unripe" condition of which was, in varying measure, reproduced and passed down by the first copies . . .' (trans. mine).

Structure and sources

For present purposes, Kornexl's hypothesis allows by implication that multiple versions of the text may have circulated, and that Ælfric's copy might have differed in more than incidental ways from *RC* (Ti) and (Fa).[16] Where the *LME* disagrees with the two extant manuscripts of the *Concordia*, the latter may not represent the source exactly as Ælfric knew it. Both copies of the *Concordia* and the single copy of the *LME* are, moreover, of mid-eleventh-century date and at an unknown number of removes from their originals, so distinguishing variants in Ælfric's exemplar from subsequent copying errors is often impossible.[17] In a few instances, a reading preserved in the *LME* agrees with one manuscript of the *Concordia* against the other, but the evidence of conjunctive readings does not yield any clear patterns of correspondence.[18] Additional witnesses to the *Concordia*, including the anonymously compiled eleventh-century extracts titled *De ecclesiastica consuetudine* (= *DEC*), elucidate the problem only occasionally.[19]

See also *ibid.*, pp. lix and cvii–cviii, and Kornexl, 'The *Regularis Concordia* and its Old English Gloss', pp. 108–9.

[16] Minor instances in which Ælfric's copy of the *Concordia* differed from either version have long been acknowledged; see, e.g., Clemoes's 'Supplement to the Introduction', *Hirtenbriefe*, ed. Fehr, p. cxlvi, n. 94; but cf. commentary to *LME* 32 (at n. 170). See also below, n. 33.

[17] A comparison between the *LME* and manuscripts of the source reveals that the most common variants are fluctuations between singular and plural verb forms (though such discrepancies might hinge only on a scribe's forgetting or wrongly supplying a *titulus*) and between indicatives and subjunctives.

[18] For example, *LME* 18 and *RC* (Fa) 46 *si nondum diei* [*dies LME* manuscript] *aurora eluxerit*, agreeing against *RC* (Ti), where the phrase is omitted. The omission of the phrase in (Ti) is probably the result of a scribe's anticipation of a similar phrase introducing the next sentence; see *RC* (Kornexl), p. 261 (commentary to lines 695–6). Elsewhere, Ælfric's reading is closer to the Tiberius manuscript; e.g., *LME* 68 and *RC* (Ti) 101 *epistola* agree against *RC* (Fa) *episticula*.

[19] The excerpts – which combine extracts from the *Concordia* with additions from Amalarius's *Liber officialis* and other sources – constitute a significant analogue to the *LME*. The similarities led Fehr to attribute them, plus adjacent extracts from Amalarius in Cambridge, Corpus Christi College 190 (see below, n. 178), to Ælfric himself. Partial editions are included as 'Anhang III: Teile aus Aelfrics Priesterauszug', in *Hirtenbriefe*, ed. Fehr, pp. 234–43. Clemoes rejected the attribution to Ælfric, pointing out that the *LME* and 'commonplace book' excerpts draw on the same sources but often in different ways; see his 'The Old English Benedictine Office' and 'Supplement to the Introduction', *Hirtenbriefe*, ed. Fehr, pp. cxlvi–cxlvii. For textual links between the *DEC* and Eynsham 'letter', see commentary to *LME* 16 (at n. 74), 32

Because collation of the several Latin witnesses proves inconclusive, it is fortunate that Ælfric used the *Concordia* elsewhere in his writings. Faint echoes are present in his *Catholic Homilies* (First Series) for Candlemas and Palm Sunday.[20] More extensive use is evident in his description of the Offices of the Triduum in the *LME*, the pastoral letter to Wulfsige (Brief I) and the second Old English pastoral letter to Wulfstan (Brief III), all of which draw from the same part of the *Concordia* and overlap to a great extent.[21] The pastorals take certain details from the source that figure minimally or not at all in the *LME*, so the Old English letters are valuable witnesses to Ælfric's knowledge of other parts of the text.[22] Each time he used the *Concordia*, he appears to have returned directly to the source rather than to one of his earlier treatments of it, for he tends to adapt the text in slightly different ways on each occasion. Speculation about the content of his exemplar must therefore take account of all available witnesses. When describing communion in the mass of the Easter Vigil, for instance, *LME* 46, *RC* (Fa) 77 and *DEC* 9 all omit the phrase, found in *RC* (Ti) 77, *et pacem non dare nisi qui communicent*. The common absence, along with Kornexl's arguments that the addition in (Ti) lacks authority,[23] leads to the reasonable conclusion that Ælfric's exemplar would not have contained the additional phrase. But in the teeth of all the evidence, the corresponding provision in the second Old English pastoral letter for Wulfstan appears to include part of the detail

---

(at n. 170), 43 (at n. 219) and 46 (at nn. 232 and 234), and further discussion in Jones, 'Two Composite Texts'.

[20] *CH* I.ix and xiv, ed. Thorpe I, 150 and 218.

[21] See *Hirtenbriefe*, ed. Fehr, Briefe I.120–32 and III.23–63 and 178–81. The latter of the two pastorals is thought to stand quite close in date to the *LME*, and the similarities between the two are indeed strong; see Clemoes, 'Supplement to the Introduction', *Hirtenbriefe*, ed. Fehr, p. cxlv; but on the chronology, see also below, n. 26.

[22] The pastorals are occasionally closer in detail to the *Concordia* than to the *LME*; see Brief III.39–41 (lessons, chants and prayers for Good Friday) and III.43–9 (Veneration of the Cross), and cf. *RC* 73 and *LME* 43. Also compare Brief III.23–5 and *RC* 61 (no close correspondences in *LME*).

[23] Kornexl makes a strong case that the phrase is a later addition: it is not glossed in *RC* (Ti) and contradicts teaching elsewhere in the *Concordia*; see *RC* (Kornexl), pp. 320–2 (commentary to lines 1196–7). The phrase is also grammatically troubled; Symons and the CCM editors emend by supplying a finite verb *non <debent> dare*, etc.

Structure and sources

found in (Ti): 'Ac ge ne scylan singan offerendan on þæm dæge ne agnus dei ne communia *ne gan to pacem.*'[24]

Similarly, for his teaching on the Mass of the Presanctified on Good Friday,[25] Ælfric adapted *RC* 75 in slightly different ways for the letter to Wulfsige (Brief I.122–6), the *LME* (44) and the second Old English letter to Wulfstan (Brief III.50–4).[26] The versions agree in outline, and their common indebtedness to the wording of the *Concordia* is obvious. Some of their differences reflect nothing more than varying audiences: the *Concordia* and *LME* are monastic customaries, while the Old English pastoral letters take the form of an address to be delivered by a bishop to his secular clergy and therefore make (though not consistently) such substitutions as *preost* or *mæssepreost* for *abbas*.[27] Of greater weight is Ælfric's mention in all three texts of the corporal (the small square of linen placed on the altar beneath the bread and wine), which finds no analogue in the *Concordia* or the *DEC*. Here the difficulty is of a different sort: the detail may derive from Ælfric's exemplar or from a supplementary source, or it may be his own.[28] Also unaccounted for is his teaching

---

[24] Brief III.60 (emphasis added): 'And on that day you shall not sing the offertory nor the "Agnus Dei" nor exchange the peace.' The provision is the same in all four manuscripts. For the more problematic remainder of the phrase in (Ti), *nisi qui communicent*, there is no support at all.

[25] That is, the communion service that is a part of the liturgy of Good Friday. Because priests cannot consecrate the eucharist on this day, they distribute communion from the reserve sacrament blessed on the previous day, Maundy Thursday.

[26] The relative chronological order Brief I (992 × 1002), then (*c.* 1005) Briefe 2 and 3 and the *LME*, followed (*c.* 1006) by Briefe II and III, has been generally accepted since Fehr (*Hirtenbriefe*, p. xlvii), although his arguments are questionable to the extent that they assume dependence of Brief III on the *LME*. I incline toward Hill's view that Ælfric drew from the *Concordia* directly for Brief III; see her 'Monastic Reform and the Secular Church', p. 107, n. 10.

[27] Some fluctuation of these terms may go back to the source (*RC* 75). Conversely, Brief III.54, in a supposedly secular context, refers to the presence of brothers (*gebroþru*), though the term might apply to secular communities. The omitted reference to an assisting deacon in the letter to Wulfsige (at Brief I.122; cf. *LME* 44 and Brief III.50) may also hint at an intended audience of priests who celebrated the liturgy unassisted in parish churches rather than in secular communities.

[28] The consistency of the reference seems to favour a written source, as does the strange word order of the earliest version, Brief I.122, suggestive of a translation error: 'Gange se preost syððan to þam Godes weofode mid þære husl-lafe, þe he halgode on þunresdæg and mid ungehalgodum wine mid wætere gemenged and behelie mid corporale' ('Then the priest shall go to God's altar with the remnant of the eucharist that he

25

that the unconsecrated wine brought from the sacristy shall be mixed with water ('mixto uino' / 'wine mid wætere gemenged'), a detail shared by the letter to Wulfsige and the *LME*, but present in neither the *Concordia* nor the second Old English letter to Wulfstan. Rarely the two Old English pastorals may agree with the *Concordia* against the *LME*,[29] but the similarities between the *LME* and the second Old English letter to Wulfstan are consistently stronger – confirmation, perhaps, of their supposedly proximate composition (*c.* 1005 and 1006, respectively).[30]

Most decisive are the few points at which all three of Ælfric's texts agree against one or both manuscripts of the *Concordia*. On the manner in which the priest shall intone the various parts of the Lord's Prayer in the aforementioned communion service of Good Friday, the Ælfrician texts all give specific instructions which, despite slightly varying terminology, impose a uniform practice. Yet the *Concordia* offers only one of the three directions (and that in only one manuscript):[31]

RC 75 (Ti only)	DEC (CCCC 190)	Brief I.123–4	LME 44	Brief III.51–2
uoce sonora	*uoce sonora*	*be sone*	*sonora uoce*	*be sone*
–	–	*digellice*	*secrete*	*fægre*
–	–	*hlude*	*alta uoce*	*be sone*

The addition preserved in *RC* (Ti) could account for only the first of Ælfric's points; the presence of the other two in all three texts strongly suggests, once again, a fuller exemplar or a supplementary source.[32]

blessed on Thursday, and with unblessed wine mixed with water, and he shall cover [?it ?them] with a corporal'). Fehr's translation ('... und bedecke [sie] mit dem Korporale') makes the bread and wine the objects of *behelie*, but the implied object should be *altare*, as it correctly is in the *LME* and Brief III.

[29] For example, subjunctive *dicat* (RC 75), *cwæðe* (Brief I.123) and *cweðe* (Brief III.51) instead of the indicative at *LME* 44 (*dicit tunc abbas*).

[30] See above, n. 26.

[31] On the status of the phrase *uoce sonora*, see *RC* (Kornexl), p. 313 (commentary to line 1137). Its absence in (Fa) and lack of a gloss in (Ti) suggest to her that the phrase was not part of the 'original' text.

[32] The three Ælfrician texts also exhibit strong similarities in their restatement of the final provisions about placing the particle of consecrated bread (or *sanctum*) in the chalice and about the order of communion. All three agree against the source by: (a) using a single verb in place of the compound predicate *sumat . . . et ponat* of the first sentence; (b) using a single verb and compound subject in place of the plural verb

Structure and sources

Though so close a comparison is neither possible nor warranted in every instance where the *LME* and *pastoralia* overlap, the preceding examples demonstrate the risks in drawing conclusions about Ælfric's exemplar solely from a comparison of the *LME* and extant manuscripts of the *Concordia*. Even when further evidence from the pastoral letters or homilies is available, reconstruction of Ælfric's copy of the source remains unsure since he often adapted it differently from one occasion to the next.

Re-organization of the source

Kornexl's theory – that the extant versions of the *Concordia* transmit a stage or stages of a work in progress – might well explain that text's occasionally troubled organization. Æthelwold may have intended to return to the work and smooth its rough edges, and perhaps did so in some versions that have not survived. In any case, the *LME* suggests that some frustration with the arrangement of the *Concordia* may not be an entirely modern symptom. Even if his exemplar did not look exactly like *RC* (Ti) or (Fa),[33] Ælfric evidently re-arranged and rewrote parts of the source so completely that his dissatisfaction with the *Concordia* seems plain. His re-organization and synthesis of topics illustrate the intelligence and editorial skill familiar from his treatment of sources for the homilies, saints' lives and other works.

In the main, the *LME* follows the progression of topics in the *Regularis concordia* from its initial description of the monastic day through the many proper ceremonies of the liturgical year. Ælfric's most significant modifications of the source's plan occur at the very beginning of his customary (*LME* 1–12). This portion corresponds generally to the first major division of the *Concordia* (*RC* 15–38), where the customary proper begins with the words *a Kalendis Octobris*[34] and proceeds to describe in

---

communicent of the final clause; (c) inserting an adverb of time (*syððan/tunc/þonne*) where the source has none.

[33] Differences between Ælfric's exemplar and *RC* (Ti) and (Fa) best account for the otherwise inexplicable departures in *LME* 69, on which see the commentary at nn. 315–17. See also above, n. 16.

[34] *RC* 15: 'A kalendis enim octobris religiosorum morum domini opitulante gratia exordium sumendo omnia, quae usu regulari et sanctorum patrum imitatione spiritualia siue corporalia humili ac necesario [*sic*] agenda sunt officio, cum benedictione inchoentur.'

detail a typical feria, then a typical feast day, in the winter horarium – including the various parts of the Divine Office, as well as periods for work (*obedientia*), reading (*lectio*) and meals. Chapter two of the *Concordia* (*RC* 39–44) then proceeds from 1 November, when, according to the *Rule*, the length and arrangement of various parts of the horarium undergo further change to accommodate the longer nights and shorter days of winter.[35] The chore of describing the monks' daily round is complicated not only by these seasonal adaptations, but by the more frequent variation between ferial and Sunday or festal arrangements, as well as by the large number of extra prayers and devotions that had crowded into the horarium since St Benedict's time.[36] With so many variables to consider, the opening segments of the *Concordia* must frequently digress and backtrack.[37]

Ælfric re-organizes and greatly simplifies most of this material. He begins, for example, by condensing the sequence of the diurnal Offices into the first few sentences of the customary:

Kalendis enim Octobris, exceptis dominicis et festiuis diebus, primo diluculo prima canenda est cum septem psalmis et letaniis, deinde uacent lectionibus usquequo signum tertie insonuerit. Calceant se tunc et lauent et orationes faciant – scola simul et seniores singillatim – et spargant se aqua benedicta. Finita tertia fiat prima missa, postea capitolum. Post sextam horam faciant missam de die, qua finita decantent nonam. Nam de ceteris regula sancta dicit.[38]

---

[35] These seasonal adaptations are an essential feature of the monastic horarium as established in *RSB*, c. VIII. Because of the difference in latitude, the English obviously experienced even longer winter and shorter summer nights than did the Italian monks for whom Benedict wrote – a practical difficulty Ælfric acknowledges at *LME* 57.

[36] For example, the *trina oratio*, the chanting of the gradual psalms before Nocturns, special Offices for the Dead and All Saints, as well as some devotions unique to the *Concordia*, such as the frequent prayers for the royal house. On liturgical accretions to the monastic liturgy between the fifth and tenth centuries, see *RC* (Symons), pp. xlviii–l, and *RC* (Kornexl), pp. lxiii–lxiv.

[37] The simplest overview is still provided by Symons's outlines of the horaria (both winter and summer) inferred from the *Concordia*; see *RC* (Symons), pp. xliii–xliv; repr. with minor alterations by Knowles, *Monastic Order*, pp. 714–15 (Table XVIII).

[38] *LME* 2: '[From] the Kalends of October, excluding Sundays and feast days, Prime should be sung at first light, together with the seven psalms and the litanies. Then they [*scil.* the monks] shall retire to their reading until the bell for Terce rings. Then let them put on their day shoes, wash and say their prayers – the children together as a group, the senior monks individually – then sprinkle themselves with holy water. When Terce is over, the first mass shall take place, then Chapter. After the hour of Sext

He omits the source's wordy description of the monks' rising and their devotions before Nocturns (*RC* 15–18) and, for the present, omits altogether the Offices of Nocturns and Lauds with their several supplementary devotions. Perhaps influenced by the Benedictine *Rule*'s distribution of the psalms for the Office, he begins instead with Prime.[39] Ælfric then proceeds briskly through the horarium but alerts his readers from the outset that this is the order for ferias only.[40] The qualifying remark is another small but helpful modification of the *Concordia*, which does not acknowledge the ferial–festal distinction until far into its first chapter, where the reader must suddenly assimilate the new data to the already tortuous description.[41] The perceived abruptness of the turn highlights one of the weaknesses of this portion of the *Concordia*: the compiler does not separate the various components of the horarium for summary treatment, but attempts to describe in sequence all of the liturgical and extra-liturgical activities of the day, from the monks' rising for Nocturns until their going to bed after Compline. Given the sheer number of activities and the author's expectation – apparent from the amount of detail he provides[42] – that some of these will be unfamiliar to his audience, this plan buckles under its own weight. From the maze of detail no clear view of the horarium's structure emerges. The *LME* does not wholly escape the consequences of this disorienting arrangement,[43] but Ælfric does manage to unravel and follow the relevant threads with some consistency.

The brevity of Ælfric's instructions for the remainder of the day – especially his laconic mention of Chapter (which merits a lengthy, separate description at *RC* 26) – suggests that all of this material is familiar to his audience, either from the *Rule* itself or from their own experience.[44] Although the preface states that the Eynsham monks do not

---

they shall celebrate the mass of the day and, when that is finished, chant None. The holy *Rule* tells of the rest.'

[39] The recitation of the psalter from Ps. I begins on Monday at Prime in the Benedictine *cursus*; see *RSB*, c. XVIII.4.

[40] He says, 'exceptis dominicis et festiuis diebus'. He will return to these provisions soon, at *LME* 5 and 7–10.

[41] *RC* 27: 'Ista uero omnia [*scil.* the preceding detailed provisions for the matutinal mass and Chapter] quae diximus post Tertiam his temporibus [*scil.* the period of the winter horarium] agenda, dominicis diebus omni tempore ante Tertiam agantur . . .'

[42] For example, the full prayer texts provided for the *trina oratio* collects at *RC* 17.

[43] See, e.g., commentary to *LME* 6 (at n. 37).

[44] New monasteries would usually be staffed by a vanguard of experienced monks

know Æthelwold's customary,⁴⁵ Ælfric does presuppose their knowledge of the *Rule* and of certain devotional practices described in full by the *Concordia*.⁴⁶ He also assumes the monks will possess all or most of the necessary liturgical books and the skill to use them properly.⁴⁷

Succeeding passages of the *LME* bring to light the further usefulness of Ælfric's re-organization. After outlining the diurnal Offices, he pauses to treat summarily a number of supplementary devotions that the *Concordia* describes one by one, as they would actually occur through the day. For the first of these, the *trina oratio* (*LME* 3), consisting of varying psalms, prayers and collects recited at different times, Ælfric compresses into a single sentence information that sprawls over four places in the source.⁴⁸ Following this summary, he takes up another important set of devotions, the so-called *psalmi familiares* or *psalmi pro benefactoribus*⁴⁹ chanted after each of the liturgical hours (*LME* 4) for the monastery's friends and benefactors, including the king.⁵⁰ As prescribed by the *LME*, the devotion consists of two psalms (one for the king, plus one for the king and all benefactors), the Lord's Prayer, a series of short petitions (called

---

transplanted from some major house: thus Abingdon was reformed from Dunstan's Glastonbury, the Old and New Minsters from Æthelwold's Abingdon, Ramsey from Oswald's Westbury-on-Trym, and so on; see Knowles, *Monastic Order*, pp. 49–52 and 721 (Table I).

⁴⁵ *LME* 1: 'hactenus predictus libellus uestrae fraternitati incognitus habetur'.

⁴⁶ On the *Rule*, see mentions at *LME* 1, 2, 57, 62(2x) and 63. For a devotion whose practice is assumed by Ælfric but detailed in the *Concordia*, see *LME* 3 (the *trina oratio*) and commentary.

⁴⁷ This is evident throughout: e.g., *LME* 17 (martyrology), 52 (antiphoner), 51 (sacramentary) and 54 (hymnal). Apparent exceptions, perhaps indicative that Ælfric is introducing new material or updating old, include: (1) his thorough instructions for the order of hymns (*LME* 13, 50 and 54); (2) his provision of antiphons to take the place of 'Alleluia' in the second Nocturn of Vigils through Septuagesima and Lent (*LME* 26); and (3) his provisions for the occurrence of saints' days and Sundays (*LME* 55). See below, pp. 35–6, as well as the commentary to each of these sections.

⁴⁸ Cf. *RC* 16–17 (before Nocturns), 24 (before Terce in winter), 37 (after Compline) and 82 (before Prime in summer). Twice (*RC* 17 and 37) the *Concordia*'s basic instructions are swollen, moreover, with the full texts of the collects to be said at the end of each devotion. That Ælfric feels at liberty to omit these may indicate that a practice novel in the 970s was well established by *c.* 1005.

⁴⁹ *RC* (Symons), p. 12, n. 7: 'The MSS of the Concordia draw no consistent distinction between *familiares* and *benefactores*.'

⁵⁰ See commentary to *LME* 4 (at n. 18).

preces) and a collect. Ælfric's version of this custom differs in some interesting respects from that found in the *Concordia*,[51] but it is his re-arrangement of the material that is most striking. The provisions for the *trina oratio* were culled from four separate places, those for the *psalmi familiares* from as many as seven.[52] The *Concordia* introduces the first instalment of the devotion after Nocturns, specifying the particular psalms for this hour and three collects to be used every time the devotion is said.[53] Following these instructions, the *Concordia* says, 'Et sic finitis omnibus regularibus horis semper agatur',[54] obscuring the fact that the two psalms differ for each hour and that the collects quoted will not, it seems, be needed after Lauds, Vespers and Compline. These additional details only emerge gradually and dimly as the *Concordia* plods through the monastic day. Ælfric's presentation begins with a one-sentence summary of the devotion's purpose, its placement in the horarium and its constituent parts.[55] Then follows a clear outline of the proper psalms and hours to which they are assigned; along the way Ælfric states explicitly how the devotions are to terminate (i.e., with their own collect or, at Lauds, Vespers and Compline, with that 'of the hour').[56] The essential features of the custom, however scattered in the source, are thus conveniently brought together in one place.

This practice of distillation continues, if less noticeably, through most of the early sections of *LME* that describe the horarium and its

---

[51] For example, on his omission of the queen from the specific intentions, see *RC* (Kornexl), p. lxiv, n. 33.

[52] *RC* 19, 21–2, 24, 33–4 and 37.

[53] The *Concordia* quotes in full the three collects (one for the king, one for the queen, one for the king, queen and benefactors). Ælfric does not quote these prayer texts but refers to only one *oratio* (*LME* 4), hinting again that he expects his readers to know them, or at least know where to find them.

[54] *RC* 19: 'And they shall always do in like manner after each of the regular hours.' After Prime alone do the intentions of the devotion change (*RC* 22: 'pro carnis temptatione' and 'pro defunctis fratribus'); Ælfric includes the same stipulations (*LME* 4). Symons concludes (*RC* (Symons), p. 14, n. 3) that there were no devotions on the king's behalf after Prime, but cf. *RC* (Kornexl), p. lxiv, n. 33.

[55] *LME* 4: 'Pro rege et pro benefactoribus omnibus horis duo psalmi canendi sunt cum dominica oratione et precibus et oratione.'

[56] As at *RC* 21, 34 and 37, where the *psalmi familiares* are incorporated into other devotions following these hours and so do not need their own collect.

variations.[57] The details are further discussed in the commentary, but an overview of the the opening segments of the *LME* in relation to the order of corresponding material in the source is given here in tabular form. Numbers refer to the sections of the present edition of the *LME* and the Symons–Spath edition of the *Concordia* in the CCM:

LME	RC
1 Ælfric's preface	–
2 diurnal order, from Prime	15, 22–6 and 33
3 *trina oratio*	17–18, 24 and 37–8
4 *psalmi familiares*	19, 21–2, 24, 33–4 and 37
5 Sunday/festal order	[26] and 27–8 [58]
6 five psalms after Chapter *pro defunctis fratribus*	32
7 Sunday confession	[28] and 27 [59]
8 communion on Sundays/feasts	29
9 admonitions[60]	–
10 matutinal mass intentions, Sundays and ferias	28 and 25
11 mass of the day, Friday and Saturday	31
12 votive antiphons of Holy Cross and BVM after Lauds and Vespers	21, 34 and 42

The relative successes and failures of Ælfric's methods in this part of the *LME* are clear. The attempt at a lucid, summary presentation of the elements and variations of the horarium, if such was his design, appears to have broken down at *LME* 5, after which only occasional regroupings of points (as in *LME* 10 and 12) occur.

Subsequent portions of the *LME* do not demonstrate so complex a relationship to the *Concordia* as do these early sections. Beginning with his description of changes to the full winter horarium (1 November through Easter), Ælfric follows the order of the source much more closely.

---

[57] On these variations, see commentary to *LME* 5–12. Ælfric's re-arrangement does not prove so effective as in *LME* 2–4, for it seems to interject two or three points out of their logical order (see commentary to *LME* 6). It must also be admitted that *RC* 27–9 presents a more logical, if also wordier, digest of the festal horarium.

[58] The substance of *LME* 5 is from *RC* 27–8, but Ælfric introduces the passage with words borrowed from the opening of *RC* 26; on this compositional method, see below, pp. 51–8.

[59] *LME* 7 is from *RC* 27, but with a key phrase borrowed from *RC* 28.

[60] Sources uncertain, but see commentary to *LME* 9 (at n. 48).

The next segment (*LME* 13–15) moves to the full winter horarium 'a Calendis [*sic*] Nouembris', including an expanded overview of the winter hymnal (with proper hymns from Advent through Passiontide).[61] But extensive interpolations of this sort remain the exception in the *LME*, and Ælfric's adherence to the *Concordia* carries through to the following segments: the description of customs proper to the period from Advent to Candlemas (*LME* 16–25) and, more fully still, from Septuagesima through Easter (*LME* 26–48).[62] Among the details of these latter seasons, Ælfric interjects teaching from the *Liber officialis* of Amalarius of Metz and from other sources,[63] but without disturbing the essential order of provisions from the *Concordia*. The ten weeks from Septuagesima through the Easter Octave, with their complex variations in the liturgy, required particularly careful exposition, and Ælfric's allotment of so much space to these seasons mirrors the emphases of both the *Concordia* and Amalarius.[64]

After the liturgical climax of Easter, the *LME*, like the *Concordia*, lapses into a less detailed survey of the transition to the summer horarium (*LME* 49–54). Ælfric continues to follow the source (*RC* 81–91), but with greater freedom than in preceding sections. Again he fleshes out the skeletal order of hymns provided by the *Concordia*,[65] but otherwise the *LME* proceeds quite casually through a number of topics, only some of

---

[61] *LME* 13. The *Regularis concordia*, by contrast, specifies only the hymns for Vespers, Compline, Nocturns and Lauds on Sunday, assuming the reader's knowledge of the rest (*RC* 39). See commentary to *LME* 13.

[62] Corresponding to *RC* 44–54 and 55–80, respectively.

[63] See below, pp. 59–68. This supplementary material is usually separated from the customs derived from the *Regularis concordia* by citation-tags: see, e.g., *LME* 30: 'Amalarius: In Quadragessima . . . Consuetudo: In diebus Quadragessime . . .' The distinction is not always observed, however: e.g., at *LME* 22 (Holy Innocents) there is a silent transition from the *Concordia* to Amalarian teaching, and similarly at *LME* 25 (Candlemas); see commentary (at nn. 88 and 103, respectively).

[64] By their very nature – dramatic and rare – the ceremonies surrounding the high points of the liturgical year attracted a disproportionate share of attention in customaries, *ordines*, sacramentaries, pontificals and *expositiones*. For Anglo-Saxon evidence, see Ælfric's pastoral letters, Briefe I.120–32 and III.23–63; also the anonymous *DEC* (see above, n. 19). A fragmentary mid-eleventh-century Old English translation of the *Concordia*, limited to customs for Palm Sunday through the beginning of Good Friday, is preserved in Cambridge, Corpus Christi College 201, pp. 1–7; see 'Ein weiteres Bruchstück', ed. Zupitza, and Hill, 'The "Regularis Concordia"', pp. 309–11.

[65] *LME* 50 (Paschaltide) and 54 (summer), only the latter corresponding to *RC* 91.

which are directly tied to the seasons after Easter and Pentecost.[66] Despite the occasional pooling of instructions to good effect,[67] by its end the work resembles only a gathering of miscellaneous points. Interestingly, it is to these negligible surroundings that Ælfric relegates (at *LME* 63–4) his only direct borrowings from Æthelwold's ostentatious, politically charged proem to the *Concordia*.[68] The customary proper of the *LME* concludes, like the *Concordia*, with directions for the care of the dying or recently deceased members of the community, the circulation of the *breue* and confraternal obligations (*LME* 65–9).[69] If Ælfric knew the so-called epilogue to the *Concordia* (an exemption of monasteries from the tax known as the heriot), he did not use it.[70]

Evaluating Ælfric's adaptations

Many departures from the *Concordia* suggest differences of substance between the two texts, their respective audiences and the circumstances of their composition. Some of Ælfric's changes, like his aforementioned tendency to regroup instructions, accord with the aim of clarifying or expanding received material. The expansions are of particular importance for the historical study of liturgy, since evidence about the details of the Office in Anglo-Saxon monasteries is scarce.[71] Because Ælfric usually followed the *Concordia* rather closely, however, the worth of the *LME* as an independent liturgical witness has more often than not been undervalued.

---

[66] A similar lack of coherence is seen near the end of the *Concordia* itself, which presents a relatively loose collection of miscellaneous points.

[67] For example, *LME* 58, on the ringing of bells at Nocturns, the mass of the day and Vespers on major feasts (claimed to be a native English custom), is a synthesis and interpretation of *RC* 50 and 18.

[68] On the possible awkwardness of the proem for Ælfric, see below, pp. 42–51, and commentary to *LME* 63–4.

[69] Cf. *RC* 98–102.

[70] The exemption aimed to remove any pretext for abbots and abbesses to hoard their surplus wealth rather than disburse it to the poor. On this portion of the source (*RC* 104), see *RC* (Kornexl), pp. lxxxii–lxxxiii and cviii–cix. The absence of this section from *RC* (Fa) raises the possibility that it was omitted from some copies of the text in circulation and so, perhaps, from Ælfric's exemplar.

[71] For summaries of surviving evidence, see Gatch, 'The Office'; Gneuss, 'Liturgical Books', pp. 110–31, 136 and 139–41; and A. Corrêa, 'Daily Office Books: Collectars and Breviaries', in *Liturgical Books*, ed. Pfaff, pp. 45–60.

Only its most conspicuous departures – such as the outline of the monastic hymnal or the supplement on the readings and responsories for the Night Office – have featured prominently in studies of Anglo-Saxon liturgy. The importance of these additions is beyond dispute, but the *LME* contains many quieter modifications of the source which also repay careful study. The identification of differences, no matter how slight, recalls that agreement between Ælfric and the *Concordia* cannot be taken for granted. And even where substantial differences are not at stake, Ælfric's decisions about what his audience does and does not need to be told shed light on his expectations and theirs.

Additions to the source

Many additions seemingly prompted by a lack of detail in the source do not indicate exceptional practices at Eynsham. Ælfric's outlines of the order of winter and Paschaltide hymns (*LME* 13 and 50, respectively), for example, and his quotation of the full series of antiphons for the second Nocturn of Vigils from Septuagesima through Lent (*LME* 26) expand the corresponding but meagre provisions of the *Concordia*.[72] For these additions Ælfric drew on outside liturgical sources, most likely the hymnal and antiphoner directly. The mere fact of expansion does not reveal Ælfric's motive; if the community's hymnal and antiphoner were seriously defective, common sense would seem to urge correction of the liturgical books themselves. Even complete books, on the other hand, could be difficult to use because of confusing organization or faulty rubrics, or because an arrangement once correct had become obsolete with changes in liturgical fashion. Since he provides only incipits, Ælfric seems concerned to revise or correct the use of existing texts in already available books. Other additions sent Ælfric to quite different sources. His teaching at *LME* 55 on the relative precedence of major feasts and Sundays when these coincide (or 'occur'), though not without precedent in monastic customaries, does not come from the *Concordia*. More noticeably, he also draws from Amalarius's *Liber officialis* to supplement the virtual silence of the *Concordia* regarding observance of pre-Lent (*LME*

---

[72] Cf. *RC* 39 and 91 (hymns) and 56 (antiphons from Septuagesima). In a few minor points, Ælfric's hymnal is unusual; see esp. commentary to *LME* 13 (at nn. 62–3).

26–8),[73] and uses the same treatise to explain and emphasize the importance of Lent, Passion Sunday (not mentioned at all in the *Concordia*), Palm Sunday and the *triduum sacrum* (*LME* 29–46). He also adds material that his monks, from a strictly practical viewpoint, do not need, such as a fulsome explanation of the Chrism Mass (*LME* 39), which would not have taken place at Eynsham.[74]

Most of these additions confirm or vaguely imply that Ælfric's liturgy was what the available evidence suggests was typical for an early eleventh-century Anglo-Saxon monastery touched by the influence of the 'Benedictine revival'. Of similar weight is the appended supplement (*LME* 70–80) to the customary proper, outlining the readings and responsories for the Night Office. The order of lections there represented is closely related to *Ordo romanus XIII A*, which was certainly known in late Anglo-Saxon England.[75] As in his outline of the hymnal, Ælfric's provision here of incipits only presupposes that the texts and music are already available in some form. Even so, the need to discuss at length such basic features of the Office might raise questions about the training of the Eynsham monks and their access to up-to-date and well-ordered liturgical books.[76]

Omissions from the source

The loss of Ælfric's exemplar of the source urges caution when speaking of 'changes' to it, let alone 'his changes'. The following remarks build on the cautious premise that Ælfric's copy of the *Regularis concordia*, while it probably was not identical to, at least did not differ radically from the version of the text known to us from *RC* (Ti) and (Fa). During his years as a monk at the Old Minster, Ælfric would have

---

[73] That is, Septuagesima, Sexagesima and Quinquagesima Sundays; cf. the spare provisions of *RC* 55–6.

[74] See the commentary to *LME* 39 (at n. 196).

[75] See Hall, 'Some Liturgical Notes', and present commentary to *LME* 70–7. English copies of the *ordo* are preserved in CCCC 190, pp. 212–13, and Rouen, Bibliothèque Municipale, 1382, 173r. The latter was collated as manuscript S (misidentified as Rouen 1372) by Andrieu, *Les Ordines romani* II, 481–8.

[76] Ælfric claims to be addressing a need voiced by the monks themselves: 'Quia rogastis fratres scribi uobis qualiter legere siue cantare per anni circulum in ecclesia debeatis, exponam uobis' (*LME* 70). On the dearth of surviving evidence for Anglo-Saxon Office lectionaries and antiphoners, see Gneuss, 'Liturgical Books', pp. 117 and 120.

witnessed for himself many of the customs described in the *Concordia*,[77] so memory, too, could compensate for possible deficiencies in his exemplar. From everything that is known of his working methods, however, his omissions from the *Concordia* are more likely to reflect deliberate editorial choices. In the preface Ælfric clearly states that the *LME* is, like most of his known writings, an abridgement and synthesis of authorities.[78] If his exemplar resembled the two extant copies of the source, then Ælfric's omissions fall into two groups: (1) those permitted by an assumption that his audience is already acquainted with monastic life, Benedict's *Rule*, the elements of the Office and the proper use of liturgical books; and (2) omissions that suggest actual divergence from the practices laid down in the *Concordia*.

It bears repeating that no customary was meant to serve as a wholly self-sufficient text, but to codify and regulate aspects of the monastic life about which Benedict's *Rule* is silent. In his preface and twice elsewhere, Ælfric obliquely reminds the reader of his text's function ancillary to the *Rule* (at *LME* 1, 2 and 55), which he otherwise takes for granted. His reorganization of the opening chapter of the *Concordia*, discussed above, refers to the diurnal hours in the most general terms in order to devote more care to the supplemental devotions.[79] He does not mention the monks' rising for Nocturns or, for that matter, the entire period from Nocturns to Lauds (cf. *RC* 15–16 and 20–1); similarly absent are the Offices of Vespers and Compline (cf. *RC* 34 and 36–8).[80] Given that the Benedictine *cursus horarum* and the divisions of the psalter are amply treated in the *Rule*, Ælfric drops the thread after listing the hours from

---

[77] See *LME* 1, where Ælfric refers to observances 'quae in scola eius [*scil*. Æthelwoldi] degens multis annis de moribus seu consuetudinibus didici'. In addition to the observance of the *Rule* and, presumably, the customs of the *Regularis concordia*, Æthelwold imposed on his monks a number of additional devotions (see *Life of St Æthelwold*, ed. Lapidge and Winterbottom, pp. lxviii–lxxvii), though there is no trace of these in the *LME*.

[78] *LME* 1: '*haec pauca* de libro consuetudinum . . . scriptitando demonstro' (emphasis added). On Ælfric's methods as an abbreviator, see below, pp. 51–8.

[79] The *Concordia*'s initial method of plodding through the horarium is, in fairness, primarily a way of describing the order not of the liturgical hours but of the devotions and other activities surrounding them.

[80] *LME* 3 mentions Compline and some attendant ceremonies (prayers and asperges) only in the context of describing the *trina oratio*.

Prime to None and refers his readers to that text.[81] Later, where the *Concordia* pauses to outline the summer horarium (*RC* 83), Ælfric's customary offers no comparable summary, although relevant instructions are inserted elsewhere.[82] The *LME* rarely mentions such essential activities as work (*obedientia*) or meals (*prandium, cena* or *mensa*).[83] The important rule of silence from Vespers to Chapter on the following day, as well as during periods for *lectio*, is merely implied.[84]

Absent, too, are certain customs not contained in the *Rule* but widespread by the later tenth century. The daily routine at Chapter, not explicitly given in the *Rule*, is outlined at *RC* 26 in such detail as to suggest, if not the introduction of new customs, at least the standardization of existing ones.[85] Other liturgical forms are omitted, it seems, because they are presumed known or written down in obvious, accessible places. At *LME* 4, for example, Ælfric leaves out the texts of the *psalmi familiares* collects quoted in full at *RC* 19 and 37.[86] Similarly, for the

---

[81] *LME* 2: 'Nam de ceteris regula sancta dicit'; cf. *RSB*, cc. VIII–XVIII (outline of the daily and nightly *cursus*).

[82] *LME* 5 (the ferial order 'ab octauis Pentecosten': Prime + matutinal mass + Chapter), 12 (Vigils of the Dead after Vespers) and 57 (the summer interval between Nocturns and Lauds).

[83] See *RC* (Symons), pp. xxxiii–xxxvi, and references at *RC* 32, 33, 53 and 83 (work), and *RC* 14, 33, 44, 70, 83, 88 and 92 (meals); see also *RSB*, cc. XLVIII and XXXIX–XLI, which Ælfric probably takes for granted. From Easter to 14 September, and on Sundays and feasts of twelve lessons throughout the year, the *Concordia* allows two meals, *prandium* at noon and *cena* after Vespers. From 14 September to the beginning of Lent, the monks take one meal only, between None and Vespers; during Lent itself and on Ember Days, this single meal (again termed *cena*) is postponed until after Vespers. See also D. A. Bullough, 'What Has Ingeld to Do with Lindisfarne?', *ASE* 22 (1993), 93–125, at p. 108.

[84] That is, in the provision (*LME* 60) that the monks have a separate place (*auditorium*) in which to carry on conversation. See *RC* (Symons), p. xxxviii, and *RSB*, cc. VI and XLII.

[85] The *Concordia*'s prescriptions for Chapter are similar to those in the *Memoriale qualiter*; see Hallinger's apparatus to *RC* 26, 86.15–87.24. According to *RC* 26, Chapter includes a reading from the martyrology, various prayers and responses, a reading from the *Rule* (or, on major feasts, the gospel of the day) and the public confession and correction of faults. The meeting ends (*RC* 32) with the five extra psalms *pro defunctis fratribus*, also mentioned by Ælfric at *LME* 6 (though his abridgement may be faulty there; see the commentary).

[86] It is possible, however, that Ælfric's vague *oratio* (*LME* 4, first sentence), without a specified intention, is part of a larger, deliberate down-playing of the emphasis on the royal house; see below, pp. 43–9.

elaborate description of the Veneration of the Cross on Good Friday, including the long devotional prayers quoted *in extenso* at *RC* 73, Ælfric substitutes the terse instructions 'deportetur crux ante altare a cantoribus cantantibus uersus et cetera, ut omnes eam per ordinem salutent'.[87] The chants or *uersus* mentioned would be found in the gradual (the mass antiphoner), and perhaps additional instructions in the rubrics of the sacramentary.[88] Again, in place of the full outlines of lections, chants and prayers for the Vigils of Easter and Pentecost (*RC* 77 and 88), Ælfric simply refers his readers to the sacramentary and (implicitly) the gradual.[89]

More significant, however, are those omissions from Æthelwold's customary that point to actual differences in practice.[90] Although Ælfric saw the *Concordia* as a useful model, he was not at all timid about adapting and supplementing the source where necessary. In the preface he claims, with a hint of pride, that to observe all of the customs of Æthelwold's Winchester, his own *alma mater*, would be too much for his present charges.[91] Behind his avowedly paternal concern must also lie a practical awareness that recently refounded Eynsham could not vie with Winchester in splendour or resources. Certain observances are therefore

---

[87] *LME* 43: 'a cross shall be carried down before the altar by cantors as they chant the verses and the rest, so that all may venerate it [*scil.* the cross] in due turn'. Ælfric's wording may also be influenced by Amalarius; see the commentary to *LME* 43 (at n. 220).

[88] See Gneuss, 'Liturgical Books', pp. 102–4 (graduals) and 99–102 (sacramentaries).

[89] See *LME* 46 and 51 with commentary (at nn. 228 and 265, respectively), although interesting interpretative or textual cruces may lurk in both passages; on Ælfric's 'Gregorian' system of readings for the Easter Vigil, see Hall, 'Some Liturgical Notes', pp. 301–3, and Remley, *Old English Biblical Verse*, pp. 78–87. On the notorious confusion surrounding the Pentecost Vigil in the *Concordia* and most texts derived from it, see *RC* (Kornexl), pp. 353–6.

[90] On the difficulty of distinguishing real from apparent departures, Gatch's warning is well taken: 'It is clear on cursory examination that the "Letter" is not merely an abbreviation of the *Concordia*, and it is extremely uncertain which observances of the latter not mentioned in the "Letter" were to be omitted at Eynsham' ('Old English Literature and the Liturgy', p. 241).

[91] *LME* 1: 'nec audeo omnia uobis intimare, quae in scola eius degens multis annis de moribus seu consuetudinibus didici, ne forte fastidientes districtionem tante obseruantiae nec saltem uelitis auditum prebere narranti'. On Æthelwold's customization of the Office, see above, n. 77; on evidence for his contributions to other parts of the liturgy, see *Life of St Æthelwold*, ed. Lapidge and Winterbottom, pp. lx–lxxxv.

shorter and less demanding; roles are doubled and clerical ranks, where not of immediate consequence, left unspecified. Ælfric's brief instructions concerning the Veneration of the Cross on Good Friday, for example, suggest a much simpler ceremony, perhaps without the lengthy private devotions recommended in the *Concordia*. Nor, in the same ceremony, does he assign the antiphonal singing of the *uersus* to deacons and subdeacons as in the source, but to two unspecified cantors,[92] and he omits altogether the rite of 'burying' the cross (*depositio crucis*) that immediately follows in the *Concordia* (*RC* 74).[93] Practical considerations, such as the length of the Night Office or the number of available participants at Eynsham, may also have prompted Ælfric to leave out one of the most celebrated passages in the *Concordia*, the so-called *Visitatio sepulchri* 'play' at Easter Nocturns.[94] He quite naturally omits a further provision allowing additional time for the monks to wash and shave on Good Friday, 'if the number of the community is so great that Saturday, the next day, would not suffice for this'.[95] Such would obviously not be the case at Eynsham.

Interpreting other apparent omissions requires greater caution. Unlike the *Concordia*, for instance, the *LME* does not indicate the presence of a lay congregation at the mass of the day;[96] but to conclude from this that laymen were not present or that Eynsham priests served no parochial functions clashes with other indications in the text.[97] Ælfric also omits a

---

[92] See *LME* 43, trans. above at n. 87.

[93] Arguably, the rite might be included at the end of the veneration service in the sacramentary (or wherever else the rubrics for that ceremony were found). The *depositio crucis* was never so widespread a custom as the veneration, however, and neither Ælfric's instructions here nor any known to me in his other writings hints that he observed this ceremony. Even at *RC* 74, moreover, the redactor (probably Æthelwold himself) stresses that the *depositio* is optional.

[94] At *RC* 79; the origins and contemporary perceptions of this rite are much disputed in modern scholarship. Representative studies include K. Young, *The Drama of the Medieval Church*, 2 vols. (Oxford, 1933) I, 249; Hardison, *Christian Rite*, pp. 178–219; and, more recently, G. B. Bryan, *Ethelwold and Medieval Music-Drama at Winchester: The Easter Play, its Author, and its Milieu*, European University Studies, Series 30: Theatre, Film and Television 10 (Bern, 1981).

[95] Trans. *RC* (Symons) 47, p. 46 (= *RC* 76: 'si tanta fuerit cohors societatis ut sabbati crastini ad hoc non sufficiat dies').

[96] Cf. *RC* 28: 'signorum <motu> fidelem aduocantes plebem missam inchoent'; see also *RC* 68.

[97] For example, his remarks on infant baptisms at the Easter Vigil (*LME* 46). The other

Structure and sources

reference to the wearing of chasubles by the priest, deacon and subdeacon at mass during Lent and on Ember Days; the absence could suggest that either this provision from the *Concordia* has become commonplace or is being suppressed deliberately.[98] Another equivocal silence concerns the officer known as the *circa*, whose duties are the subject of an entire chapter in the *Concordia* (*RC* 86–7), but of whom Ælfric says nothing. Far more significantly, for unstated reasons the *LME* departs from its source on the recommended frequency of receiving holy communion: Ælfric urges reception on Sundays and feasts only (*LME* 8), the *Concordia* daily (*RC* 29).[99] Other unexplained departures include a shortening of the period in the year during which a procession takes place before the principal mass on Wednesdays and Fridays (ending 14 September instead of 1 October) and the chanting of the fifteen gradual psalms (Pss. CXIX–CXXXIII) upon the death of a brother in confraternity (instead of the seven penitential psalms designated by the *Concordia*).[100]

Finally, whether considering Ælfric's additions or omissions, it should be remembered that pragmatic reduction was not his only concern. On one major point the *LME* sets a higher standard than its sources do – not just the *Concordia*, but St Benedict himself. Thus in the summer period, when the *Rule* prescribes only one reading at Nocturns on ferias, Ælfric retains three (*LME* 80).[101] Such rigour befits Ælfric, whose pragmatism

---

occasion on which Ælfric implies a lay presence is at the Chrism Mass (see *LME* 39), but the fact that this would never have taken place at Eynsham raises the possibility that other parts of his customary, too, reflect an 'academic' interest in the liturgy more than in the actual customs at Eynsham. On other limitations of the *LME* as evidence, see below, pp. 68–70.

[98] The source (*RC* 58) also directs that the subdeacon shall remove his chasuble before reading the epistle, while the deacon, before reading the gospel, shall fold his and wear it over the left shoulder (the style termed *casula duplicata*). These customs were widespread, however; see Hallinger's apparatus to *RC* 58, 104.8–15. If a house such as Eynsham did not have a sufficient number of chasubles, the custom would be impractical. For another possible hint about the availability of liturgical vestments, see commentary to *LME* 66 (at n. 306).

[99] See commentary to *LME* 8 (at n. 45).

[100] *LME* 29 (cf. *RC* 57) and 69 (cf. *RC* 102), with commentary (at nn. 133 and 315, respectively).

[101] Noted by Gatch, 'Old English Literature and the Liturgy', p. 242, and *RC* (Kornexl), p. cliv, n. 26. Ælfric's teaching about repetition of Sunday masses (also at *LME* 80) may also be supererogatory, but the provision is difficult to interpret (see commentary at nn. 369–70). Another stricture not found in the *Concordia* is the fast enjoined on

never lost sight of, and in some cases raised, the standards of the monastic reform that he had inherited.

Further responses and changing ideas of 'reform'

The preceding summary has compared the *Concordia* and *LME* according to their shared function: to convey detailed instructions about the liturgy. It is well known, however, that the *Regularis concordia* represented much more than a functional guide. Both in its lengthy proem and in certain features of the customary proper, the *Concordia* was also a monument to the religious and political ideology of Æthelwold and the dominant parties of the tenth-century reform movement. 'Reform' from its beginnings was a complex and pliable notion, and even its three great proponents, Dunstan, Æthelwold and Oswald, appear to have fostered their own individual standards.[102] Certain common emphases, however, stand out among tenth-century sources: a uniform observance of the Benedictine *Rule* in all English monasteries; the professed cultivation of royal over local aristocratic patronage; a harsh polemic against secular clerks and their expulsion from some cathedral chapters and minsters; the 'restoration' of a monastic episcopacy as witnessed by Bede in the 'golden age' of the Anglo-Saxon church; and, fuelled by that nostalgia, a pride in the 'native' element in Anglo-Saxon

those who read the lesson or carry the paten at mass (*LME* 56; see commentary at n. 282).

[102] The differences reflected, in part, their various ties to continental monasticism (Dunstan's to Ghent, Oswald's and (indirectly) Æthelwold's to Fleury). Liturgical differences aside, serious ideological divisions, especially between Dunstan and Æthelwold, have also been suggested; see D. Parsons, 'Introduction', in *Tenth-Century Studies*, ed. Parsons, pp. 1–9, at 3; also *RC* (Kornexl), pp. xxvii–xxviii. According to *RC* 5, monks from Ghent and Fleury advised the Council of Winchester that drew up the *Concordia*. For the traditional analysis, which favoured the influences of Ghent and Lotharingian customs, see Symons, 'Sources', and *idem*, '*Regularis Concordia*: History and Derivation', in *Tenth-Century Studies*, ed. Parsons, pp. 37–59; see also *RC* (Symons), pp. xlv–lii, and Knowles, *Monastic Order*, pp. 39 and 721 (Table I). A recently discovered customary by Thierry of Amorbach, reflecting the observances of late tenth-century Fleury, suggests that the influences of that house were stronger than previously believed. See *Consuetudines Floriacenses antiquiores*, ed. Davril and Donnat, in CCM 7.3, 7–60. The source-debate is well summarized in *Life of St Æthelwold*, ed. Lapidge and Winterbottom, pp. lviii–lx, and *RC* (Kornexl), pp. lxxxix–xcv.

monasticism relative to continental trends of revival and liturgical embellishment.[103]

All of these themes have been detected, in one form or another, in the *Concordia*, and yet all of them are muted in, or simply absent from, Ælfric's customary. If, in fact, the *LME* were the only surviving witness to the *Concordia*, our impressions of the latter would be much distorted. Apart from his prefatory acknowledgement of Æthelwold's role in drafting the *Concordia*, Ælfric's pride in the living legacy of reform is curiously non-specific. This could be the result of a pragmatic mind at work: the politics and polemic of the source were not, after all, essential to the yearly round of work and prayer at Eynsham. But a closer look at the vast difference in attitude between the two works might perceive in Ælfric's editorial decisions some compromise between his master's ideologically pure programme of the 970s and the realities of the new millennium. Recent study of Ælfric's writings in their historical and literary contexts has emphasized their singularity not just against 'unreformed' traditions, but within the reform movement itself. While he might not parade his dissent, Ælfric was not timid about asserting his own standards where he felt those of his colleagues to be inadequate, especially touching the authority of written sources.[104] The same rigorist impulse extended to liturgical practice, as already seen in his retention of three readings in the summer Night Office. A comparable exercise of independent judgement about politics, as they impinged on the welfare of the church and Christian society, may explain the most conspicuous omission of all from the source.[105]

Despite its designation as a 'proem', the introduction that Æthelwold penned for the *Concordia* (*RC* 1–14) is no empty preface, but a manifesto outlining some essential policies of the reform movement. It lays particular emphasis on the marriage of reformed-monastic and royal interests: the king shall sanction and protect the monks' endeavours, and uniformity of monastic observance shall be a national political concern. The monks, for their part, shall support the royal house with their

---

[103] These four aspects are well covered in Wormald, 'Æthelwold and his Continental Counterparts', and Gransden, 'Traditionalism and Continuity'.

[104] On Ælfric's self-definition within his own party, see Clayton, *The Cult of the Virgin Mary*, pp. 260–5, and Hill, 'Reform and Resistance', pp. 33–8.

[105] The political implications of certain aspects of the *LME* were first suggested by Gatch, 'The Office', p. 343.

prayers, specifically the *psalmi familiares* after every Office. A further, unwritten benefit to King Edgar may have been the expansion of royal patronage – and the loyalties it purchased – to areas whose control had traditionally been the prerogative of regional aristocracies. Thus the *Concordia* absolutely prohibited *saecularium prioratus* 'the lordship of laypersons', commending in its place 'regis tantumodo [*sic*] ac reginae dominium ad sacri loci munimen et ad aeccliasticae possessionis augmentum'.[106]

Part of this emphasis on the royal house does inform the *LME*. Ælfric clearly retains the *psalmi familiares* with the rubric 'pro rege et benefactoribus' (*LME* 4),[107] but the distribution of collects and intentions, which in the source heavily favour the king over the queen and benefactors, is not specified and so, perhaps, effectively levels the distinctions among them. Similarly, where the source specifies that the matutinal mass on ferias shall be 'for the king or whatever impending need' (*RC* 25), Ælfric suppresses the former option.[108] But it is the near-total avoidance of matter from the proem to the *Concordia* that most undercuts Æthelwold's celebration of the king as patron and protector of monks. From the entire proem, Ælfric excerpted only two provisions: one against lay dominion (*LME* 63) and one forbidding laymen to eat in, or monks to eat outside, the refectory (*LME* 64). Both provisions are, in some practical sense, relevant to the good order of a monastery, but Ælfric's effort to disengage them from their original programmatic context is evident in their thorough revision and relegation to the miscellaneous catch-all section near the end of his customary.[109] His treatment of the issue of lay control

---

[106] *RC* 10: 'the sovereign power of the King and Queen – and that only . . . both for the safeguarding of the holy places and for the increase of the goods of the Church' (trans. *RC* (Symons) 10, p. 7). The rendering of *saecularium prioratus* as 'lordship of laypersons' – especially in the sense of 'lay abbacies' – is Wormald's ('Æthelwold and his Continental Counterparts', p. 35). The view of royal *dominium* as an instrument to curtail local aristocratic power is most fully articulated by John, 'The King and the Monks', pp. 162–72, and *idem*, 'The Age of Edgar', in *The Anglo-Saxons*, ed. Campbell, pp. 160–91, at 185; but cf. Wormald, 'Æthelwold and his Continental Counterparts', p. 33.

[107] Cf. *RC* 19 and 37. Ælfric's may simply be an imprecise formulation of the same usage dictated by the source.

[108] *LME* 10: 'Nam ferialibus diebus de quacumque necessitate euenerit facienda est.'

[109] Cf. *RC* 10 and 13 (+ 95), and see commentary to *LME* 63–4 (at nn. 297–300). Other practical directions from the proem are left out of the *LME*, most notably *RC* 9 (on

over monasteries also differs suggestively from that in the *Concordia*-proem by stating that the monks shall recognize the king's dominion 'ad munimen loci, *non ad tirannidem*'.[110] The proem could have supplied the first, but not the second half of the phrase. The derivation of Ælfric's wording here is complicated by the presence of a very similar phrase in the Eynsham 'foundation charter' and in one other charter.[111] But the formulaic ring of the words does not void the possibility that they are cited at *LME* 63 with pointed intent. Ælfric probably found many details in the proem irrelevant to the running of Eynsham, yet he may also have taken a quietly skeptical view of its royalist and polemical zeal, which must have seemed less convincing, if not, at times, outright embarrassing, to some early eleventh-century heirs of reform. Relationships between the church and secular powers (including the king) had been less than ideal since Edgar's death in 975. The royal–monastic partnership suffered from a deeply divisive succession dispute between Edgar's two sons, Edward the Martyr and Æthelred,[112] and from a simultaneous 'anti-monastic'

---

the election of abbots, in which the king shall have right of consent), 11 (rules for monks on journeys) and 12 (behaviour towards the *pueri* of the monastery). The possibility that Ælfric's exemplar of the *Concordia* preserved a deeply corrupt version of the proem, as in the extant *RC* (Fa), should also be acknowledged.

[110] *LME* 63: 'for the protection of the place, *not the exercise of tyranny over it*' (emphasis added).

[111] Cf. S 911: 'rex autem non ad tirannidem, sed ad munimen loci & augmentum . . . dominium . . . custodiat' (*EC* I, 21). This section, in turn, is repeated almost verbatim in S 792, a grant of lands in Edgar's name to Æthelwold's monastery at Thorney (dated 973, though of doubtful authenticity); see above, p. 14, n. 47. If the phrase *non ad tirannidem* in S 911 does reflect contemporary sentiment in the reign of Æthelred, an intriguing parallel (kindly pointed out to me by Dr Greg Rose) may be found in the reference to *tyrannica contumacia* in the so-called *Orthodoxorum* group of charters. Simon Keynes has argued that this group of five charters (S 658, 673, 786, 788 and 812), though dated to Edgar's reign, are probably forgeries drafted in the 990s, so that their pointed reference to 'tyranny' may recall the depredations suffered by the monasteries in the reign of Edward the Martyr (*Diplomas*, pp. 98–100). By contrast, a reference to 'tyranny' in c. XIV of the unquestionably authentic New Minster privilege (S 745), probably written by Æthelwold himself, is significantly distanced from King Edgar ('Reges . . . quicumque nostri fuerint successores nullam exstraneam personam ius tirannidis super monachos exercentem imponant'; see *Councils and Synods*, ed. Whitelock *et al.*, pp. 119–33, at 128).

[112] See B. Yorke, 'Æthelwold and the Politics of the Tenth Century', in *Bishop Æthelwold*, ed. Yorke, pp. 65–88, at 84–6; Stafford, *Unification and Conquest*, pp. 57–9; and *RC* (Kornexl), p. liv.

backlash. The latter is now commonly viewed less as an 'anti-monastic' movement than as a re-assertion of aristocratic privileges, among them control over monastic estates that had been appropriated as part of Edgar's benefactions to the monks.[113]

In this troubled period Ælfric remained a monk at Winchester, where his spiritual and intellectual formation would have been already far advanced.[114] There, until his transfer to Cernel (c. 987), he was well placed to observe the monastic theology of kingship undergo gradual changes that quietly distanced the monks' fortunes from those of a ruler less popular and, in some cases, less dependable than Edgar had been.[115] Although Æthelred II (978–1016) favoured and enriched many monasteries during his long rule, for a period of several years after the death of Æthelwold in 984, the monarch reduced the privileges and alienated the property of some of the most venerable churches in the kingdom, including Abingdon, the Old Minster, Glastonbury and the see of Rochester.[116] These actions in no way amounted to a wholesale reversal of monastic patronage, but they must have alerted the second generation

---

[113] The most violent 'anti-monastic' seizures took place in western Mercia, under Ealdorman Ælfhere; see D. J. V. Fisher, 'The Anti-Monastic Reaction in the Reign of Edward the Martyr', *Cambridge Historical Journal* 10 (1952), 254–70; John, 'The Return of the Vikings', pp. 192–3.

[114] The usual date for his birth is given as *c.* 955, but cf. *Ælfric's Prefaces*, ed. Wilcox, p. 7, 'by 940 or 945'.

[115] On the telling later developments in monastic 'ruler theology', see John, 'The Return of the Vikings', pp. 203 and 206, and *idem*, 'The World of Abbot Ælfric', in *Ideal and Reality in Frankish and Anglo-Saxon Society: Studies Presented to J. M. Wallace-Hadrill*, ed. P. Wormald, D. Bullough and R. Collins (Oxford, 1983), pp. 300–16, at 313. On comparable developments, along rather different lines, in the writings of Wulfstan, see D. Bethurum Loomis, '*Regnum* and *sacerdotium* in the Early Eleventh Century', in *England Before the Conquest*, ed. Clemoes and Hughes, pp. 129–45.

[116] On the period of Æthelred's 'youthful indiscretions', see Keynes, *Diplomas*, pp. 176–82, and P. A. Stafford, 'The Reign of Æthelred II, a Study in the Limitations on Royal Policy and Action', in *Ethelred the Unready: Papers from the Millenary Conference*, ed. D. Hill, BAR British Series 59 (Oxford, 1978), 15–46, at p. 27. The years of 'youthful indiscretion' aside, monasticism generally flourished and produced some of its most lasting monuments in Æthelred's reign (see Keynes, *Diplomas*, pp. 198–200), but the king was seldom credited for these successes. It was, ironically, the Danish conquerer, Cnut, who would come nearer to attaining the status of a 'second Edgar'; see Gransden, 'Traditionalism and Continuity', p. 84, and M. K. Lawson, *Cnut: The Danes in England in the Early Eleventh Century* (London and New York, 1993), pp. 117–60.

Structure and sources

of reformers to the precariousness of too great a dependence on royal support. When, in the late 980s, Scandinavian raids followed close upon this early souring of the royal–monastic partnership, the king's critics within the church did not hesitate to view the events as cause and effect. When Ælfric himself implicitly rebukes Æthelred for failing to ward off the attacks, his criticism is, tellingly, couched in nostalgic praise of Edgar. As a postscript to his Life of St Swithun, Ælfric draws an implicit comparison between the two kings, the point of which is that Edgar's unwavering support of the monks had kept foreign enemies at bay during *his* reign.[117] Æthelred emerges the obvious loser by the comparison. In another homily, also from the *Lives of Saints*, Ælfric strengthens the contrast in an often-quoted passage:

Wel we magon geðencan hu wel hit ferde mid us, þaða þis igland wæs wunigende on sibbe, and munuc-lif wæron mid wurðscipe gehealdene, and ða woruld-menn wæron wið heora fynd, swa þæt ure word sprang wide geond þas eorðan. Hu wæs hit ða siððan ða þa man towearp munuc-lif, and godes biggengas to bysmore hæfde, buton þæt us com to cwealm and hunger, and siððan hæðen here us hæfde to bysmyre.[118]

The reference (from 'Hu wæs hit . . .') is probably to the 'anti-monastic

---

[117] *Ælfric: Lives of Three English Saints*, ed. G. I. Needham (London, 1966), p. 80, lines 369–74: 'se tima wæs gesælig and wynsum on Angelcynne, þa ða Eadgar cyningc þone cristendom gefyrðrode and fela munuclifa arærde, and his cynerice wæs wunigende on sibbe, swa þæt man ne gehyrde gif ænig scyphere wære, buton agenre leode þe ðis land heoldon' ('the time was blessed and joyful among the English people when King Edgar advanced Christendom and established many monasteries; and his kingdom remained at peace, so that no one heard if there were any naval force, save that of the people who possessed this land' (trans. mine)); see also *ibid.*, p. 81, lines 381–6. Likewise in the epilogue to Ælfric's paraphrase of the book of Judges, praise of victorious kings includes Alfred, Æthelstan and, most fulsomely, Edgar, but then falls conspicuously silent; see *The Old English Version of the Heptateuch, Ælfric's Treatise on the Old and New Testament and his Preface to Genesis*, ed. S. J. Crawford, EETS o.s. 160 (London, 1922; repr. with a supplement by N. R. Ker, 1969), 416. On Ælfric's changing views of the Viking incursions, see M. R. Godden, 'Apocalypse and Invasion in Late Anglo-Saxon England', in *From Anglo-Saxon to Early Middle English*, ed. Godden *et al.*, pp. 130–62.

[118] *LS* xiii (*De oratione Moysi*), ed. Skeat I, 294, lines 147–55 (quoted with modern punctuation, ignoring Skeat's verse-line division): 'Well may we think how well it fared with us when this island was dwelling in peace, and the monastic orders were held in honour, and the laity were ready against their foes, so that our report spread widely throughout the earth. How was it then afterward when men rejected monastic

reaction' in the reign of Edward the Martyr. That the sufferings of the nation continue into the present, however, only underscores that the monks' injuries remain unredressed under Æthelred.[119] Less obviously, the passage may recall that the present king, too, had done injury as one who 'overthrew monasteries' (*towearp munuclif*).

The actual experience of 'royal dominion' by the turn of the millennium bore only an erratic resemblance to the ideal that confronted Ælfric and his contemporaries in the proem to the *Concordia*. Royalism may, for that matter, have been a malleable principle from the start. Just as the 'anti-monastic reaction' did not likely object to monasticism as such, the earlier royal–monastic partnership had never excluded – and had, in fact, greatly depended on – the participation of powerful lay magnates and lesser nobles.[120] While Edgar was still alive, St Oswald was busy cultivating the patronage of Ealdorman Æthelwine of East Anglia, who would donate the site and much of the endowment for Oswald's monastery at Ramsey.[121] Clearly, aristocratic patrons and protectors proved no less desirable than kingly ones, so long as they did not try to replace monastic with secular communities or intrude themselves or their relations as lay-abbots. Ælfric's mature career owed much to aristocratic patronage: his immediate benefactors, Ealdorman Æthelweard and his son, Æthelmær, endowed both foundations where he spent his career after leaving Winchester. From Cernel, the first of these, Ælfric was transferred to Eynsham where Æthelmær personally appointed him abbot.[122] Ælfric probably felt a special allegiance, personal and political, to Æthelweard and his son, and to the king only indirectly. The political causes (if such they were) of Æthelmær's retirement to Eynsham would also have

life and held God's services in contempt, but that pestilence and hunger came to us, and afterward the heathen army had us in reproach?' (trans. Skeat).

[119] Cf. the depiction of an Edgarian golden age in the anonymous Old English 'rhythmical prose' translation of Edgar's privilege to the monks of Ely. J. C. Pope, following a suggestion by A. McIntosh, has made a strong case for Ælfric's authorship of the translation; see Pope's 'Ælfric and the Old English Version of the Ely Privilege', in *England Before the Conquest*, ed. Clemoes and Hughes, pp. 85–113, at 103–4.

[120] On the continuing importance and complexity of lay patronage, see Wormald, 'Æthelwold and his Continental Counterparts', pp. 35–7, and Stafford, *Unification and Conquest*, pp. 188–94.

[121] Barrow, 'Community of Worcester', p. 95.

[122] '[Æthelmær] abbatem sanctę monachorum congregationi preferre se uiuente instituit' (*EC* I, 20); see above, pp. 6–11.

coloured Ælfric's perception of royal authority.[123] Other works from late in his career convey firm disapproval of Æthelred's reign in general and of the violent politics of 1005–6 in particular.[124] The *LME* belongs, roughly, to this more outspokenly 'political' phase in Ælfric's work, as does the remarkable text beginning 'Wyrdwriteras us secgað'. This fragmentary treatise commends the sharing of military and political responsibilities between king and ealdorman, just as between David and Joab, Moses and Joshua, or Constantine and Gallicanus.[125] Ælfric's exact motives in the piece are uncertain, although its potential relevance to contemporary politics is hard to overlook.[126] Its argument establishes the figures of Joab, Joshua and the rest as types of the Christian ealdorman. In this way 'Wyrdwriteras' may intend to pay indirect homage to Ælfric's patrons and incidentally justify his loyalties, perhaps because they do not lie altogether where earlier polemic, including Æthelwold's proem, demanded they ought.

The language of 'royal dominion' was not the only feature of the proem from which Ælfric might wish to retreat. Another sensitive issue may have been that the *LME* was admittedly something less ambitious than the *Regularis concordia*. Ælfric's decision to compose the *LME* in the first place, rather than simply impose the source as written, amounted to a compromise of the strict liturgical uniformity that the *Concordia* had been designed to achieve.[127] The imperial pretensions of Edgar's reign went hand in hand with Æthelwold's zeal for total unity in worship and religious discipline, all in self-conscious imitation of Carolingian

---

[123] See above, pp. 12–15.
[124] M. Godden, 'Ælfric's Saints' Lives and the Problem of Miracles', in *Sources and Relations*, ed. Collins *et al.*, pp. 83–100, at 95–7; M. Clayton, 'Of Mice and Men: Ælfric's Second Homily for the Feast of a Confessor', *Leeds Studies in English*, n.s. 24 (1993), 1–26, at pp. 19–23.
[125] *Supplementary Collection*, ed. Pope II, 728–32 (no. xxii). See also Ælfric's discussion of the term *subregulus* in the late Temporale homily for the twenty-second Sunday after Pentecost in *Old English Homilies*, ed. Irvine, pp. 19–25, at 20–1, lines 36–60, and pp. 11–15 (introduction).
[126] *Supplementary Collection*, ed. Pope II, 726–7 and additional note on 733. The fragment is also discussed by Keynes, *Diplomas*, pp. 206–8, Stafford, *Unification and Conquest*, p. 13, and in *Old English Homilies*, ed. Irvine, pp. 11–13.
[127] Thus *RC* 4: '[Edgar] monuit, ut concordes aequali consuetudinis usu . . . nullo modo dissentiendo discordarent, ne impar ac uarius unius regulae ac unius patriae usus probrose uituperium sanctae conuersationi irrogaret.'

models.¹²⁸ How widely and with what success the resulting 'national customary' was ever imposed on Anglo-Saxon monasteries remain disputed questions. Some critics have viewed the mere existence of the *LME* as evidence that, even if the ideal of uniformity enshrined in the *Concordia* was an actual intention, it did not long outlive the drafters of that document.¹²⁹ If the difference between the theory and practice of royal dominion troubled Ælfric, the closely associated rhetoric of liturgical uniformity may have sounded equally hollow and impractical. We have already seen that such changes as Ælfric introduced can hardly be described as scandalous; more often, they bespeak a sound judgement that the *Concordia* required adaptation if it was to serve at Eynsham. But his position was made awkward by (among other things) the proem's account of an oath, sworn in council by those who drafted the *Concordia*, to maintain without variance the customs therein adopted.¹³⁰ That council not only imposed this strict adherence to the document; it also forbade any subsequent additions or modifications, except those adopted temporarily for urgent need, or by the consent of a future synod.¹³¹ The mandate was doubly solemn, in as much as it made the issue of uniformity a matter of holy obedience, the cornerstone of Benedictine monasticism.

---

[128] Wormald, 'Æthelwold and his Continental Counterparts', p. 32.

[129] Robinson, *Times of Saint Dunstan*, p. 156, and Knowles, *Monastic Order*, pp. 66–7, both doubt the legislative impact of the document and consider Ælfric's free treatment of it further evidence that the *Concordia* represented only an 'ideal for houses which aimed at highest observance' (Robinson, p. 156); but cf. *RC* (Kornexl), pp. cliv and li–lvi. If the Council of Winchester occurred as late as 973, dissemination of the text could barely have gotten underway before Edgar's death (975) and its aftermath, the effects of which on the spread of the *Concordia* are likewise much disputed; see *RC* (Kornexl), pp. liv–lv, and Hill, 'The "Regularis Concordia"'.

[130] *RC* 6 (but quoted here from *RC* (Kornexl) 6, lines 77–86): 'Ne igitur singuli, si suam . . . adinuentionem suapte presumptuosi eligerent, excellentissimum sancte obedientię fructum, alicuius arrogantię fastu inopinate seducti, miserabiliter amitterent ac Sarabitę potius quam monachi aut homines uiderentur legitimi, uotum Domino nostro Ihesu Christo unanimes <u>ouerunt pactoque spirituali confirmauerunt: se uita comite iugo regulę deditos has adnotatas morum consuetudines communi palam custodire conuersatione.'

[131] *RC* 8: 'Si autem pro qualibet necessitate quid extra communem regularis consuetudinis usum addendum fuerit, tamdiu agatur quoadusque negotium pro quo agatur Christi opitulante gratia melioretur'; and slightly later, '. . . nisi concilio synodali electum traditumque cum discretione uirtutum omnium matre ab uniuersis fuerit catholicis'.

Structure and sources

Ælfric had little choice but to omit an emphasis that would contradict his present efforts and, more seriously, threaten the credibility he enjoyed by styling himself as Æthelwold's faithful disciple.

Still other emphases of the reform movement, such as the nostalgia for a Bedan golden age, with its monastic episcopacy, or the interest in distinguishing an 'English' character of reform amidst the infusion of so many continental customs, find only oblique expression in the *LME*. Ælfric's general reticence here, as on matters of politics, reflects the practical nature of his customary. The few discernible traces of these concerns only remind us that a reformer could, at the turn of the millennium, take for granted what had been controversial one or two generations earlier. In addition to Ælfric's scholarly interest, the successful re-establishment of a monastic episcopacy, for example, probably lies behind his otherwise strange inclusion of a pontifical rite, the Chrism Mass (*LME* 39), in a customary not intended for a monastic cathedral. Similarly, his comparative lack of pride in specifically 'English' customs – such as sustained bell-ringing on important feasts, mentioned at *LME* 22 and 58 (cf. *RC* 50) – sounds not a less patriotic note but a less defensive one, as though many of the foreign practices imported from the Continent and enshrined in the *Concordia* are, after a generation, sufficiently patriated that the 'English' character of reform need not depend on a few relatively trivial customs.[132]

Stylistic changes

More obviously than in matters of liturgy or politics, Ælfric parted company with many of his fellow reformers over the issue of Latin prose style. Michael Lapidge has demonstrated that cultivation of a difficult 'hermeneutic' Latinity was a hallmark of learning among the leaders of reform and their disciples. Here again, as in other aspects of the movement, Ælfric went his own distinctive way. Seemingly alone among later tenth-century Anglo-Latin authors, he rejected exotic vocabulary, overly long sentences and convoluted word order.[133] He was a competent

---

[132] On the importance of native traditions even in periods of greatest continental influence, see Gransden, 'Traditionalism and Continuity'.

[133] Thus M. Lapidge, 'The Hermenuetic Style in Anglo-Latin Literature', *ASE* 4 (1975), 67–111, at p. 101 (repr. with addenda in his *Anglo-Latin Literature*, pp. 105–49 and 474–9, at 139): 'It is not simply that Ælfric did not affect the hermeneutic style; he

Latinist, however, to judge from his compositions in that language and his bilingual *Grammar*, and from the depth of understanding manifest in his translations of Latin sources.[134] The style of his Latin compositions has been praised for its 'brevity, clarity, and simplicity'[135] – the very qualities that readers of his Old English homilies would be prone to detect. If hermeneutic Latin was the preferred mode among the reforming elite, Ælfric's departure from the norm cannot represent a casual decision. As Lapidge concludes, Ælfric very likely wrote plain Latin for the same pragmatic reasons he wrote extensively in Old English: to bring before the widest possible audience the fruits of his learning.[136]

For his much-studied Old English style, Ælfric had a model in Æthelwold, whose translation of the Benedictine *Rule* shows a clarity and restraint untouched by the hermeneutic excesses typical of his Latin writings.[137] Æthelwold's segregation of styles appropriate to each

---

reacted vigorously against it. Thus in the Latin preface to his *Catholic Homilies* he explains that he has written in English rather than Latin so that his meaning will penetrate more directly to the hearts of his readers or listeners: "ideoque nec obscura posuimus verba, sed simplicem Anglicam". His reference to *obscura uerba* is clearly a rejection of the contemporary stylistic fashion.' See also *idem*, 'Æthelwold as Scholar and Teacher', pp. 183–94 and 200–1, and *Life of St Æthelwold*, ed. Lapidge and Winterbottom, p. xcviii. Even Ælfric's lay patron, Ealdorman Æthelweard, adopted this style for his Latin translation of the *Anglo-Saxon Chronicle*; see *Chronicon Æthelweardi*, ed. Campbell, pp. xlv–lv, and M. Winterbottom, 'The Style of Æthelweard', *Medium Ævum* 36 (1967), 109–18.

[134] On Ælfric's Latin canon, see *Life of St Æthelwold*, ed. Lapidge and Winterbottom, pp. cxlvii–cl; Clemoes, 'Chronology', pp. 244–5; and Jones, '*Meatim sed et rustica*'.

[135] Gatch, *Preaching and Theology*, p. 131, discussing the set of excerpts compiled by Ælfric from Julian of Toledo's *Prognosticon futuri saeculi*. Cf. Ælfric's abbreviation of another Latin source to produce his *Vita S. Æthelwoldi*, discussed at length in *Life of St Æthelwold*, ed. Lapidge and Winterbottom, pp. cli–cliii, and in the notes to their edition of Ælfric's text, pp. 71–80 (Appendix A).

[136] For another possible intepretation, see Jones, '*Meatim sed et rustica*'.

[137] For Æthelwold's vernacular compositions, see *Die angelsächsischen Prosabearbeitungen der Benediktinerregel*, ed. A. Schröer, BaP 2 (Kassel, 1885–8; repr. with a supplement by H. Gneuss; Darmstadt, 1964), and the prose tract on 'King Edgar's Establishment of the Monasteries', in *Councils and Synods*, ed. Whitelock *et al.*, pp. 142–54. Essential studies, all by M. Gretsch, are *Die Regula Sancti Benedicti*, summarized in English as 'Æthelwold's Translation of the *Regula Sancti Benedicti* and its Latin Exemplar', *ASE* 3 (1974), 125–51; and 'The Benedictine Rule in Old English: a Document of Bishop Æthelwold's Reform Politics', in *Words, Texts and Manuscripts: Studies in Anglo-Saxon Culture Presented to Helmut Gneuss on the Occasion of his Sixty-Fifth*

language established that a simple vernacular was the fit medium for teaching the unlearned (who included monks and clergy). Ælfric accepted but modifed this view by narrowing the artificial disparity between an unadorned vernacular and an over-adorned Latin style. His mentor's rather plain Old English he improved by experimenting with rhythmical cadences, alliteration and the occasional 'poetic' word.[138] His Latin shows no inclination towards full-blown 'hermeneuticism', though he sometimes attempts longer, self-consciously elevated sentences, especially in the prefaces.[139]

Because of its technical nature, the *LME* is not the best choice of texts in which to consider Ælfric's Latin style. But it serves very well to illustrate his methods as a redactor of Latin texts, and this issue is of first importance in the evaluation of the *LME* as liturgical evidence. The *Concordia* presented Ælfric with a range of styles, from the hermeneutic to the plain.[140] The distinction is strongest between the elevated register of the proem and (in *RC* (Ti) only) the epilogue, on one hand, and the language of the customary proper, on the other.[141] Quite apart from its

Birthday, ed. M. Korhammer, K. Reichl and H. Sauer (Woodbridge, 1992), pp. 131–58. For Æthelwold's Latin works, see Lapidge, 'Æthelwold as Scholar and Teacher', pp. 189–95, and *Life of St Æthelwold*, ed. Lapidge and Winterbottom, pp. lxxxvi–xci.

[138] On Ælfric's 'rhythmical prose', see *Supplementary Collection*, ed. Pope I, 105–36. On the 'poetic' element in his vocabulary, see M. Godden, 'Ælfric's Changing Vocabulary', *English Studies* 61 (1980), 206–23, at pp. 217–19, and R. Frank, 'Poetic Words in Late Old English Prose', in *From Anglo-Saxon to Early Middle English*, ed. Godden *et al.*, pp. 87–107, at 91, 96–8, 104–5 and 106, n. 31.

[139] In the *LME*, sentences that are, by Ælfric's standards, long and syntactically complex occur in §§ 1 and 80. He rarely admits the exotic word (e.g., *LME* 46 'thimiama'). The *Colloquy* includes 'mathites' (emend. of manuscript *machites*) (ed. Garmonsway, p. 48, line 308), while the *Glossary* sometimes appended to the *Grammar* is full of unusual words, but in these works the difficulty of distinguishing Ælfric's original from the additions of his pupil, Ælfric Bata, complicates the evidence; see D. Porter, 'Ælfric's *Colloquy* and Ælfric Bata', *Neophilologus* 80 (1996), 639–60.

[140] The most complete study of the Latinity of the *Concordia* is *RC* (Kornexl), pp. clxx–clxxxiii; see also her 'The *Regularis Concordia* and its Old English Gloss', pp. 115–16; Lapidge, 'Æthelwold as Scholar and Teacher', pp. 98–100; and *Life of St Æthelwold*, ed. Lapidge and Winterbottom, p. lxxxviii.

[141] Kornexl has also shown that isolated hermeneutic passages in the body of the *Concordia* are probably the asides of Æthelwold himself. See *RC* (Kornexl), pp. clxxv–clxxvii and xlv–l, and 'The *Regularis Concordia* and its Old English Gloss', p. 116, referring to examples in *RC* 15, 45, 61, 74 and 95.

content, the proem to the *Concordia*, on stylistic grounds alone, would hardly have commended itself to Ælfric.[142] Fortunately, the body of the *Concordia* was, for the most part, written in a less obscure style that clearly reflects the language of its liturgical sources. Pervasive stylistic features of liturgical *ordines* are a heavy reliance on jussive subjunctive verbs (and these often in the passive voice) and the presentation of a sequence of actions by a string of qualifying phrases at the head or tail of a main clause. The latter tendency is most apparent in the heaping up of ablative absolutes, temporal clauses, prepositional phrases and predicative participles to describe the circumstances or sequence of events that shall precede, attend or follow the main action, as in: 'Hoc expleto, facto signo a priore, conuenientes ad capitulum, ipso precedente, uersa facie ad orientem salutent crucem';[143] or 'Tota namque aestate, exceptis dominicis et festiuis diebus, Prima decantata matutinalique missa celebrata capitulo etiam peracto pulsetur tabula.'[144] These are extreme examples, but they illustrate features of style characteristic of the *Concordia* and of *ordines* generally. They also demonstrate that, even where no hermeneutic elements are present, the density of the source demanded careful attention.

The *LME* does not depart radically from this typical *ordo*-style Latin, probably because the two texts are so similar in content. Frequent verbatim quotation indicates that Ælfric was often satisfied with the wording he found in the source.[145] Just as often, however, he opts for simple paraphrase

---

[142] The only material drawn from the proem (for *LME* 63–4) has been completely rewritten; see above, pp. 44–5. The 'epilogue' in *RC* (Ti), on the payment of the heriot, is also written in the hermeneutic style and has no correlate in the *LME*. There is a good possibility that this section was not in Ælfric's exemplar of the source, the ending of which also diverged from *RC* (Ti) and (Fa) in other respects; cf. above, nn. 70 and 33.

[143] *RC* 26, but here quoted from *RC* (Kornexl) 21, lines 389–91: 'After the Morrow Mass, at a sign from the prior, all shall come together for the Chapter, the prior leading. Turning to the east they shall salute the Cross' (trans. *RC* (Symons) 21, p. 17).

[144] *RC* 83: 'During the entire summer, Sundays and feast days excepted, when Prime has been sung, the Morrow Mass celebrated and the Chapter carried out, the *tabula* shall be struck' (trans. *RC* (Symons) 55, p. 54).

[145] Substantial instances of quotation that have undergone no or only minor revision occur in: *LME* 17–22, 29, 30 (slightly re-arranged), 32–4, 36, 40, 45–6, 49, 52, 65–6 and 68–9. This list would swell considerably if it were to include the many less extensive verbal echoes.

Structure and sources

or abridgement to avoid difficult vocabulary and word order.[146] While the goal of 'simplification' in this limited, grammatical sense cannot account for all of Ælfric's changes,[147] brevity and clarity, whether in Latin or Old English, were paramount. As a typical example, consider his changes to *RC* 40, a custom providing the monks a place of warmth and refuge during the winter (italics indicate lexical and syntactic parallels):

RC 40	LME 14
Ab eisdem kalendis [*scil*. Nouembris] *concedatur fratribus accessus ignis*, dum *necessitas compulerit* et *frigoris nimietas incubuerit* . . . In huius quoque hiemis tempore propter nimiam imbrium asperitatem locus aptus fratribus designetur, cuius <cecaumenes> refugio hibernalis algoris et intemperiei aduersitas leuigetur. *Si autem temperies tranquilla* fuerit, *claustro* uti libuerit cum Christi benedictione utantur.[148]	Brumali uero tempore *concedatur fratribus accessus ignis*, si *necessitas compulerit* . . . Et si *frigoris nimietas incubuerit*, in domo legant omnes simul et canant. *Sin autem temperies tranquilla* aderit, sedeant pariter omnes in *claustro*.[149]

Ælfric has broken up the redundant compound verb of the opening *dum*-clause and used each member separately to introduce two conditionals, one on the privilege of the *accessus ignis*, and another on the place appointed for the monks' refuge. On the latter point, he rejects the verbosity of the

---

[146] On Ælfric's Latin *breuitas*, see *Life of St Æthelwold*, ed. Lapidge and Winterbottom, pp. cl–clii and cix.

[147] The popular labelling of the *LME* as a mere abridgement or digest implies that Ælfric was motivated as much by the often obscure language of the *Concordia* as by the complexity of its observances. This assumption dates back at least to Bateson, who observed, 'Ælfric did his best to interpret Æthelwold [*scil*. the *Concordia*] whose language revels in obscurity' ('Rules for Monks', p. 703).

[148] 'From the Calends of November aforesaid the brethren shall be allowed to have a fire as long as necessity demands and excess of cold lasts . . . Thus in winter, when storms are harsh and bitter, a suitable room shall be set aside for the brethren wherein, by the fireside, they may take refuge from the cold and bad weather. When, however, the weather is fair, they shall be free to use the cloister with Christ's blessing' (trans. *RC* (Symons) 29, pp. 25–6).

[149] 'During the winter period the brothers shall be granted access to a fire, should necessity require it . . . And should the severe cold persist, let them all read and chant together in the *domus*. But should the weather be mild, let them all sit together in the cloister.'

source ('nimiam imbrium asperitatem . . . hibernalis algoris et intemperiei aduersitas') and the bizarre grecism *cecaumenes* (or whatever form occurred in his exemplar).[150] Perhaps by having his monks 'sit' in rather than 'use' the cloister, he also disposes of the easily misconstrued *uti* (= *ut*) so close to the ablative object ('claustro') of 'utantur'.

The *LME* offers numerous instances of abbreviation similarly prompted by the long-windedness of the source. Often only a glance at the corresponding passages in the *Concordia* will explain the desire for a more lucid text.[151] Ælfric also took special care with word order, unravelling some of the more affected arrangements: thus, at *LME* 33, he replaces the source's 'agant tacitas genu flexo more solito preces' (*RC* 61) with 'agant tacitas preces, flexis genibus, solito more'. The revision uses all of the same words but avoids postponement of the direct object and changes the number of *genu flexo*, perhaps better to distinguish, by dissimilar endings, the individual ablative phrases from each other.

Ælfric's method also occasionally suggests an effort to distinguish primary from circumstantial actions in the liturgy, even when the result was a grammatically *more* complex sentence. A tendency, for example, to cluster adverbial information at the head of his rewritten version[152] leads once to the subordination of what stood as an independent clause in the source:

RC 54:

Et intrantes aecclesiam agant orationem cum antiphona et collecta ad *uenera-tionem ipsius sancti cui ecclesia ipsa ad quam itur dedicata est*. Deinde *abbas stola et cappa indutus benedicat candelas* . . .[153]

LME 25:

Et decantata antiphona cum oratione in *uenerazione ipsius sancti cui ecclesia illa ad quam itur dedicata est*, benedicat abbas, indutus stola et cappa, candelas . . .[154]

---

[150] The CCM edition adopts the reading *caumene* of *RC* (Ti) (glossed by OE *fyrhyses*) over the obviously corrupt *cacumenae* of (Fa), but the underlying form was probably *cecaumenes* (Greek genitive singular); see Lapidge, 'Æthelwold as Scholar and Teacher', p. 100, n. 75, and *RC* (Kornexl), pp. 248–9 (commentary to line 634).

[151] Other good examples occur in *LME* 12 (cf. *RC* 21), *LME* 25 and 32 (cf. *RC* 54 and 60) and *LME* 61 (cf. *RC* 93).

[152] For examples see also *LME* 18 (third and fourth sentences; cf. *RC* 46) and 32 (first sentence; cf. *RC* 60).

[153] 'On entering the church, having prayed awhile, they shall say the antiphon and collect in honour of the saint to whom this same church is dedicated. Then the abbot, vested in stole and cope, shall bless the candles . . .' (trans. *RC* (Symons) 33, p. 31).

[154] 'And when the antiphon, together with its collect, has been sung in honour of the

Ælfric's use of subordination may convey more clearly the hierarchy of actions as he perceived it. The information of the first sentence in the *Concordia* has been converted into a long ablative absolute (with its own dependent members) describing the circumstances attending the central act, the abbot's blessing of the candles.[155]

Other parts of the *LME*, by contrast, reveal a freer engagement of the *Concordia* and its language: at many points where Ælfric did not have to intervene for the sake of brevity or clarity, he frequently did. If such differences do not simply reflect variants in his exemplar of the *Concordia*, they would seem to indicate stylistic preferences. At least ten times, for example, his rewriting calls for a substitution of finite for infinite verbs,[156] or of active for passive constructions.[157] These changes might suggest the influence of Old English syntax, but Ælfric's practice in totality is by no means consistent enough to reveal the contours of a vernacular substrate.[158] His methods of rewriting the *Concordia* cannot

saint to whom that church is dedicated which is the destination of the procession, the abbot, vested in a stole and cope, shall bless the candles . . .'

[155] The word order introduced into the revised version bears a slight resemblance to the 'verb second' principle in Old English; see Mitchell, *Old English Syntax*, § 3929, and J. McLaughlin, *Old English Syntax: a Handbook*, Sprachstrukturen, Reihe A: Historische Sprachstrukturen 4 (Tübingen, 1983), § 9.3. On 'inverted order' in Ælfric's Old English writings, see C. R. Barrett, 'Studies in the Word-Order of Ælfric's Catholic Homilies and Lives of the Saints', *Department of Anglo-Saxon, Occasional Papers* 3 (Cambridge, 1953), 1–3 and 7–37. (Of course in Latin a 'verb second' tendency would not necessarily imply 'inversion', since Latin relies on implied subjects more often than English does.) At least once (*LME* 65: 'eant'; cf. *RC* 98) the verb has moved to initial position after a simple co-ordinating conjunction *et*, for which, again, there exists an analogous tendency in Old English; see Mitchell, *Old English Syntax*, § 3934.

[156] For finite verbs from participles or participial phrases, see *LME* 25 *induant . . . eant*, 29 *incipiant*, 32 *intrent*, 46 *detur* and 48 *reuertentur* (cf. *RC* 54, 57, 60, 77 and 80); from ablative absolutes, see *LME* 35 *lauent*, 37 *deportetur*, 47 *dicat* and 69 *pulsetur* (cf. *RC* 65, 67, 79 and 102); from gerunds, see *LME* 42 *propinet* (cf. *RC* 67).

[157] For changes of voice only, see *LME* 38 *dat*, 42 *legat*, 47 *inchoet* and 48 *eant* (cf. *RC* 68, 71, 79 and 80); for change of voice accompanied by substitution of a different verb, see *LME* 16 *nec . . . mittant pinguedinem* (*RC* 44 *pinguedo interdicitur*), 18 *canant* (*RC* 46 *celebrentur*), 24 *decantent* (*RC* 52 *dicantur*), 29 *debent inchoare* (*RC* 57 *dicatur prima*), 32 *procedant . . . ad . . . processionem* (*RC* 60 *agitur . . . processio*) and 51 *uesperam . . . psallimus* (*RC* 88 *Vesperae . . . celebrantur*).

[158] On the use of co-ordinated finite verbs in Old English to translate Latin appositive participles, see M. Callaway, Jr, 'The Appositive Participle in Anglo-Saxon', *PMLA*

finally be reduced to simple formulas, for he ranged widely, and not always predictably, between quotation and paraphrase. Perhaps the *Concordia* in particular, because of its length, complex structure and varying levels of style, discouraged a uniform editorial method.

If there is a consistent feature of his method in the *LME* (and in all Latin writings attributed to Ælfric), it is a strong tendency to re-use the language of the source. As may be seen from the parallel passages quoted above, this appears to have been done by excising words or phrases, discarding the unwanted scraps, then splicing the retained pieces together, touching up the morphology and syntax as required. To describe the technique of Ælfric's abridged *Vita S. Æthelwoldi*, Lapidge has used a similar metaphor: '[Ælfric] need have done no more than draw a red pencil (so to speak) through the words in Wulfstan's text which he regarded as superfluous and then copy the remainder. He need hardly have altered a word.'[159] The occasionally mechanical appearance of this method is one of the most significant differences between Ælfric's compositions in Latin and in Old English. The process of translation demanded a more active and analytical approach, but his Latin-to-Latin compositions seem to have favoured 'short-cuts' that did not always yield good grammar or logical transitions. Some of the liturgically problematic features of the *LME* look very much like the results of an uncritical or over-hasty reliance on a source's wording.[160] The method would also explain some grammatically and organizationally awkward points, where Ælfric has imperfectly fused together provisions from separate parts of the source or transplanted irrelevant details along with the relevant.[161]

---

16 (1901), 141–360, at p. 321. On the tendency of Old English translations to substitute active for passive constructions, see M. Kilpiö, *Passive Constructions in Old English Translations from Latin, with Special Reference to the OE Bede and the Pastoral Care*, Mémoires de la Société Neophilologique de Helsinki 49 (Helsinki, 1989), 203–29 and 234–43. Other possible vernacular influences are mentioned above, n. 155.

[159] *Life of St Æthelwold*, ed. Lapidge and Winterbottom, p. cliii.
[160] See below, pp. 68–70.
[161] For example, see commentary to *LME* 3 (at n. 17), 6 (at n. 37) and 12 (at n. 55).

ÆLFRIC AND THE *LIBER OFFICIALIS*

More than any other single feature, the interpolation of liturgical commentary from the *Liber officialis* of Amalarius of Metz[162] distinguishes the *LME* as a project quite distinct from the *Concordia*. Just as the technicality of the subject did not prevent Ælfric from tacitly pressing his views of reform, the occasion also did not force him to set aside his familiar role of teacher and exegete. His use of Amalarius's work, both in the *LME* and elsewhere, can be seen in the context of the Anglo-Saxon reformers' esteem for Carolingian scholarship and its role in church reform.[163] It is ironic, then, that Amalarius's *magnum opus*, which exercised enormous influence throughout the Middle Ages, was in some respects a curiosity of the Carolingian renaissance. Although Amalarius's 'Romanizing' urge was well matched with the imperial agenda of political and liturgical unity, the essential character of the *Liber officialis* was encyclopedic, scholarly and antiquarian rather than practical or catechetical, like the older *expositiones missae* it would soon surpass in popularity.[164] In effect, Ælfric was again confronted with a source that held great appeal but required significant adaptation if it was to serve his purpose. At least some of the job of revision, however, had already been done for him by one or more anonymous editors of Amalarius's work. The textual history of the *Liber officialis* has been impressively reconstructed from the large number of surviving manuscripts, but against this background Ælfric's exemplar represents something of a special case, of major importance in source study of the *LME*.

---

[162] Ed. by Hanssens in *AEOLO* II, with prolegomena and indices in vols. I and III, respectively. My references employ Hanssens's book, chapter and section numbers.

[163] On the importance of Carolingian authorities and their different uses by the reformers, see Hill, 'Reform and Resistance', pp. 20 and 36.

[164] For the broader context of Amalarius's work, see A. Wilmart, 'Expositio Missæ', *Dictionnaire d'archéologie chrétienne et de liturgie*, ed. F. Cabrol and H. Leclercq, 15 vols. in 30 (Paris, 1907–53) V, cols. 1014–27; R. E. Reynolds, 'Liturgy, Treatises on', *DMA* VII, 624–33; and D. L. Mosey, 'Allegorical Liturgical Interpretation in the West from 800 A.D. to 1200 A.D.' (unpubl. Ph.D. thesis, Univ. of St Michael's College, Toronto, 1985).

Amalarius and the history of the Liber officialis

Amalarius was born *c.* 770 × 775, perhaps in or near the city of Metz.[165] A student of Alcuin,[166] towards the end of 809 he succeeded Archbishop Wizo as metropolitan of the ancient see of Trier (Trêves). In the spring of 813 Amalarius was sent by Charlemagne on an embassy to Constantinople; but upon his return, coincident with the death of the emperor in 814, he found himself deprived of his see. This still unexplained demotion freed him to devote much of the next two decades to liturgical studies, culminating in the publication of the *Liber officialis* (sometimes called *De ecclesiasticis officiis*) through several editions.

The earliest identifiable form of the work consisted of a dedicatory preface to Louis the Pious (*Gloriosissime imperator*) and a text in three books.[167] The first treats the liturgies of the church year from Septuagesima Sunday through the Octave of Pentecost, with particular attention to the solemn services of Holy Week. The second book begins with a discussion of the origins and significance of the Ember Days, then proceeds to a detailed analysis of the eight ecclesiastical grades and the principal liturgical vestments. The third book is a step-by-step commentary on the actions and prayers of the mass, subjects Amalarius had perhaps already treated in less detail elsewhere.[168] A second, revised edition of the *Liber officialis* appeared near the end of the 820s.[169] Its manuscripts evidence Amalarius's significant revision of certain points

---

[165] This sketch of Amalarius's life is based on *AEOLO* I, 58–82, as well as Hanssens, 'Le texte', and Cabaniss, *Amalarius*.

[166] Though where is not known; Hanssens (*AEOLO* I, 62–3) inclines towards the Palace School, under Alcuin's direction from 792–6, while Cabaniss (*Amalarius*, pp. 12–21) assumes that all such references are to St Martin's, Tours, whither Alcuin retired as abbot until his death in 804. Nowhere in his writings does Amalarius claim to have lived anywhere as a professed monk, although arguments have been advanced that he held the office of commendatory abbot of Hornbach (Cabaniss, *Amalarius*, p. 24; *AEOLO* I, 71).

[167] The first edition was probably published in the early 820s (Hanssens's date; see *AEOLO* I, 134). Cabaniss (*Amalarius*, p. 52, n. 1) argues for a slightly earlier date.

[168] Namely, the *Missae expositionis codices I & II* and *Canonis missae interpretatio* (*c.* 815); Hanssens attributes these to Amalarius, though their authenticity has been doubted.

[169] Again, the precise date is disputed: Hanssens argues for 830 or 831 (*AEOLO* I, 135 and 68), while Cabaniss posits an earlier date of 826 or 827 (*Amalarius*, p. 71). In any event, the *terminus ante quem* would appear to be 831.

from the prior edition and, more importantly, include a new, fourth book devoted entirely to the Divine Office.

Separating the second edition of the *Liber officialis* from the third is the watershed event in Amalarius's career as a liturgist: his journey to Rome in 831. In that year, or the closing months of the preceding one, Louis the Pious dispatched Amalarius on a diplomatic visit to Pope Gregory IV (827–44). The reasons for the mission are not recorded, but Amalarius took advantage of the occasion to study at first-hand the liturgical customs of the city's ancient churches. There he gathered enough new material to warrant yet another, thoroughly revised and – in keeping with the spirit of Carolingian *renouatio* – 'Romanized' edition of the *Liber officialis*. This version must have been published sometime between Amalarius's return home (the latter part of 831) and his disastrous assignment in 835, again by the Emperor Louis, to serve as interim administrator of the troubled see of Lyons. There his enemies began a series of attacks that led to the eventual condemnation of the *Liber officialis* as newfangled, heretical teaching.[170] Amalarius was removed from his office, but no further action was taken against him. He continued to write about the liturgy, producing in the last phase of his career yet another important work, the *Liber de ordine antiphonarii*. He died on 29 April 852 or 853, probably at Metz, where he was buried in the church of St Arnulf. Despite the charges of heresy, the *Liber officialis* continued to be read, copied, cited and epitomized for centuries,[171] although the manuscript evidence does suggest that the dissemination of the third edition suffered from the controversies of 835–8.[172]

---

[170] The controversy may have had political roots. The previous archbishop of Lyons, Agobard, had been deposed for his support of a failed rebellion led by Louis's son, Lothar, in 833. The clergy of Lyons, who remained devoted to the exiled Agobard, would probably have resented anyone whom Louis chose to oversee the archdiocese, but they found an easy target in the academically inclined Amalarius and his eccentric scholarship. After three years of bitter complaint, voiced most stridently by the deacon Florus, the anti-Amalarian party finally obtained from a synod at Quierzy (September 838) a condemnation of the *Liber officialis*. Florus's own account of the synod is quoted at length in *AEOLO* I, 77–9

[171] See *AEOLO* I, 83–91, and for a specific case study, R. W. Pfaff, 'The "Abbreviatio Amalarii" of William of Malmesbury', *Recherches de théologie ancienne et médiévale* 47 (1980), 77–113, and 48 (1981), 128–71 (edition).

[172] Only four manuscripts of the complete third edition survive, compared to sixteen of

Ælfric's exemplar

Of more than twenty separate *loci* in the *LME* clearly drawn from the *Liber officialis*, only about one third bear citation-tags such as 'Amalarius: . . .', 'Amalarius dicit . . .' or 'secundum disputationem Amalarii',[173] but most of the borrowings, elaborative in character, stand out strongly against the more technical matter of the customary. Textual evidence indicates that, until the mid-eleventh century, the *Liber officialis* was known in England only in an abridged version derived from Amalarius's third edition. Called the *Retractatio prima* by the modern editor of the *Liber officialis*, Jean-Michel Hanssens, this two-book abridgement was probably compiled in northern France or Brittany in the decades shortly after Amalarius's death.[174] The close associations of early Breton and English copies argue that the *Retractatio prima* first crossed the Channel in the early tenth century, perhaps in the baggage of Breton refugees who were fleeing Viking attacks.[175] These displaced Bretons have long been acknowledged as a source of innovation in the early tenth-century Anglo-Saxon church,[176] which gratefully received the two-book redaction of Amalarius's *Liber officialis*. The work was 'treated with considerable respect' in English scriptoria decades before the beginning of monastic revival in the mid-tenth century.[177] By the time Ælfric wrote the *LME*,

---

the first edition and ten of the second. For inventories, see *AEOLO* I, 120–4, and Hanssens, 'Le texte'.

[173] See *LME* 24, 26, 30–2, 35 and 43. The tag can likewise introduce material of doubtful authenticity that was nevertheless in Ælfric's exemplar of the *Liber officialis*, as at *LME* 37.

[174] *AEOLO* I, 162–3.

[175] Edward the Elder (899–924) received these refugees into his protection, and his successor, Athelstan (924–39), actively promoted the re-establishment of the Breton dynasty in the 930s; see Dumville, 'The English Element', p. 12.

[176] For example, in the establishment of the cult of St Judoc at the New Minster, Winchester, or in the large number of Breton relics that found their way into Athelstan's eager hands; see Dumville, *Liturgy and Ecclesiastical History*, pp. 110 and 112–16, and Ortenberg, *The English Church*, pp. 231–2. For a possible reference to Breton liturgical influence in the Old English poem *The Seasons for Fasting*, see Sisam, *Studies*, p. 55.

[177] Quotation from Dumville, *Liturgy and Ecclesiastical History*, p. 116, referring to the execution of Cambridge, Trinity College B. 11. 2, an early example of 'phase II' Anglo-Saxon Square minuscule; see *idem*, 'English Square Minuscule Script: the Mid-Century Phases', *ASE* 23 (1994), 133–64, at pp. 136–42. The Anglo-Breton subgroup of *R1*

Structure and sources

Amalarius's text had been known at some Anglo-Saxon centres for the better part of a century.[178]

First suggested by Milton McC. Gatch, the identification of the *Retractatio prima* as Ælfric's intermediate source helps explain why some material in the *LME* is organized differently than in the modern printed text of Amalarius's third edition, and how some apparently non-Amalarian material must have stood alongside passages from the authentic *Liber officialis* in Ælfric's exemplar.[179] After considering the extant Anglo-Saxon and Breton manuscripts and the interpolations common to them,

manuscripts includes (by Hanssens's sigla): Q = Paris, Bibliothèque Nationale, nouv. acq. lat. 1983 (Brittany, *c*. 900); B = Boulogne-sur-Mer, Bibliothèque Municipale, 82 (England, *c*. 930); T = Cambridge, Trinity College B. 11. 2 [241] (St Augustine's, Canterbury, *c*. 930); and F = Cambridge, Corpus Christi College 192 (Landevennec, Brittany, 952). The Breton manuscript CCCC 192 was probably copied from an English exemplar, as argued by Dumville, 'The English Element', pp. 6–7. Dumville has refined Hanssens's stemma (*AEOLO* I, 198), suggesting a more precise filiation: both English manuscripts and the later of the two Breton ones (F) ultimately derive from a hyparchetype collateral with Q, though whether that hyparchetype (now lost) was an English or Breton copy cannot be known; see D. N. Dumville, 'Breton and English Manuscripts of Amalarius's *Liber officialis*', in *Mélanges François Kerlouégan*, ed. D. Conso, N. Fick and B. Poulle (Paris, 1994), pp. 205–14.

[178] Further evidence of the *R1*-tradition includes excerpts preserved as the *Institutio beati Amalarii de ecclesiasticis officiis* in two manuscripts of Archbishop Wulfstan's 'commonplace book', where it is found alongside the excerpts from the *Concordia* titled *De ecclesiastica consuetudine* (see above, n. 19). Other excerpts from the *Liber officialis*, also probably derived from an *R1* copy, occur on fols. 102–21 of London, BL, Cotton Vespasian D. xv (? Worcester, *c*. 1000; see Dumville, *Liturgy and Ecclesiastical History*, p. 136), a portion of which (on the significance of church bells) was elsewhere translated into Old English; see T. Graham, 'The Old English Prefatory Texts in the Corpus Canterbury Pontifical', *Anglia* 113 (1995), 1–15. Additional Amalarian excerpts preserved in the later part (s. xi/xii) of the *LME* manuscript itself (CCCC 265), however, must have been drawn from the whole *Liber officialis*, not the abridgement; see below, p. 74, n. 13.

[179] See Gatch, 'The Office', p. 349. The order of items in manuscripts of the *R1* (especially its second book) often does not follow that of the third edition itself; for a detailed overview of this redaction, see *AEOLO* I, 163–8. Hanssens prints the post-Amalarian interpolations from *R1* at *AEOLO* II, 560–5. Several passages in the *LME* evidence significant *R1* variants; see full quotations and commentary at *LME* 25 (at n. 103), 27 (at n. 117), 28 (at n. 120), 30 (at n. 142), 32 (at n. 169) and 43 (at n. 212). Furthermore *LME* 26 shows by its ordering of ideas the influence of the prior abridgement and omission of material carried out for the *R1* (see commentary at n. 105).

63

however, one is still left with a significant amount of 'Amalarian'-style exposition in the *LME* at variance with both the complete *Liber officialis* and its later *Retractatio prima*. Once, for example, Ælfric explicitly attributes to Amalarius a point (about the striking of a new fire on each day of the Triduum) that bears no resemblance to anything in the *Liber officialis* or among its better-attested interpolations.[180] Such evidence raises the challenge that, at this and numerous other points, Ælfric's exemplar was surprisingly unlike any other extant member of the basic Anglo-Breton *Retractatio prima* family.[181]

Just such a variant version of the *Retractatio prima*, containing almost all of Ælfric's extra 'Amalarian' teaching, happens to survive in a manuscript that escaped the notice of Hanssens as he was preparing his edition. The main text of Salisbury, Cathedral Library, 154 (Salisbury, s. xi^{ex}) is that of the *Retractatio prima*, but with considerable re-arrangement and interpolation.[182] The antecedents of this version and its relationship to other English and Breton copies of the recension are as yet undetermined. It would be useful to know, at least, whether this variant *Retractatio prima* preserves the work of a tenth-century Anglo-Saxon scholar or represents a separate textual tradition, imported ready-made from the Continent. The immediate significance of this copy, however, is that it confirms the existence of an augmented version of the *Retractatio prima* from which Ælfric's exemplar, like Salisbury 154, clearly derived.[183] For present purposes, the crucial 'extra' material in the

---

[180] See commentary to *LME* 37 (at n. 191).

[181] See commentary to *LME* 33 (at n. 176), 35 (at n. 188), 39 (at nn. 197–204) and 44 (at n. 222).

[182] The peculiarities were first noted by N. R. Ker, 'The Beginnings of Salisbury Cathedral Library', in *Medieval Learning and Literature: Essays Presented to Richard William Hunt*, ed. J. J. G. Alexander and M. T. Gibson (Oxford, 1976), pp. 23–49, at 46–7; repr. in Ker's *Books, Collectors and Libraries*, ed. Watson, pp. 143–73, at 170–1. The manuscript is also noticed by Webber, *Scribes and Scholars*, pp. 70–1 and 152–3.

[183] Salisbury books copied from pre-Conquest English exemplars are far outnumbered by those that reflect newly imported continental traditions, but see Webber, *Scribes and Scholars*, pp. 68–75. Salisbury 154 is a good example of the transition from native to imported exemplars: to the core text (the *Retractatio prima*, long known to the Anglo-Saxons), contemporary scribes have added parts of the complete *Liber officialis* not known to have been in England before the later eleventh century (*ibid.*, p. 71, n. 112).

Structure and sources

Salisbury version begins on p. 18 of the manuscript, with a question-and-answer dialogue now supplementing, now replacing outright, the discussion of Maundy Thursday, Good Friday and Holy Saturday found in other copies of the *Retractatio prima*. Selected quotations from the Salisbury version are provided in the commentary, below, to illustrate how its variant discussion of the *triduum sacrum* informs nearly all of the 'Amalarian' teaching in the *LME* that cannot be traced to Hanssens's edition or to other manuscripts of the *Retractatio prima*.

Adaptations and informing concerns

The allegorical method of liturgical exposition that drew loud rebuke from some quarters in Amalarius's own lifetime seems, ironically, to have been the very aspect that commended his work to later generations. Ælfric knew and admired the *Liber officialis* from early in his career, since the text figures as a source in both series of *Catholic Homilies*.[184] In the Old English homily for Septuagesima (Second Series) he cites the text and author by name: 'Sum wis lareow hatte Amalarius. se awrat ane boc be cyrclicum ðeawum, hwæt ða gesetnyssa godes þenunga on gearlicum ymbryne getacniað.'[185] Such praise from the pen of one whose writings show only an occasional interest in the liturgy is best explained by the similarity between Amalarius's project and Ælfric's more accustomed sphere, the exposition of scripture. Ælfric's use of the *Liber officialis* when

---

[184] From the First Series, see portions of *CH* I.xviii (*In letania maiore*) and I.xxii (Pentecost), ed. Thorpe I, 244 and 326, borrowing from *Lib.off.* I.xxxvii.3–4 and I.xxxix.1, respectively (both passages are included in *R1*). For the Second Series, see *CH* II.v, ed. Godden, pp. 41–51, at lines 234–87. The Amalarian source of these three passages was noted long ago by Förster, 'Über die Quellen', pp. 48–9. Other alleged identifications of the *Liber officialis* among the *Catholic Homilies* are less convincing; see B. Fehr, 'Über einige Quellen zu Aelfrics Homiliae Catholicae', *Archiv* 130 (1913), 378–80. Because Ælfric demonstrates a familiarity with the *Liber officialis* from the earliest stage in his career, it is plausible to count Amalarius's text among the books he studied as a monk at Winchester.

[185] *CH* II.v, ed. Godden, p. 49, lines 237–8: '[There was] a certain wise teacher named Amalarius, who wrote a book concerning ecclesiastical customs, [that is,] what the regulations of God's services betoken through the course of the year.' The homily proceeds with a selection and adaption of material almost identical to that used in *LME* 26 (see commentary at nn. 104–8). The identification of the homiletic source was given by Förster, 'Über die Quellen', pp. 48–9.

composing the *LME* closely parallels his use of commentary by Bede, Gregory, Augustine, Jerome and others in the exegetical homilies. His ease, moreover, in moving from biblical to liturgical commentary reflects a broader contemporary trend.[186] An allegorical 'reading' of ritual appealed to an age of liturgical elaboration and increasingly affective modes of piety, while also imposing a transcendent order on what was, in actuality, an often disorderly universe of practices. This spiritual and exegetical unity of the liturgy may even have offered a theoretical substitute for the literal uniformity of custom that, I have suggested, was a sensitive point for Ælfric as he modified the *Concordia*.

Ælfric's choice of the *Liber officialis* as a supplementary source accords well with everything that is known of his scholarly and pedagogical tastes. All of the material adapted from it serves to elaborate bare liturgical instructions on important holy days or, in some cases, fill in gaps left by the *Concordia*.[187] The adaptation of Amalarian passages illustrates a command of the whole (abridged) source and remarkable confidence in quoting or paraphrasing the material in a way that best suits his needs.[188] The practical sensibility that informed Ælfric's treatment of the *Concordia* also stands out here, most notably in the silent adaptation of secular liturgical customs to a monastic context.[189] Familiar from the homilies, too, is a careful attention to biblical quotation and a

---

[186] Thus Gatch: 'beginning with the Carolingian scholars whose work came to its fruition in the monastic-liturgical movement of the tenth century, the most original applications of the theory of multiple meanings were applications to the words and actions of the liturgy . . . Explication, like other theological disciplines and the arts, became a handmaid of the liturgy' (*Preaching and Theology*, p. 11). The essential similarity of biblical and liturgical exposition is underscored by Ælfric's reminiscences in the *LME* of his earlier, homiletic treatments of the scriptural passages pertinent to the liturgical occasion; see, e.g., commentary to *LME* 25 (at n. 103). On the kinship of biblical and liturgical exegesis, see T. M. Thibodeau, '*Enigmata Figurarum*: Biblical Exegesis and Liturgical Exposition in Durand's *Rationale*', *Harvard Theological Review* 86 (1993), 65–79.

[187] See, e.g., *LME* 27 (Sexagesima) and 28 (Quinquagesima).

[188] On Ælfric's treatment of sources generally, see Clemoes, 'Ælfric', and Pope's remarks in *Supplementary Collection* I, 150–63. The Amalarian passages in the *LME* also show a close reliance on the wording of sources, which is characteristic of Ælfric's rewriting of Latin texts; see above, pp. 51–8.

[189] Amalarius was probably not a monk, and the form of the liturgy presupposed in his works is secular, not monastic. See discussion in the commentary to *LME* 24 (at n. 94); but cf. below, p. 70 and n. 199.

seeming preference for the authentic wording of scripture over the vague echo.[190] At least twice, exegetical details intrude that are best explained by reminiscence or direct consultation of his earlier homilies.[191]

Ælfric may have been drawn to the *Liber officialis* because he found its method familiar and stimulating, but he also refashioned its teaching according to a larger design. Certain changes which he consistently introduced suppress the scholarly and antiquarian emphases of Amalarius's work and exploit its imaginative and dramatic potential. In effect, Ælfric's rewriting of the text often involves a shift from Amalarius's ostensibly objective and 'historical' discourse to a near-affective and hortatory one. The result, not surprisingly for Ælfric, sometimes sounds more like a sermon than a liturgical exposition.[192] Amalarius usually maintains, for example, the pretense of a historical 'author of the liturgy' (*compositor officii*) who has designed observances to correspond in rational and intricate ways to typological patterns laid down in the Old and New Testaments. Ælfric (or, in a few cases, the prior redactor whose work is preserved in the 'Salisbury version') always deletes this human intermediary. The result is a rhetorical trick that recasts present liturgical acts as a kind of participation in the biblical events being commemorated.[193] Amalarius's historicism, which is at once both encyclopedic and chaotically inconsistent, objectifies and distances the liturgy as sublime artifice. Ælfric's choice and adapation of material collapse this distance and

---

[190] See commentary to *LME* 24 (at n. 93) and 30 (at n. 141); see also *LME* 33 (at n. 171) and 43 (at n. 219), where the 'restorations' appear already to have been carried out in his peculiar version of *R1*.

[191] See commentary to *LME* 25 (at n. 103) and 32 (at n. 169). On 'reminiscence' in Ælfric's homilies, see Cross, 'Ælfric – Mainly on Memory', and *idem*, 'The Literate Anglo-Saxon', pp. 85–8 and 92.

[192] On a similar discourse 'shift' in Ælfric's *Lives of Saints*, see M. R. Godden, 'Experiments in Genre: the Saints' Lives in Ælfric's *Catholic Homilies*', in *Holy Men and Holy Women*, ed. Szarmach, pp. 261–87. In his first preface to the *Liber officialis*, Amalarius had virtually claimed for his insights the authority of a private revelation: 'uidebatur mihi, quasi in crypta posito, fenestratim lucis scintillas radiare ad nostram paruitatem de re [*scil*. the rationale of the liturgy] quam desiderabam. Longa esurie auidus, non frenum passus sum alicuius magistri, sed ilico . . . scripsi quod sensi' ('Gloriosissime imperator', 1–2). In the body of the work, however, a (pseudo-) historical mode predominates.

[193] See commentary to *LME* 22 (at n. 88), 24 (at n. 93), 25 (at n. 103), 26 (at n. 106), 32 (at n. 168), 33 (at n. 171), 39 (at n. 204) and 43 (at n. 219).

encourage a view of the monks' liturgy as an immediate response to events in Christian history.

SOURCE STUDY AND FURTHER INTERPRETATIVE PROBLEMS

When interpreting what the *LME* says, relative to its sources, about Ælfric's own liturgy, one is frustrated to have to qualify difference after suggestive difference as only 'apparent' or 'possible'. But the loss of Ælfric's exemplars and the complex textual histories of both his major sources necessitate such caution. As noted above, the omission of some extravagant rituals in the *Regularis concordia*, such as the famous *Visitatio sepulchri* 'play' at Easter Nocturns, might indicate something about the size, resources or liturgical competence of the new community. Or the absence of much matter from the proem to the *Concordia* might be explained by tacit shifts between first- and second-generation ideals of 'reform'. But such conclusions ultimately rest on arguments from silence and so remain speculative to a high degree. No customary could include every detail of observance, and an abridgement of a customary was bound to be more selective and allusive still.

No less troubling for the historian of the liturgy are numerous instances in which Ælfric *should* depart from his sources but does not. Here his tendency to cut and splice Latin sources, while attempting to preserve much of the lexis and even the syntax of the originals, has crucial implications. Some passages follow the sources slavishly even where changes were obviously called for. The result is most noticeable, if innocuous, in blank liturgical formulas quoted directly from the *Regularis concordia*. The blanks in the original here presumably reflect Æthelwold's intention that the *Concordia* would serve as a template for reformed houses, whose scriptoria would fill in such details in their own copies. Because Ælfric did not tailor these formulas, the *LME* never reveals even such basic facts as the dedication of the monastic church at Eynsham or the name of the saint(s) whose relics were enshrined in its altar(s).[194] Ælfric, in a word, did not fully customize his customary. Whether he was not as thorough an adaptor as one would like to think, or whether from the very outset he imagined that the 'Eynsham letter' would be read and

---

[194] See the examples discussed in the commentary to *LME* 12 (at n. 53), 25 (at n. 98) and 68 (at n. 313).

used by a wider audience,[195] the assumption that he has so fully integrated his sources that every detail in the *LME* necessarily reflects Eynsham practices does not always withstand scrutiny.

More seriously, his occasional failure to modify what (contemporary evidence strongly suggests) must have been outdated or otherwise inappropriate customs undermines the assumption that the *LME* is always reliable in those details it does provide. A close reading of the *LME* against its sources quickly reveals that the extent of Ælfric's editing fluctuates considerably, and the cutting-and-splicing method that served him adequately when abridging homiletic and narrative sources could have serious consequences when applied to more technical matter. Doubt will therefore linger that misplaced or antiquated customs in the *LME* are merely the vestiges of an imperfectly modified source rather than evidence of exceptional practice at Eynsham.[196] At least twice, for example, Ælfric provides liturgical incipits that can hardly be correct: one of these is taken over as part of an extensive direct quotation from Amalarius, the other (less certainly) from a derivative of *Ordo romanus XIII*.[197] Elsewhere an instruction about the Night Office readings in Advent, also from *Ordo romanus XIII*, appears to conflict with an earlier statement in the First Series of *Catholic Homilies*.[198]

More interesting than these cases, which betray only incidental lapses of attention, are discrepancies that suggest Ælfric's makeshift adaptation of secular Office materials to a monastic context. The substitution of the secular for the monastic form of the Office during the most solemn parts of the church year (especially the *triduum sacrum* and Easter) was a widespread custom by Ælfric's day. Yet three times his *ordo lectionum* (*LME* 70–80) implies the framework of a secular Office (with nine instead of twelve readings) on feasts that did not substitute the secular for

---

[195] By this possibility the *LME* would resemble the pastoral letters, of which at least four were supposedly written near the year 1005 and which, though addressed to specific persons, were also evidently intended for a wider audience; see Hill, 'Monastic Reform and the Secular Church'. The fact that the *LME* survives only in a Worcester copy of Archbishop Wulfstan's 'commonplace book' indicates that Ælfric's customary was known outside Eynsham at a relatively early date, though the manuscript context allows varying interpretations; see below, ch. 3.

[196] Instances of structural confusion attributable to the method have already been noted; see above, n. 161.

[197] See commentary to *LME* 27 (at n. 118) and 71 (at n. 338), respectively.

[198] See commentary to *LME* 75 (at n. 355).

the monastic form.[199] The Eynsham monks probably did not do so either, but Ælfric has adopted the potentially misleading formulation wholesale from some version of the secular *Ordo romanus XIII*. Even if he could depend on the monks' Office lectionary and antiphoner to prevent any confusion, the very fact that, late in the second generation of the 'Benedictine revival', a monastic *ordo lectionum* was not available for his use is remarkable. To witness, at this period and place, the monastic tradition turning to the secular for such a basic resource is perhaps only another indication that 'reform', as Ælfric understood it, was of necessity pragmatic and synthetic, its fortunes more closely bound to the non-monastic church than earlier polemic had been able to admit.

[199] The interpretation is difficult; see commentary to *LME* 71 (at n. 337), 76 (at n. 358) and 77 (at n. 363). By contrast, cf. commentary to *LME* 24 (at n. 94) for a very expert adaptation of secular to monastic contexts. On the substitution of the secular for the monastic Office, see commentary to *LME* 34 (at n. 181), 46 (at n. 238) and 47 (at nn. 243–4).

3

The manuscript

The sole extant copy of Ælfric's *Letter to the Monks of Eynsham* survives on pp. 237–68 of an extraordinarily complex manuscript, Cambridge, Corpus Christi College 265 (formerly K. 2). This composite volume has been much studied, but earlier published accounts are in need of considerable revision.[1] The present discussion can only touch on those aspects of the manuscript's contents and structure where these pertain to the unique survival of the *LME*, its possible relevance to those who copied it and the assumptions made by modern scholars regarding its place in the tradition of Archbishop Wulfstan's 'commonplace book'.[2]

DESCRIPTION

CCCC 265 is made up of 275 parchment leaves, plus one parchment flyleaf of s. xi^2 at its beginning, and two of s. xiii at its end.[3] The volume

---

[1] The foundational treatment is by Bateson, 'A Worcester Cathedral Book', which formed the basis of the entry in James's *Descriptive Catalogue* II, 14–21. For other significant notices, see *Les Ordines romani*, ed. Andrieu I, 99–101; *Hirtenbriefe*, ed. Fehr, pp. xiv and cxxviii; Ker, *Catalogue*, pp. 92–4 (item 53); R. A. Aronstam, 'The Latin Canonical Tradition in Late Anglo-Saxon England: the *Excerptiones Egberti*' (unpubl. PhD dissertation, Columbia Univ., 1974), pp. 20–2; *Theodulfi Capitula*, ed. Sauer, pp. 45–50; Dumville, *Liturgy and Ecclesiastical History*, pp. 137–8. Most useful and accurate of recent publications is Sauer, 'Zur Überlieferung'.

[2] For an updated inventory and discussion of the whole manuscript, see Jones, 'Ælfric's Letter', pp. 42–98.

[3] The leaves of quires 24–7 are slightly smaller, as James noted (*Descriptive Catalogue* II, 16). The manuscript's pagination is faulty; after page 115 the enumerator skipped a folio, and resumed his numbering on the recto of the following folio (117, etc.). A similar mishap occurred in the later part of the manuscript, where the pagination omits

measures *c.* 265 mm × 165 mm, with a written space of *c.* 205 mm × 110 mm.[4] Its texts were copied over the course of nearly a century by a number of scribes. The present bound codex is actually a composite volume made up of at least three distinguishable sections, the first two of which also seem to have been made up incrementally before joining each other and the third. All parts must have been combined, however, by the time a thirteenth-century scribe added a crude table of contents on the verso of the first flyleaf (p. 2).[5]

A recent codicological re-examination of pp. 3–268, or 'Part A', at whose end the unique copy of the *LME* is preserved, has corrected and supplemented the entry in M. R. James's *Descriptive Catalogue of Manuscripts in the Library of Corpus Christi College, Cambridge* on a number of points.[6] Palaeographical evidence and later medieval provenance suggest that this portion was copied at Worcester in the middle or third quarter of the eleventh century.[7] The contents of Part A distinguish it as one of a group of manuscripts associated with the Old English homilist Wulfstan, bishop of London (996–1002), then archbishop of York (1002–23; with

---

numbers 331–40. To avoid unnecessary confusion, however, I continue to use the manuscript's faulty pagination. A revised codicological description of the whole codex is forthcoming in M. Budny, *Insular, Anglo-Saxon, and Early Anglo-Norman Manuscript Art at Corpus Christi College, Cambridge* (Kalamazoo). I am grateful to Dr Budny for allowing me to read her entry on CCCC 265 in typescript.

[4] *Theodulfi Capitula*, ed. Sauer, p. 46.

[5] James, *Descriptive Catalogue* II, 16; Ker, *Catalogue*, p. 94.

[6] *Theodulfi Capitula*, ed. Sauer, p. 46: Part A contains 134 leaves in seventeen quires, collation: $1-14^8 + 15^6 + 16-17^8$, with two singletons each in gatherings 3 and 12–14.

[7] Ker, *Catalogue*, p. 92, 's. xi med.'; see also *idem*, *Medieval Libraries of Great Britain: A List of Surviving Books*, 2nd ed., Royal Historical Society Guides and Handbooks 3 (London, 1964), 206; H. Gneuss, 'A Preliminary List of Manuscripts Written or Owned in England up to 1100', *ASE* 9 (1981), 1–60, at p. 9 (item 73); and McIntyre, 'Early-Twelfth-Century Worcester Cathedral Priory', pp. 202–9 and 211–15 (Appendix A.i–ii). Gameson ('Book Production', p. 238) separates and dates the constituent parts differently: pp. 1–208 's. xi med' and pp. 209–68 's. xi^2'. On the Worcester 'house style' of Latin script, see Bishop, *English Caroline Minuscule*, p. 20, n. 1. In addition to the resemblance of certain hands in CCCC 265 to this 'house style', other evidence supporting a Worcester origin includes: (1) the profession of chastity, added to p. 1 during s. xi^2 and including the phrase 'domno presule uulstano [i.e., St Wulfstan II, bishop of Worcester 1062–95] presente'; (2) Old English additions to pp. 41, 74, 77 and 78 in the hand of Coleman, St Wulfstan's chancellor, deputy preacher and eventual biographer (see references below, at n. 75).

The manuscript

Worcester, 1002–16).[8] Wulfstan assembled a reference book of canonistic, liturgical and homiletic materials from which he drew throughout his career. The collection appears to have changed considerably over time and perhaps never had a fixed, authoritative form. Consequently it survives in markedly different versions as the core of several manuscripts whose precise interrelations are now difficult to recover.[9] Some or all of Part A witnesses this collection; its contents are so various and drawn from so many sources that they are difficult to characterize, but there appears to be a basic division between canon law and penitential texts (pp. 3–208) and liturgical texts (pp. 209–68).[10] On closer examination, the strongest links to the 'commonplace book' family are limited to the canon collections and penitential texts in the first thirteen quires (pp. 3–208), which for convenience may be identified separately as Part A_1. A rough outline of the notable contents in this portion would include: the canon law collection erroneously known as the *Excerptiones Ecgberti*, plus (or including) a great many canons from Insular and Carolingian sources;[11] a type of 'confessor's handbook' in Latin and Old English; a collection of letters, including some addressed to Wulfstan, on the subject of penitential pilgrimages; the episcopal capitularies of Radulf and Theodulf; Ælfric's two Latin pastoral letters to Wulfstan, plus Wulfstan's own Latin 'sermons' on baptism and the chrism; three composite Latin texts on the ecclesiastical grades, attributed to Ælfric; and short excerpts from Hrabanus Maurus's *De clericorum institutione*.

---

[8] In addition to works by Bateson and Sauer cited above, n. 1, see Bethurum, 'Archbishop Wulfstan's Commonplace Book'. On Wulfstan's career, see *Sermo Lupi*, ed. Whitelock, pp. 7–17, along with her 'Archbishop Wulfstan' and 'Wulfstan at York'. See also the introduction to *Homilies of Wulfstan*, ed. Bethurum, pp. 54–87.

[9] The complexities are well demonstrated by stemmata in Sauer, 'Zur Überlieferung'.

[10] There are obvious exceptions, such as the law code *IV Edgar* (pp. 216–27) or the extensive liturgical matter included among canon law excerpts in, among others, Ælfric's second Latin pastoral letter to Wulfstan (pp. 174–80).

[11] The difficulties of identifying discrete text-groups within this material are enormous. For editions and cross-references to other members of the 'commonplace book' family, see Jones, 'Ælfric's *Letter*', pp. 44–59. P. Wormald has argued forcibly that the canon law excerpts, including the so-called *Excerptiones Ecgberti*, actually reveal a methodical effort by someone, probably Wulfstan himself, to compile a comprehensive canon law collection from texts available at early eleventh-century Worcester Cathedral Priory. I am grateful to Mr Wormald for providing me with a typescript of a paper on this topic delivered at the 1996 Congress on Medieval Studies at Kalamazoo.

The remainder of Part A (pp. 209–68), or A_2, contains a lengthy form of excommunication,[12] the Latin-Old English law code *IV Edgar*, an incomplete *ordo* for the bishop's Chrism Mass on Maundy Thursday and, finally, the *LME* itself. The transition from canonical to primarily liturgical documents becomes more pronounced in the ten quires of Part B (pp. 269–442). These quires, datable on palaeographical grounds to the late eleventh or early twelfth centuries, contain excerpts from Amalarius's *Liber officialis*,[13] a block of texts drawn from the Romano-German Pontifical,[14] the supposedly Amalarian *Eclogae de ordine romano* and Bernold of Constance's *Micrologus de ecclesiasticis obseruationibus*. Part C (pp. 443–550), a twelfth-century copy of Hugh of Fleury's *Chronicon* bearing a false attribution to Ivo of Chartres, is not relevant to the following discussion.

An overview of the diverse parts of CCCC 265 reveals that Part A_2 is closer than B or C in date to the material copied on pp. 3–208, but shares with other manuscripts of the 'commonplace book' family only one text, the excommunication rite on pp. 211–15.[15] Arguably, the liturgical content of A_2, especially the Chrism Mass *ordo* and the *LME*, form a neater fit with the later additions of Part B (extracts from Amalarius, etc.). Part A_2 also distinguishes itself from the preceding 'commonplace book' core by a relative diversity of scribal hands. A single 'irregular and uncalligraphic hand'[16] (Scribe 1) is responsible for almost all of A_1 (i.e.,

---

[12] Unlike many formulas, this text contains additions referring to a particular offence that merited excommunication; see Sauer, 'Die Exkommunikationsriten'.

[13] *Lib.off.* II.xvii–xviii, xxv, xxii, xx–xxi, xix, xxiii–xxiv and xxvi; III.v–xxii, xxvii, xxxii and xxxiv–xxxv. Because some of this material could not have been found in the *Retractatio prima* (see above, pp. 62–5), these excerpts indicate the arrival of the full text of the *Liber officialis* in England some time in the second half of the eleventh century.

[14] This important tenth-century liturgical compilation does not appear to have reached England before the mid-eleventh century; see M. Lapidge, 'The Origin of CCCC 163', *Transactions of the Cambridge Bibliographical Society* 8 (1981), 18–28; idem, 'Ealdred of York and MS. Cotton Vitellius E. XII', *Yorkshire Archaeological Journal* 55 (1983), 11–25; repr. with addenda in his *Anglo-Latin Literature*, pp. 453–67 and 492.

[15] This rite, without the customizing details mentioned above (n. 12) and with an altered ending, occurs in the late 'commonplace book' manuscript, Oxford, Bodleian Library, Barlow 37, 40v–41v. The table of contents in CCCC 190 suggests that the same excommunication formula may also have occurred among material that was lost from the exemplar of that manuscript; see Sauer, 'Die Exkommunikationsriten', p. 285.

[16] Ker, *Catalogue*, p. 94; cf. James, *Descriptive Catalogue* II, 16.

The manuscript

pp. 3–207, the first thirteen quires).[17] A different scribe added a few canons on the last page and a half of the thirteenth quire (p. 207, line 14–p. 208, line 16).[18] The latter writes a heavy, rotund 'Style IV' Anglo-Caroline minuscule characteristic of later eleventh-century manuscripts copied in Anglo-Saxon scriptoria.[19] A highly artificial and legible script, Style IV appears to have emanated from Canterbury in the second quarter of the eleventh century, perhaps from the celebrated scribe known as 'Eadui Basan'.[20] It quickly spread to Exeter and other important scriptoria all over the kingdom, although it appears to have been taken up at Worcester only in the 1050s during the pontificate of Ealdred (1046–62).[21] Notably, the general appearance of Scribe 1's writing in A_1 has little in common with the script of other later eleventh-century Worcester books, which show the cultivation of a distinctive 'house style' of Style IV Anglo-Caroline.

The texts that immediately follow in A_2, rituals for excommunication and reconciliation (pp. 211–15) and customizing additions to them (p. 209), appear to be the work of multiple scribes,[22] as does the next item,

---

[17] James, *Descriptive Catalogue* II, 16–17; *Theodulfi Capitula*, ed. Sauer, pp. 46–7. According to Ker this scribe also wrote the Anglo-Saxon minuscule on pp. 72–83 (the Old English 'confessor's handbook' = Ker's *Catalogue*, p. 94, item 53, articles a.i–viii). Part of a letter from Gregory I to Maximianus, written on the originally blank p. 199, appears to be the work of another hand. There are also a number of glosses and marginal additions, some extensive, in several contemporary hands.

[18] James, *Descriptive Catalogue* II, 17; *Theodulfi Capitula*, ed. Sauer, p. 46.

[19] The term 'Style IV' was coined by Dumville as an elaboration of earlier categories devised by Bishop in his *English Caroline Minuscule*. See Dumville's *English Caroline Script*, pp. 111–40.

[20] The identification of 'Eadui' rests on the equivocal evidence of a colophon in Hanover, Kestner-Museum W. M. xxi a, 36, 183v. In addition to Dumville (preceding note), see Bishop, *English Caroline Minuscule*, p. 22, and R. W. Pfaff, 'Eadui Basan: Scriptorum Princeps?', in *England in the Eleventh Century*, ed. Hicks, pp. 267–83.

[21] On the relatively late arrival of Style IV at Worcester, see Dumville, *English Caroline Script*, pp. 136–7. The evidence for both Latin and vernacular scripts at Worcester in the first half of s. xi does not reveal a single, clear line of development; see Dumville, *English Caroline Script*, pp. 68–75, and N. R. Ker, 'Hemming's Cartulary: a Description of the Two Worcester Cartularies in Cotton Tiberius A.XIII', in *Studies in Medieval History Presented to F. M. Powicke*, ed. R. W. Hunt, W. A. Pantin and R. W. Southern (Oxford, 1948), pp. 49–75, at 51–2; repr. in his *Books, Collectors and Libraries*, ed. Watson, pp. 31–59, at 34–5.

[22] Cf. James, *Descriptive Catalogue* II, 17, who seems to attribute all the ritual texts (up to

the law code *IV Edgar*.²³ The following Maundy Thursday *ordo* (pp. 228–31, written in red ink) breaks off abruptly in mid-course, and the last two-and-a-half folios (= pp. 232–6) of quire 15 are blank. The writing resumes on p. 237, the first folio of quire 16, where the *LME* begins in a heavy Style IV hand similar but not identical to that of the preceding *ordo*. The scribal stints of A_2 still await a thorough sorting out, but the main point should be clear: while one scribe copied, probably from a single exemplar, the entire portion of texts exemplifying the 'commonplace book', the succeeding four quires witness a mix of hands copying, mostly in a new style of script, texts of miscellaneous character, perhaps even from several different exemplars. The hand of the *LME*-scribe makes no significant appearance elsewhere in the manuscript, and, unlike other texts in Part A, the *LME* fits neatly in the space of two complete quires (16 and 17).²⁴ These quires, moreover, are ruled in a manner slightly different from the ones before and after them.²⁵ The gathering that holds the *LME* thus begins to look very much like a separate section not originally copied to be part of the preceding manuscript.²⁶ Because of the incremental growth of the whole book,

---

p. 215) to a single hand, neglecting at the very least a marked change in script at p. 211, line 16.

²³ In the Latin of *IV Edgar* the hand changes perceptibly at the top of p. 219; Ker (*Catalogue*, p. 94) had noticed a change of hand in the Old English version of the laws, but did not remark that the two hands also divided the copying of the Latin.

²⁴ The hand of the *LME*-scribe is, however, very similar to, and may be the same as that which added the extra canons to pp. 207–8. Because these additions occur at the end of quire 13 in space left blank by Scribe 1, however, they do not necessarily indicate co-operation between the two scribes.

²⁵ They contain the same number of lines per page (26), but their double-ruled vertical boundary lines extend only the length of the written area, not all the way to the top and bottom of the folio, as in the preceding quires.

²⁶ Evidence that the *LME* actually constituted a separate 'booklet' that enjoyed independent circulation (suggested by Gatch, 'Old English Literature and the Liturgy', p. 241, n. 4) is less compelling. There is considerable wear and soiling on some leaves (especially p. 268, which must have been the last verso of the volume for a time), but only in the second quire of the work (no. 17), wherein the parchment was, it seems, already of much poorer quality than in the first (no. 16). There is no evidence of additional folding or creasing in either quire. On the distinguishing marks of 'booklets', see P. R. Robinson, 'Self-Contained Units in Composite Manuscripts of the Anglo-Saxon Period', *ASE* 7 (1978), 231–8.

The manuscript

these last two quires could have joined the rest of Part A at any time before Part B was added to it, probably near the turn of s. xi/xii.

The single scribe who copied the *LME* was competent, and the text rarely calls for emendation. Punctuation is inconsistent, with a single point used for differing degrees of medial pause and occasionally for full stops; in a few instances, a fuller hierarchy is introduced by the use of the *punctus eleuatus* and *punctus uersus*.[27] Some proper names appear in a hybrid display script,[28] and a few unpretentious two- and three-line initials occur,[29] but the presentation of the text is otherwise quite unremarkable. The sense-divisions or 'Sinnabschnitte' introduced by Nocent and Hallinger for the 1984 edition in the CCM (and retained for convenience in the present edition) have no manuscript authority. Rather, the text is unbroken by paragraph divisions or chapter headings; unlike the manuscripts of the *Concordia*, the *LME* lacks a table of contents (or provisions for one). Nothing about this unique copy suggests, then, that Ælfric's original plan for the text included a division into chapters, much less into chapters corresponding to the divisions found in the body of the *Concordia*.

THE *LME* AND ARCHBISHOP WULFSTAN'S 'COMMONPLACE BOOK'

In 1895 Mary Bateson pointed out the striking parallels, both in content and arrangement, of five manuscripts: CCCC 265; CCCC 190; London, BL, Cotton Nero A. i; Oxford, Bodleian Library, Bodley 718; and Paris, Bibliothèque Nationale, lat. 3182. She correctly linked the collection to Worcester, *c.* 1000, though not to the figure of Archbishop

---

[27] For example, in the preface (*LME* 1), with the *punctus eleuatus* after *scriptis*, *demonstro*, *praesumere*, *didici* and *narranti*, and the *punctus uersus* after *habetur*. See B. Bischoff, *Latin Palaeography: Antiquity and the Middle Ages*, trans. D. Ganz and D. Ó Cróinín (Cambridge, 1990), p. 169, and P. Clemoes, 'Liturgical Influence on Punctuation in Late Old English and Early Middle English Manuscsripts', *Department of Anglo-Saxon, Occasional Papers* 1 (Cambridge, 1952); repr. as *Old English Newsletter* Subsidia 4 (Binghamton, 1980).

[28] Rustic capitals, with occasional uncial and minuscule forms: e.g., p. 237, *eADGARI*, p. 254, *SECUNDUM IOHANNEM*; p. 260, *MARIE* and *MichAhEliS*; cf. p. 264, *ORATIO PRO DEFUNCTO FRATRE* and *FINIUNT CONSUETUDINES*.

[29] See p. 237 (*LME* 1–2) *Ælfricus* and *Kalendis*; and p. 264 (*LME* 69–70) *Satisfaciat* and *Quia*. On the use of colour and rubrication, see above, p. 19, n. 3.

Wulfstan.[30] In 1942 Dorothy Bethurum associated the collection with Wulfstan the homilist by demonstrating numerous instances in which he drew from these materials for the composition of his own Latin and Old English works. To Bateson's list of manuscripts, Bethurum added: Oxford, Bodleian Library, Junius 121 and Barlow 37; Copenhagen, Kongelige Bibliotek, Gl. Kgl. Sam. 1595; and London, BL, Cotton Vespasian A. xiv.[31] Both Bateson and Bethurum recognized, however, that there could be no easy explanation of the relationships among the several manuscripts, since none appeared to be a direct copy of any of the others; in fact, some differences among them seemed so great as to deny that all the manuscripts could have descended from a single archetype. Striking agreements in variant readings and the internal arrangement of entire text-groups, on the other hand, ruled out the attribution of their similarities to mere coincidence.

This puzzling array of evidence has led to the conclusion that Archbishop Wulfstan's 'commonplace book' existed from the very beginning in more than one version, that Wulfstan himself was at least partly responsible for the different versions and that he did not use any one version to the exclusion of the others.[32] These conclusions usefully reconcile otherwise contradictory evidence. First, three extant manuscripts of the 'commonplace book' appear to be products of one of Archbishop Wulfstan's own scriptoria and contain additions, corrections and occasional titles in his own hand.[33] Yet even these three manuscripts – all demonstrably used by Wulfstan and copied, it seems, under his direction – present differing versions of the collection, both in their choice and arrangement of material. Second, a recent, painstaking study of the structure of one of these three manuscripts, Copenhagen 1595, reveals that it is made up of several sections produced independently of one another, and that the many scribes 'contributed to their individual Sections as ends in themselves and with no initial notion of forming the collection as it now stands'.[34] As a first-generation witness to the

---

[30] 'A Worcester Cathedral Book'.   [31] 'Archbishop Wulfstan's Commonplace Book'.
[32] Sauer, 'Zur Überlieferung', p. 379.
[33] Cotton Nero A. i, Cotton Vespasian A. xiv and Copenhagen 1595; the identification of Wulfstan's hand was made by N. R. Ker, 'The Handwriting of Archbishop Wulfstan', in *England before the Conquest*, ed. Clemoes and Hughes, pp. 315–31; repr. in his *Books, Collectors and Libraries*, ed. Watson, pp. 9–26.
[34] *The Copenhagen Wulfstan Collection*, ed. Cross and Tunberg, pp. 27–8 and 60 (quotation

'commonplace book', the Copenhagen manuscript demonstrates how Wulfstan may have employed his own scriptorium to produce a copy of the collection. In that manuscript the basic increment appears to have been the section – a quire or quires containing a complete group or 'block' of texts.[35] How these blocks were afterwards 'stacked' may have mattered less than the internal composition of each block. The construction of Copenhagen 1595 sheds new light on the 'commonplace book' puzzle, for it allows that, at the source (perhaps in Wulfstan's possession), several different 'archetypes' of the collection might have existed side by side.[36] The arrangement by section may represent the texts as they occurred in Wulfstan's own copy or in a copy he ordered made; these sections would be variously distributed for copying, and the resulting copies then bound together in particular sequences and/or in combination with extraneous texts. Depending on the arrangement of these sections, the process could produce a number of different exemplars which, especially after further recopyings, omissions and interpolations, would explain the survival of the 'commonplace book' in such widely differing versions.[37]

The shifting foundations of the 'commonplace book' and its contents deserve close attention since manuscript context offers what may be the only available clues to the early reception of the *LME*. The survival of the work in CCCC 265 alongside texts of known derivation from the 'commonplace book' has been interpreted as evidence that the *LME*

---

from p. 27). A similar union of independently copied sections or 'booklets' is also suggested by the coincidence of scribal stints with gatherings in the Alcuin letter-books on 114r–171v of another first-generation copy of the 'commonplace book', Cotton Vespasian A. xiv (Worcester or York, s. xi^1); see *Two Alcuin Letter-Books*, ed. C. Chase, Toronto Medieval Latin Texts 5 (Toronto, 1975), 8–9.

[35] For example, in Copenhagen 1595: Amalarius's *Eclogae* (section 1 = quires i–ii), sermons by Abbo of Saint-Germain (section 3 = quires iv–v) and so on. Sauer's analysis of the 'commonplace book' structure also relies on 'blocks' of texts, the restacking of which may explain certain differences in the internal arrangements of CCCC 265 and Barlow 37 ('Zur Überlieferung', pp. 371–2).

[36] Whitelock ('Wulfstan at York', pp. 215–16) offers a salutary reminder that 'at the source' in Wulfstan's case need not mean Worcester. Some of the 'commonplace book' manuscripts, including Copenhagen 1595, may well come from York.

[37] Sauer's collations of individual items in several manuscripts point to at least four different 'original' versions in Wulfstan's possession. They are represented by: (1) Copenhagen 1595 and (2) Cotton Nero A. i, as well as the exemplars from which descend (3) CCCC 190 and (4) the closely related CCCC 265 and Barlow 37 ('Zur Überlieferung', p. 377).

entered Wulfstan's collection either because Ælfric sent the archbishop a copy or Wulfstan sought one out. Bernhard Fehr, editor of Ælfric's *pastoralia*, reasoned that Ælfric sent Wulfstan a copy of the *LME* 'because it would have to have been of interest to him [*scil.* Wulfstan], the former abbot'.[38] Quite apart from the fact that Wulfstan is titled 'abbot' only in a late and unconfirmable source,[39] Fehr underestimated the complexity of the relationships among the 'commonplace book' manuscripts and greatly overstated the collection's ties to Ælfric.[40] Deftly correcting these misconceptions, Peter Clemoes nevertheless allowed Fehr's judgement of the *LME*'s reception to stand, though he added the qualifier that Wulfstan might have acquired his copy not from Ælfric directly, but through some other channel.[41] Clemoes's modified but still confident attribution of the *LME* to the 'commonplace book' tradition is typical.[42]

Because analysis of the contents and structure suggest a division of Part A into texts that exemplify the 'commonplace book' and those that do not, the dangers of a circular argument now loom. The *LME* is associated with the 'commonplace book' tradition in part because of its survival in the final two quires of CCCC 265, Part A;[43] at the same time, the presence of the *LME* there has been cited as one piece of evidence to support the argument that the last four quires of Part A, like the first thirteen, exemplify the 'commonplace book' tradition. Acknowledging

[38] Fehr, 'Das Benediktiner-Offizium', p. 343: 'weil er ihn, den früheren abt, ebenfalls interessieren mußte'.

[39] See *The Chronicle of John of Worcester II: The Annals from 450 to 1066*, ed. R. R. Darlington and P. McGurk, trans. J. Bray and P. McGurk (Oxford, 1995), p. 452. At the date he is called 'abbas' by John of Worcester (*s.a.* 1002), Wulfstan was already bishop of London, although he may have been an abbot earlier in his career; see *Sermo Lupi*, ed. Whitelock, p. 7, and *Homilies of Wulfstan*, ed. Bethurum, pp. 56–7.

[40] Fehr ('Das Benediktiner-Offizium') originally believed that the Latin portion of CCCC 190, or its exemplar, was compiled under Ælfric's direction and sent to Wulfstan, who in turn incorporated large portions of that manuscript into CCCC 265. In her seminal article on the 'commonplace book' (1942), Bethurum did not rule out Fehr's hypotheses, though Fehr himself later retreated from his original views on CCCC 190.

[41] Clemoes, 'The Old English Benedictine Office': because the *LME* occurs in a manuscript 'drawing on Wulfstan's collection of texts', he writes, 'it can be assumed that Wulfstan knew Ælfric's letter to the monks of Eynsham' (pp. 282–3).

[42] Implied, for example, by Whitelock, 'Archbishop Wulfstan', p. 33, n. 1; and Cross, 'A Newly-Identified Manuscript', p. 67.

[43] The argument also rests on other verifiable evidence of intellectual exchange between Ælfric and Wulfstan; see Clemoes, 'The Old English Benedictine Office', pp. 282–3.

The manuscript

this danger, recent discussions of CCCC 265 have been more guarded about claiming for unique texts in the later 'commonplace book' manuscripts descent from one of the versions of Wulfstan's 'original' collection.[44] Further comparative study of the several manuscripts only underscores the need for caution. In showing, for example, that CCCC 265 stands quite close to an even later 'commonplace book' manuscript, Barlow 37, Sauer has argued strongly that 'commonplace book'-portions of both manuscripts descend from a single exemplar (now lost), which was itself a copy at one or more removes from a manuscript used by Wulfstan.[45] The absence of the *LME* from Barlow 37, a manuscript in other respects so close to CCCC 265, necessarily raises doubt as to whether the text was present in their common ancestor. Of the *LME* and other texts found in CCCC 265 but not Barlow 37, Sauer will only say, 'one cannot rule out that at least a portion of the material in manuscript C [= CCCC 265] . . . was already in Wulfstan's collection, especially pp. 216–27 [= *IV Edgar*] and 237–68 [= *LME*]'.[46] CCCC 265, Part A, having been written between twenty-five and fifty years after the archbishop's death, is decidedly not a first-generation witness to Wulfstan's reference book. By its very nature the collection appears to have invited, in any case, the addition of new texts and abridgement or omission of matter from the exemplar. While the traditional association of the *LME* with the 'commonplace book' remains plausible and, one must admit, attractive for its preservation of a contemporary link between Ælfric and Wulfstan, the evidence when re-examined allows for the possibility that the *LME* falls

---

[44] See Dumville, *Liturgy and Ecclesiastical History*, p. 138.

[45] 'Zur Überlieferung', p. 380. The point is illustrated by a number of Sauer's collations; see, for example, his stemma for Wulfstan's Homily *De baptismo* (Bethurum's Homily VIIIa), 'Zur Überlieferung', p. 368.

[46] 'Zur Überlieferung', pp. 369–70: 'Bei Hs. C [= CCCC 265] ist es . . . nicht ausgeschlossen, daß zumindest ein Teil des Materials . . . schon in Wulfstans Sammlung war (bes. S. 216 bis 227 [= *IV Edgar*] u. 237–268 [= *LME*]).' Both here and in a later remark (p. 372), where he tentatively allows the *LME* a place in the reconstructed common exemplar, Sauer's tone contrasts strikingly with the traditional view (cf. Clemoes's 'it can be assumed . . .', quoted above, n. 41). On the case for and against *IV Edgar* as part of the 'commonplace book' tradition, see Whitelock, 'Archbishop Wulfstan', p. 32, n. 2, and 'Wulfstan at York', pp. 216 and 224. A second copy of this law code extant in London, BL, Cotton Nero E. i (Worcester, s. xi[ex]) hints that Worcester, rather than Archbishop Wulfstan's personal attention, may be the common factor in the survival of this text.

outside the 'commonplace book' tradition. This possibility invites renewed speculation about the reception of Ælfric's customary and the significance of its sole surviving copy.

As already stated, CCCC 265, Part A, is a Worcester manuscript of the middle to third quarter of the eleventh century. The book's contemporary associations are therefore entirely with the career of another Wulfstan, Wulfstan II of Worcester (hereafter 'St Wulfstan' to distinguish him from the archbishop).[47] If, as one scholar has suggested, CCCC 265 was a 'handbook of canonical and liturgical texts used by Wulfstan II during his episcopate',[48] the *LME* perhaps owes its survival more to the interest of this later Wulfstan than of his namesake, the archbishop. Peculiar circumstances at Worcester Cathedral Priory in the later tenth and eleventh centures would accommodate this view. Following the pattern of his fellow reformers, at some time between 966 and 977 St Oswald, then bishop of Worcester, had introduced monks into the cathedral close, though it is difficult to say exactly when the older secular community ceased to function there, or if it existed in some form until well into the eleventh century.[49] Whatever the relative status of the monks and seculars at Worcester, when St Wulfstan was appointed prior of the cathedral monastery (*c.* 1055 × 1057) by Bishop Ealdred (1046–62), his policies suggest dissatisfaction with what he found there. He immediately set about reviving the community which, by his own account, had dwindled to twelve monks.[50] A decline in numbers and discipline would have

---

[47] Thus the monastic profession 'presule uulstano presente' copied on the recto of the front flyleaf (p. 1). The Old English *Life of St Wulfstan*, written by his chancellor and sometime chaplain, Coleman, has not survived, although a Latin translation and partial abridgement by William of Malmesbury has (*Vita Wulfstani*, ed. Darlington). Valuable re-assessment of Wulfstan II and eleventh-century Worcester is provided by Mason, *St Wulfstan*.

[48] Dumville, *Liturgy and Ecclesiastical History*, p. 138.

[49] Some sources claim that Oswald, like Æthelwold, expelled the secular clergy in a single, dramatic move, while others suggest he built up the monastic community gradually. The opposing views and their documentary bases are clearly laid out by Barrow, 'Community of Worcester'.

[50] See *The Cartulary of Worcester Cathedral Priory*, Register I, ed. R. R. Darlington, Pipe Roll Series 76 (London, 1968), no. 3; and Mason, *St Wulfstan*, pp. 62, n. 85, and 130. There is some disagreement over the date of St Wulfstan's election as prior. Given that Ealdred was elevated to Worcester only in 1046 and did not immediately replace the existing prior, the suggestions 1043 (A. E. E. Jones, *Anglo-Saxon Worcester* (Worcester,

The manuscript

resulted in part from the political turmoil that drained the resources of the see during the reigns of Edward the Martyr, Æthelred and Cnut. But the more damaging influence remained the custom of plurality which allowed archbishops of York to hold both the York and Worcester dioceses at the same time.[51] Given the importance of Worcester, the community over which St Wulfstan became prior was relatively small and poor and may have still included both monks and clerks. In such a setting, even the monks might not know the full observance instituted by St Oswald, including the liturgical customs of the *Regularis concordia*. Because Ælfric's customary was written for a modest community, some of whose members supposedly did not know the *Concordia*, the *LME* might have served St Wulfstan well as he set about re-introducing the regular life in all its fullness.[52] The compilation of CCCC 265, Part A, or at least the addition of texts in A_2, may date to the years of St Wulfstan's priorate, since reform of the Worcester scriptorium and adoption of Style IV Anglo-Caroline had apparently already begun during Ealdred's pontificate.[53]

Nor would the usefulness of the *LME* have ceased when St Wulfstan became bishop in 1062: even then he made a point of living in the monastic community and, so far as possible, acting as its abbot. During his pontificate the *LME* could have served as a reference text to consult, and perhaps even adapt and use, when establishing smaller dependencies. Ælfric's customary bore witness to an earlier period of monastic colonization, when many new or refounded houses required some record of the customs in their parent foundations. From St Wulfstan's Worcester emanated an analogous, if less ambitious, revival, the success of which

---

1958), p. 155) and 1046 (Bannister, 'Note on MS Hatton 113', p. lxii) are untenable. Mason says (*St Wulfstan*, p. 61, n. 80) that Wulfstan became prior 'evidently not later than 1055'. For an alternative date of 1057, cf. D. Knowles, C. N. L. Brook and V. C. M. London, *The Heads of Religious Houses: England and Wales, 940–1216* (Cambridge, 1972), p. 83.

[51] Mason, *St Wulfstan*, pp. 21–3

[52] The *LME* would require some modification to suit a cathedral monastery, although the custom of plurality (and, in Ealdred's case, sheer absenteeism) meant that Worcester's bishop would ordinarily play little part in the monks' day-to-day worship. The prior was, in effect, head of the community. On the other hand, *LME* 39 does include the episcopal liturgy of the Chrism Mass, which would probably have meant more to the monks of Worcester than to Ælfric's original audience.

[53] On the introduction of Style IV Anglo-Caroline and the Romano-German Pontifical, see above, nn. 21 and 14, respectively.

must have required authoritative models of liturgical observance, though on a scale less grand than at Worcester Cathedral Priory. An epitome such as the *LME* would serve as an ideal model for the transplanting of liturgical custom to a small dependency, such as Westbury-on-Trym, which St Wulfstan refounded sometime before 1093.[54]

Whether or not the *LME* served on such specific occasions as these, its context in CCCC 265 points to the larger cultural significance of St Wulfstan's pontificate, which prolonged the life of native ecclesiastical customs in the decades of transformation from Anglo-Saxon to Anglo-Norman England. It is well known that the copying of Old English manuscripts continued and perhaps even increased at St Wulfstan's Worcester; additionally, some English liturgical practices were preserved there, and confraternities established with other houses retaining Anglo-Saxon heads fostered a recusant identity.[55] But even among his Norman colleagues, St Wulfstan enjoyed a high reputation not only for his sanctity but for his thorough knowledge of pre-Conquest church tradition. When Anselm became archbishop of Canterbury in 1093, St Wulfstan was the last Anglo-Saxon bishop and, as such, the last living authority on native English customs.[56] Wulfstan took seriously his role as a preserver of the old ways, especially the traditions of Anglo-Saxon monasticism. Tellingly,

---

[54] *Vita Wulfstani*, ed. Darlington, p. 52. Founded by St Oswald, the house had suffered greatly in the aftermath of King Edgar's death and the 'anti-monastic reaction'. St Wulfstan rebuilt the monastery, endowed it with lands and provided service books for its church. Coleman was active there as prior by 1093; the house was disbanded, however, by Wulfstan's successor, Samson (1096–1112), in 1096. On the date of the refoundation (before 1093), see Mason, *St Wulfstan*, pp. 168–9, n. 47. Though he did not actually refound the house, Wulfstan also exercised influence over the struggling foundation at Great Malvern (*Vita Wulfstani*, ed. Darlington, p. 26).

[55] Mason, *St Wulfstan*, pp. 206–9 and 130; on post-Conquest changes in the Worcester liturgy, see *ibid.*, pp. 116–17 and 204; on the confraternity, *ibid.*, pp. 197–200. For a broader view of the Norman impact on English monastic life, see Knowles, *Monastic Order*, pp. 122–4, and J. A. Robinson, 'Lanfranc's Monastic Constitutions', *Journal of Theological Studies* 10 (1909), 375–88.

[56] Thus Eadmer: 'Supererat adhuc beatæ memoriæ Wulstanus ... Wigornensis episcopus, unus et solus de antiquis Anglorum patribus, uir in omni religione conspicuus et antiquarum Angliæ consuetudinum scientia apprime imbutus' (*Historia nouorum in Anglia*, ed. M. Rule, Rolls Series 81 (London, 1884), 45–6: 'Of the ancient fathers of the English [church], only one was still living: Wulfstan of blessed memory ... bishop of Worcester, a man celebrated for every sort of piety and utterly steeped in the knowledge of the ancient customs of England').

his first public act after being ordained bishop was the dedication of a church to the Venerable Bede. Coleman's Old English Life of Wulfstan, which survives only in a Latin translation by William of Malmesbury, interprets the significance explicitly:

> Altera enim ordinationis die beato Bede dedicauit ecclesiam, pulchre illi prime dedicationis prebens principium, qui fuisset literature princeps de gente Anglorum. Eo enim die tam proflua predicatione populum irrorauit, ut non dubitaretur Wlstanum per spiritum sanctum eadem niti facundia, que quondam linguam mouisset in Beda.[57]

Like the great monk-bishops of Bede's *Historia ecclesiastica*, St Wulfstan ideally balanced his episcopal and monastic roles. But the nostalgia for a golden age of Anglo-Saxon monasticism was, of course, received through the ideology of the tenth-century reformers, with whose role St Wulfstan also consciously identified his own. His pontificate represented a deliberate return to certain ideals of his Worcester predecessors, Dunstan (957–9) and Oswald (961–92).[58] In another revealing episode, St Wulfstan's biographer recounts how the bishop, armed only with copies of the *Vitae* of his two saintly predecessors, successfully defended his see from the proprietary claims of the newly elected Norman archbishop of York, Thomas (1070–1100).[59] Dunstan and Oswald proved valuable symbols not only for their Worcester connections, but because they recalled the long tradition of English monasticism and epitomized the virtues of a monk-bishop.

Although the *LME* boasts no immediate link to either of St Wulfstan's predecessors at Worcester, Ælfric's preface, with its mention of Æthelwold's school, flaunts in a general way the badge of the reforming party to which they belonged. Perhaps more to the point, liturgical and other ties between reformed Winchester and Worcester broaden the context for

---

[57] *Vita Wulfstani*, ed. Darlington, p. 20: 'On the day following his ordination he dedicated a church to blessed Bede, appropriately offering the priority of his first dedication to him who had been foremost in learning among the English. For on that day he bedewed the people with such fluent preaching that there could be no doubt but that Wulfstan was, through the Holy Spirit, drawing on that same eloquence that had once inspired the tongue of Bede.'

[58] See Mason, 'St Oswald and St Wulfstan'.

[59] *Vita Wulfstani*, ed. Darlington, p. 25. For details of this dispute, which culminated at a Windsor synod on Pentecost, 1072, see Mason, *St Wulfstan*, pp. 110–13, and *idem*, 'St Oswald and St Wulfstan', pp. 269 and 277.

reception of the *LME*. The form of the 'New Hymnal' still in use at Worcester during St Wulfstan's pontificate, for example, was essentially that of Æthelwold's Winchester nearly a century before, and of the *LME* itself.[60] Other evidence for the liturgical influence of Winchester includes: the prominence of SS Birinus, Swithun and Judoc in the calendar of St Wulfstan's 'Portiforium';[61] the textual affinities of two manuscripts of Æthelwold's bilingual version of the Benedictine *Rule*;[62] the type of script written at both centres in the later tenth century ('Style I' Anglo-Caroline);[63] and, less certainly, the presence of an Old Minster sacramentary at Worcester in the later eleventh century,[64] as well as the

[60] See Gneuss, *Hymnar*, pp. 69–74; idem, 'Latin Hymns in Medieval England', p. 413; also Milfull, pp. 9–10 and 45. Apart from the relatively meagre provisions in the *Concordia* itself, the *LME* is the oldest representative of the 'Winchester–Worcester' group, the most complete representative of which is CCCC 391 – the so-called Portiforium of St Wulfstan, written in 1065. On the hymnal of the *LME*, see the commentary to §§ 13, 50 and 54. On the general subject of Winchester–Worcester ties, it should be noted that some earlier assumptions are now being reconsidered; see Dumville, *English Caroline Script*, pp. 4–5, n. 15.

[61] For the calendar of the 'Portiforium', see *English Kalendars before A. D. 1100*, ed. F. Wormald, HBS 72 (London, 1934), 212–23 (no. 17); for the prayers and *commune sanctorum*, see *The Portiforium of Saint Wulstan*, ed. Hughes; for the collectar, hymnal, calendar and various other materials, see vol. II of *The Leofric Collectar*, ed. Dewick and Frere, as well as Milfull, pp. 43–7; the litany is also re-edited in *Anglo-Saxon Litanies of the Saints*, ed. Lapidge, pp. 115–19 (no. VI). On the Winchester saints in the Portiforium calendar, see also Turner, *Early Worcester MSS*, p. lviii.

[62] Gretsch, *Die Regula Sancti Benedicti*, pp. 118–19. The two manuscripts are Oxford, Corpus Christi College 197 (Bury-St-Edmunds provenance, s. x²) and CCCC 178 (Worcester, s. xi¹). Gretsch suggests that the textual affinities stem from a common link to Winchester – directly for Worcester, indirectly (via Ely) for Bury. Dumville, claiming that the usually cited date for the refoundation of Bury (1022) is far too late, has argued for a direct Worcester–Bury link via Ramsey; see his *English Caroline Script*, pp. 7–78.

[63] Bishop, *English Caroline Minuscule*, pp. xxi–xxii. Now see also Gameson, 'Book Production'.

[64] Worcester, Cathedral Library, F. 173 (Old Minster, Winchester, s. xi^med). On these fragments' ties to Winchester, see the *Catalogue of Manuscripts Preserved in the Chapter Library of Worcester Cathedral*, ed. J. K. Floyer, rev. and ed. S. G. Hamilton (Oxford, 1906), pp. 98–100; also C. H. Turner, 'The Churches at Winchester in the Early Eleventh Century', *Journal of Theological Studies* 17 (1915–16), 65–8. The presence of this book at Worcester in the earlier Middle Ages is questioned by Gameson, 'Book Production', p. 243, but accepted by K. D. Hartzell, 'An English Missal Fragment in the British Library', *ASE* 18 (1989), 45–97, at pp. 84–9. The direct Winchester–

liturgical division of Ps. LXXVII at verse 40 rather than 36 – supposedly a Winchester symptom – in a *de luxe* psalter probably written at Ramsey, a Worcester dependency since its founding by St Oswald *c.* 966.[65] Regarding Æthelwold's own reputation at Worcester, it is significant that Coleman may have drawn elements for his Life of Wulfstan from a *Vita* of Æthelwold.[66] If the *LME* was not already in the exemplar of CCCC 265, then the prominence of the names 'Æthelwold' and 'Winchester' at the head of the work and its extensive use of the *Regularis concordia* would have commended the text to historically sensitive, post-Conquest Worcester.

It may also be wondered whether or not the contrast between the two Wulfstans and the emphases of their respective pontificates argues against the linking of the *LME* to the 'commonplace book' tradition. Neither the contents of Archbishop Wulfstan's collection nor his original writings indicate any deep or lasting interest in monastic life and liturgy. Apart from preaching (not necessarily a liturgically based activity), the archbishop's liturgical interests centred on rites associated with the episcopacy.[67] Among the several 'commonplace book' manuscripts, the only traces of any interest in the specific details of monastic liturgy (disallowing the equivocal evidence of the *LME* itself) are the excerpts *De ecclesiastica consuetudine*, found in CCCC 190 and Rouen 1382; even these, however, have been adapted (if imperfectly) for secular use.[68] Archbishop Wulfstan's overriding interest was the formation and discipline of the

---

Worcester link long perceived in the 'Samson Pontifical' (= CCCC 146, s. xi^in), has been challenged by a revised palaeographical analysis; see Dumville, *Liturgy and Ecclesiastical History*, pp. 72–3.

[65] The psalter is London, BL, Harley 2904; on its alleged Winchester connection, see *The Salisbury Psalter*, ed. C. and K. Sisam, EETS o.s. 242 (London, 1969), 4–5, and A. Corrêa, 'The Liturgical Manuscripts of Oswald's Houses', in *St Oswald*, ed. Brooks and Cubitt, pp. 285–324, at 292–6.

[66] Suggested by A. Gransden, *Historical Writing in England, c. 550 to c. 1307* (London, 1974), p. 88; see also her 'Cultural Transition at Worcester in the Anglo-Norman Period', in *Medieval Art and Architecture at Worcester Cathedral: The British Archaeological Association Conference Transactions for the Year 1975* (London, 1978), pp. 1–14, at 5, as well as her 'Traditionalism and Continuity', pp. 199–200.

[67] See *Homilies of Wulfstan*, ed. Bethurum, nos. XIV, XV and XVIII.

[68] These excerpts and their associations with Wulfstan or Ælfric pose notorious difficulties; see above, p. 23, n. 19, and p. 63, n. 178.

secular clergy:[69] canons, not monks, formed his own cathedral chapter at York. As for his dealings with Ælfric (insofar as we can infer the archbishop's side of the exchange from Ælfric's responses), Wulfstan sought in the pastoral letters elaboration only of such major observances as Candlemas and the Triduum – that is, celebrations enjoined on both monks and seculars. Whether or not Archbishop Wulfstan was a monk himself (not to mention an abbot), his pontificate as a whole reflects a greater concern with the world than with the cloister: he is remembered as a preacher, a counsellor to kings and an author of law codes. His associations with particular monasteries are few and difficult to explain, except perhaps by personal or political ties.[70] In his own see of Worcester, Archbishop Wulfstan was later reviled for his alleged pursuit of secular interests at the expense of the cathedral priory. No contemporary monastically produced *uita* of Archbishop Wulfstan survives.

St Wulfstan's cultivation of the monastic life, deliberately patterned after the tenth-century reformers, offers a rather more accommodating prospect for the reception of Ælfric's customary. Some potential applications for the text have already been noted. Evidence also indicates that St Wulfstan and his Worcester monks knew Ælfric by reputation and so may even have prized the *LME* as a work of the abbot's pen. As prior, St Wulfstan distinguished himself as a preacher, and as bishop he clearly viewed preaching to the laity as one of the essential duties of his office.[71] Several vernacular homily collections survive from Worcester of the second half of the eleventh century.[72] The most important of these –

---

[69] Thus the ostensible purpose of Ælfric's Old English pastorals to Wulfstan, and Wulfstan's own *Canons of Edgar* (ed. R. Fowler, EETS o.s. 266 (London, 1972)).

[70] Wulfstan was buried at Ely, where miracles at his tomb were claimed; he was also revered at Peterborough for an alleged donation. Yet Archbishop Wulfstan does not appear to have been a monk at either of these houses, leading Whitelock to speculate that he had family ties to the Fenland monasteries; see the introduction to her *Sermo Lupi*, pp. 7–8. The modest use of the Benedictine *Rule* in Wulfstan's works is discussed by K. Jost, *Wulfstanstudien*, Schweizer anglistische Arbeiten 23 (Bern, 1950), 51, n. 2, and *Homilies of Wulfstan*, ed. Bethurum, p. 325.

[71] *Vita Wulfstani*, ed. Darlington, pp. 13–14. This duty would later pass to his chancellor and future biographer, Coleman (*ibid.*, pp. 39–40), whose annotations turn up in a number of Worcester manuscripts from the period; see below, n. 75.

[72] On vernacular manuscripts and preaching at St Wulfstan's Worcester, see Gatch, *Preaching and Theology*, pp. 56–7 and 209, n. 101; also W. Keller, *Die literarischen Bestrebungen von Worcester in angelsächsischer Zeit*, Sprach- und Culturgeschichte der

The manuscript

now separated as Oxford, Bodleian Library, Hatton 113 and 114 – was very likely compiled under St Wulfstan's direction and for his own use.[73] Although the first half of the collection favours catechetical and generally admonitory sermons deliverable *quando uolueris*, the second part contains pieces arranged for the Temporale from Christmas to Pentecost and drawn largely from Ælfric's two sets of *Catholic Homilies*.[74] More relevant to the present discussion is the smaller collection of homilies preserved in CCCC 178 (s. xi^1, origin unknown). Although probably not written at Worcester, after the mid-eleventh century this manuscript was certainly in use there, where it received a belligerent annotation by Coleman on p. 229, and where it may also have served as an exemplar for certain items in the more extensive collection, Hatton 113–14.[75] As in the Hatton manuscript, the homilies of CCCC 178 are divided into those for use *quando uolueris* and those designated for specific occasions; moreover, in CCCC 178 the latter group is drawn entirely from Ælfric's series for the Temporale and prefaced by a compiler's short notice: 'In hoc codicello continentur duodecim sermones anglice. quos accepimus de libris quos ælfricus abbas anglice trans-

---

germanischen Völker 84 (Strassburg, 1900), 63–6. For a broader survey, including Latin as well as Old English homiliaries, see McIntyre, 'Early-Twelfth-Century Worcester Cathedral Priory', pp. 98–103.

[73] See Ker, *Catalogue*, item 331; also *Supplementary Collection*, ed. Pope I, 70–7. Hatton 113–14 was originally the companion volume of Oxford, Bodleian Library, Junius 121 (Ker item 338). For Hatton 113–14, a more precise date of 1070 has been argued, based on obits inserted into the calendars that precede both Hatton 113 and CCCC 391; see Bannister, 'Note on MS Hatton 113', p. lxii.

[74] *Supplementary Collection*, ed. Pope I, 74–6. The arrangement of this large collection suggests that, by the mid-eleventh century, 'at Worcester exegetical preaching on the pericope was practiced only in the chief Dominical seasons and that most preaching there was catechetical; hence the emphasis on materials which are useful at will rather than seasonally' (Gatch, *Preaching and Theology*, p. 56). The movement towards catechetical preaching at some centres is better exemplified by Hatton 115 (Ker, *Catalogue*, item 332; origin unknown, s. xi^2), the thirty-two items of which, though all by Ælfric, are all designated *quando uolueris*; see *Supplementary Collection*, ed. Pope I, 53–9.

[75] Ker, *Catalogue*, item 41(A). On Coleman's marginalia, see the list by Ker, 'Old English Notes Signed "Coleman"'. Significant additions to Ker's list are offered by McIntyre, 'Early-Twelfth-Century Worcester Cathedral Priory', pp. 40–2. On the possible relation of CCCC 178 to Hatton 113–14, see *Supplementary Collection*, ed. Pope I, 76–7.

tulit.'⁷⁶ Although Ælfric's homilies enjoyed a wide circulation, they appear in most manuscripts without attribution.⁷⁷ An ascription such as the one in CCCC 178 is a rarity, and rarer still for its accuracy – the twelve items that follow are indeed by Ælfric. The compiler's note in CCCC 178 attests that, at least in some centres, Ælfric's name did not pass from memory, but remained linked to his genuine works. The Worcester Old English homiliaries bear signs of significant use in the later eleventh century,⁷⁸ and a note such as the attribution in CCCC 178 would not escape notice. St Wulfstan or some other compiler may even have chosen particular pieces for the Hatton 113 and 114 collection on the basis of Ælfric's prestige.

Ælfric's reputation at post-Conquest Worcester is further attested by a fragmentary early Middle English poem, the 'First Worcester Fragment' or 'St Bede Lament'.⁷⁹ These crude alliterative verses were copied at the end of an early thirteenth-century manuscript of Ælfric's *Grammar* and *Glossary* (Worcester, Cathedral Library, F. 174) by the famous 'Tremulous Hand'.⁸⁰ The poem laments the supplanting of native English teachers by 'oþre leoden' ('other peoples') – French-speaking churchmen, perhaps – and claims that many English souls are daily being lost for want of preaching in their own tongue. Immediately following the Venerable

---

⁷⁶ 'In this little book are contained twelve *sermones* in English, which we have taken from the books that Abbot Ælfric translated into English'; see Ker, *Catalogue*, item 41(A), art. 19.

⁷⁷ The prefaces that name Ælfric as author of the First and Second Series of *Catholic Homilies* are found in only one manuscript (Cambridge, University Library, Gg. 3. 28), apart from which there is no manuscript evidence for the circulation of the prefaces; see Gatch, *Preaching and Theology*, pp. 47–54, and *Ælfric's Prefaces*, ed. Wilcox, pp. 74–7. On CUL Gg. 3. 28, see Sisam, *Studies*, pp. 165–71, and *Supplementary Collection*, ed. Pope I, 34–5.

⁷⁸ On the evidence of late eleventh-century annotations and corrections, see McIntyre, 'Early-Twelfth-Century Worcester Cathedral Priory', pp. 52–82 and 218–23 (Appendix B).

⁷⁹ The most recent edition and commentary are by Brehe, 'Reassembling the *First Worcester Fragment*'; still useful, too, are the edition and notes by Hall, *Selections from Early Middle English* I, 1 (text) and II, 223–8 (notes).

⁸⁰ See C. Franzen, *The Tremulous Hand of Worcester: A Study of Old English in the Thirteenth Century*, (Oxford, 1991), pp. 12–14, 70–1, 84–94 and pl. X; also 'An Edition of the Early Middle English Copy of Ælfric's "Grammar" and "Glossary" in Worcester Cathedral MS. F.174', ed. M. S. Butler (unpubl. PhD dissertation, Pennsylvania State Univ., 1981), pp. 1–8 and 81–9.

The manuscript

Bede, and preceding some of the most illustrious names in the Anglo-Saxon church (Wilfrid, Cuthbert, Aldhelm, Dunstan, Æthelwold, Oswald and others), the poet inserts Ælfric and praises him as the translator of the Pentateuch into English.[81] The orthography of the 'Fragment' points to a now-lost Old English original, perhaps itself from Worcester.[82] Regardless of where the Old English antecedent was written, the extant poem bears witness to Ælfric's enduring reputation as a teacher and translator on a par with some of the greatest Anglo-Saxon churchmen. Like few other late eleventh-century communities, St Wulfstan's Worcester nurtured an audience capable of appreciating the importance of the name 'Ælfricus abbas' (begun prominently with a three-line red capital) in the salutation of the *LME*. To this attraction add the prestige of Ælfric's link to Æthelwold's reform and the long line of native monastic tradition, and there is little about the *LME* that would not appeal to St Wulfstan's personal interests or the reactionary temper of later eleventh-century Worcester.

---

[81] Lines 6–9. Ælfric did not in fact translate all of the Pentateuch; see *The Old English Illustrated Hexateuch*, ed. C. R. Dodwell and P. Clemoes, EEMF 18 (Copenhagen, 1974), 42–53. Strangely, the 'Fragment' also gives Ælfric the cognomen Alcuin, though this may simply reflect a muddled knowledge of Ælfric's translation of Alcuin's *Interrogationes Sigewulfi*; see Hall, *Selections from Early Middle English* II, 226, and Brehe, 'Reassembling the *First Worcester Fragment*', pp. 531–2.

[82] Hall (*Selections from Early Middle English* II, 224) argues against a Worcester origin, citing the absence from the poem of such local worthies as Bishop Wærferth (872–915) and Archbishop Wulfstan (1002–16), not to mention the great preacher St Wulfstan. For a corrective and more plausible interpretation of the list of bishops, see Brehe, 'Reassembling the *First Worcester Fragment*', pp. 531–5.

4

Critical and editorial history

The *LME* has won notice chiefly as an ancillary witness to the *Regularis concordia*, of which it is usually assumed to be a straightforward abridgement, and as a fixed point of reference in discussions of Ælfric's identity or the chronology of his career. Otherwise, the text has drawn little attention and has, through a remarkable series of accidents and misunderstandings, often been confused in secondary literature with the *Regularis concordia* or any of the Latin or Old English reflexes thereof. Lucia Kornexl's survey of the editorial history of the *Concordia* has laid bare centuries of confusion surrounding that text;[1] only a brief word remains to be said about the implications of this peculiar history for the modern reception of the *LME*. The earliest reference to Ælfric's text occurs on the verso of a parchment flyleaf bound at the beginning of CCCC 265 itself. There a thirteenth-century hand has added a brief table of contents, of which the fifth item is, 'Epistola Alfrici de consuetudine monachorum'.[2] It is doubtful that this brief title alone accounts for the centuries-long tradition of calling Ælfric's customary a 'letter', but noteworthy that the inclination antedates modern scholarship.

In the sixteenth century the *LME* caught the attention of Matthew Parker's Latin secretary, John Joscelyn (1529–1603). Joscelyn's annotations occur in portions of CCCC 265, and he may be responsible for a few marginal notes added to the opening pages of the *LME*.[3] The preface to

---

[1] *RC* (Kornexl), pp. clvi–clxix.   [2] Printed by James, *Descriptive Catalogue* II, 16.
[3] On Joscelyn's hand in CCCC 265, see Ker, *Catalogue*, p. 94. On pp. 237–8 of the *LME* the annotations 'prima hora', 'tertia hora', 'sexta hora' and 'nona hora' appear to be Joscelyn's, referring to the corresponding names of the hours that he or another reader has underlined in the text of *LME* 2 (I am grateful to Tim Graham and Catherine Hall for assistance with the identification). In addition to Joscelyn's hand are at least three

Parker's celebrated *Testimonie of Antiquitie*, probably written by Joscelyn, refers to CCCC 265 ('an ancient book of canons from Worcester') and, in the course of establishing Ælfric's identity, to the *LME* specifically: 'And truly [Ælfric] calleth himself abbot in diuers of his epistles, although he neuer named of what place as in that he wryteth Egneshamensibus [sic] fratribus, de consuetudine monachorum; To the monkes of Egnesham, of the order and manner of monkes.'[4] That Joscelyn had studied the entire *LME* and not just the epistolary preface is evident from an annotation he added to yet another manuscript. At the foot of what is now 176v in London, BL, Cotton Tiberius A. iii, the last page of an incomplete Old English translation of the *Regularis concordia*, Joscelyn wrote the caption: 'Liber de consuetudine monachorum, qui est aut idem quem Æthelwoldus Wintoniensis episcopus cum coepiscopis et abbatibus tempore Eadgari regis Anglorum collegit (de quo mentionem facit Ælfricus Abbas in epistola ad Egneshamenses [sic] fratres) aut certe ex eodem est desumptus.'[5] Joscelyn intended to attach the title *De consuetudine monachorum* not to the preceding Old English translation, however, but to the copy of the Latin *Regularis concordia* that originally followed on the next (facing) folio and was still present when he annotated the manuscript. The note indicates his recognition of the link beween Ælfric's 'epistola' and the 'liber de consuetudine monachorum' (= the *Regularis concordia*). Joscelyn could only have reached this conclusion after comparing the content of both texts, since the copy of the *Concordia* to which he was referring bears no title that would alone suggest the *liber consuetudinum* mentioned by Ælfric as a source (*LME* 1). Through a series of accidents, centuries would pass before

---

layers of later medieval and early modern annotation in the *LME*. Two notes in a glossing hand of s. xii (?) have been partially cropped away on p. 264 (pertaining to *LME* 69). Very faint late medieval cursive notes in pencil, usually beginning 'Nota', occur on pp. 247–52 and 254, and quite frequently elsewhere in the whole manuscript. Finally, a modern hand has added line numbers on each page.

[4] 'The Preface to the Christian Reader', in *A Testimonie of Antiquitie, shewing the auncient fayth in the Church of England touching the sacrament of the body and bloude of the Lorde . . . aboue 600. yeares agoe* (London, 1566 or 1567), 5r–v (on CCCC 265) and 7v (reference to the *LME*).

[5] Quoted from *RC* (Kornexl), p. xxxv, n 17: 'A book concerning monastic custom, which is either the same [book] that Æthelwold, together with his fellow bishops and abbots, compiled in the time of Edgar, king of the English (mentioned by Abbot Ælfric in his letter to the brothers of Eynsham), or certainly a derivation thereof.' Joscelyn's wording clearly echoes *LME* 1.

the relation of Ælfric's text to the *Concordia* was rediscovered. Sir Robert Cotton dismembered the codex containing the Old English translation, including Joscelyn's note, and bound it into another miscellany (the present Cotton Tiberius A. iii); the folios containing the Latin text of the *Concordia* to which Joscelyn had referred were bound with others as Cotton Faustina B. iii.[6] Later readers naturally assumed that Joscelyn's note, now on 176v of the Tiberius manuscript, referred to the Old English translation that it *followed*. The resulting confusion would have serious consequences for future scholarship on the *Concordia* and texts derived from it.

In the works of the antiquaries of the seventeenth through the earlier nineteenth centuries, the *LME* remains a marginal text without a fixed title. In his catalogue of Anglo-Saxon manuscripts, Humphrey Wanley (1672–1726) singled out the *LME* in CCCC 265 (then K. 2), quoting the preface in full.[7] James Nasmith (1740–1808) did not draw on Wanley's work when compiling his catalogue of manuscripts at Corpus Christi College, Cambridge, and his entry for CCCC 265 offers a further variation on the title: 'Excerpta ex institutionibus monasticis Ethelwoldi episcopi Wintoniensis compilata in usum fratrum Egneshamnensium per Ælfricum abbatem.'[8] (Nasmith's descriptive title would later resurface at the head of Mary Bateson's edition of the *LME* in 1892.) In the eighteenth century, confusion over the identity of Ælfric the homilist still reigned, and in a treatise devoted to the question, Edward-Rowe Mores (1730–78) re-asserted a claim that the homilist was none other than Ælfric, archbishop of Canterbury (995–1005).[9] Then forced to explain

---

[6] On the codicology of the Faustina manuscript before and after its mutilation, see now *RC* (Kornexl), pp. cxii–cxvi.

[7] 'Notandum quoque in pag. huiusce Cod. 237 exstare *Excerpta Ælfrici ex libro Athelwoldi Wintoniensis Episcopi de Consuetudine Monachorum*, cuius Epistolam nuncupatoriam describere haud grauatus sum: . . . [here follows *LME* 1 quoted in full]' (*Librorum Veterum Septentrionalium, qui in Angliæ Bibliothecis extant nec non multorum Veterum Codicum Septentrionalium alibi extantium Catalogus Historico-Criticus*; vol. II of G. Hickes's *Linguarum Veterum Septentrionalium Thesuarus Grammatico-Criticus et Archæologicus* (Oxford, 1705), p. 110).

[8] J. Nasmith, *Catalogus librorum manuscriptorum quos Collegio Corporis Christi et B. Mariae Virginis in Academia Cantabrigiensi legauit reuerendissimus Matthæus Parker, Archiepiscopus Cantuariensis* (Cambridge, 1777), p. 312 (item 17). Nasmith's description of CCCC 265 is reprinted by James, *Descriptive Catalogue* II, 14–16.

[9] Mores, *De Ælfrico* (1789), published posthumously by G. J. Thorkelin. The identification with Archbishop Ælfric of Canterbury had been popular among the Elizabethan

why the archbishop would style himself 'abbot' in a document datable to c. 1005, Mores resolved the difficulty by claiming the *LME* as the work of the homilist's pupil, Ælfric Bata.[10] Mores nevertheless deserves credit for reading beyond the epistolary conventions of the *LME*-preface and recognizing that the 'Ælfricus abbas' of the *LME* is almost certainly addressing the Eynsham community not as an outsider but as its head.[11] Other scholars had been and would continue to be hesitant about identifying Ælfric the homilist as the abbot of Eynsham.[12]

The publications of Eduard Dietrich signal the advent of the modern era in Ælfric scholarship.[13] It is ironic, then, that Dietrich's treatise, 'Abt Ælfrik', while laying the foundations for much of what is now taken for granted about Ælfric's career and canon, introduced a new element of confusion about the *LME*. Dietrich not only misattributed to Ælfric the Old English translation-fragment in Cotton Tiberius A. iii, but so confused this vernacular version with the Latin *LME* that he appears to speak of them as being different manuscripts of the same text, which he refers to as 'Ælfric's extract . . . for beginners'.[14] On the one hand, Dietrich was clearly led astray by ubiquitous references to the *LME* as

---

Anglo-Saxonists, but was challenged in the late seventeenth century by the 'Dissertatio de Elfrico Archiepiscopo Cantuar[.], utrum is fuerit Elfricus Grammaticus', included by H. Wharton (1664–95) in his *Anglia sacra, siue collectio historiarum . . . de archiepiscopis et episcopis Anglia* [*sic*] *a prima fidei Christianae susceptione ad annum MDXL*, 2 vols. (London, 1691) I, 125–34. Mores's arguments are directed chiefly against Wharton's thesis; see the summary by White, *Ælfric*, pp. 183–5.

[10] Mores, *De Ælfrico*, pp. 66–7. Mores also attributes to Bata the *Vita S. Æthelwoldi* and the pastoral letters to Wulfstan.

[11] Mores, *De Ælfrico*, pp. 66–7: 'postea cœnobio Benedictinorum Egneshamensi ab Æthelmero recens fundato præponebatur abbas [*scil.* Ælfric Bata] anno MV[;] ibi excerpta ex Atheluuoldi *libro* de *consuetudine* monachorum fratribus *nuper rogatu Æthelmeri ad monachicum habitum ordinatis scriptando demonstrauit*' (emphasis added to indicate echoes of *LME* 1).

[12] This vacillation continued until Dietrich's publications of 1855–6 ('Abt Ælfrik'); see, e.g., T. Wright, *Biographia Britannica Literaria, or Biography of Literary Characters of Great Britain and Ireland arranged in Chonological Order*, 2 vols. (London, 1842–6) I, 482–3 (*s.v.* 'Alfric of Canterbury'). Wright suggests that Ælfric (of Canterbury) visited Eynsham and acted, while archbishop, as its head; it was, then, in this capacity that 'he abridged the "Rule" of Ethelwold' (p. 482). For a recent instance of doubt, see Hohler, 'Some Service Books', p. 73.

[13] 'Abt Ælfrik', published in two parts in 1855 and 1856.

[14] 'Abt Ælfrik', p. 541: 'Ælfriks Auszug . . . für Anfänger'.

Ælfric's 'excerpts' from a work known as *De consuetudine monachorum*, and, on the other, by the widespread misinterpretation of Joscelyn's aforementioned note. Dietrich's error was partially remedied by the dissertation of Edward Breck,[15] who distinguished once more the vernacular Tiberius-fragment from the Latin *LME*. Moreover, he claimed to have discovered what Joscelyn had realized over three centuries before – that the link between the *LME* and the Old English fragment is their mutual dependence on Æthelwold's *Regularis concordia* (which Breck continued to call the *De consuetudine monachorum*). Unfortunately, Breck persisted in attributing to Ælfric the Old English translation in the Tiberius manuscript and devised an ingenious theory to explain the relation of that text, which he called 'Ælfric's fragment', to the *LME*, which he called 'Ælfric's Latin Abridgment'. Breck theorized that Ælfric began a translation of the *De consuetudine* (i.e., the *Concordia*) for his monks at Eynsham, but soon gave up the project in favour of a Latin abridgement of the same (i.e., the *LME*). Breck's theory about the relation of the Old English and Latin texts is untenable, since Ælfric's authorship of the former can no longer be upheld.[16] But his characterization of the motives and methods underlying the *LME* retains some value: Breck was one of the first scholars to demonstrate an appreciation for the *LME* as something more than mere 'excerpts' or an abridgement in the simplest sense.[17] To his dissertation Breck also appended a transcription of the first two manuscript pages of the *LME*, the largest portion of the text to appear in print so far.[18] Breck's errors were soon challenged by Frederick Tupper's survey of the

---

[15] Breck, 'Fragment of Ælfric's Translation' (1887). The Old English text edited here had also been printed in the previous year by A. Schröer, 'De Consuetudine Monachorum', *Englische Studien* 9 (1886), 290–6.

[16] *Hirtenbriefe*, ed. Fehr, p. cxxvi, n. 1; also *RC* (Kornexl), p. cli.

[17] 'By doing this he was enabled to offer them a far more practical guide, freed from all unnecessary matter, and more fitted to their particular wants as he knew them; and he secured in addition the opportunity of making other suggestions taken from the writings of Amalarius, and, in all probability, from his own experience. This accounts for the very free style of his Abridgment [i.e., the *LME*], as he absorbed the matter of the De Consuetudine and wrote out the gist of it, not at all in the order of the original, and wove much foreign matter into his work' (Breck, 'Fragment of Ælfric's Translation', p. 12).

[18] Wanley had printed the entire preface in his *Catalogus*, and many studies had quoted from the preface (either from Wanley or directly from the manuscript), but no other portions of the *LME* had been edited.

principal texts of the Anglo-Saxon monastic reform. Drawing on the work of Julius Zupitza that appeared shortly after Breck's dissertation, Tupper firmly rejected Ælfric's authorship of any Old English translation of the *Regularis concordia*.[19] Along the way, he sorted out much of the confusion caused by use of the vague term 'Ælfric's Extract' to describe both the Tiberius translation-fragment and the *LME*.[20]

Tupper's article appeared in 1893 but must have gone to press before he was alerted to Mary Bateson's *editio princeps* of the *LME* that appeared in the previous year, with Nasmith's catalogue entry for its title: *Excerpta ex institutionibus monasticis Æthelwoldi episcopi Wintoniensis compilata in usum fratrum Egneshamnensium per Ælfricum abbatem*.[21] At the beginning of the edition proper, Bateson supplied the heading: 'Ælfric's Abridgement of St. Æthelwold's Concordia Regularis', while repeating Nasmith's Latin title in a footnote. In her brief introduction Bateson's up-to-date knowledge of the *Concordia* and related texts is evident, knowledge to which she herself would contribute in no small measure.[22] She characterizes the *LME* as a letter 'containing a selection of passages from, or rather an abbreviation of [Ælfric's] master's treatise'.[23] There follows a summary of the monastic reform movement, then a brief statement about the significance of the *LME*:

Ælfric's Letter gives us a brief account of the regulations under which the Monks of St. Swithun's [*scil.* the Old Minster] lived in the early years after their restoration; it throws abundant light on the daily course of their lives and on the exact nature of the religious services which played so large a part therein. It also assists materially in the interpretation of the 'Concordia', the Latinity of which might well be obscure even to the Monks themselves.[24]

Concerning Ælfric's relationship to the monks addressed in the letter, Bateson will say only that he 'appears to have been at one time their

---

[19] Tupper, 'History and Texts', col. 357. See also 'Ein weiteres Bruchstück', ed. Zupitza, who claimed (p. 24) that the Old English Tiberius fragment, with its considerable translation errors, could hardly be the work of Ælfric, author of the *Grammar* and *Colloquy*.

[20] Tupper, 'History and Texts', col. 357; see also *RC* (Kornexl), p. xxxv, n. 18.

[21] Published as 'Appendix VII' to *Compotus Rolls of the Obedientiaries of St. Swithun's Priory, Winchester*, ed. G. W. Kitchin (London, 1892), pp. 171–98.

[22] As in her 'Rules for Monks', which re-identified the second extant manuscript of the *Regularis concordia* in Cotton Faustina B. iii; see *RC* (Kornexl), p. cxvi, n. 81.

[23] *Excerpta ex institutionibus*, ed. Bateson, p. 173.   [24] *Ibid.*, p. 174.

head'.²⁵ Bateson printed a quasi-diplomatic transcription, though her punctuation, where it differs from the scribe's, at times suggests a lack of comprehension of the text.²⁶ She inserted paragraph breaks (sometimes without regard for context) and added helpful English captions in the margins that alert the reader to the general movement from topic to topic, but otherwise the edition respects the presentation of the *LME* in the manuscript. Bateson's *apparatus fontium* is impressive, given the unavailability of critical editions of the pertinent texts,²⁷ but she inevitably left a great deal of material unidentified or claimed as Ælfric's own teaching statements that can now be attributed to other sources. Though she did not translate the *LME*, in a subsequent article of 1894 she offered a summary of its contents – amounting, at times, to an English paraphrase of the text.²⁸ This article presented a fuller description of the Eynsham letter and its setting than had appeared in the headnote to the edition itself, and also employed – apparently for the first time – the English title by which the work has come to be known: 'Ælfric's Letter to the Monks of Eynsham'.²⁹ In the following year, Bateson would

---

[25] *Ibid.* The rest of Bateson's remarks have stood up less well. She suggested, for example, that the copy in CCCC 265 may be Ælfric's autograph, and she accordingly tried to date the manuscript (and not just the composition of the *LME*) to 'before the year 1005'. Note her implied realization, however, that the evidence of S 911 requires Æthelmær's monastery to have been built and manned before the date of the charter. Cf. above, pp. 5–10.

[26] For example, *Excerpta ex institutionibus*, p. 192 (second paragraph): 'ac uictualia quibus fratres utuntur ipsis prebere cui obedientię adsit, ipse abbas quotienscumque ei uacauerit, nam de susceptione hospitum regula docet'. The scribe correctly put a stop after *prebere*; cf. edition, below, at *LME* 62.

[27] For the Latin text of the *Concordia*, she cites the edition from Cotton Tiberius A. iii by Logeman, 'De Consuetudine Monachorum'; for Amalarius's *Liber officialis* (which Bateson calls *De ecclesiasticis officiis*), she had to rely on Melchior Hittorp's *De diuinis catholicae ecclesiae officiis* (Cologne, 1568).

[28] Bateson, 'Rules for Monks', pp. 703–7. This English summary must be used with caution. See, for example, her paraphrase of Ælfric on the bishop's anointing of the newly baptized (*LME* 46): 'quia episcopus debet in fronte unguere ubi laminam auream pontifex ferebat' (referring to Exod. XXVIII.36–8), rendered by Bateson, 'because it is left to the bishop to anoint on the forehead where the pope would put the gold leaf' ('Rules for Monks', p. 706).

[29] Bateson, 'Rules for Monks', p. 702. She appears to accept (p. 707, n. 57) the theory of Dietrich and Breck that Ælfric wrote the Old English Tiberius-fragment, although she questions the likelihood that such a translation could have been meant for the Eynsham monks, who obviously could read Latin.

round out her study of the *LME* with a detailed analysis of its manuscript, CCCC 265.[30]

In 1898 Caroline White's book-length study of Ælfric's life and works (heavily indebted to Dietrich's publications of 1855–6) did not draw on Bateson's edition and articles, nor do these appear in her extensive bibliography.[31] Instead, White's discussion of the *LME* is based almost entirely on the works of Breck and Tupper.[32] Not surprisingly, then, she refers to the *LME* as the 'Excerpts from Æthelwold's De Consuetudine'.[33] In her final chapter, White prints all of Ælfric's prefaces, including that to the *LME*, as well as part of the Eynsham foundation charter.[34]

The close associations between the *LME* and liturgical matter in Ælfric's pastoral letters to Archbishop Wulfstan encouraged Bernhard Fehr to reconstruct a more precise chronology of these works in the introduction to his edition of the *pastoralia* (1914). Although Fehr's chronology has won the endorsement of Clemoes and most modern scholars, it rests in part on the questionable assumption that the second Old English pastoral letter to Wulfstan (Brief III) is at numerous points a translation of the *LME* (called by Fehr 'Ælfrics Klosterauszug aus Aethelwold' or, more often, simply 'Klosterauszug'), and that the Latin *LME* was composed as 'a useful preparatory work' to facilitate the writing of Brief III.[35] To support this claim, Fehr's edition of Brief III includes extensive quotations from the 'Klosterauszug' (= *LME*) at the foot of each

---

[30] 'A Worcester Cathedral Book'.

[31] White, *Ælfric*, pp. 199–211 (bibliography); Bateson's publications are noted in Godden's 'Supplementary Classified Bibliography' appended to the 1974 reprint of White's book (p. 231).

[32] 'Fragment of Ælfric's Translation' and 'History and Texts', respectively.

[33] See, White, *Ælfric*, pp. 62–3 and 159–64. At pp. 63–4, White claims that the *De consuetudine* from which Ælfric drew his 'excerpts' was a vernacular text, but she corrects herself on p. 159, n. 1. Her error reflects the widespread confusion among previous scholars caused by the misinterpretation of Joscelyn's note in Cotton Tiberius A. iii. White repeats (p. 164) Breck's arguments for and Zupitza's against Ælfric's authorship of the Tiberius fragment but does not favour one position over the other.

[34] White, *Ælfric*, pp. 181–2. The portion of S 911 printed is the Old English summary of the terms of Æthelmær's gift, including his appointment of an unnamed abbot (*ealdor*) and his pledge to live among the monks; see *EC* I, 24 (from 'Ic Æþelmær cyðe . . .').

[35] *Hirtenbriefe*, ed. Fehr, p. xlvii: 'eine nützliche Vorbereitungsarbeit'. It is far more likely that Ælfric returned to his original sources when composing Brief III. Cf. above, pp. 24–7, and Hill, 'Monastic Reform and the Secular Church', p. 107, n. 10.

page. The rest of Fehr's discussion of the *LME* concerns its relationship to still another text, a compilation of liturgical customs drawn from the *Regularis concordia* and other sources and adapted for use in non-monastic churches. Fehr saw in this, the *De ecclesiastica consuetudine* (his 'Priesterauszug'), yet another work by Ælfric preparatory to the pastoral letters for Wulfstan. Whether or not Ælfric had anything to do with these excerpts, they are more likely to represent an important analogue to the *LME* than a direct source.[36] Fehr's edition was reprinted in 1966 with a new supplement to the introduction prepared by Peter Clemoes, whose remarks concerning the *LME* aimed chiefly to refute Fehr's theory about the 'Priesterauszug'; on the relation of the *LME* to Brief III, however, Clemoes left Fehr's hypothesis to stand.[37]

Following the publication of Bateson's edition, references to the *LME* gradually multiply. Liturgists were quick to recognize the significance of Ælfric's customary, and the *LME* figures prominently in three major works of liturgical scholarship published in the middle decades of the twentieth century. J. B. L. Tolhurst included the *LME* (usually cited as 'the Eynsham customs') among the sources for the study of the medieval Office surveyed and compared in his *Introduction to the English Monastic Breviaries*.[38] Thomas Symons cited Ælfric's work freely in the explanatory notes to his edition and translation of the *Concordia* (1953).[39] Finally, Ælfric's fuller picture of the hymnal at *LME* 13 and 50 provided important evidence for Helmut Gneuss's reconstruction of the 'Winchester–Worcester' liturgy in a ground-breaking study of 1968.[40]

In recent decades a resurgence of interest in all things related to the monastic revival of the tenth century has greatly advanced understanding of the *Regularis concordia* and, if only by implication, the *LME*. New editions of both texts were published in 1984 in the Corpus Consuetudinum Monasticarum, a collaborative series of scholarly editions of

---

[36] See Jones, 'Two Composite Texts'.
[37] In an earlier publication ('Chronology', pp. 241 and 245) Clemoes had already accepted the essence of Fehr's chronology, on which see also Clemoes's 'Supplement to the Introduction', *Hirtenbriefe*, ed. Fehr, p. cxlv. Cf. above, p. 25, n. 26.
[38] Vol. VI of *The Monastic Breviary of Hyde Abbey* (1932–42).
[39] See *RC* (Symons), pp. xxix, lvi and *passim*. The notes to his edition refer to the *LME* by the siglum 'AE'.
[40] *Hymnar*, esp. pp. 119–20. Gneuss refers to the *LME* as 'Ae'.

the major Benedictine customaries from the eighth through fifteenth centuries.[41] The important advance in the CCM edition by Adrien Nocent and Kassius Hallinger (titled *Aelfrici abbatis epistula ad monachos Egneshamnenses directa*) is not the text itself but the accompanying commentary. This *apparatus explicatiuus*, as the editors call it, combines extensive references to sources and analogues with explanatory notes and bibliography, while the comparative study of monastic customs is greatly facilitated by cross-references to the many continental texts edited in the CCM. The editors have also helpfully divided the text into eighteen major sections (indicated by roman numerals and descriptive titles supplied in angled brackets), which are further divided into sense-units ('Sinnabschnitte'), indicated by arabic numerals in the margin.[42]

While Nocent's edition of 1984 did a great service for comparative liturgical scholarship, all who are interested in the *LME* specifically as a part of Ælfric's canon are likely to be frustrated by the presentation of the text in the CCM. The editors declare from the outset that they include Ælfric's customary in the series chiefly as a textual and interpretative aid to the more important *Regularis concordia*. This attitude reflects centuries of dismissive characterization of the *LME* as little more than an 'abridgement' of, or 'excerpts' or 'extracts' from, the *Concordia*. In the CCM, for example, the *LME* does not merit an introduction of its own, instead receiving only slight notice in the discussion of witnesses drawn upon to establish the text of the *Concordia*.[43] The scope of the series provided no forum in which to discuss the relation of the *LME* to Ælfric's career and other works, and the explanatory apparatus does not comment on the implications of the many choices Ælfric made in adapting his sources. The importance of the *LME* for the study of the

---

[41] The project was begun at Rome in 1955, the first volume appearing in 1963. A statement of the origins, scope and editorial principles is included in *Initia consuetudinis Benedictinae*, CCM 1 (Siegburg, 1963), lxxv–lxxix and lxxxv–xcviii.

[42] The present edition retains the CCM division and numbering of 'Sinnabschnitte'. The larger organizational divisions (following the CCM only in part) are noted in the commentary but not in the body of the edition.

[43] See, for example, CCM 7.1, 157: 'Text der (verkürzten) *Reg.Conc.*'; also p. 158: '... dieses für die Textkontrolle der *Reg.Conc.* wichtigen Faszikels'; and p. 160: 'Auch der nach 1004 verfaßte Ælfric-Brief erweist sich mitunter als brauchbare textkritische Hilfe.'

Regularis concordia has occasioned the only significant notices of Ælfric's customary, by Joyce Hill and Lucia Kornexl, since the publication of the CCM edition.[44]

The tendency to subordinate the *LME* to the *Concordia* has admitted rare exceptions. Tolhurst, Symons and Gneuss had demonstrated that Ælfric occasionally supplemented the *Concordia* in important ways, but the first study devoted exclusively to the *LME* only appeared in 1975 with J. R. Hall's collection of notes on some of its liturgical features.[45] Two subsequent articles by Milton McC. Gatch included ample and enthusiastic mention of Ælfric's text. The first of these, published in 1977, amplified Hall's plea for further study of the *LME* and its sources and called special attention to the importance of *LME* 70–80 for the understanding of Ælfric's Old English canon.[46] Gatch returned in 1985 to a detailed analysis of Ælfric's *ordo lectionum* for the Night Office in a useful survey of primary sources available for the study of the Office in Anglo-Saxon England.[47] There he also mentioned other features of Ælfric's text that merit closer study, including the tailoring of the *Concordia* to the needs of a new, modest house; the lessened emphasis on royal patronage; and, finally, Ælfric's adaptation of Amalarius's allegorical teaching about the liturgy.[48] The reader will recognize that Gatch's agenda has informed the course of these pages considerably.

[44] 'The "Regularis Concordia"', pp. 302–5, and *RC* (Kornexl), pp. clii–cliv. A recent broadly based liturgical study, much in the tradition of Tolhurst and Gneuss, constitutes the only exception: see Roper, *Medieval English Benedictine Liturgy*, citing the *LME* as 'Ccc 265' or 'Aelfric'.

[45] Hall, 'Some Liturgical Notes'. See commentary to *LME* 46 (at n. 228) and 70 (at n. 320).

[46] 'Old English Literature and the Liturgy', pp. 240–2.

[47] 'The Office', esp. pp. 348–9 and 352–62. In this article Gatch announced his intention to publish a new edition and full study of the *LME*.

[48] *Ibid.*, p. 349.

Editorial principles

THE TEXT

The survival of the *LME* in only one manuscript precludes the establishment of a critical text. It is fortunate, then, that the unique witness in CCCC 265, pp. 237–68, appears to be fairly sound, showing few manifest corruptions. Emendation is rarely necessary and usually amounts to the correction of what are probably late scribal errors. Because the text has already seen two conservative editions, my editorial procedures are slightly more intrusive than those of Bateson and the CCM.[1] Emendations are incorporated directly into the text, with manuscript readings recorded in the critical apparatus at the foot of each page, to which a sequence of superscript letters (a, b, c, etc.) within each numbered section refers. Improvements adopted from Nocent's edition are so noted ('*em. Nocent*').

Gaps in sense are rare, but where it has been necessary to supply a word not present in the manuscript, the conjecture is enclosed within angled brackets. All abbreviations are silently expanded. Caudate or 'tailed' *e* is transcribed as either *e* or *ae*, as phonologically correct, though Classical *ae* is invariably used in abbreviations where the scribe might have used *e*, caudate *e*, *ae* or *æ*, had he written the word out (e.g., pr*ae*-, qu*ae*sum*us*, p*ap*ae). Otherwise, the edition follows the eleventh-century orthography (e.g., *Septuagessima*, *Bryttannia*, *euuangelium*), although a few spellings have been normalized that, although not unusual in medieval Latin,

---

[1] See above, pp. 97–9 and 100–2. Bateson's is nearly a diplomatic edition. The CCM editors deal more freely with the presentation of the text, especially in the use of supplied chapter and section headings, but their principles of transcription and emendation remain conservative, as is common when treating a *codex unicus*.

produce false homographs (e.g., *hostium* for *ostium*, *expoliamus* for *exspoliamus*) or appear to exceed the limits of variation normal for this scribe (e.g., *chatholicorum*). The normalized forms are treated as emendations. Punctuation and capitalization have been modernized throughout, and the majuscule form of *u* (used by the scribe invariably for both the vowel and the consonant) is transcribed as V.

Biblical quotations and liturgical incipits are enclosed within single quotation marks and further identified in the commentary. The pagination of the manuscript is indicated by numbers in square brackets inserted in the Latin text at the page breaks. Nothing suggests that Ælfric intended a division of the *LME* into chapters, but for consistency and ease of reference the text is divided into paragraphs and sections, the latter (indicated by arabic numerals) corresponding to the sections of Nocent's edition in the CCM. My edition does not include chapter headings and subheadings comparable to those supplied by Nocent and Hallinger, although I have supplied brief sectional and subsectional headings in English throughout the commentary. The reader searching for a particular topic in Ælfric's customary is referred to the overview of the organization of the text in ch. 2, as well as to the index of liturgical *formae* and general index at the end of the volume.

THE TRANSLATION

An invariably paratactic or 'recipe-like' style is characteristic of liturgical *ordines*, and the facing-page translation does not aspire to introduce a polish or syntactic diversity not present in the original. Words in square brackets are not found in Ælfric's Latin but have been supplied to complete the sense or to accommodate modern English idiom. For the sake of stylistic consistency, Ælfric's frequent verbatim borrowings from the *Regularis concordia* have been translated afresh, although my debt to Symons's translation and notes is great throughout.

The translation also takes the liberty of imposing some artificial consistency on Ælfric's technical language. For certain components of the mass and Office, he may, in accordance with the practice of his time, use various terms interchangeably. In such instances it has seemed preferable to use the same modern English equivalent throughout. The reader will therefore observe that English 'collect', for example, translates not only *collecta*, but also *prima oratio missae*, or simply *oratio* or *prex* where 'collect'

Editorial principles

is clearly meant. Similarly fluid are Ælfric's names for certain of the liturgical seasons and hours. Here, too, I have opted for consistency, so *Pascha* or *Pascha Domini* = 'Easter'; *in Natiuitate* (or *Natale*) *Domini* (or *Christi*) = 'Christmas', and so on. To avoid the confusion often caused by the English term 'Matins', I have rendered *matutinales laudes, (laudes) matutinae, (officium) matutinum,* etc. uniformly as 'Lauds'. There is no similar ambiguity surrounding terms for the Night Office, which I simply call 'Nocturns' or 'Vigil(s)', following Ælfric's own practice.

Biblical quotations in English, including psalm incipits, are taken from the Douai-Reims translation of the Vulgate (1582–1609) as revised by Richard Challoner (1749–50; repr. Baltimore, 1899, and Rockford, IL, 1971). Other liturgical incipits have required variable treatment: for *formae* drawn directly from scripture, I have simply quoted the Douai Bible; for those that only echo scripture or are completely non-biblical, I have often relied on English translations in the dual-language *Ideal Daily Missal, with Vespers for Sundays and Feasts, Compiled from the Missale Romanum*, ed. S. P. Juergens (Montreal, 1934). Obviously, incipits so 'Englished' may not translate the Latin directly but aim to give a version approximate in length and sense. For the first responsory at Nocturns in Pentecost week, for example, Ælfric gives the incipit 'Dum complerentur' (*LME* 72), which I render by the Douai translation of the biblical source (Acts II.1) as 'When [the days of the Pentecost] were accomplished'. Any loss of literal accuracy is justified by the avoidance of a nonsensically terse 'When were accomplished', and square brackets may again indicate words not present in the Latin. Because there are no standard English translations of the Office hymns that would be widely identifiable by their opening lines, I leave these incipits in their more familiar Latin. They, and almost all quoted matter, are further identified in the commentary. Where foreign words or phrases appear in the English translation, I have normalized the spelling and made such minor substitutions as 'Kyrie eleison' for the manuscript *Kyr(r)ieleison*. Capitalization of liturgical terms and the *nomina sacra* in the translation follow standard English practice as outlined by the editors of this series.

THE COMMENTARY

Superscript numbers running in a single series through the Latin text indicate words and phrases further discussed in the appended commentary, which aims to complement rather than supersede Hallinger's notes to the CCM edition. The latter help to situate the *LME* in the wider development of Western monastic liturgy and so will remain indispensable for all who wish to study Ælfric's customary in those terms.[2] The present commentary continues, rather, the emphasis of the preceding introductory chapters: namely, that the *LME*, while occasionally significant from the broad perspective of comparative liturgy, is fascinating throughout as a witness to the reception of specific, identifiable liturgical sources. The aims of my notes are twofold: first, to document these immediate sources and distinguish them from analogues. There is, in fact, very little in the *LME* that Ælfric could not have drawn from the *Concordia*, Amalarius and the liturgical books proper. My emphasis on written sources in the commentary is especially relevant if, as I have suggested, Ælfric's *LME* is (typically for its author) a scholarly, editorial production – a work, as it were, of the library as much as of the choir.[3] My second aim has been to supply as much as possible of the information that the text takes for granted, and so make the content of the *LME* more accessible to Anglo-Saxonists and others who, though perhaps interested in Ælfric, may lack the degree of familiarity with the medieval mass and Office presumed by the CCM editors.[4] Explanations of this order will, I fear, try the patience of knowledgeable liturgists, but they also usefully demonstrate the extent of technical knowledge demanded by the *LME* of its readers. Even with such modest goals, opportunities for comment and elaboration are almost infinite. Clearly, some limits have had to be imposed, but I hope to have

---

[2] The comparisons, however, are mostly indirect, through the *Concordia* and its sources and analogues; see above, p. 42, n. 102.

[3] See especially above, pp. 58 and 68–70, on the possible effects of Ælfric's compositional method.

[4] The present commentary does assume a basic knowledge of the mass, Office, horarium and liturgical calendar, such as may be gained from Harper, *Forms and Orders*. Also helpful are Hardison, *Christian Rite*, pp. 48–77 (the mass); P. Salmon, *L'Office divin*, Lex orandi 27 (Paris, 1959; English trans. as *The Breviary through the Centuries*; Collegeville, MN, 1962); S. J. P. van Dijk, 'The Bible in Liturgical Use', in *The Cambridge History of the Bible. II: The West from the Fathers to the Reformation*, ed. G. W. H. Lampe (Cambridge, 1969), pp. 220–52 (mass and Office); R. E. Reynolds, *s.v.* 'Mass, Liturgy of the', *DMA* VIII, 181–201; *idem*, *s.v.* 'Divine Office', *DMA* IV, 221–31. On the medieval English monastic Office, especially useful are Tolhurst's *Introduction to the English Monastic Breviaries* and *RC* (Symons), pp. xxix–xlv.

Editorial principles

provided in the space available a balanced discussion that throws into relief the unique, interesting and problematic features of the *LME*.

Although the method of the commentary is not broadly comparative, the attempt to supply information that is understood in the text necessarily relies on external liturgical sources of appropriate date and provenance. Turning to the English manuscripts that might serve this function, one finds that sacramentaries, collectars, hymnals and pontificals survive in small numbers, but evidence of some very pertinent types of book – antiphoners, Office lectionaries and other customaries – is meagre or nonexistent. The following external sources are frequently cited; the classification, date and origin (or provenance) of each follows Gneuss's inventory of Anglo-Saxon liturgical books.[5]

Ben.ARob. — *The Benedictional of Archbishop Robert*, ed. Wilson. Rouen, Bibliothèque Municipale, 369 (Y. 7). Pontifical and benedictional: New Minster, Winchester, s. x^2. Cited by page number of edition.

Cant.Ben. — *The Canterbury Benedictional*, ed. Woolley. London, BL, Harley 2892. Benedictional: Christ Church, Canterbury, s. xi^1. Cited by page number of edition.

Claud.Pont.I — *Claudius Pontificals I*, ed. Turner, pp. 1–88. London, BL, Cotton Claudius A. iii, fols. 31–86 and 106–50. Pontifical and benedictional: Worcester or York, s. x/xi and xi^1. Cited by page number of edition.

Corp.41 — Cambridge, *Corpus Christi College 41*, ed. Grant. Portions of a sacramentary copied into the margins of a manuscript of the Old English version of Bede's *Historia ecclesiastica gentis Anglorum*: Exeter provenance, s. xi^1. Cited by page number of edition, or manuscript page (for unedited material).

DEC — *De ecclesiastica consuetudine*. Extracts from the *Regularis concordia* and other sources; two versions in manuscripts of s. xi (CCCC 190, and Rouen, Bibliothèque Municipale, 1382 [U. 109]). Cited by section numbers of Jones, 'Two Composite Texts'.

IBA — *Institutio beati Amalarii de ecclesiasticis officiis*. Extracts from Amalarius's *Liber officialis* and other sources in two manuscripts

---

[5] Gneuss, 'Liturgical Books', supplemented by updated references in *Liturgical Books*, ed. Pfaff.

Editorial principles

of s. xi (listed under *DEC*, above). Cited by section numbers of Jones, 'Two Composite Texts'.

Leofr.Coll. — *The Leofric Collectar*, ed. Dewick and Frere. London, BL, Harley 2961. Collectar and hymnal (secular usage): Exeter, s. xi^{med}. Cited by volume and page number of edition.

Leofr.Miss. — *The Leofric Missal*, ed. Warren. Oxford, BL, Bodley 579. Sacramentary etc.: northeastern France, s. ix^{2}, with additions from ?Glastonbury, s. x^{2}, and Exeter, s. xi^{med}. Cited by page number of edition.

Miss.NMin. — *The Missal of the New Minster, Winchester*, ed. Turner. Le Havre, Bibliothèque Municipale, 330. An early *missale plenum*: New Minster, Winchester, s. xi^{2}. Cited by page number of edition.

Miss.RJum. — *The Missal of Robert of Jumièges*, ed. Wilson. Rouen, Bibliothèque Municipale, 274 (Y. 6). Sacramentary: ?Christ Church, Canterbury, s. xi^{1}. Cited by page number of edition.

Miss.StAug. — *The Missal of St Augustine's Abbey, Canterbury*, ed. Rule. CCCC 270. Sacramentary: St Augustine's, Canterbury, s. xi^{2}. Cited by page number of edition.

Pont.Egb. — The 'Egbert Pontifical', in *Two Anglo-Saxon Pontificals*, ed. Banting, pp. 3–153. Paris, Bibliothèque Nationale, lat. 10575. Pontifical: origin and English provenance unknown, s. x^{2}. Cited by page number of edition.

Pont.Lan. — *Pontificale Lanaletense*, ed. Doble. Rouen, Bibliothèque Municipale, 368 (A. 27). Pontifical: Crediton, s. xi^{in}. Cited by page number of edition.

Port.Wulst. — *The Portiforium of Saint Wulstan*, ed. Hughes. CCCC 391. A 'proto-breviary', including calendar, psalter, hymnal, collectar and various offices (monastic usage): Worcester, s. xi^{2}. Cited by volume and page number.

Winch.Sacr. — *The Winchcombe Sacramentary*, ed. Davril. Orléans, Bibliothèque Municipale, 127 (105). Sacramentary: Winchcombe, s. x^{2}. Cited by text number of editon.

Worc.Ant. — The 'Worcester Antiphoner', facs. ed. as *Antiphonaire monastique, xiiie siècle*. Worcester, Cathedral Library, F. 160. Worcester, s. xiii. Cited by page number of the facsimile edition.

Editorial principles

Abbreviations used for the several editions of the *Regularis concordia* are given in the general list at the beginning of the volume. Even though Kornexl's Latin text is often superior, I usually refer to the Symons–Spath section numbers so that my notes will better mesh with the CCM apparatus and other indices. (A table for the conversion of section numbers in the CCM edition to those of *RC* (Symons) and (Kornexl) is included at the end of this book.) Quotations from Amalarius (*Lib.off.*) are from Hanssens's critical edition, among which significant variants from the *Retractatio prima* (*R1*) are occasionally noted. Pseudo-Amalarian material preserved in Salisbury, Cathedral Library, 154 (= *R1(Sa)*) is quoted from that manuscript, with modern punctuation and capitalization added. All biblical references follow *Biblia sacra iuxta uulgatam uersionem*, ed. R. Weber *et al.*, 3rd ed. (Stuttgart, 1983). The Vulgate numbering and 'Gallican' version of the psalter are assumed throughout, unless otherwise noted.

Ælfric's *Letter to the Monks of Eynsham*

TEXT

1   Ælfricus[a] abbas Egneshamnensibus fratribus salutem in Christo.[1]
Ecce, uideo uobiscum degens uos necesse habere, quia nuper rogatu Æþelmæri[2] ad monachicum habitum ordinati estis, instrui ad mores monachiles dictis aut scriptis. Ideoque haec pauca de libro consuetudinum[3] quem sanctus Aðelwoldus Wintoniensis episcopus[4] cum coepiscopis et abbatibus tempore Eadgari[b] felicissimi regis Anglorum undique collegit ac monachis instituit obseruandum,[5] scriptitando demonstro, eo quod hactenus predictus libellus uestrae fraternitati incognitus habetur.[6] Fateor me ualde timide id praesumere, sed nec audeo omnia uobis intimare, quae in scola eius degens multis annis de moribus seu consuetudinibus didici,[7] ne forte fastidientes districtionem tante obseruantiae nec saltem uelitis auditum prebere narranti. Tamen, ne expertes[c] tam salubris doctrine remaneatis, aliqua quae regula nostra non tangit huic cartule insero uobisque legenda committo, addens etiam aliqua de libro Amalarii presbiteri.[8] Valete feliciter in Christo.

2   Kalendis[a] enim Octobris, exceptis dominicis et festiuis diebus, primo diluculo prima canenda est[9] cum septem psalmis et letaniis,[10] deinde uacent lectionibus usquequo signum tertie insonuerit.[11] Calceant se tunc et lauent et orationes faciant[12] – scola simul[13] et seniores singillatim – et spargant [p. 238] se aqua benedicta. Finita tertia fiat prima missa, postea capitolum. Post sextam horam faciant missam de die,[14] qua finita decantent nonam. Nam de ceteris regula sancta dicit.

3   Omni die ter faciende sunt orationes tres in oratorio:[15] tres in nocte, audito primo signo;[16] tres ante primam tota estate (et in hieme ante tertiam);

1 a Ælfricus] Æ *three-line initial in red*
  b Eadgari] *capitals*
  c expertes] expertis MS; *em. Nocent*
2 a Kalendis] K *three-line initial in blue*

Ælfric's *Letter to the Monks of Eynsham*

TRANSLATION

1   Abbot Ælfric to the brothers of Eynsham: Greetings in Christ.

Behold, while dwelling with you I observe that, because you have recently been ordained to the monastic habit at Æthelmær's request, you need to be instructed in monastic customs by both the spoken and the written word. I am therefore setting forth in writing these few things from the customary that St Æthelwold, bishop of Winchester, together with his fellow bishops and abbots in the time of most blessed Edgar, king of the English, compiled from various sources and established for monks to observe, because until now the aforesaid little book has been unknown to your brotherhood. It is, I confess, with great trepidation that I presume to do so, nor do I dare to convey to you all those things that I learned about customs and usages while abiding for many years in his [*scil.* Æthelwold's] school, lest you draw back at the strictness of so great an observance and not even wish to give me a hearing as I speak. Nevertheless, in order that you should not remain deprived of such salubrious teaching, I include in this document certain matters upon which our *Rule* does not touch. These I entrust to you to read, adding, too, certain points from the book of the priest Amalarius. I bid you health and happiness in Christ.

2   [From] the Kalends of October, excluding Sundays and feast days, Prime should be sung at first light, together with the seven psalms and the litanies. Then they [*scil.* the monks] shall retire to their reading until the bell for Terce rings. Then let them put on their day shoes, wash and say their prayers – the children together as a group, the senior monks individually – then sprinkle themselves with holy water. When Terce is over, the first mass shall take place, then Chapter. After the hour of Sext they shall celebrate the mass of the day and, when that is finished, chant None. The holy *Rule* tells of the rest.

3   Every day three prayers are to be said thrice in church: three at night, at the sound of the first bell; three before Prime during the entire summer period

tres post completorium, cum conpunctione spiritali ac benedictione commendantes se Deo et aspergentes se aqua sanctificata et lectulos eorum omni nocte.[17]

4   Pro rege et pro benefactoribus[18] omnibus horis[19] duo psalmi canendi sunt cum dominica oratione et precibus et oratione.[20] Statim post nocturnam decantent 'Domine ne in furore tuo' primum, 'Exaudiat te Dominus';[21] post matutinas 'Beati quorum', 'Inclina Domine'[22] coniunctim^a sub una collecta illius hore;[23] post primam 'Domine ne in furore tuo' (ii) pro temptatione, 'Miserere mei, Deus'[24] pro defunctis fratribus; post tertiam 'Vsquequo Domine', 'Miserere mei, Deus, miserere mei';[25] post sextam 'Deus misereatur nostri', 'Domine exaudi' (i).[26] Post missam etiam 'Exaudiat te Dominus', 'Ad te leuaui oculos meos',[27] cum precibus tantum et oratione congrua; post nonam 'Qui regis Israel', 'De profundis';[28] post uesperam 'Benedixisti Domine', 'Domine exaudi' (ii)[29] coniunctim sub una^b oratione ipsius sinaxis;[30] post completorium 'Deus in adiutorium meum intende', 'Leuaui oculos meos'[31] similiter sub una collecta.

5   Dominicis uero diebus et festiuis[32] semper post primam, facto signo a priore,[33] eant fratres ad capitolum.[34] Quo expleto [p. 239] fiat prima missa, deinde signum ad tertiam, et sanctificent salem et aquam pergentes ad processionem, dominicis diebus tantum.[35] Similiter a Pascha post primam capitulum agendum est, uerum ab octauis Pentecosten tota estate ferialibus diebus statim post primam, finita letania, matutinalis missa agenda est, et deinde eant ad capitulum.[36]

6   Surgentes a capitulo[37] canant quinque psalmos pro defunctis fratribus: 'Verba mea',[38] 'Domine ne in furore tuo',[39] 'Dilexi quoniam', 'Credidi propter', 'De profundis',[40] quos sequatur dominica oratio cum collecta.[41]

7   Dominicis tamen diebus[42] protendatur prima.[43] Et sedeat abbas in claustro una cum fratribus et exeant singuli ad confessionem,[44] humiliter illi confitentes quicquid tota ebdomada inpugnante aduersario commiserint.

8   Omni dominica die siue sollempni eant fratres ad pacem et eucharistiam accipiant,[45] exceptis his qui antea missam fecerunt.[46] Si forte alicui hoc displicuerit, audiat quid beatus Augustinus de hoc dicat: 'Qui cotidie', inquit, 'non meretur accipere, non meretur post annum accipere.'[47]

9   Ergo regularium monachorum consuetudo[48] non sinit ut aliquis frater neglegenter occurrat horis canonicis, sed facto signo conueniant omnes ad

---

4 a coniunctim] cumiunctim *MS*
   b una] uno *MS; em. Nocent*

(and before Terce in the winter period); three after Compline, as every night [the monks] commend themselves to God with compunction of spirit and a blessing and sprinkle themselves and their beds with holy water.

4   For the king and benefactors two psalms are to be sung, together with the Lord's Prayer, *preces* and a collect, at every one of the hours. Immediately after Nocturns they shall sing the first 'O Lord, [rebuke me] not in thy indignation' [and] 'May the Lord hear thee'; after Lauds 'Blessed are they' [and] 'Incline [thy ear], O Lord' together under the single collect of that hour; after Prime '[Rebuke me] not, O Lord, in thy indignation' (ii) against temptation [and] 'Have mercy on me, O God' for departed brothers; after Terce 'How long, O Lord' [and] 'Have mercy on me, O God, have mercy on me'; after Sext 'May God have mercy on us' [and] 'Hear, O Lord' (i). After mass, too, 'May the Lord hear thee' [and] 'To thee have I lifted up my eyes' with the *preces* only and the appropriate collect; after None '[Give ear], O thou that rulest Israel' [and] 'Out of the depths'; after Vespers 'O Lord, thou hast blessed' [and] 'Hear, O Lord' (ii) combined under the single collect of that hour; after Compline 'O God, come to my assistance' [and] 'I have lifted up my eyes' likewise under a single collect.

5   But always on Sundays and feasts at the prior's signal the brothers shall proceed to Chapter after Prime. When Chapter has concluded, the first mass shall take place, followed by the bell for Terce, and, on Sundays only, they shall bless salt and water and carry on with the procession. Similarly, from Easter [onwards] Chapter is to be held after Prime, but, on ferias after the Octave of Pentecost and in the entire summer period, the matutinal mass is to be said immediately after Prime (when the litany has ended), and then they shall go to Chapter.

6   Rising from Chapter they shall sing five psalms for the departed brothers: '[Give ear, O Lord, to] my words', 'O Lord, [rebuke me] not in thy indignation', 'I have loved, because', 'I have believed, therefore' [and] 'Out of the depths', followed by the Lord's Prayer and a collect.

7   On Sundays, however, Prime shall be prolonged; and the abbot shall sit in the cloister together with the brothers, and one by one they shall go to confession, humbly confessing to him whatever they have done at the Enemy's instigation during the entire [past] week.

8   On every Sunday or solemnity the brothers shall exchange the peace and receive the eucharist, except for those who have already said mass. Should this displease anyone, let him listen to what blessed Augustine says on the matter: 'He who does not deserve to receive daily does not deserve to receive once a year.'

9   The custom of monks living under the *Rule*, then, does not permit any brother to be negligent in attending the canonical hours; but at the bell they shall

orationem, et intenti incipiant simul sinaxim simulque finiant, omnes stantes exceptis egrotantibus aut qui in minutione sunt sanguinis.[49]

10   Dominicis diebus matutinalis missa de sancta Trinitate[50] celebranda est, [p. 240] nisi alia festiuitas occurrerit. Nam ferialibus diebus de quacumque necessitate euenerit[51] facienda est.

11   Igitur sexta feria tota estate de sancta cruce principalis missa facienda est, et in sabbato de sancta Maria,[52] nisi alia festiuitas occurrerit.

12   Et omni die, decantatis matutinalibus laudibus, dicatur antiphona de sancta cruce et de sancta Maria et de sancto cuius reliquie ibi habentur.[53] Similiter finita uespera faciant usque Aduentum Domini.[54] Vigilia quoque pro defunctis[55] more solito, exceptis festiuis diebus, facienda est.

13   A Calendis Nouembris[56] dominica uespera[57] canatur hymnus[58] 'O lux beata', ad completorium 'Christe qui lux es', ad nocturnas uero 'Primo dierum'. Et ad matutinas dicatur 'Aeterne rerum', et ad uesperum 'Lucis creator'.[59] Iste ordo hymnorum omni die dominica tenendus est usque duas septimanas ante Pasca Domini.

Omnibus diebus toto anno canatur ad primam 'Iam lucis orto sidere', ad tertiam 'Nunc sancte nobis Spiritus', ad sextam 'Rector potens', ad nonam 'Rerum Deus'.[60]

De Aduentu Domini ad uesperam 'Conditor alme siderum', ad nocturnas 'Verbum supernum', ad matutinas 'Vox clara'.[61] In Natiuitate Christi ad uesperam 'Christe redemptor omnium', ad nocturnas 'A Patre unigenitus', ad matutinas 'A solis ortus cardine' usque 'Hostis Herodes',[62] quia 'Veni redemptor' et 'Audi redemptor' non uidentur sapientibus honeste esse compositos.[63] In uigilia Epiphaniae 'Hostis Herodes impie', ad noc- [p. 241] turnas item 'A Patre unigenitus', ad matutinas 'Iesus refulsit omnium'.[64] In Purificatione sanctae Mariae ad uesperam 'Quod chorus uatum', ad nocturnas 'Quem terra', ad matutinas 'A solis ortus'.[65]

In Septuagessima ad uesperam 'Alleluia dulce carmen', ad nocturnas 'Alleluia piis edite laudibus', ad matutinas 'Almum sidereæ[a] iam patrie decus'.[66] In Quadradgessima ad uesperam 'Audi benigne conditor', ad nocturnas 'Clarum decus ieiunii', ad matutinas 'Iesu quadragenarie',[67] per quattuor ebdomadas continue.[68] In Passione Domini ad uesperam 'Vexilla regis', ad nocturnam 'Arbor decora', ad matutinum 'Auctor salutis'.[69] In tota Quadragessima ferialibus diebus canatur ad tertiam 'Dei fide qua uiuimus', ad sextam 'Meridie orandum est', ad nonam 'Perfecto trino numero'.[70]

14   Brumali uero tempore concedatur fratribus accessus ignis, si necessitas

13 a sidereæ] sidere MS

all assemble for prayer and attentively begin the Office together and finish it together, all standing except for those who are sick or undergoing bloodletting.

10   The matutinal mass celebrated on Sundays shall be that of the Holy Trinity unless some other feast should occur. On ferias [the matutinal mass] is to be celebrated for whatever need should befall.

11   Accordingly on Fridays in the summer period the mass of the day shall be that of the Holy Cross and on Saturdays that of St Mary, unless some other feast should occur.

12   And after Lauds have been sung every day, antiphons of the Holy Cross, of St Mary and of the saint whose relics are kept there shall be said. At the end of Vespers [the monks] shall do the same, until Advent. Vigils of the Dead, too, are to be celebrated in the usual way except on feast days.

13   From the Kalends of November, at Vespers for Sunday the hymn 'O lux beata' shall be sung, [and] at Compline 'Christe qui lux es', but at Nocturns 'Primo dierum'. And at Lauds 'Aeterne rerum' shall be said, and at Vespers 'Lucis creator'. This arrangement of hymns shall be observed every Sunday up until the two weeks before Easter.

At Prime 'Iam lucis orto sidere', at Terce 'Nunc sancte nobis Spiritus', at Sext 'Rector potens' [and] at None 'Rerum Deus' shall be sung daily throughout the entire year.

In Advent: at Vespers 'Conditor alme siderum', at Nocturns 'Verbum supernum', at Lauds 'Vox clara'. At Christmas: at Vespers 'Christe redemptor omnium', at Nocturns 'A Patre unigenitus', at Lauds 'A solis ortus cardine' as far as 'Hostis Herodes', because to the experts 'Veni redemptor' and 'Audi redemptor' do not seem worthily composed. At the Vigil of Epiphany: [at Vespers] 'Hostis Herodes impie', at Nocturns 'A Patre unigenitus' [and] at Lauds 'Iesus refulsit omnium'. On the Purification of St Mary: at Vespers 'Quod chorus uatum', at Nocturns 'Quem terra' [and] at Lauds 'A solis ortus'.

In Septuagesima: at Vespers 'Alleluia dulce carmen', at Nocturns 'Alleluia piis edite laudibus' [and] at Lauds 'Almum sidereae iam patriae decus'. In Lent: at Vespers 'Audi benigne conditor', at Nocturns 'Clarum decus ieiunii' [and] at Lauds 'Iesu quadragenariae', repeatedly through the [first] four weeks. In Passiontide: at Vespers 'Vexilla regis', at Nocturns 'Arbor decora' [and] at Lauds 'Auctor salutis'. On ferias throughout the whole of Lent, at Terce 'Dei fide qua uiuimus' shall be sung, at Sext 'Meridie orandum est' [and] at None 'Perfecto trino numero'.

14   During the winter period the brothers shall be granted access to a fire,

compulerit; in refectorio tamen hoc minime agatur. Et si frigoris nimietas incubuerit, in domo[71] legant omnes simul et canant. Sin autem temperies tranquilla aderit, sedeant pariter omnes in claustro.

15   A festiuitate sancti Martini[72] post nonam non bibant fratres[73] festiuis diebus usque ad Purificationem sanctae Mariae.

16   In Aduentu Domini non canant 'Gloria in excelsis Deo'[74] nec in cibos mittant pinguedinem.[75] Festiuis tamen diebus licet uti pinguedine.

17   Vigilia Natalis Domini dum eiusdem natalis mentio a lectore recitetur in capitulo,[76] omnes pariter surgentes genua flectent, gratias agentes [p. 242] propter eius ineffabilem pietatem qua mundum a laqueis diaboli redempturus descendit.[77] Sabbato quoque Sancto Pasce idipsum agendum est, quamuis in martirlogio hoc non habeatur.

18   Vespere Natiuitatis Domini canantur antiphone congrue de ipsa completione temporis[78] ad psalmos. In cuius noctis uigilia in quarto responsorio,[79] ut honorificentius agatur, duo simul cantent. Et post euuangelium[80] lauent se et fiat missa de nocte,[81] deinde matutinales laudes de die. Et, si nondum diei[a] aurora eluxerit, cantent laudes de omnibus sanctis; si autem eluxerit, celebrent missam matutinalem quae in lucis crepusculo celebranda est, et dehinc canant de omnibus sanctis.

19   Ipso namque die in capitulo prosternant se fratres, abbati confessionem facientes ex intimo corde, et abbas respondeat 'Misereatur'.[82] Deinde ipse solotenus se prosternens idipsum faciat et fratres singuli dicant 'Misereatur', et abbas compleat confessionem cum precibus et oratione congrua. Idem quoque modus confessionis prima a Pascalis sollempnitatis die agatur.

20   Facto signo ad tertiam induant se fratres et[a] sint ornati ad tertiam.[83] Et omni die, quando missa celebratur, sint ministri ante sinaxim induti, ne uideantur inhoneste discurrere dum opus Dei celebratur. Ad uesperam ipsius diei dicantur antiphone 'Tecum principium' et reliquae.[84]

21   Reliquis uero tribus diebus dicantur antiphone de ipsis sanctis [p. 243] cum psalmis ipsi sollempnitati competentibus.[85] His peractis rursum repetatur 'Tecum principium' usque Octauas Domini.

22   His autem diebus inter Innocentium festiuitatem et Octauas Domini, quia 'Gloria in excelsis Deo' ob tante festiuitatis honorificentiam ad missam

18 a diei] dies *MS*
20 a et] *? for* ut; *cf. RC* 48

should necessity require it; this shall not be done in the refectory, however. And should the severe cold persist, let them all read and chant together in the *domus*. But should the weather be mild, let them all sit together in the cloister.

15   From the feast of St Martin until the Purification of St Mary, the brothers are not to take a drink after None on feast days.

16   In Advent they shall not sing 'Glory to God in the highest' or put lard in their food. On feast days, however, it is permitted to use lard.

17   On the Vigil of Christ's Nativity, when the reader in Chapter makes mention of that same birth, all shall rise together and genuflect to give thanks for his [*scil*. Christ's] ineffable kindness, whereby he descended in order to save the world from the Devil's snares. This same [custom] is to be done on Holy Saturday, too, even though it is not [prescribed] in the martyrology.

18   At Vespers of Christmas, antiphons appropriate to the fullness of time shall be sung at the psalms. At Vigils on this night, two shall sing the fourth responsory together, in order that it may be done with greater reverence. And after the gospel they shall wash, then the mass *in nocte* shall take place, followed by Lauds of the day. And if the day has not yet dawned, they shall sing Lauds of All Saints; but if it has dawned, they shall celebrate the matutinal mass (which is to be celebrated at daybreak) and then sing [Lauds] of All Saints.

19   In Chapter on that day [*scil*. Christmas], the brothers shall prostrate themselves, making their confession to the abbot from the depths of their hearts, and he shall respond with 'May [almighty God] have mercy'. Then he, prostrating himself on the ground, shall do the same, and one by one the brothers shall say 'May [almighty God] have mercy', and the abbot shall finish the confession with *preces* and an appropriate collect. This same order of confession shall also be observed on the first day after the solemnity of Easter.

20   At the bell for Terce, the brothers shall dress and be vested for Terce. And every day, when mass is celebrated, the ministers are to be vested before the service [of Terce], lest they seem to be scurrying about irreverently during the celebration of the Divine Office. At Vespers of the same day [*scil*. Christmas], the antiphons 'With thee is the principality' and the rest are to be said.

21   But on the three remaining days, [proper] antiphons of the saints themselves shall be said, together with the psalms appropriate to the solemnity [of Christmas]. When these days are over, [the series] 'With thee is the principality' shall be repeated until the Octave of Christmas.

22   Moreover, on these days between the feast of the Holy Innocents and the Octave of Christmas, because 'Glory to God in the highest' is sung at mass to

celebratur, ad nocturnam et ad uesperam uti ad missam omnia signa pulsentur,[86] licet 'Te Deum laudamus' non cantetur nec euuangelium legatur. Cerei etiam[a] accendantur et turibulum turificando deportetur.[87] In festiuitate Innocentium non canitur 'Gloria in excelsis Deo' nec 'Alleluia' ad missam propter mestitiam plangentium matrum illorum necem crudelem.[88]

23   Ab Octauis Domini non cantetur 'Gloria in excelsis Deo' nec sonentur signa simul, exceptis festiuis diebus, sed agatur obedientia[89] et psallantur cum antiphona[a] ad uesperam psalmi feriales[90] usque octauas Epiphaniae.

24   In uigilia uero Epiphanie non teneatur ieiunium,[91] et ad uesperam decantent psalmos ipsius uespere cum antiphonis de eadem sollempnitate.[92]

Amalarius dicit: In Epiphania Domini omittimus inuitatorium ut distinguamur ab inuitatione Herodis, qui congregauit scribas et principes sacerdotum ut disceret ab eis ubi Christus nasceretur, quem cogitabat interficere.[93] Ad nocturnas canimus psalmum 'Deus noster refugium' preposter ordine, quia magi uenerunt adorare Dominum antequam baptizatus esset; et ideo cantamus antiphonam 'Venite adoremus eum' prius et postea 'Fluminis [p. 244] impetus laetificat'.[94]

25   In Purificatione[95] sanctae Mariae, audito signo ad tertiam,[96] induant se fratres albis et eant, si aura sic permiserit,[97] ad processionem. Et decantata antiphona cum oratione in ueneratione ipsius sancti cui ecclesia illa ad quam itur dedicata est,[98] benedicat abbas, indutus stola et cappa, candelas et conspergat[a] aqua benedicta et turificet. Et sic, accepto cereo ab edituo, psallentibus cunctis, accipiant singuli singulas acceptasque accendant, reuertentes uero ad ecclesiam cantando.[99] Post antiphonam 'Responsum accepit Symeon'[100] dicatur oratio ad ostium[b] 'Erudi quaesumus Domine'.[101] Et intrantes ecclesiam canant 'Cum inducerent' cum dominica oratione,[102] quam sequatur tertia. Et teneant luminaria donec ea offerant sacerdoti post euuangelium, hoc significante, ut unusquisque clarus et lucidus appareat bonis operibus in Presentatione Domini, qui est lux mundi.[103]

26   In Septuagessima[104] dimittimus cantica caelestia,[105] hoc est 'Alleluia' et 'Gloria in excelsis Deo', usque in uigiliam Pascae. Et humiliamur sponte pro peccatis nostris sicut humiliatus est Hebraicus populus inuitus, septuaginta annis seruiens regi Babilonis sine uoce gaudii et letitiae, uoce sponsi et

---

22 a etiam] *cf. RC* 50 tamen; *see commentary*
23 a antiphona] *cf. RC* 51 antiph̄ *usu. expanded as plural; see commentary*
25 a conspergat] conspergit *MS; cf. RC* 54
   b ostium] hostium *MS*

Translation

show reverence for so great a feast, all the bells are to be rung at Nocturns and Vespers just as they are at mass, even though the [hymn] 'We praise thee, O God' is not sung, nor the gospel read. Candles shall also be lit, and a thurible with burning incense shall be carried. On the feast of the Innocents neither 'Glory to God in the highest' nor 'Alleluia' is sung at mass on account of the sadness of the mothers lamenting their [*scil.* the Innocents'] cruel slaughter.

23   Beginning with the Octave of Christmas, 'Glory to God in the highest' is not sung nor are the bells rung together, save on feast days; but work shall be done, and the ferial psalms with their antiphon shall be chanted at Vespers until the Octave of Epiphany.

24   But on the Vigil of Epiphany no fast shall be kept, and at Vespers they shall sing the psalms of that [day's] Vespers with antiphons of the same solemnity.

Amalarius says: On Epiphany we omit the invitatory, that we may be distinguished [in our invitation] from the invitation of Herod, who gathered the scribes and the chief priests in order to learn from them where Christ would be born, whom he was planning to kill. At Nocturns we sing the psalm 'Our God is our refuge' out of sequence, because the Magi came to worship the Lord before he had been baptized; and we therefore sing the antiphon 'Come let us praise [the Lord with joy]' first, and afterwards 'The stream of the river maketh [the city of God] joyful'.

25   On the Purification of St Mary, at the sound of the bell for Terce, the brothers shall vest in albs and make their way to the procession, weather permitting. And when the antiphon, together with its collect, has been sung in honour of the saint to whom that church is dedicated which is the destination of the procession, the abbot, vested in a stole and cope, shall bless the candles, sprinkle them with holy water and cense them. And so, after [the abbot] has received his candle from the sacristan, and as all are chanting, every man shall receive his own candle and light it, and they shall make their way, while singing, back to the [main] church. After the antiphon 'Simeon received an answer', the prayer 'Teach [us], we implore thee, O Lord' shall be said at the entrance [of the church]. And entering the church they shall sing 'When [his parents] brought in [the child Jesus]', followed by the Lord's Prayer, then Terce. And they shall keep holding their candles until they offer them to the priest after the gospel reading [at mass], thereby signifying that each and every person should appear bright and shining in good works at the Presentation of the Lord, who is the light of the world.

26   In Septuagesima we dismiss the heavenly songs, that is, 'Alleluia' and 'Glory to God in the highest', until the Vigil of Easter, and we humiliate

sponse.¹⁰⁶ Ergo officia ipsa in Septuagessima monent nos preparare nosmetipsos ad bellum spiritale, cum dicitur in ipsa oratione misse 'ut qui iuste pro peccatis [p. 245] nostris affligimur', et in introitu 'Circumdederunt me gemitus mortis', et in epistola 'Omnis enim qui in agone contendit ab omnibus se abstinet.'¹⁰⁷ Nam Septuagessima secundum disputationem Amalarii dominica die nouem ebdomadas ante Pascha Domini incipit et post Pascha Domini in septima sabbati finitur.¹⁰⁸

Consuetudo dicit intermittere pinguedinem¹⁰⁹ a Septuagessima. Et hoc sciendum est, quod, dimissa 'Alleluia', sex posteriores psalmi ad nocturnam cum antiphonis canendi sunt:¹¹⁰ secunda feria uidelicet .i. antiphona 'Vt non delinquam in lingua mea', .ii. antiphona 'Sana Domine animam meam, quia peccaui tibi', .iii. antiphona 'Eructauit cor meum uerbum bonum'.¹¹¹ Feria tertia .i. antiphona 'Auertit Dominus captiuitatem plebis sue', .ii. antiphona 'Intende in me et exaudi me Domine', .iii. antiphona 'Iuste iudicate filii hominum'.¹¹² Feria quarta .i. antiphona 'Quaerite Dominum et uiuet anima uestra', .ii. antiphona 'Domine Deus in adiutorium meum intende', .iii. antiphona 'Quam bonus Israel Deus'.¹¹³ Feria quinta <.i.>ᵃ antiphona 'Exultate Deo adiutori nostro', .ii. antiphona 'Tu solus altissimus super omnem terram', .iii. antiphona 'Benedixisti Domine terram tuam'.¹¹⁴ Feria sextaᵇ .i. antiphona 'Cantate Domino et benedicite nomini eius', .ii. antiphona 'Quia mirabilia fecit Dominus', .iii. antiphona 'Iubilate Deo omnis terra'.¹¹⁵ Sabbato .i. antiphona 'Visita nos Domine in salutari tuo', .ii. antiphona 'De necessitatibus meis eripe me Domine', .iii. antiphona 'Confitebor Domino nimis in ore meo'.¹¹⁶

27 In Sexagessima¹¹⁷ circumdati sumus tribulationibus quam maximis ac si non esset locus euadendi. Vendidimus nos sub peccato; in nobis non est uirtus soluendi. [p. 246] Vnde dicitur in prima oratione Sexagessimae 'Deus qui conspicis quia ex nulla nostra uirtute subsistimus';¹¹⁸ similiter in ceteris officiis ipsius diei.

28 Quinquagessima¹¹⁹ in tertio gradu consistit. Antea dubitabamus utrum Dominus propiusᵃ¹²⁰ nobiscum esset an non. Modo¹²¹ tenemus illum et dicimus 'Esto mihi in Deum protectorem et in locum refugii'¹²² et cetera. Sic et in reliquisᵇ officiis eiusdem diei.

Consuetudo docet abstinere a Quinquagessima a cibis qui de lacte siue de ouis fiunt.¹²³

29 Consuetudo: Quarta feria Capitis Ieiunii, nona decantata,¹²⁴ abbas ornatus stola benedicat cineres et imponat capitibus singulorum, quia legimus in

---

26 a .i.] *om. MS*
   b sexta] sextam *MS*
28 a propius] *cf. Lib.off.* I.iii.1 proprius; *see commentary*
   b reliquis] reliquiis *MS*

ourselves willingly for our sins, just as the Hebrew people was humiliated unwillingly for seventy years, serving the king of Babylon without the voice of joy and happiness, the voice of the bridegroom and the bride. The liturgy itself of Septuagesima therefore admonishes us to prepare ourselves for spiritual warfare, when it is said in the mass collect, 'that we who are justly afflicted for our sins', and in the introit, 'the groans of death have surrounded me', and in the epistle, 'everyone that striveth for the mastery refraineth himself from all things'. According to the reckoning of Amalarius, Septuagesima begins on the Sunday nine weeks before Easter and ends on the Saturday after Easter.

The customary says to give up lard from Septuagesima onwards. This, too, must be known, that, in the absence of 'Alleluia', the second six psalms at Nocturns are to be sung with antiphons: namely, on Monday the first antiphon [shall be] 'That I sin not with my tongue', the second 'Heal my soul, O Lord, for I have sinned against thee', the third 'My heart hath uttered a good word'. On Tuesday the first antiphon [shall be] 'The Lord hath turned away the captivity of his people', the second 'Be attentive to me and hear me, O Lord', the third 'Judge justly, ye sons of men'. On Wednesday the first antiphon [shall be] 'Seek ye God, and your soul shall live', the second 'Lord God, come to my assistance', the third 'How good is God to Israel'. On Thursday the [first] antiphon [shall be] 'Rejoice to God our helper', the second 'Thou alone art the most high over all the earth', the third 'Lord, thou hast blessed thy land'. On Friday the first antiphon [shall be] 'Sing ye to the Lord and bless his name', the second 'Because he hath done wonderful things', the third 'Sing joyfully to God, all the earth'. On Saturday the first antiphon [shall be] 'Visit us, O Lord, with thy salvation', the second 'Deliver me, O Lord, from my necessities', the third 'I will give great thanks to the Lord with my mouth'.

27   In Sexagesima we are surrounded by the greatest tribulations possible, as if there were no way of escape. We have sold ourselves under sin; the power of release does not lie within us. Wherefore it is said in the collect for Sexagesima, 'O God, you see that by no power of our own do we stand firm', and similarly in the other Offices of the day.

28   Quinquagesima is the third step. Previously we doubted whether or not the Lord was near to us. Now we cling to him and say, 'Be thou unto me a God, a protector and a house of refuge', and similarly in the remaining Offices of the same day.

From Quinquagesima onwards, the customary teaches to abstain from foods made of milk or eggs.

29   The customary: On Ash Wednesday, after None has been sung, the abbot, vested in a stole, shall bless ashes and put them on the heads of each and every

ueteri et in nouo testamento paenitentes semetipsos cynere aspersisse, demonstrantes humanam naturam esse reuersuram in puluerem ob culpam prime preuaricationis.[125] Incipiat interim cantor antiphonam 'Exaudi nos Domine'[126] cum psalmo[127] et 'Gloria', 'Kyrieleison', 'Pater noster', psalmo 'Deus misereatur nostri', collecta.[128] Eant tunc ad processionem reliquas antiphonas decantando.[129] Venientes uero ad ecclesiam quo eunt,[130] cantent antiphonam de ipso sancto et dominicam orationem, flexis genibus,[131] et psalmum[a] 'Ad te leuaui oculos meos'[132] cum precibus et oratione. Incipiant tunc cantores letaniam reuertentes ad matrem ecclesiam et induant se ministri ad missam.

Igitur iste ordo processionis teneatur quarta et sexta feria usque in Cenam Domini [p. 247] et ab octauis Pentecostes usque ad Exaltationem sanctae crucis,[133] semper discalciatis pedibus.[134] Sed excepto Capite Ieiunii[b] debent inchoare processionem cum antiphona 'Exsurge Domine'[135] cum psalmo et 'Gloria'.

30   Amalarius: In Quadragessima[136] aliqua pars pugne peracta est. Dicit nobis quem[a] in Quinquagessima protectorem inuocauimus 'Inuocauit me et ego exaudiam eum'[137] et cetera. Epistola ita 'Tempore accepto exaudiui te et in die salutis adiuui te.'[138] In responsorio angeli Domini custodiunt nos.[139] In tractu scuto ueritatis circumdati sumus.[140] In euuangelio ad triumphum tendimus, ut dicamus inimico 'Vade retro Satanas.'[141]

In Quadragessima reliquie et cruces occultantur[142] et uelamen inter sancta sanctorum et populum ponitur, quia absurdum putamus crucem adorare dum 'Alleluia' relinquimus. Si quis crucem adorare uult in Quadragessima, non habet opus in die Passionis Domini eam adorare nobiscum.

Consuetudo: In diebus Quadragessime aliquid nobis augendum[143] diuine seruituti ad solitum pensum nostrae seruitutis censuimus (ut regula sancta hortatur), ita ut a capite Quadragessime usque ad Cenam Domini, festiuis exceptis diebus, cotidie post expletionem uniuscuiusque hore duos psalmos prostrati solo oratorii peroremus deuoti,[144] eo scilicet ordine ut, matutinis finitis, mox dicantur duo psalmi 'Domine ne in furore tuo' et 'Ad Dominum',[145] 'Kyrieleison', 'Pater noster', et preces pro peccatis[146] et oratio.[b] [p. 248] Ad primam psalmi 'Beati quorum', 'Leuaui'[147] et reliqua ut supra. Ad tertiam psalmi 'Domine ne in furore tuo' (ii) et 'Letatus sum'.[148] Ad sextam psalmi 'Miserere mei Deus' et 'Ad te leuaui oculos meos'.[149] Ad nonam psalmi 'Domine exaudi' et 'Nisi quia Dominus'.[150] Ad uesperam psalmi 'De profundis', 'Qui confidunt'.[151] Ad completorium psalmi 'Domine exaudi' (ii) et 'In conuertendo'.[152]

29 a psalmum] psalmo *MS; em.* Nocent
    b Capite Ieiunii] Capitis Ieiunio *MS*
30 a quem] quia *MS; em.* Nocent; *cf. Lib.off.* I.iv.1
    b oratio] oratione *MS*

Translation

person, because we read in the Old and New Testaments that penitents dusted themselves with ashes, showing that human nature would return to dust, on account of guilt for [man's] primordial transgression. Meanwhile the cantor shall begin the antiphon 'Hear us, O Lord' with a psalm, [then] 'Glory [be to the Father]', 'Kyrie eleison', 'Our Father', the psalm 'May God have mercy on us' [and a] collect. They shall then go to the procession singing the remaining antiphons. When they reach the destination church, they shall sing the antiphon of its saint and then, kneeling, the Lord's Prayer and the psalm 'To thee have I lifted up my eyes', with the *preces* and a collect. Then the cantors shall begin the litany as they [all] make their way back to the mother church, and the ministers shall vest for mass.

This order of procession, then, shall be kept on Wednesdays and Fridays up until Maundy Thursday, and from the Octave of Pentecost until [the feast of] the Exaltation of the Holy Cross, and always in bare feet. But, except on Ash Wednesday, they should begin the procession with the antiphon 'Arise, O Lord' with the psalm and 'Glory [be to the Father]'.

30   Amalarius: In Lent a certain part of the fight is finished. He whom we called upon as a protector in Quinquagesima [now] says to us, 'He hath called upon me, and I shall hear him', and so on. The epistle [says], 'In an accepted time have I heard thee; and in the day of salvation have I helped thee.' In the [gradual] response the Lord's angels protect us. In the tract we are surrounded by the shield of truth. In the gospel we head towards victory, that we may say to the Enemy, 'Begone, Satan!'

In Lent the relics and crosses are concealed, and a veil is placed between the Holy of Holies and the people, for we think it illogical to venerate the cross while we give up 'Alleluia'. If anyone wishes to venerate the cross in Lent, he has no need to venerate it together with us on the day of the Lord's Passion [*scil*. Good Friday].

The customary: We have thought it right in the days of Lent, as the holy *Rule* admonishes, to add something to our divine service beyond the accustomed measure of our duty; accordingly, every day from Ash Wednesday until Maundy Thursday (feast days excepted), at the conclusion of every [liturgical] hour we are to prostrate ourselves on the floor of the church and fervently recite two psalms. This shall be the order: namely, that at the end of Lauds the two psalms 'O Lord, [rebuke me] not in thy indignation' and '[In my trouble I cried] to the Lord' shall be said immediately, [then] 'Kyrie eleison', 'Our Father' and the *preces pro peccatis* and a collect. At Prime the psalms [shall be] 'Blessed are they' [and] 'I have lifted up [my eyes]', and the rest as above. At Terce the psalms '[Rebuke me] not, O Lord, in thy indignation' (ii) and 'I rejoiced'. At Sext the psalms 'Have mercy on me, O God' and 'To thee have I lifted up my eyes'. At None the psalms 'Hear, O Lord' and 'If it had not been that the Lord [was with us]'. At Vespers the psalms 'Out of the depths' [and] 'They that trust'. [And] at Compline the psalms 'Hear, O Lord' (ii) and 'When [the Lord] brought back [the captivity of Sion]'.

Text

In tota Quadragessima ferialibus diebus offerat unus chorus ad primam missam et alter ad missam maiorem.[153] Sabbato uero mediante Quadragessima tantum radent se fratres.[154]

31   Amalarius: Dies Passionis Domini[155] computantur duobus ebdomadibus ante Pascha Domini. In illis diebus omittimus inuitatorium[156] et in responsoriis 'Gloriam' sanctae Trinitatis, quoniam per humilitatem ueniendum est ad Passionem Christi. Conformat se sancta ecclesia capiti suo et de glorificatione eius reticetur usque dum exaltetur per triumphum uictoriae. Due ebdomade passionis Christi duo tempora sunt huius mundi ante legem et sub lege. Dies uero Pasche in tertia ebdomada est, hoc est in tertio tempore gratiae Christi, in qua restauratur omnis amissa glorificatio. Nam in duobus prioribus temporibus Passio Christi prophetata est, et in tertio, ea adimpleta, redemptionem et glorificationem et gratiam inuenimus.

32   In Die Palmarum, interim dum matutinalis missa canitur,[157] agatur a sacerdote cum quodam <puero>[a] processio in claustro, et finita missa procedant fratres ad maiorem processionem ubi palme benedicendae sunt,[158] albis induti si aura permiserit.[159] Et fi- [p. 249] nita oratione[b] processionis[160] legat diaconus euuangelium 'Turba multa' usque 'Ecce mundus totus post eum abiit',[161] quo expleto sequatur benedictio palmarum.[162] Et aspergantur benedicta aqua et turificentur et diuidentur, inchoantibus pueris antiphonas 'Pueri Hebreorum'.[163] Transacta processione[164] subsistant ante ecclesiam et decantent pueri deintus 'Gloria laus' cum uersibus, omnibus respondentibus sicut mos est.[165] Quibus finitis, incipiente cantore responsorium 'Ingrediente Domino',[166] intrent ecclesiam agantque tertiam, sicut supradictum est.[167] Et teneant palmas in manibus usque dum offertorium cantetur, et eas post oblationem offerant sacerdoti.

Amalarius: Die Palmarum in memoriam illius rei[168] qua Israeliticus populus processerunt obuiam Domino cum ramis palmarum, clamantes 'Osanna, benedictus qui uenit in nomine Domini, rex Israel,' nos per ecclesias solemus portare ramos et clamare 'Osanna' propter triumphalem uictoriam Christi.[169]

Eadem die ad Passionem Domini[170] diaconus dicat 'Dominus uobiscum' et respondent omnes 'Et cum spiritu tuo'; sed cum dicit 'Passio Domini' et reliqua, nullus respondeat 'Gloria tibi Domine.' Similiter ad illam Passionem quae legitur in quarta feria. Ad illam uero quae legitur in sexta feria non dicatur 'Dominus uobiscum' nec 'Gloria tibi Domine.'

---

32 a puero] *not in MS;* quodam *followed by an erasure of 4–5 letters; descender of initial* p *is partially visible*
    b oratione] orationis MS; *em.* Nocent

Translation

On ferias throughout the whole of Lent, one choir shall make the offering at the first mass, the other at the principal mass. The brothers shall shave on mid-Lent Saturday only.

31   Amalarius: The days of the Lord's Passion are reckoned as the two weeks prior to Easter. In those days we omit the invitatory and the 'Glory [be]' to the Holy Trinity in our responsories, because it is necessary to approach the Passion of Christ in humility. The holy church patterns itself after its head, and silence is kept concerning his glorification until he is exalted through [his] triumphant victory. The two weeks of Christ's Passion are the two ages of this world, before and under the Law. But Easter day is in the third week, that is, in the third age, [that] of the grace of Christ, in which all the glory that was lost is restored. For in the two prior ages Christ's Passion was foretold, and, upon its fulfilment in the third, we have found redemption, glory and grace.

32   On Palm Sunday, while the matutinal mass is being sung, the procession in the cloister shall be carried out by a priest, with a boy [as server]. When the mass is ended, the brothers, dressed in albs if the weather permits, shall conduct the greater procession [to that place] where the palms are to be blessed. And after the processional collect, the deacon shall read the gospel 'A great multitude', up to the words 'Behold, the whole world is gone after him'. When this has been done, the blessing of the palms shall follow: they are to be sprinkled with holy water, censed and divided up while the boys begin the antiphons 'The Hebrew children' [and the rest]. At the end of the procession they shall stop before the church where, from within, boys shall sing 'All glory, laud and honour' with its verses, while the rest respond in the usual way. When these things have been done, they shall enter the church while the cantor begins the responsory 'As the Lord entered [the holy city]', and they shall celebrate Terce, as described above. And they shall hold the palms in their hands until the offertory is sung and, after the offering, present them to the priest.

Amalarius: On Palm Sunday, in memory of that occasion when the people of Israel went forth with branches of palm to meet the Lord, crying 'Hosanna, blessed is he that cometh in the name of the Lord, the king of Israel', it is our custom to carry branches through our churches and cry 'Hosanna' on account of Christ's triumphant victory.

On the same day, at [the reading of] the Lord's Passion, the deacon shall say 'The Lord be with you,' to which all respond 'And with thy spirit'; but when he says 'The Passion of the Lord' and so on, no one is to answer 'Glory be to thee, O Lord,' and similarly at that Passion which is read on Wednesday. But at that [Passion] which is read on Friday, neither 'The Lord be with you' nor 'Glory be to thee, O Lord' shall be said.

33   In Cena Domini[171] non dicimus ad nocturnas 'Domine labia mea aperies' nec 'Deus in adiutorium meum intende'[172] cum 'Gloria Patri', quia haec sunt officia principis congregationis, et noster [p. 250] princeps Christus in hac nocte traditus est. Inuitatorium non canimus quia disperse sunt oues et non est pastor qui congreget. 'Gloria Patri' non canimus, quia Filius Patris inter iniquos deputatus est. Ante lectiones non petimus benedictionem nec dicimus 'Tu autem Domine',[173] quia pastor noster qui benedictionem dare solet conprehensus est, et 'discipuli omnes relicto eo fugerunt'.[174] Similiter facimus propter supradictas causas omnibus illis tribus noctibus.

In quibus noctibus etiam uiginti quattuor candelas accendimus quas ad singulas antiphonas et ad singula responsoria extinguimus[175] propter discessum ueri solis, qui Christus est. Nam uiginti quattuor horis unus dies adimpletur, et nos hanc extinctionem totidem candelarum per tres noctes frequentamus, quia et noster sol triduo sepulchro uelatur.[176]

Consuetudo docet debere, finita ultima antiphona in euuangelio[177] in Cena Domini, duos pueros psallere sonora uoce 'Kyrrieleison' in australi porticu duosque respondere 'Christeleison' in boreali porticu, et in occidentali parte duos fratres reboare 'Domine miserere nobis', et omnem chorum simul respondere 'Christus Dominus factus est obediens usque ad mortem.'[178] Faciant sic omnes ter et agant tacitas preces, flexis genibus, solito more. Qui mos cantilenae tribus noctibus uniformiter teneatur. Et si matutine ante lucem fuerint finite, fratres qui uoluerint ad suam redeant requiem.[179]

34   Mane autem facto pulset edituus tabulam[180] [p. 251] et cantent primam more canonico,[181] scilicet 'Deus in nomine tuo',[182] 'Beati inmaculati' usque 'Legem pone'[183] et cetera more solito. His tribus diebus, peracta prima, psallant psalterium ex integro unanimiter in choro et letanias agant prostrati,[184] et ceteras horas psallant more canonico. Ipso namque die psallant omnes horas simul sonoriter et preces singillatim tacite, Parasceue uero et sabbato singillatim et tacite, exceptis nocturnis.[185] Parasceue etiam debent exercere nudipedalia usquequo crux adoretur.[186]

35   Facto namque capitulo in Cena Domini, discalciant se fratres et lauent sacerdotes altaria et ceteri pauimenta ecclesiae, et non sit ea die celebratio missae in aliquo altari donec lauetur.[187] In quo facto, dicit Amalarius, intellegimus lauationem quam exercuerat Christus erga discipulos suos, per quam iterum intellegimus remissionem quam debet unusquisque exercere erga fratrem suum.[188]

Translation

33   At Nocturns of Maundy Thursday we do not say 'O Lord, thou wilt open my lips' or 'O God, come to my assistance' or 'Glory be to the Father' because these are the duties of the head of our community, and our head, Christ, was betrayed on this night. We do not sing the invitatory, because the sheep have been scattered and there is no shepherd to gather them. We do not sing 'Glory be to the Father' because the Son of the Father was reviled among the wicked. Before the readings we do not seek a blessing, nor do we say 'But thou, O Lord, [have mercy]' because our shepherd who usually gives the blessing has been seized, and all of the disciples have 'abandoned him and fled'. We do these same things for the aforesaid reasons on all three nights.

On these nights we also light twenty-four candles, which we extinguish one by one at each antiphon and responsory because of the departure of the true sun, which is Christ. For a single day is made up of twenty-four hours, and we repeat this extinguishing of that same number of candles for three nights, because our sun, too, lies hidden in the tomb for three days.

The customary teaches that on Maundy Thursday, after the concluding antiphon of the [canticle] 'Blessed [be the Lord God of Israel]', two boys are to sing from the southern porch of the church 'Kyrie eleison' in full voice, and two respond from the northern porch 'Christe eleison', and from the western side two brothers sing back 'Lord have mercy on us', and the whole choir responds as one 'Christ became obedient unto death.' They shall all do this three times and, kneeling, say the *preces* in the usual way [but] silently. This choral custom is to be observed in the same way for three nights. Should Lauds conclude before daylight, the brothers who so desire may return to their beds.

34   But at daybreak the sacristan shall sound the *tabula*, and they shall sing Prime according to the secular Office, namely '[Save me,] O God, by thy name' [and] 'Blessed are the undefiled', as far as 'Set [before me] for a law', and the rest in the usual way. After Prime on these three days they shall chant the entire psalter together in choir, and they shall perform the litanies prostrate, and the rest of the hours they shall chant according to the secular Office. On this day [*scil.* Maundy Thursday] they are to sing all the hours together and out loud, and the *preces* individually and silently; but on Good Friday and [Holy] Saturday [they shall recite all the hours] individually and silently, except Nocturns. On Good Friday they should also go barefoot until the cross is venerated.

35   After Chapter on Maundy Thursday the brothers shall remove their shoes, and the priests shall wash the altars while the rest wash the church floor; and on that day no mass is to be celebrated on any altar until it has been washed. In this act, Amalarius says, we understand that washing which Christ carried out among his disciples, by which we also understand the forgiveness which every man ought to extend to his brother.

36   Consuetudo: Sexta peracta celebretur missa pauperibus ante ad hoc collectis,[189] secundum numerum quem abbas praeuiderit. Et lauent pedes uirorum tantum[190] et extergant atque osculentur et, data aqua manibus illorum, dentur eis etiam cibaria et quicquid abbas praeuiderit.

37   Amalarius: Ipso namque die et duobus sequentibus diebus, hora nona, ad ostium[a] ecclesie nouus ignis de lapide excutiendus est et in ecclesiam portandus, quia in illa massa[b] fragili quae ducta est ex primo homine extinctus est commemoratus ignis. Quapropter [p. 252] conuenit ut de lapide qui excisus est 'de monte sine manibus' idem ignis requiratur.[191]

Consuetudo dicit ut, si ita placuerit, decantata nona habeatur imago serpentis preparata, hastae adfixa, candelam habens in ore suo, quae accensa a praedicto igne deportetur cum hasta illis tribus diebus in ecclesiam, et accendantur luminaria ex ea.[192]

38   Ipsa die non dicatur 'Dominus uobiscum' ad missam,[193] nisi ab episcopo ubi crisma conficitur. Ipse etiam, decantato ter 'Agnus Dei', pacis osculum presbiteris solummodo licenter dat. Ipso etiam die post celebrationem missae et uespertinalis sinaxis altaria exspoliamus,[a] ut stent denudata usque in sabbatum, quia Dominus noster exspoliatus[b] est uestimentis suis.[194] Nuda sint altaria eo tempore in quibus solemus Deo oblationes offerre, quoniam exspoliatus est ille per quem acceptabilis fit Deo oblatio nostra.[195]

39   In Cena Domini crisma ab episcopo sacrandum est,[196] quia eo die sacramenta ecclesiae Dominus discipulis contradidit.[197] Tria uascula inpleantur oleo in secretario, et uno eorum, quod honestius uidetur ceteris esse, debet episcopus balsamum miscere. Precipitur enim ut primum uas benedicatur ante communionem, quod est pro medicamento afflictorum et infirmorum membrorum, quia hoc uas significat antiquos patres, qui habebant magnam gratiam curationum.[198] Tunc, una ampulla benedicta, communicet episcopus solus et, accepto sacrificio, benedicat duas reliquas ampullas, quia Christus [p. 253] solus suum corpus obtulit Deo Patri et calicem Passionis bibit,[199] et postea peracta sunt sacramenta crismatis et olei sui.[200] Duo uero uascula benedicantur post communicationem episcopi, quorum unum, in quo balsamum mixtum est, Christum intelligimus significari,[a] in quo 'misericordia et ueritas sibi obuiauerunt',[201] in secundo corpus Christi demonstrari quod est in nouo

---

37 a ostium] hostium *MS*
   b massa] missa *MS; em. Nocent; cf. R1(Sa)*
38 a exspoliamus] expoliamus *MS*
   b exspoliatus] expoliatus *MS*
39 a significari] *? for* significare

Translation

36   The customary: After Sext one shall celebrate the mass for the poor, who have been assembled beforehand for this purpose in numbers determined by the abbot. [The monks] shall wash and dry and kiss the feet of the men only, and, after pouring water over their hands, they [*scil*. the poor] shall also be given food and whatever [else] the abbot deems appropriate.

37   Amalarius: At the ninth hour on this day and the two following, at the doorway of the church a new fire is to be struck from a rock and [then] carried inside, because the aforesaid fire was extinguished in the fragile substance that descended from the first man. It is therefore fitting that the same fire [now] be sought from a stone 'cut without hands out of a mountain'.

The customary says that, if it be pleasing, after None they shall have ready the figure of a serpent attached to [the end of] a shaft; in its mouth is a candle which, when lit from the aforesaid fire on these three days, shall be carried atop the shaft into the church, and from it [other] candles shall be lit.

38   On that same day 'The Lord be with you' is not to be said at mass, except by the bishop when the chrism is blessed. He alone also has license to give the kiss of peace to the priests, once 'Lamb of God' has been sung three times. Also on that day after the celebration of mass and the service of Vespers, we should strip the altars so that they stand bare until Saturday, because our Lord was stripped of his garments. The altars on which we are wont to make our offerings to God should be bare at that time, because he was stripped, through whom our offering is made acceptable to God.

39   On Maundy Thursday chrism is to be blessed by the bishop, because on that day the Lord passed down to his disciples the sacraments of the church. In the sacristy three small vessels should be filled with oil, and the bishop should mix balsam into the one that appears worthier of reverence than the others. It is stipulated that the first vessel, which is for the remedy of sick and afflicted members, should be blessed before communion, because this vessel signifies the ancient fathers, who possessed the great gift of healing powers. Then, when one ampoule has been blessed, the bishop alone shall communicate and, after receiving the sacrifice, bless the two remaining ampoules, because Christ alone offered his body to God the Father and drank the cup of his Passion, and afterwards the sacraments of his chrism and oil were established. Two vessels, moreover, should be blessed after the bishop's communion, one of which – that in which the balsam was mixed – we understand to represent Christ, in whom 'mercy and truth have met each other'; in the second is signified the body of Christ that exists under the new dispensation, that is, the church under the grace of Christ. Two of the vessels are consecrated in silence, that is, the first and the third; but the middle one, in which balsam was mixed, should be blessed aloud,

testamento, hoc est ecclesia sub gratia Christi. Due enim ampulle tacite consecrantur, id est prima[b] et tertia.[c] Media[d] uero, in qua balsamum est mixtum, excelsa uoce benedicatur, quoniam Christum predicamus, sicut dicit Paulus: 'Non nosmetipsos[e] predicamus, sed Iesum Christum.'[202] Postquam salutent ipsa uascula sancta, communicet omnis populus. Et seruent de ipso sacramento oblationes tantum usque in crastinum, quia non licet eo die, quo Dominus passus est, sanctificare sacrificium.[203]

In Cena Domini et in Parascheue et in sabbato non pergimus ad pacem propter osculum ficte pacis, quo Iudas tradidit Christum.[204]

40   Consuetudo: Peracta misse celebratione omnes ad mixtum[205] pergant. Post mixtum quos uoluerit abbas secum ex fratribus assumens suum peragat mandatum,[206] quo peracto uesperam celebrant.

41   Deinde ad refectionem pergant[207] et tempore congruo agatur mandatum fratrum <ab>[a] abbate ac ministris. Tunc, lotis fratribus, exhibeant priores eandem humilitatem abbati.

42   Factoque signo collationis[208] sit diaconus ebdomadarius indutus dalmatica et ceteri ministri [p. 254] altaris albis induti. Veniat tunc diaconus portans textum euuangelii, praecedentibus ministris cum cereis[a] et turibulo, et legat euuangelium secundum Iohannem[b] 'Ante diem festum'[209] usquequo intrent more solito in refectorium. Legat tunc diaconus stans cum ministris sequentia euuangelii, inposito libro super ambonem, et abbas propinet fratribus caritatem,[210] deosculans singulorum manus. Et finita lectione praecedant ministri ut se exuant sintque cum reliquis ad completorium.

43   Amalarius: Feria sexta est[a] Parasceue, hoc est praeparatio Iudeorum, quia eo die preparabant Iudei sibi necessaria quae in sabbato habere debuissent, quando non licuit eis operari.[211] Ipso namque die, hora nona, sedente abbate in sede sua preparato[b] ad officium diei, legatur lectio Oseae prophetae 'In tribulatione sua mane',[212] quam sequitur tractus 'Domine audiui' et collecta 'Deus a quo et Iudas'.[213] Deinde legatur lectio libri Exodi 'Dixit Dominus ad Moysen et Aaron', in qua agnus, qui die dominica Hierusalem ad immolandum

   b prima] priman *MS*
   c tertia] tertiam *MS*
   d media] mediam *MS*
   e nosmetipsos] uosmetipsos *MS*
41 a ab] *om. MS; em. Nocent*
42 a cereis] ceteris *MS*
   b secundum Iohannem] *capitals*
43 a est] que est *MS; see commentary*
   b preparato] preparatus *MS;* preparata *em. Bateson*

Translation

because it is Christ we are proclaiming, as Paul says: 'We preach not ourselves, but Jesus Christ.' After they reverence these holy vessels, the entire people shall communicate. And from that same eucharist they [*scil.* the ministers] shall preserve offerings only until the next day, because it is not permitted to consecrate the sacrament on the day the Lord suffered.

On Maundy Thursday, Good Friday and Holy Saturday we do not exchange the peace, on account of the kiss of false peace by which Judas betrayed Christ.

40   The customary: After the celebration of mass all shall proceed to [take] the *mixtum*. After the *mixtum*, the abbot shall carry out his own maundy, taking with him from among the brothers those whom he wishes. After this they shall [all] celebrate Vespers.

41   Then they shall proceed to take their meal, and at the proper time the brothers' maundy shall be carried out by the abbot and his ministers. Then, when the brothers have been washed, the foremost among them shall offer the same act of humble service to the abbot.

42   At the signal for *collatio* the hebdomadary deacon shall be vested in a dalmatic, and the other ministers of the altar be vested in albs. Then the deacon, preceded by the [other] ministers with candles and a thurible, shall come bearing the gospel book, and he shall read, [from] the gospel according to John, 'Before the festival day' until they enter the refectory in the usual manner. Then the deacon, standing with the ministers, shall place the book on the ambo and read the gospel sequence, and the abbot shall serve the *caritas* to the brothers, kissing the hands of each one [as he goes]. At the end of the reading, the ministers shall go out first in order to remove their vestments and so join the rest for Compline.

43   Amalarius: Friday is the *Parasceue* (that is 'preparation') of the Jews, because on that day the Jews used to prepare for themselves those necessities that they required for the Sabbath, when they were not permitted to work. Now on this same day, at the ninth hour, when the abbot has taken his seat in readiness for the liturgy of the day, the lesson shall be read from the prophet Hosea, 'In their affliction [they will rise] early'. The tract 'O Lord, I have heard' follows, and the collect 'O God, from whom Judas [received the punishment of his guilt]'. Then the lesson shall be read from the book of Exodus, 'The Lord said to Moses and Aaron', in which the lamb is sacrificed which, on [the previous] Sunday, entered Jerusalem in order to be sacrificed. The tract 'Deliver me, O Lord' follows this reading and, after the tract, [the reading of] the Lord's Passion. For the tract takes its name from *trahendo* ['drawing'], and the Lord did not die immediately when hung on the cross, but rather 'drew out' the time of his dying

intrauit, immolatur.²¹⁴ Hanc lectionem sequitur tractus 'Eripe me Domine'²¹⁵ et, finito tractu, Passio Domini; nam tractus a 'trahendo' dicitur, et Dominus suspensus in cruce non continuo obiit, sed trahebat in cruce tempus mortis suae usque ad horam^c quam dispositam habebat emittendi spiritum. Tractus sit ante euuangelium; in euuangelio 'emisit spiritum'.²¹⁶ [p. 255] In eadem Passione, quando legitur 'Partiti sunt uestimenta mea' et reliqua, duo diaconi trahant uestem quae iacet sub euuangelio in modum furantis, quia milites crucifixo Christo uestimenta eius diuiserunt sibi sortem mittentes.²¹⁷

Finita^d Passione incipit abbas orationes sollempnes quae sequuntur, quoniam et eadem die saluator noster pro tota ecclesia orauit in cruce.²¹⁸ Omnes orationes cum genuflexione fiant excepta quando oramus pro perfidis Iudeis. Illi enim inridentes Christum genu flexo^e ante eum inludebant, dicentes 'Aue rex Iudeorum', et nos fugimus eorum consensu qui Dominum inrident, non flectentes genua pro eis orando.²¹⁹ Deinde, finitis orationibus sollempnibus, deportetur crux ante altare a cantoribus cantantibus uersus et cetera, ut omnes eam per ordinem salutent.²²⁰

44   His finitis ponat diaconus corporale super altare cum corpore Christi quod pridie remansit et calicem cum mixto uino non consecrato.²²¹ Corpus Christi solummodo seruatur a Cena Domini in Parasceue, quia credimus eum uere mortuum esse corpore; et item in Parasceue uinum cum aqua in calice mittitur, quia credimus ueram resurrectionem eius, ut habeamus sacramenta uiuentis hominis in nobis per corpus et sanguinem eius.²²² Dicit tunc abbas stans ad altare 'Oremus: Preceptis salutaribus' et 'Pater noster' sonora uoce, et secrete 'Libera nos, quaesumus Domine, ab omnibus malis' finetenus, et alta uoce 'Per omnia saecula saeculorum'. [p. 256] Mittat tunc silens de corpore Christi in calicem et communicet ipse et omnes, quia in his tribus festis diebus communicare oportet.²²³

45   His expletis canant singuli uespertinalem sinaxim more canonico,²²⁴ scilicet 'Confitebor tibi Domine', 'Domine probasti me', 'Eripe me Domine', 'Domine clamaui', 'Voce mea' et cetera.²²⁵ Tunc demum calceant se et refectorium petant. His uero tribus diebus in refectorio et in capitulo omnia more solito agantur.

46   Sabbato Sancto, hora nona decantata, sanctificet diaconus primitus cereum honorifice, et accendatur nouo igne benedicto;²²⁶ qui cereus Christi humanitatem praefigurat, qui lux mundi ueraciter cognoscitur esse.²²⁷ Sequantur tunc lectiones secundum constitutionem sancti Gregorii^a papae²²⁸ cum tractibus

   c horam] oram *MS*
   d Finita] Finito *MS*
   e genu flexo] geno fle *with* xo *written in the margin by the same hand*
46 a sancti Gregorii] *capitals*

Translation

on the cross until the hour he had appointed for the yielding up of his spirit. The tract shall be before the gospel, [for] in the gospel he 'gave up the ghost'. In the same Passion [reading], at the words 'They have parted my vestments', etc., two deacons shall, in the manner of thieves, pull away the cloth lying beneath the gospel book, because after crucifying Christ the soldiers divided his vestments among themselves by casting lots.

At the conclusion of the Passion, the abbot begins the *orationes solemnes* that follow, because on that same day our Saviour also prayed from the cross for the whole church. All the *orationes* should be performed with genuflexions, except for the one wherein we pray for the treacherous Jews. For they derided and mocked Christ by going down on bended knee before him, saying 'Hail, king of the Jews.' By not kneeling when we pray for them, we flee the fellowship of those who mock the Lord. Then, when the *orationes solemnes* have ended, a cross shall be carried down before the altar by cantors as they chant the verses and the rest, so that all may venerate it [*scil*. the cross] in due turn.

44   When these things are completed, the deacon shall place a corporal upon the altar, together with the Body of Christ left over from the previous day and a chalice of unconsecrated wine mixed [with water]. Because we believe that he did truly die in body, only the Body of Christ is reserved from Maundy Thursday to Good Friday; and again, on Good Friday, because we believe that his resurrection was genuine, wine mixed with water is put in the chalice, in order that by [receiving] his Body and Blood we might have [in us] the sacraments of a living person. Then, standing at the altar, the abbot shall say in an audible voice 'Let us pray: [Instructed] by thy saving precepts' and 'Our Father', and, inaudibly, 'Deliver us, we beseech thee, O Lord, from all evils' to [that prayer's] end; then aloud, 'World without end'. Then, without speaking, he shall place a portion of Christ's Body in the chalice. He himself shall receive communion, then shall all, because it is fitting to communicate during these three solemn days.

45   When these things have been done, they shall individually sing the service of Vespers according to the secular Office, namely, 'I will praise thee, O Lord', 'Lord, thou hast proved me', 'Deliver me, O Lord', 'I have cried [to thee,] O Lord', '[I cried to the Lord] with my voice' and so forth. Then at last they shall put on their shoes and proceed to the refectory. In these three days everything in the refectory and in Chapter is to be done in the usual way.

46   On Holy Saturday, after None has been sung, the deacon shall first reverently bless the [Paschal] candle, and it shall be lit from the new fire which has been blessed. The candle stands for the humanity of Christ, who is truly acknowledged to be the light of the world. Then shall follow the readings, with tracts and collects, according to the arrangement of holy Pope Gregory, then a sevenfold

et collectis, deinde septene letaniae²²⁹ canantur. Postea descendat sacerdos siue abbas cum ministris ad fontem benedicendum, canendo quinas letanias.

Infantes, quando baptizantur, in cerebro unguendi sunt a presbitero, quia episcopus debet in fronte unguere ubi laminam auream pontifex ferebat.²³⁰ Cereus qui infanti baptizato datur in manum coadunatur lampadibus sapientium uirginum.²³¹

Finita benedictione fontis redeant ad altare cum letania terna et, antequam incipiatur 'Gloria in excelsis Deo', canatur alta uoce a magistro scole siue cantore 'Accendite' ter,²³² et inluminentur omnia luminaria et pulsentur omnia signa [p. 257] dum canitur 'Gloria in excelsis Deo'. Sequitur collecta, epistola, 'Alleluia: Confitemini', tractus 'Laudate', euuangelium.²³³ In ipsa missa non portantur cerei ante euuangelium sed thimiama (siue thus) tantum, ad imitationem mulierum quae aromata detulerunt.²³⁴ In ipso die non cantatur offertorium nec 'Agnus Dei' nec communio,²³⁵ sed interim dum communicantur canant 'Alleluia' sonoriter et psalmum 'Laudate Dominum omnes gentes';²³⁶ dehinc antiphona 'Vespere autem sabbati', 'Magnificat'. Sic sacerdos missam ac uespertinalem sinaxim una compleat oratione.²³⁷ Eodem uespere ad mandatum aqua manibus tantum detur, et cantant completorium more canonicorum.²³⁸

47   Ad nocturnas in dominica sancte Pascae more canonicorum dicatur primitus 'Domine labia mea aperies' semel, 'Deus in adiutorium meum intende'²³⁹ cum 'Gloria'. Tunc cantor incipiat inuitatorium; posthinc tres antiphone cum tribus psalmis, secundum auctoritatem beati Gregorii papae,²⁴⁰ deinde uersus et dominica oratio cum prece. Sequantur tres lectiones de tractu euuangelii cum tribus responsoriis; et, finita 'Gloria', incipiat prior hymnum²⁴¹ 'Te Deum laudamus', post cuius finem dicat sacerdos uersum uerbotenus 'Surrexit Dominus',²⁴² et sic incipiat matutinas dicens 'Deus in adiutorium meum intende'. Tunc cantor ilico inchoet antiphonam cum psalmo 'Dominus regnauit', quia 'Deus misereatur nostri' debet sequi [p. 258] 'Deus Deus meus' more canonicorum.²⁴³ Finitis quinque psalmis cum antiphonis, dicat sacerdos capitolum et puer uersum. Tunc antiphona in euuangelio, qua finita dicatur statim collecta. Nam his septem diebus non canimus de omnibus sanctis nec ymnos.²⁴⁴

48   Ad primam dicantur cum 'Alleluia' 'Deus in nomine tuo', 'Confitemini', 'Beati inmaculati', 'Retribue', 'Quicumque uult', uersus 'Haec dies', 'Kyrrieleison', dominica oratio, 'Viuet anima mea', 'Erraui', et simbolum cum precibus et collecta.²⁴⁵ Ad tertiam 'Legem pone', 'Memor esto', 'Bonitatem'²⁴⁶ cum 'Alleluia' canantur; tunc gradalem 'Haec dies' canant sine capitulo et sine uersu,²⁴⁷ deinde collectam. Ad sextam eodem ordine 'Defecit', 'Quomodo

litany shall be sung. Afterwards, accompanied by the singing of a fivefold litany, the priest or abbot shall go down with his ministers to bless the font.

When infants are baptized they should be anointed on the top of the head by the priest, because the bishop should anoint on the forehead, where the high priest used to wear a plate of gold. The candle that is placed in the hand of the baptized infant is likened to the lamps of the wise virgins.

After the blessing of the font they shall return to the altar while a threefold litany [is sung], and, before 'Glory to God in the highest' is begun, *'Accendite'* ['set ablaze!'] shall be sung three times by the choir master or cantor, and all the lights shall be set ablaze, and all the bells shall be set ringing while 'Glory to God in the highest' is sung. [Then] follow the collect, epistle, 'Alleluia' [with its verse] 'Give praise [to the Lord]', the tract 'O praise [the Lord]' [and] the gospel. In the mass itself candles are not carried before the gospel, but only *thymiama*, or incense, in imitation of the women who brought perfumes [to Jesus's tomb]. On this same day the offertory, 'Lamb of God' and communion [chant] are not sung; rather they shall sing in full voice 'Alleluia' and the psalm 'O praise the Lord, all ye nations'. Then [shall follow] the antiphon 'And in the evening of the Sabbath' [and the canticle] '[My soul] doth magnify [the Lord]', and so the priest shall conclude both mass and Vespers with a single collect. At the maundy on this same evening, water shall be poured over the hands only, and [the monks] shall sing Compline according to the secular Office.

47   At Nocturns of Easter Sunday, 'O Lord, thou wilt open my lips' shall be said first and one time only, [then] 'O God, come to my assistance' with the 'Glory [be to the Father]', [all] as in the secular Office. Then the cantor shall begin the invitatory, after which [follow] three antiphons with three psalms as ordained by blessed Pope Gregory, then the versicle, Lord's Prayer and collect. [Then] follow three readings from homilies on the gospel with three responsories, [at the end of which,] when the 'Glory [be to the Father]' is finished, the prior shall begin the hymn 'We praise thee, O God'. After that is finished, the priest shall say the versicle 'The Lord is risen' straight through and so begin Lauds by saying 'O God, come to my assistance'. Then the cantor shall immediately begin the antiphon with the psalm 'The Lord hath reigned', because 'May God have mercy on us' should follow 'O God, my God' as in the secular Office. After the five psalms and their antiphons the priest shall say the capitulum and a boy the versicle, then the antiphon [for the canticle] 'Blessed [be the Lord God of Israel]' [is sung]. After [the final repetition of] that antiphon, the collect is to be said immediately following. In these seven days we do not sing hymns or the Offices of All Saints.

48   At Prime '[Save me, O God,] by thy name', 'Give praise', 'Blessed are the undefiled', 'Give bountifully' [and] 'Whosoever wishes [to be saved]' are to be said with 'Alleluia'; [then] the versicle 'This is the day', the 'Kyrie eleison',

dilexi', 'Iniquos'.²⁴⁸ Ad nonam simili modo 'Mirabilia', 'Clamaui', 'Principes'.²⁴⁹

Ad uesperam 'Dixit Dominus', 'Confitebor', 'Beatus uir'²⁵⁰ cum antiphonis sine capitulo, gradalisᵃ 'Haec dies' sine uersu, 'Alleluia' cum uersu et sequentia.²⁵¹ Postea inchoetur antiphona in euuangelio et collecta, dehinc eant ad fontem²⁵² cum psalmo 'Laudate pueri Dominum' et antiphona, quam sequatur collecta. Iterum reuertentur ad chorum canendo psalmum 'In exitu Israel' cum antiphona et collecta.²⁵³

Ad completorium psalmus 'Cum inuocarem', 'In te Domine speraui', 'Qui habitat', 'Ecce nunc',²⁵⁴ capitolum, uersus, 'Nunc dimittis' cum antiphona, 'Kyrrieleison', dominica oratio, uersus 'In pace in idipsum', symbolum, preces cum collecta et benedictione.²⁵⁵

Nam iste ordo²⁵⁶ sex reliquis diebus tenendus est, [p. 259] hoc excepto, quod non canimus 'Confitemini Domino' ad primam nisi dominica die, nec antiphonas ad nocturnas sedᵇ cum 'Alleluia'.

49   Vespera uero octauarum Pasce ordo iam regularis pleniter inchoetur.²⁵⁷ De omnibus sanctis una antiphona canatur usque in octauas Pentecosten.²⁵⁸ Et omnes sinaxes cum 'Alleluia' psallantur, et ad missam pro gradale una 'Alleluia' canatur ferialibus diebus, festiuis ueroᵃ diebus due 'Alleluia' canende sunt usque praedictum tempus.²⁵⁹ His etiam diebus genuflexionem non facimus nec letanias canimus²⁶⁰ more ecclesiastico.

50   In octauis sanctae Pascae ad uesperam canimus hymnum 'Ad cenam Agniᵃ prouidi', ad nocturnam 'Iesu nostra redemptio', ad matutinum 'Aurora lucis rutilat'²⁶¹ usque Ascensionem Domini. Tunc canimus ad uesperam 'Hymnum canamus gloriae', ad nocturnam 'Optatus uotis omnium', ad matutinas 'Aeterne rex altissime'²⁶² usque Pentecosten. Tunc canimus ad uesperam 'Iam Christus astra ascenderat', ad nocturnam 'Veni creator Spiritus', ad matutinum 'Beata nobis gaudia'.²⁶³

48 a gradalis] *capitals*
    b sed] s& *abbrev. MS*
49 a uero] uera *MS*
50 a Agni] magni *MS*

Lord's Prayer, [*preces*] 'My soul shall live' [and] 'I have gone astray', and the Creed, *preces* and collect. At Terce 'Set [before me] for a law', 'Be thou mindful' [and] '[Thou hast done] well' are to be sung with 'Alleluia'; [the monks] shall then sing the gradual 'This is the day' without the capitulum and versicle, then the collect. At Sext, by the same arrangement, '[My soul] hath fainted', 'O how [have I loved thy law]' [and] '[I have hated] the unjust'. At None, in similar fashion, '[Thy testimonies are] wonderful', 'I cried [with my whole heart]', 'Princes [have persecuted me]'.

At Vespers 'The Lord said', 'I will praise [thee]' [and] 'Blessed is the man' with antiphons but no capitulum, [then] the gradual 'This is the day' with no verse, [then] 'Alleluia' with its verse and the sequence hymn. After that, the antiphon [of the canticle] '[My soul] doth magnify [the Lord]' shall begin, and [after the final repetition of that antiphon,] the collect. Then they shall proceed to the font during the [chanting of the] psalm 'Praise the Lord, ye children' and its antiphon, which is to be followed by a collect. Likewise they shall return to the choir singing the psalm 'When Israel went out [of Egypt]' with its antiphon and a collect.

At Compline the psalm 'When I called [upon him]', 'In thee, O Lord, have I hoped', 'He that dwelleth [in the aid of the Most High]' [and] 'Behold now [bless ye the Lord]', [then] the capitulum and versicle, the [canticle] 'Now thou dost dismiss [thy servant]' with its antiphon, the 'Kyrie eleison', the Lord's Prayer, the versicle 'In peace in the selfsame', the Creed [and] *preces* with a collect and a blessing.

This order is to be kept on the six remaining days [of Easter week], with the exception that we sing 'Give praise to the Lord' at Prime on Sunday only, and we do not sing antiphons at Nocturns, but 'Alleluia'.

49 But at Vespers of the Octave of Easter, the regular order [of the Office] shall begin in full. In the [Offices] of All Saints, a single antiphon shall be sung until the Octave of Pentecost. All the liturgical hours shall be chanted with 'Alleluia', and at mass on ferias a single 'Alleluia' shall be sung in place of the gradual; but on feast days, up until the aforementioned time [*scil.* the Octave of Pentecost], two 'Alleluias' are to be sung. Also, in conformity with church custom, we do not genuflect or sing the litanies during these days.

50 On the Octave of Easter at Vespers we sing the hymn 'Ad cenam Agni prouidi', at Nocturns 'Iesu nostra redemptio' [and] at Lauds 'Aurora lucis rutilat', until [the feast of] the Ascension. Then we sing at Vespers 'Hymnum canamus gloriae', at Nocturns 'Optatus uotis omnium' [and] at Lauds 'Aeterne rex altissime', until Pentecost. Then we sing at Vespers 'Iam Christus astra ascenderat', at Nocturns 'Veni creator Spiritus' [and] at Lauds 'Beata nobis gaudia'.

51   In uigilia Pentecosten[264] in primordio legatur prima lectio 'Temptauit Deus Abraham', collecta 'Deus qui <in>[a] Abrahe' et cetera sicut in missali habentur,[265] et septenas et quinas et ternas letanias sicut in uigilia Pascae canimus.[266] Nam uesperam eo die congruo tempore psallimus cum responsorio et ymno more solito.[267]

52   Illa dominica nocte tribus psalmis totidemque lectionibus cum responsoriis agitur nocturna laus, [p. 260] ut in antiphonario[a] titulatur.[268] Ceteris uero horis diei et ebdomade sequentis regularis ordo teneatur.[269] Et illa ebdomada canatur ad missam 'Gloria in excelsis Deo', exceptis ieiuniorum diebus.[270]

53   In octauis Pentecosten non repetatur officium 'Spiritus Domini', eo quod septem[a] diebus celebremus tantummodo aduentum Spiritus sancti,[271] sed agatur illa ebdomada de sancta Trinitate.[272]

54   In tota estate[273] usque Kalendas Nouembris dominicali sabbato canitur ymnus 'Deus creator omnium', ad nocturnas 'Nocte surgentes', ad matutinas 'Ecce iam noctis', ad uesperam 'Lucis creator', ad completorium omnibus noctibus 'Te lucis ante terminum'.[274] Ferialibus uero diebus feriales hymnos canant semper,[a] et festiuis congruos ipsi festiuitati, et in toto anno tria cantica conuenientia ipsi tempori uel sollempnitati, sicut in hymnario habentur.[275]

55   Si Natiuitas sancti Iohannis baptiste in dominica die euenerit, omnes lectiones et omnia responsoria de ipso Iohanne uolumus tenere.[276] Similiter de Adsumptione et Natiuitate sanctae Mariae[a][277] et festiuitate sancti Michaelis:[b][278] si dominica die occurrerint pleniter de illis tenere uolumus. Item in festiuitate omnium sanctorum[279] et omnium apostolorum idipsum facimus, nisi quae in Aduentu Domini aut a Septuagessima usque Pasca occurrerint. In aliis uero festiuitatibus quas populus non celebrat, si plenam habent hystoriam, si dominicis diebus aduenerint, primam [p. 261] sedem et tertiam de illis recitemus et secundam de dominica.[280]

56   Ferialibus namque diebus more solito ante missam letanie canende sunt,[281] et qui epistolam legit et qui patenam portat ieiuni id faciant.[282]

57   Regula sancta dicit teneri interuallum estiuis noctibus,[283] sed nos in Bryttannia degentes, breuiores noctes habentes estate Beneuentanis,[284] dicimus sufficere nobis pro interuallo quattuor psalmos quos canimus pro rege, duos post

---

51 a in] *om. MS; em. Bateson; cf. Sacr.Greg., no.* 508
52 a antiphonario] antiphanario *MS*
53 a septem] .vi.[tem] *abbrev. MS; see commentary*
54 a semper] seper *MS*
55 a Mariae] *capitals*
   b Michaelis] Michahelis *MS; capitals*

Translation

51 At the beginning of the Vigil of Pentecost, the first lesson 'God tempted Abraham' is to be read, [followed by] the collect 'O God, who in [the deed] of thy [servant] Abraham' and so forth, as found in the sacramentary, and we sing sevenfold, fivefold and threefold litanies, just as at the Easter Vigil. But on this day, at the proper time, we chant Vespers with the responsory and hymn in the usual way.

52 During the night before [Pentecost] Sunday, the Office of Nocturns is said with three psalms and the same number of readings and responsories, as in the antiphoner. But at the rest of the hours of the day and in the following week the regular order shall be observed. During that week, 'Glory to God in the highest' shall be sung at mass, except on the days of fasting.

53 On the Octave of Pentecost, the liturgy [beginning] 'The Spirit of the Lord' shall not be repeated, because we should celebrate the coming of the Holy Spirit for seven days only. On that [Sunday and in the following] week, rather, [the liturgy] of the Holy Trinity shall be celebrated.

54 In the entire summer period, until the Kalends of November, the hymn 'Deus creator omnium' is sung [at Vespers] on Saturday evening, at Nocturns 'Nocte surgentes', at Lauds 'Ecce iam noctis', at Vespers 'Lucis creator' and every night at Compline 'Te lucis ante terminum'. But on ferias they shall always sing ferial hymns, and on feast days [hymns] proper to the feast, as well as three canticles proper to the season or solemnity throughout the entire year, as in the hymnal.

55 If the Nativity of St John the Baptist should fall on a Sunday, we desire to retain all the readings and all the responsories about John himself. The same [rule applies] for [the feasts of] the Assumption and Nativity of St Mary and the feast of St Michael: should [any of these] occur on a Sunday, we desire to retain [their liturgies] in full. Again, we do the same for the feast of All Saints and [the feasts] of all the apostles, except for those which occur in Advent or [in the period] from Septuagesima to Easter. But as for other feasts not observed by the laity, if they fall on Sunday and have a full history [of their own], let us read about them in the first and third position, and about the Sunday in the second.

56 On ferias litanies are to be sung before mass in the usual way, and he who reads the epistle and he who carries the paten are to fast.

57 The holy *Rule* says that, on summer nights, an interval is to be observed [between Nocturns and Lauds], but we who live in Britain, having shorter nights in the summer than they do in Benevento, say that the four psalms we sing for the king – two after Nocturns and two after Lauds – together with Lauds of All Saints are for us a sufficient substitute for the [prescribed] interval.

nocturnam et duos post matutinales laudes, et insuper matutinales laudes quas de omnibus sanctis canimus.[285]

58   Consuetudo docet debere sonari primum signum ad nocturnam semper et ad uesperam tamdiu usquequo scola ingrediatur in ecclesiam ad orationem.[286] Mos etiam apud nos inoleuit omnibus festiuis diebus, in quibus ab opere cessatur, pulsare omnia signa ad nocturnas, ante missam, ante uesperam.[287]

59   Si deficiant nobis officia aestate,[288] nos repetamus iterum decantata, quantum nobis sufficit, sed non canimus 'Dicit Dominus: Ego cogito cogitationes pacis' nisi una ebdomada ante Aduentum Domini.[289]

60   Consuetudo quoque docet auditorium habendum in monasterio,[290] ut in eo[a] liceat loqui pro necessitate aliqua quando fratres uacant lectionibus seu post uesperam.

61   Quattuor Temporibus ieiuniorum[291] dicatur ad missam 'Flectamus genua',[292] et eadem abstinentia quae in Quadragessima fit[293] custodiatur.

62   Mandatum omni sabbato faciendum fratribus regula sancta satis monet,[294] [p. 262] sed insuper consuetudo docet omni die trium pauperum ex his, qui in monasterio iugiter pascuntur,[295] fratres uicissim debere lauare pedes et aquam[a] manibus infundere loco apto, ac uictualia, quibus fratres utuntur, ipsis praebere. Cui obedientiae adsit ipse abbas quotienscumque ei uacauerit, nam de susceptione hospitum regula docet.[296]

63   Monet etiam consuetudo ut nullus laicorum habeat dominium[a][297] super monasterium ubi regula sancta tenetur, nisi rex solus ad munimen loci, non ad tirannidem.[298]

64   Nec quispiam secularium in refectorio manducet aut bibat, excepto rege et filiis eius,[299] aut abbas seu fratres extra refectorium manducent uel bibant, nisi causa infirmitatis, siue secularia conuiuia temerario ausu adire presumant.[300]

65   Cum quislibet frater infirmatur,[301] si senserit suam creuisse inbecillitatem, indicetur hoc abbati[302] et fiat missa matutinalis pro eo. Et eant ministri illius missae induti albis cum eucharistia et cereis et turibulo cum omni congregatione ad uisitandum infirmum,[303] canentes psalmos paenitentiales, consequente letania[304] et orationibus ac unctione olei (prima tantum die). Tunc demum communicetur. Quod si infirmitas leuigata fuerit, intermittatur et hoc; sin alias, prosequatur uisitatio usque ad exitum.

60 a eo] *corr. from* ea, *with* a *not expunged*
62 a aquam] aqua *MS*
63 a dominium] dñm *(? dominum) abbrev. MS; cf. RC* 10

Translation

58 The customary teaches that the first bell for Nocturns and for Vespers always ought to be rung for as long as it takes the *schola* to enter the church to pray. The custom has also grown up among us of ringing all the bells at Nocturns, before mass and before Vespers on all feast days when no work is done.

59 Should we run out of liturgies in the summer period, we are to repeat a sufficient number of those that have already been sung; but we do not sing [the mass beginning] 'The Lord saith: I think thoughts of peace' except in the week before Advent.

60 The customary also teaches that there is to be an *auditorium* in the monastery, so that one may, for some pressing need, converse in that place after Vespers or when the brothers have retired to their reading.

61 On Ember Days, 'Let us kneel' shall be said at mass, and the same abstinence shall be observed as during Lent.

62 The holy *Rule* plainly admonishes that the brothers are to carry out the maundy every Saturday, but in addition to this the customary teaches that every day, in a place suited to this purpose, the brothers should take turns washing the feet and pouring water over the hands of three of the paupers who are regularly fed in the monastery, and that they should provide them with the same food that the brothers themselves enjoy. Even the abbot shall take part in this work of service as often as he has leisure to do so, for the *Rule* provides instruction concerning the treatment of guests.

63 The customary also warns that no layman shall have dominion over [any] monastery where the holy *Rule* is observed, save the king alone – and even he for the protection of the place, not the exercise of tyranny over it.

64 Nor shall any person of secular estate eat or drink in the refectory, except for the king and his sons. Nor shall the abbot or brothers eat or drink outside the refectory (except for reason of illness) or with reckless audacity presume to attend feasts held by secular persons.

65 When any of the brothers becomes ill, if he feels that his infirmity has increased, this shall be made known to the abbot, and the matutinal mass shall be offered for him. The ministers of that mass, vested in albs and attended by the whole community, shall proceed with the eucharist, candles and a thurible to visit the sick man, singing [the seven] penitential psalms, followed by a litany, prayers and an anointing [of the sick] with oil (this anointing is to be done on the first day only). Then, finally, [the sick man] shall be given communion. Should his sickness abate, this [visitation] shall be suspended too; otherwise it shall be carried out [daily] until his death.

66   Eo igitur in extremis agente pulsetur tabula conueniantque omnes ad tuendum exitum eius, et initient commendationem anime 'Subuenite [p. 263] sancti Dei'[305] iuxta ordinem commendationis.[a] Exempto autem homine lauetur corpus a quibus iussum fuerit. Lotum induitur mundis uestimentis − id est interula, cuculla, caligis, calceis − cuiuscumque sit ordinis. Si[b] sacerdos fuerit, circumdatur ei stola super cucullam, si ita ratio dictauerit.[306] Inde fertur in ecclesiam, psallentibus cunctis motisque omnibus signis. Et si eodem die non possit sepeliri ante refectionem fratrum, uacent fratres psalmodie pernoctantes circa corpus donec, mane facto, missam celebrent pro anima eius,[307] offerentibus cunctis, et sic cadauer terre commendetur.

67   Reuertentes uero a sepultura fratres incipiant septem psalmos, quos prostrati in choro finiant cum dominica oratione et collecta.[308] Dehinc per septem continuos dies, omnibus horis finitis, unum ex supradictis prostrati canant psalmum,[309] sequente oratione, et uigilia pleniter agatur[310] pro eo ac missa matutinalis, omnibus offerentibus. Exinde usque ad tricessimum diem agatur uigilia pro eo cum tribus lectionibus et missa matutinalis, offerente uno choro. Sacerdotum[a] quoque unusquisque triginta missas pro anima defuncti fratris deuote celebret, et alii fratres in psalmodiis, in quantum ualent, illam adiuuent.[311] Tricessimo uero die item pleniter agant uigiliam et missam primam, omnibus offerentibus pro eo. Et nomen eius notetur in anniuersariis.[312]

68   Mittatur et epistola ad uicina quaeque monasteria eiusdem depositionis denuntiatura diem, [p. 264] ut iste sit sensus: 'Dominus (ille) abbas monasterii (illius)[313] cunctis sanctae ecclesiae fidelibus, tam prelatis quam et subditis. Cum cunctos maneat sors inreuocabilis hore, notum uobis esse cupimus de quodam fratre nostro (N.), quem Dominus de ergastulo huius saeculi uocare dignatus est die (illo), pro quo, obsecramus obnixe, ut sitis strennui interuentores ad Dominum sentiatque in interuentione quibus fuerat unitus in ordinis communione.'

69   Quod si ex alio monasterio noto[314] quis frater nuntiatur defunctus, pulsetur tabula et, sonante campana, quindecim graduum psalmos[315] modulentur pro anima eius. Et prima die, septima, tricessima,[316] pleniter agatur pro eo, reliquis uero sub breuitate. Si autem ex ignoto monasterio quis frater defunctus nuntietur, commendatio anime et una dies tantum pro eo agatur.

Oratio pro defuncto fratre:[a][317] 'Satisfaciat[b] tibi, Domine Deus noster, pro

66 a ordinem commendationis] orationem commendatis MS, em. Nocent; cf. RC 99
   b ordinis. Si] ordinis nisi si MS; cf. RC 99 and RC (Kornexl), p. 376
67 a sacerdotum] sacerdotes MS; em. Nocent
69 a Oratio pro defuncto fratre] red capitals
   b Satisfaciat] S green initial

66   When he is on the verge of death, then, the *tabula* shall be struck and all shall assemble to keep watch at his passing; and they shall begin the *commendatio animae*: 'Come to [his] assistance, ye saints of God', according to the commendation rite. Once the man is dead, his body shall be washed by those on whom the task is enjoined. After being washed, the body is clothed in clean garments, namely, a shirt, a cowl, stockings and shoes – all of these regardless of his rank. If he was a priest, a stole is placed over the cowl around [his neck], if resources permit. Then he is borne into the church while all chant and all the bells are rung. And if he cannot be buried on that same day before the brothers take their meal, they shall keep watch around the body overnight and devote themselves to recitation of the psalms until, come morning, they may celebrate mass for his soul (at which all shall present the offerings), and the body be thus committed to the earth.

67   As the brothers return from the burial, they shall begin the seven psalms and finish these prostrate in choir, adding the Lord's Prayer and a collect. Then for the next seven days at the end of every [liturgical] hour they shall prostrate themselves and sing one of the aforesaid psalms, followed by a collect, and full Vigils [of the Dead] shall be said on his behalf, as well as the matutinal mass, at which all shall make the offering. From then on, up to the thirtieth day, Vigils [of the Dead] of three lessons shall be said for him, as shall the matutinal mass, but with [only] one choir making the offering. Also, every single priest shall reverently celebrate thirty masses for the soul of the deceased brother, and the other brothers are to assist [his soul] as much as they are able by reciting the psalms. But on the thirtieth day, they shall again say Vigils [of the Dead] in full on his behalf, as well as the first mass, at which [again] all shall make the offering. And his name shall be entered in the anniversaries.

68   And a letter shall be sent to all the neighboring monasteries to make known the date of his burial. The sense of [the letter] shall be: 'The lord abbot N. of the monastery N. to all the faithful of the holy church, both those in authority and those subject to them. Whereas the fate of that irrevocable hour lies in store for all, we wish to notify you concerning a certain brother of ours, N., whom the Lord has deigned to call from the prison of this world on the day N. We humbly beg that you would tirelessly intercede to the Lord on his behalf and that in your intercession he might recognize to whom he had been united in monastic fellowship.'

69   But should word come that some brother from another, familiar monastery has died, the *tabula* shall be struck and, while the bell is being rung, they shall chant the fifteen gradual psalms for his soul. And on the first, seventh and thirtieth day, [Vigils of the Dead] shall be said in full for him, but in

anima fratris nostri (N.) beatae Dei genitricis semperque uirginis Mariae atque sancti Benedicti confessoris tui omniumque sanctorum tuorum[318] oratio et praesentis familiae tuae deuota supplicatio, ut peccatorum omnium ueniam quam precamur optineat, nec eum patiaris cruciari gehennalibus flammis, quem eiusdem Filii tui Domini nostri Iesu Christi glorioso sanguine redemisti. Qui tecum.'

Finiunt consuetudines.[c][319]

70   Quia[a] rogastis fratres scribi uobis qualiter legere siue cantare per anni circulum in ecclesia debeatis, exponam uobis secundum auctoritatem ecclesiasticam [p. 265] et secundum consuetudinem in qua hucusque conuersati sumus,[320] ita ut in Septuagessima legamus Genesim usque in mediam Quadragessimam,[321] et in primis canimus una die tantum hystoriam 'Alleluia dum praesens est'.[322] Et in tota ebdomada canimus responsoria de psalmis 'Quam magna multitudo' et cetera,[323] deinde aliis ebdomadibus sicut in antiphonario habetur canimus. Media uero Quadragessima legimus Exodum et canimus 'Locutus est Dominus ad Moysen'.[324] In Passione Domini, id est <duas>[b] ebdomadas ante Pascha, legimus Hieremiam prophetam[325] usque in Cenam Domini et canimus una ebdomada 'Isti sunt dies', altera uero 'In die qua inuocaui te'.[326] Sed hoc ipsum responsorium 'Isti sunt dies' non est canendum nisi dominica die, quia fallit cantor si aliis diebus cantet, 'Quarta decima die ad uesperum Pasca Domini est', cum non sit integer numerus dierum nisi a dominica die.[327]

In Cena Domini legimus lectiones .iii. de Lamentatione Hieremie et tractatus sancti[c] Augustini de psalmo 'Exaudi Deus orationem meam cum deprecor' .iii., et tres de apostolo[328] ubi ait 'Ego autem accepi a Domino quod et tradidi uobis'. Feria .vi. in primis lectiones .iii. de Lamentatione Hieremie et tres de tractu sancti Augustini de eodem psalmo et tres de apostolo ubi ait 'Festinemus ingredi in illam requiem'.[329] In Sabbato Sancto similiter omnia[d] complenda sunt, sed in tertia sede legimus de tractu euuangelii sicut in toto anno facimus.[330] Nam his tribus noctibus canimus sicut [p. 266] antiphonarium nos docet.

71   In dominica Pascae et in tota ebdomada illa legimus tres lectiones de tractibus euuangeliorum ipsius festiuitatis,[331] et canimus in prima nocte

---

   c Finiunt consuetudines] *red capitals*
70 a Quia] Q *red initial*
   b duas] *om. MS; em. Nocent*
   c sancti] sū *abbrev. MS; em. Nocent*
   d omnia] omiam *abbrev. with titulus over* a *instead of* i *MS*

shortened form on the remaining days. Should word come, moreover, that some brother from an unknown monastery has died, only the *commendatio animae* and a single day's [commemoration] shall be performed.

A prayer on behalf of a brother who has died: 'May the prayer of the blessed Mother of God and ever Virgin, Mary, of your holy confessor Benedict, and of all your saints, together with the fervent supplication of your present family, O Lord our God, be a satisfaction to you on behalf of the soul of our brother, *N*.: that for all his sins he may obtain that mercy for which we pray, and that you would not permit him to be tormented by the flames of hell whom you have redeemed by the glorious blood of your Son our Lord Jesus Christ, who [lives and reigns] with you', etc.

Here end the customs.

70   Because you have asked, brothers, to have written down for you how you are supposed to read or sing in church through the course of the year, I will explain [it] to you according to both ecclesiastical ordinance and the custom by which we have lived up until now, to the effect that: in Septuagesima we should read Genesis until mid-Lent, and we sing the history 'Alleluia: While it is present' first and for one day only, and for the week as a whole we sing the responsories from the psalms, 'O how great is the multitude' and so forth. Then, in the other weeks, we sing what is found in the antiphoner. But [from] mid-Lent we read Exodus and sing 'The Lord said to Moses'. In Passiontide, that is, for the two weeks before Easter, we read the prophet Jeremiah until Maundy Thursday and sing in one week 'These are the days' and, in the next, 'In the day when I called upon thee'. But the aforesaid responsory 'These are the days' is not to be sung except on [Passion] Sunday, for the cantor errs if on other days he sings, 'On the evening of the fourteenth day [from now] is the Passover of the Lord', since the number is not a full [fourteen days] except from [Passion] Sunday.

On Maundy Thursday we read three lessons from the Lamentations of Jeremiah and three from St Augustine's exposition of the psalm 'Hear, O God, my prayer, when I make supplication to thee' and three from the Apostle, where he says, 'For I have received of the Lord that which also I delivered unto you'. On Friday, first [come] three readings from the Lamentations of Jeremiah, and [then] three from St Augustine's exposition of the aforementioned psalm and three from the Apostle, where he says, 'Let us hasten [therefore] to enter into that rest.' On Holy Saturday everything is to be carried out in a similar way, save that we read from an exposition of the gospel in the third position, as we do throughout the entire year. In these three nights we sing as the antiphoner instructs us.

71   On Easter and in the whole week [thereafter] we read three lessons from homilies on the gospel readings for that same feast, and on the first night we

'Angelus Domini', aliis uero noctibus canimus 'Maria Magdalene'[332] et cetera. In octauis Pasce legimus de epistolis canonicis[333] et repetamus 'Maria Magdalene'. In dominica post octauas Pasce legimus Apocalipsin usque Ascensionem Domini,[334] et canimus duobus ebdomadibus 'Ego sicut uitis'.[335] Post hoc canimus 'Narrabo nomen tuum'[336] usque Ascensionem Domini. In Ascensione Domini legimus tres lectiones de capite Actuum Apostolorum et postea sermones de eadem festiuitate,[337] et canimus 'Post Passionem Domini'[338] usque Pentecosten.

72 In Pentecosten tota ebdomada legimus tres lectiones de tractibus euuangeliorum,[339] et canimus 'Dum complerentur'.[340] In octauis Pentecosten legimus et canimus de sancta Trinitate.[341] Dominica post octabas Pentecosten ponimus Regum[342] usque in dominicam primam mensis Augusti, et canimus 'Deus omnium'.[343]

73 Omnibus uero festiuitatibus sanctorum in toto anno legimus uitas aut passiones ipsorum sanctorum siue sermones congruentes ipsi sollempnitati et responsoria propria, si habeantur. Sin alias, alia congruentia canimus et tertiam sedem de tractu euuangelii sicut et ubique semper sumimus.[344]

74 In dominica prima mensis Augusti ponimus Salomonem[345] usque in Kalendas Septembris, et canimus 'In principio'.[346] In Kalendis Septembris legimus Iob duobus ebdomadibus[347] et canimus 'Si bona'.[348] In tertia septimana eiusdem mensis legimus [p. 267] Tobiam[349] et canimus 'Peto Domine'.[350] In quarta septimana ponimus Iudith, Hester et Ezdra, et canimus 'Tribulationes'[351] et cetera. Dominica prima mensis Octobris ponimus libros Machabeorum et canimus 'Adaperiat'[352] usque Kalendas Nouembris.[a] Mense uero Nouembre legimus Ezechielem et Danielem et minores prophetas,[353] et canimus 'Vidi Dominum'[354] usque Aduentum Domini.

75 In Aduentu Domini legimus Isaiam[355] usque Natiuitatem Domini et canimus prima ebdomada[a] 'Aspiciens',[356] et 'Dominus regnauit' ad matutinales laudes sicut et in Septuagessima, sed hic omnibus dominicis et ibi Septuagessima sola.[357] Ceteris septimanis canimus sicut in antiphonario habetur.

76 In Natale Domini legimus lectiones .iii. de Esaia, quarum prima est 'Primo tempore alleuiata est', secunda 'Consolamini', <tertia>[a] 'Consurge, consurge, induere',[358] deinde sermones catholicorum[b] patrum de eodem die, et canimus 'Hodie nobis'.[359]

74 a Nouembris] Nouembrium *MS*
75 a prima ebdomada] primo ebdomade *MS; em. Nocent*
76 a tertia] .ii.[a] *sic MS*
    b catholicorum] chatholicorum *MS*

Translation

sing 'An angel of the Lord', but on the other nights we sing 'Mary Magdalene' and so forth. On the Octave of Easter we read from the canonical epistles and should repeat 'Mary Magdalene'. On the Sunday after the Octave of Easter we read the Apocalypse, until [the feast of] the Ascension, and for two weeks we sing 'I am as the vine'. After this we sing 'I will declare thy name', until Ascension Day. On Ascension we read three lessons from the beginning of the Acts of the Apostles and afterwards sermons on the same feast, and we sing 'After the Passion of the Lord', until Pentecost.

72   On Pentecost and for the entire week [thereafter] we read three lessons from homilies on the gospels, and we sing 'When [the days of the Pentecost] were accomplished'. On the Octave of Pentecost we read and sing of the Holy Trinity. To the Sunday after the Octave of Pentecost we allot the Book of Kings until the first Sunday of the month of August, and we sing 'God [hears the prayers] of all'.

73   But on all feasts of the saints, throughout the entire year, we read lives or passions of the saints themselves, or sermons appropriate to the given solemnity, and [we sing] proper responsories, if these are to be had; if not, we sing other appropriate ones and adopt for the third position [readings] from a homily on the gospel, as we do always and everywhere.

74   [From] the first Sunday of the month of August until the Kalends of September we assign [the books of] Solomon, and we sing 'In the beginning'. [From] the Kalends of September we read Job for two weeks and sing 'If [we have received] good things'. In the third week of the same month we read Tobit and sing 'I beg, O Lord'. To the fourth week we assign Judith, Esther and Esdras and sing '[We have heard] the tribulations' and the rest. [To] the first Sunday of the month of October until the Kalends of November we allot the books of the Maccabees and sing 'May he open [your heart]'. But in the month of November we read Ezechiel, Daniel and the minor prophets and sing 'I saw the Lord', until Advent.

75   In Advent we read Isaiah, until Christmas, and in the first week we sing 'I look from afar' and, at Lauds, [the psalm] 'The Lord hath reigned' just as in Septuagesima (but then on Septuagesima [Sunday] only, here [in Advent] on every Sunday). In the remaining weeks we sing what is found in the antiphoner.

76   On Christmas we read three lessons from Isaiah, of which the first is 'At the first time [the land of Zabulon, and the land of Nephtali] was lightly touched', the second 'Be comforted' [and] the third 'Arise, arise, put on [thy strength]', then sermons on the same day by the church fathers, and we sing 'To us this day'.

77   In dominica siue feria uacante ab Innocentibus usque Epiphaniam legimus et canimus de ipsa festiuitate Natiuitatis Domini.³⁶⁰ In Octauis Domini legimus sermones congruentes ipsi diei, et responsoria de Natiuitate Domini canimus.³⁶¹ Nos tenemus etiam octauas sancti Stephani et sancti Iohannis et sanctorum Innocentium, et de ipsis legimus et canimus.³⁶²

In Epiphania Domini legimus tres lectiones[a] de Isaia, primam 'Omnes sitientes', .ii. 'Surge inluminare', .iii. 'Gaudens gaudebo in Domino',³⁶³ deinde sermones de ipsa festiuitate, et sic legimus et canimus de ipsa sollempnitate usque in octauas Epiphaniae. Prima dominica post octauas [p. 268] Epiphaniae legimus epistolas Pauli uel tractus psalmorum³⁶⁴ usque Septuagessimam, et canimus 'Domine ne in ira tua'³⁶⁵ et in singulis feriis tria responsoria de psalmis, sicut in antiphonario habentur.

78   Et sciendum quod tota bibliotheca debet legi in circulo anni in ecclesia, sed quia nos pigri serui sumus et segnes, legimus in refectorio quicquid de ea in ecclesia omittimus.³⁶⁶

79   In libris quoque prophetarum in quibus increpatio et obiurgatio fit ad populum, sicut in Hieremia, Ezechiele, Isaiae, dicimus post lectiones 'Haec dicit Dominus Deus exercituum: Conuertimini ad me et salui eritis.' In aliis uero, in quibus quasi hystoria narratur, dicimus 'Tu autem Domine, miserere nostri.'³⁶⁷

80   Volo etiam uos scire, fratres karissimi, ualde gratum mihi fore quod obedienter mihi consensistis in hoc, ut tres lectiones cum totidem responsoriis tota aestate ad nocturnas sicut hieme iam preteritis annis tenuimus,³⁶⁸ quod nolumus uita comite deserere ferialibus noctibus; et quod missas dominicas in Quadragessima secunda et tertia feria ad primam missam repetitis, ut saltem ter celebrentur.³⁶⁹ Similiter omnes dominicas missas <repetatis>[a] ut, si festiuitates intercurrant, tantummodo ter celebrentur in ebdomada, ne uilescere uideantur.³⁷⁰

Valete feliciter in Christo, dilectissimi fratres.

77 a lectiones] lectionis *MS; em. Nocent*
80 a repetatis] *not in MS; see commentary*

Translation

77   From [the feast of the Holy] Innocents until Epiphany, on Sunday and on ordinary ferias we read and sing as on the feast of Christmas itself. On the Octave of Christmas we read sermons appropriate to the day and sing the Christmas responsories. We also observe the Octaves [of the feasts] of SS Stephen and John and of the Holy Innocents, and we read and sing about them.

On Epiphany we read three lessons from Isaiah: the first 'All you that thirst', the second 'Arise, be enlightened' and the third 'I will greatly rejoice', then sermons on the feast itself. And so we read and sing about the same solemnity until the Octave of Epiphany. [From] the first Sunday after the Octave of Epiphany until Septuagesima we read the epistles of Paul or expositions of the psalms, and we sing '[Rebuke me] not, O Lord, in thy indignation', and on ferias [we sing] three responsories from the psalms, as in the antiphoner.

78   And be it known that, in the course of a year, the entire canon [of Scripture] ought to be read in church, but because we are lazy and slothful servants, we read in the refectory whatever we do not cover in church.

79   Also, in the books of the prophets, in which a rebuke or reproach is delivered against the people, as in Jeremiah, Ezechiel [or] Isaiah, we say after the lessons, 'Thus says the Lord God of hosts: Turn to me and you will be saved.' But in other [lessons], in which a narrative, as it were, is recounted, we say, 'But thou, O Lord, have mercy on us.'

80   I also wish you to know, dearest brothers, how very pleased I am that you have obediently agreed with me on this matter: namely, that for years now we have retained three lessons and the same number of responsories at Nocturns for the whole summer period just as in winter – [a custom] which we do not wish to abandon on ferial nights, so long as we live; and [how pleased I am] that in Lent at the first mass for Mondays and Tuesdays you repeat the Sunday masses, so that these are celebrated at least three times. [You should repeat] all Sunday masses in this same way so that, even if feast days intervene, they are celebrated as many as three times in the week, lest their worth appear diminished.

I bid you health and happiness in Christ, most beloved brothers.

Commentary

I Preface (LME 1)

LME   Ælfric's prefatory letter

[1] *Ælfricus abbas ... salutem in Christo*   For nearly all of his published works Ælfric composed epistolary or dedicatory prefaces in Latin, Old English or both, in which he typically stated his motives for writing the text, the identity of his intended audience and a summary of the authorities on whom he has depended. For a convenient collected edition of all the prefaces and discussion of Ælfric's uses of this highly conventional form, see *Ælfric's Prefaces*, ed. Wilcox, esp. pp. 65–71. Ælfric's prefaces contain biographical information that accounts for most of what is known about his career. Although Ælfric elsewhere styles himself 'abbot', his remarks at *LME* 1, 70 and 80 provide the only specific evidence that he held this office at Eynsham. On this debate, see above, pp. 4–10.

[2] *nuper rogatu Æþelmæri*   For reasons unknown, Æthelmær, son of Ælfric's long-time patron, Ealdorman Æthelweard of the western shires, withdrew from King Æthelred's court and endowed a monastery at Eynsham. There, according to the royal charter of confirmation dated 1005 (S 911), it was his intention to live out the rest of his days 'as a father' among the monks. On the foundation, date and Æthelmær's career thereafter, see ch. 1. On the interpretation of *nuper* and its implications for the chronology of Ælfric's career, see also commentary to *LME* 80.

[3] *libro consuetudinum*   In the technical vocabulary of medieval monasticism, the terms *consuetudo* and *consuetudines* came to refer to customs which, though not explicitly prescribed by Benedict's *Rule*, were vital parts of the regular life. The *liber consuetudinum* here mentioned is the *Regularis concordia*, a collection of such customs drawn up by Ælfric's mentor, St Æthelwold. For an overview of Ælfric's adaptation of this source, see above, pp. 19–58. As used throughout the *LME*, however, the terms *consuetudo*

Commentary

and *consuetudines* seem to mean not 'monastic custom' in general but rather serve as short titles for Æthelwold's specific *liber consuetudinum*. When Ælfric tags an instruction with 'consuetudo (docet)', he is, as it were, 'footnoting' his source, the *Regularis concordia*; see instances at *LME* 26, 28–30, 33, 36–7, 40, 58, 60, 62–3 and perhaps 69.

[4] *Aðelwoldus Wintoniensis episcopus*   Æthelwold, bishop of Winchester from 29 November 963 until his death on 1 August 984. The best survey of his life and career is found in the introduction to *Life of St Æthelwold*, ed. Lapidge and Winterbottom, pp. xxxix–ci and cxii–cxliii.

[5] *undique collegit ac monachis instituit obseruandum*   On the value of Ælfric's statement as evidence for Æthelwold's authorship of the *Regularis concordia*, against the long-standing attribution to Dunstan, see *RC* (Kornexl), pp. xxxviii–xxxix.

[6] *hactenus . . . incognitus habetur*   This statement has been read as evidence that the liturgical unity by fiat, seemingly advocated in the proem of the *Concordia*, did not long outlive Æthelwold (d. 984) and Dunstan (d. 988), if it ever existed at all. Still others have cited Ælfric's statement as evidence that even in the beginning the *Concordia* was never imposed on all English monasteries as an absolute standard; see the excellent summary of the debate in *RC* (Kornexl), pp. li–lvi and cliv. Kornexl urges caution against the assumption that the *LME* indicates a waning influence of the *Concordia*.

[7] *in scola eius . . . didici*   Ælfric proudly refers several times to his training at Æthelwold's cathedral (the Old Minster), Winchester: for example, in the Latin preface to his First Series of *Catholic Homilies*, as well as in those to the *Grammar*, the *Vita S. Æthelwoldi* and the *LME* (all discussed in *Ælfric's Prefaces*, ed. Wilcox, p. 7). Such statements, however sincere as expressions of personal loyalty and indebtedness, also publicize their author's impressive credentials. Ælfric enjoyed an intellectual and ecclesiastical pedigree that would bolster his authority within the walls of his own house and establish his credibility before the wider audience of his published works.

[8] *de libro Amalarii presbiteri*   Clearly, what is being referred to is the *Liber officialis* (often called the *De ecclesiasticis officiis*) of Amalarius of Metz (d. 852 or 853). Ælfric does not appear to have known the full text, however, but the two-book post-Amalarian redaction now known as the *Retractatio prima*, and that in a further adapted version. On Amalarius's work and Ælfric's use of it in the *LME* and elsewhere, see above, pp. 59–68.

II *Basic ferial horarium* a Kalendis Octobris (LME 2–4)

LME 2   The diurnal order; cf. *RC* 15, 22–6 and 33

[9] *prima canenda est*, etc.   Departing from his source (*RC* 15) Ælfric begins not with the monks' rising for Nocturns, but with the first of the 'little hours' (Prime). His decision to do so is not easily explained, but as noted in the introduction (pp. 27–32), the opening sections of the *LME* condense and re-order provisions for: (i) the horarium in its transitional period between summer and full winter forms, and (ii) two of the major

Commentary

supplementary devotions introduced, or at least standardized, by the *Concordia*. The choice to begin with Prime may also echo the disposition of psalms in the Benedictine *cursus*, which assigns Ps. I to Prime on Monday (*RSB*, c. XVIII.4). For an overview of Ælfric's reworking of this material, see the table in ch. 2 (above, p. 32).

10 *septem psalmis et letaniis*   That is, the seven penitential psalms: VI, XXXI, XXXVII, L, CI, CXXIX and CXLII. The *Concordia* gives a fuller picture of the monks' devotions after Prime, including the penitential psalms, but with the added detail at *RC* 22, 'deuote interposito psalmo *Inclina Domine*' (Ps. LXXXV) – although where and how the extra psalm shall be 'inserted' is not clear. Neither Ælfric nor the *Concordia* ever specifies the precise form of the litany after Prime, although the latter does indicate that the litany shall be sung prostrate (*RC* 22). This devotion almost certainly took the form of a litany of the saints, numerous examples of which survive in English manuscripts from the eighth century onwards. On their function in the *Concordia*, see *Anglo-Saxon Litanies of the Saints*, ed. Lapidge, p. 44. The devotions after Prime are also mentioned by the *puer* in Ælfric's *Colloquy* (ed. Garmonsway, p. 44, lines 271–2) and are given at length in Latin and Old English in the peculiar bilingual *Benedictine Office* (ed. Ure, pp. 89–94), although the character of this document remains disputed; see J. W. Houghton, 'The Old English Benedictine Office and its Audience', *American Benedictine Review* 45 (1994), 431–45.

11 *signum tertie insonuerit*   Ælfric's expression is slightly misleading since, as context verifies, he clearly means the bell signalling the end of *lectio*, not that signalling the beginning of Terce proper. The source avoids the ambiguity (*RC* 64: 'facto signo eant ad calciendum'), as does the author of a fragmentary Old English translation of the *Concordia* in Cambridge, Corpus Christi College 201, who (in another context) coins the useful term *scocnylle* 'shoe-bell' (see 'Ein weiteres Bruchstück', ed. Zupitza, p. 10, line 115).

12 *orationes faciant*   Ælfric's vague *orationes* may imply a single established routine at Eynsham, but it should be noted that the source (*RC* 23) provides several devotions from which to choose, including the penitential psalms and the secular Office.

13 *scola simul*   Schola here is the collective term for the boys (*pueri*) who live and are schooled in the monastery. These participated fully in the liturgical life of the house and would, when grown, often join the ranks of professed monks (*RC* (Symons), p. xli). Their presence is assumed throughout the *Concordia*, and Eynsham was evidently large enough and adequately staffed to assume the responsibilities of this arrangement. In the *Concordia* the term *schola* is also used of the *schola cantorum* ('choir') in liturgical contexts. The only vestige of this sense in Ælfric's text occurs at *LME* 46 (*q.v.*, based on *RC* 77), where the cantor is given the alternate title *magister scholae*, on which term see D. A. Bullough, 'The Educational Tradition in England from Alfred to Ælfric: Teaching *utriusque linguae*', rev. and repr. in his *Carolingian Renewal*, pp. 297–334, at 309.

14 *prima missa . . . missam de die*   Two daily communal masses were the assumed norm by the time the *Concordia* was compiled. The earlier, variously termed the 'first' or 'matutinal' (or 'morrow' or 'Chapter') mass, was celebrated after Prime in the summer period, after Terce in the winter; cf. OE *capitolmæsse* in the *Dictionary of Old English: C*,

Commentary

ed. A. C. Amos *et al.* (Toronto, 1988). The second mass (also 'mass of the day' or 'principal mass') took place after Terce in the summer period, after Sext in the winter. The *Concordia* implies a lay presence at the principal mass on major feasts (*RC* 28), but no firm conclusions can be drawn from Ælfric's silence on this point.

LME 3   The *trina oratio*; cf. *RC* 17–18, 24 and 37–8

15 *ter . . . orationes tres in oratorio*   Where the *Concordia* provides a detailed breakdown of the components of this devotion (the *trina oratio*) across the horarium, Ælfric allows this greatly condensed treatment to serve once and for all. The relative economy of the *LME* at this point may indicate that the *trina oratio* was already familiar to the Eynsham monks, though whether or not as a direct result of the *Concordia* cannot be known. The devotion as described in the *Concordia* consists of three groups of psalms, each group to be said with further prayers and a special collect – given in full in the *Concordia* – for a specific intention. Thus before Nocturns the seven penitential psalms are said in the groupings: Pss. VI, XXXI and XXXVII + Lord's Prayer and collect (for the monk's own soul); Pss. L and CI + Lord's Prayer and collect (for the king); Pss. CXXIX and CXLII + Lord's Prayer and collect (for the dead). The form of the *trina oratio* before Prime (or before Terce in the winter) is not specified in the *Concordia*. After Compline the order is: Pss. XII and XLII + 'Kyrie' + Lord's Prayer + *preces* and a collect; Pss. LXVI and CXXVI + 'Kyrie', etc.; Ps. CXXIX + 'Kyrie', etc. (no intentions are specified for any of these). For a discussion of the *trina oratio* and its development, see Tolhurst, pp. 57–64; Symons, 'A Note on the Trina Oratio', *DR* 42 (1924), 67–83; *idem*, 'Notes on a History of Benedictinism', *DR* 61 (1948), 191–203, at 191–4; and Roper, pp. 37–8 and 203–5 (Table 2:4). For analogues in continental customaries, see Hallinger's apparatus to *RC* 17, 81.9–82.8.

16 *primo signo*   That is, the first bell rousing the monks for Nocturns.

17 *cum conpunctione . . . omni nocte*   Vestiges, perhaps, of Ælfric's gleaning methods, these provisions technically have nothing to do with the *trina oratio* but have been uprooted and awkwardly transferred, along with the relevant matter, from *RC* 37. The *Concordia* prescribes the order: public confession + Compline + Ps. L + *psalmi familiares* (see commentary to *LME* 4, at nn. 18–31) + *trina oratio* + asperges. It does not mention, but probably did include, Ælfric's *benedictio* presumably the dialogue 'Benedicamus Domino: Deo gratias.'

LME 4   The *psalmi familiares*; cf. *RC* 19, 21, 22, 24, 33, 34 and 37

18 *Pro rege et pro benefactoribus*, etc.   Treated here by Ælfric with the same compression as the *trina oratio* (at *LME* 3), this complex set of devotions for the royal house and benefactors, to be said after every Office (including the principal mass), has been viewed as one of the most distinctive features of the *Concordia*; see Symons, 'Sources', pp. 146–9; cf. Wormald, 'Æthelwold and his Continental Counterparts', pp. 32–3, and *RC* (Kornexl), p. xlvi, n. 59. Ælfric generally tends, however, to downplay the

Commentary

19 *omnibus horis* royalism of his source (see discussion above, pp. 43–9). The retention of these prayers would seem to indicate an entrenched custom, but cf. below, n. 20.

19 *omnibus horis* There is disagreement as to whether or not the *psalmi familiares*, strictly defined, were chanted after Prime. They are not mentioned at the relevant place in *RC* 22, where two additional psalms (with prayers) are prescribed but with different intentions: (a) 'pro carnis temptatione' = Ps. XXXVII + *preces* and collect (both specified); and (b) 'pro defunctis fratribus' = Ps. L (+ *preces*?) + collect (specified). On the basis of these instructions in the *Concordia*, Tolhurst (pp. 82–3), Symons (*RC* (Symons), p. 15 n. 6), Hallinger (apparatus to *RC* 19, 83.14–15) and Roper (p. 30) maintain that psalms for royalty were not said after Prime, in spite of the explicit instruction 'omnibus horis' at *RC* 19 and 31. Against this view, see *RC* (Kornexl), p. lxiv, n. 33. *LME* 4 seems to support the traditional view of Tolhurst and others, but Ælfric's abridgement is too drastic to permit a decisive ruling.

20 *duo psalmi . . . et oratione* Ælfric's distillation of the custom notes the two psalms after every hour but does not specify the collects except to indicate where these shall be proper and where simply 'of the hour'. Proper collects are given in full at *RC* 19, where the following intentions are also specified: the first psalm shall be for the king, the second for the king, queen and benefactors together. Of the three collects then given in full, the first is specifically for the king, the second for the queen, and the third for king, queen and benefactors. Ælfric's simple, unspecified *oratio* may reflect his gentle retreat from the more overt royalism of the *Concordia*: without the special collects and careful division of intentions given in the source, this devotion might easily lose its political cast and come to resemble any other psalm-based devotion in the horarium (of which there were many, including the *trina oratio* and psalms after Chapter). The *Concordia* does not explicitly mention as a regular part of the devotion the Lord's Prayer and *preces*, as Ælfric does. For extensive treatment of this devotion and its components, see Tolhurst, pp. 81–93; Symons, 'Sources', pp. 146–69; and Roper, pp. 35–7, 202–3 (Table 2:3) and 207 (Table 2:5).

21 *'Domine ne in furore tuo' primum*, *'Exaudiat te Dominus'* Pss. VI and XIX. *Primum* indicates that Ælfric intends Ps. VI, the first psalm in numerical sequence (I–CL) beginning 'Domine ne in furore tuo', as opposed to Ps. XXXVII, which has the same incipit.

22 *'Beati quorum'*, *'Inclina Domine'* Pss. XXXI and LXXXV.

23 *sub una collecta illius hore* The corresponding details in the *Concordia* are vague, but Ælfric's form of this devotion seems to depart from the source by incorporating the *psalmi familiares* after Lauds, Vespers and Compline into the domain of those Offices, so that the two added psalms are concluded not by proper collects (like those at *RC* 19), but with the closing prayer of the liturgical hour itself. Tolhurst theorizes that this devotion underwent substantial, gradual change from its earlier form (in the *Concordia*) to that preserved in the *LME*: 'But before the adaptation by abbot Ælfric . . . two alterations had been made: the position of the two psalms at Lauds, Vespers and Compline had been altered and their collects dropped altogether; and the devotion said at Prime had been superseded by another of a different form and said for a different intention. Ælfric, or the version of the Regularis Concordia from which he

Commentary

was working, went still further and added *Pater noster* and preces to the original form as said after Matins and the little hours, and at the same time substituted one collect for the original three' (pp. 83–4). On the other hand, the sparing treatment of the custom in the *LME* also suggests a practice already familiar to the Eynsham community, the senior members of whom would not have been trained by Ælfric, so the assignment of any 'innovations' to him must remain tentative. It also bears repeating that here and elsewhere departures from the *Concordia* may be more apparent than real, the result of arbitrary omissions on the part of Ælfric or, as in the present case, an intermediate source.

[24] '*Domine ne in furore tuo*' (ii) . . . '*Miserere mei, Deus*'   Pss. XXXVII and L. The roman numeral '(ii)' serves the same purpose as the ordinal *primum* discussed above, n. 21.

[25] '*Vsquequo Domine*', '*Miserere mei, Deus, miserere mei*'   Pss. XII and LVI.

[26] '*Deus misereatur nostri*', '*Domine exaudi*' (i)   Pss. LXVI and CI.

[27] '*Exaudiat te Dominus*', '*Ad te leuaui oculos meos*'   Pss. XIX and CXXII.

[28] '*Qui regis Israel*', '*De profundis*'   Pss. LXXIX and CXXIX.

[29] '*Benedixisti Domine*', '*Domine exaudi*' (ii)   Pss. LXXXIV and CXLII.

[30] *coniunctim . . . sinaxis*   See above, n. 23.

[31] '*Deus in adiutorium meum intende*', '*Leuaui oculos meos*'   Pss. LXIX and CXX.

III Variations for the Sunday or festal horarium (LME 5 and 7–10)

LME 5   The order after Prime; cf. RC 27–8 and 83

[32] *Dominicis uero diebus et festiuis*, etc.   At the beginning of his description of the daily horarium, Ælfric warned that the order would fall somewhat differently on Sundays and major feasts (*LME* 2: 'exceptis dominicis et festiuis diebus'), so the backtracking here at *LME* 5 is much less confusing than the corresponding about-face at *RC* 27 (see above, pp. 27–9). Even so, the *LME* presents the same basic festal order as the source. On ferias the order shall be Prime + Terce + matutinal mass + Chapter; but on Sundays and feasts, the order after Prime is reversed, i.e., Chapter + matutinal mass + Terce.

[33] *facto signo a priore*   The phrase is lifted from the *Concordia*, where it is used in the context of the description of the ferial, not the festal order (see *RC* 26; cf. *RSB*, c. XX.5).

[34] *capitolum*   The form of monastic Chapter is taken for granted in the *LME*, although extensive instructions are given within the ferial horarium of the *Concordia*, which include a reading from the martyrology, prayers, a reading from and brief exposition of the *Rule* as well as a public confession of faults (*RC* 26). On the customs for Chapter, see Tolhurst, pp. 50–5, and Knowles, *Monastic Order*, p. 412. Partial instructions in Latin and Old English also survive in the *Benedictine Office*, ed. Ure, pp. 94–5.

[35] *sanctificent salem . . . dominicis diebus tantum*   The procession with asperges pertains to the mass of the day but is mentioned at this point because there would be no pause between Terce and the principal mass. This procession and blessing of holy water are

Commentary

also required by the *Concordia*, although Ælfric's phrase *salem et aquam* is more explicit (cf. *RC* 28: 'consecrationem aspersionis').

36 *Similiter a Pascha . . . capitulum* Similarities between the Sunday order and that for ferias in Eastertide prompt this confusing digression. From these and the preceding details in *LME* 5 we may reconstruct the following horaria:

Ferias *a Kalendis* Octobris:	*Sundays per annum*; also ferias from Easter through the Octave of Pentecost:	Ferias through the summer period *ab Octauis Pentecosten* (cf. *RC* 83):
Prime	Prime	Prime
Terce	Chapter	matutinal mass
matutinal mass	matutinal mass	Chapter
Chapter	Terce	Terce
Sext	mass of the day	mass of the day
mass of the day	Sext	Sext
None	None	None

Although the source does not present this information so succinctly, these parts of Ælfric's horarium agree in outline with the *Concordia*; see *RC* (Symons), pp. xliii–xliv.

LME 6   Extra psalms after Chapter; cf. *RC* 32

37 *Surgentes a capitulo*, etc.   The hazards of a too severe abridgement are evident here. Awkwardly inserted between *LME* 5 and 7, both of which concern the Sunday horarium, this instruction implies that the five additional psalms after Chapter (a practice taken over in the *Concordia* from the eighth-century *Memoriale qualiter*) are likewise only a Sunday custom. In the *Concordia*, however, the instructions corresponding to *LME* 5 and 7 are not similarly interrupted (cf. *RC* 27–8), and the provision for the five psalms after Chapter (*RC* 32) marks a clear return to the description of the ferial horarium. Also, before the *Concordia*-author leaves the ferial to take up the Sunday horarium, he inserts the proleptic remark: 'Finito hoc spiritualis purgaminis negotio [i.e., Chapter faults] quinque psalmos *qui post notantur* pro defunctis fratribus decantent' (*RC* 26, emphasis added). It seems that Ælfric either adapted these sections carelessly for the *LME* or that he himself misunderstood the *Concordia* (but see below, n. 42).

38 *'Verba mea'*   Ps. V.

39 *'Domine ne in furore tuo'*   The clarifying (i) or (ii) is omitted from the manuscript, but the identification as Ps. VI is clear from *RC* 32. The sequence of psalms for this devotion may have been so familiar that a distinguishing number was unnecessary.

40 *'Dilexi quoniam'*, *'Credidi propter'*, *'De profundis'*   Pss. CXIV–CXV and CXXIX.

41 *quos sequatur . . . cum collecta*   These are not explicitly prescribed at *RC* 32.

156

Commentary

LME 7   Sunday horarium, resumed; cf. *RC* 27

42 *Dominicis tamen diebus*, etc.   On the apparent vacillation between festal and ferial customs, see the comments above, at n. 37. Concessive *tamen* here is the only indication that Ælfric correctly intends the five psalms after Chapter (*LME* 6) as a ferial custom.

43 *protendatur prima*   The phrase is borrowed from *RC* 28: 'In diebus festis . . . ita protendatur Prima, ut capitulo facto matutinalique missa celebrata . . . si dies dominica fuerit, mox accedant ad consecrationem conspersionis, si alia quaelibet sollemnitas mox ad Tertiam' (the blessing of holy water here mentioned accompanies the procession before the principal mass on Sundays; see comment above, at n. 35). Neither the *LME* nor its source indicates exactly how Prime is to be lengthened.

44 *sedeat abbas . . . ad confessionem*   In a few details Ælfric is more explicit than his source, which allows confession to the abbot or his appointed officer (*RC* 27: 'patri spirituali uel eius . . . uicario'; on the term *pater spiritualis* for 'abbot', see *RC* (Symons), p. xxxix, n. 2, and p. 18, n. 6). The *Concordia* also requires the *schola* (i.e., the *pueri*) to participate and does not explicitly mention the cloister as the place for sacramental confessions on Sunday. On Ælfric's specification of the cloister, see Spurrell, 'Architectural Interest', p. 173.

LME 8   Communion practices; cf. *RC* 29

45 *Omni dominica . . . eucharistiam accipiant*   In a notable departure from the *Concordia*, where daily communion is encouraged, Ælfric restricts the custom to Sundays and feasts. Daily reception would have been unusual for the time, and the *Concordia* stands virtually alone in recommending it, as Symons has noted ('Sources', p. 157). Daily communion is, moreover, one practice in which Symons detected the possible influence of 'golden-age' Anglo-Saxon tradition on the reformers, in this instance through their familiarity with Bede's Letter to Bishop Ecgberht of York (*ibid.*, p. 158). Bede there urges Ecgberht always to admonish those living in the world 'how healthful for every sort of Christian is daily reception of the Body and Blood of Christ' (trans. mine; see *Venerabilis Baedae epistola ad Ecgberctum antistitem*, c. 15, in *Bede: Historical Works*, ed. and trans. J. E. King, 2 vols. (Cambridge, MA, 1930) II, 478: 'quam salutaris sit omni Christianorum generi quotidiana Dominici corporis et sanguinis perceptio').

46 *qui antea missam fecerunt*   This stipulation, not found in the *Concordia*, would include the celebrant of the matutinal mass and perhaps those in the community who had earlier offered 'private masses', although nowhere does Ælfric explicitly refer to the latter practice (but see comment below, at n. 311). On the *missa priuata* and its evolution, see the brief sketch in Vogel, *Medieval Liturgy*, pp. 156–9.

47 *'Qui cotidie . . . accipero'*   At *RC* 29 the passage is attributed to a work called *De uerbis Domini*, supposedly by Augustine. The full quotation in the *Concordia*, however, is actually a composite of phrases from Ambrose's *De sacramentis* and any of several Augustinian or pseudo-Augustinian sermons (Symons, 'Sources', pp. 157–8, and Hallinger's apparatus to *RC* 29, 89.4–9). Admittedly, a quotation justifying daily communion does not serve Ælfric's revised teaching very well.

Commentary

LME 9   Warning against tardiness and improprieties in worship

[48] *regularium monachorum consuetudo*, etc. This section does not correspond closely to any part of the *Concordia*, even though the term *consuetudo* normally occurs in the *LME* to acknowledge a debt to Æthelwold's customary, especially to signal the end of an interpolation from another source (see above, n. 3). The spirit, and occasionally the wording (e.g., *occurrere neglegenter*), of this passage are strongly reminiscent of *RSB*, c. XLIII.4–5 and 13–14. See also *RSB*, c. XIX.7 (on standing during the psalmody) which is partially quoted in *RC* 8.

[49] *minutione . . . sanguinis* This practice is often mentioned in medieval customaries, but not in the *Concordia*; see *RC* (Symons), p. xxxix.

LME 10   Votive matutinal masses; cf. *RC* 28 and 25

[50] *missa de sancta Trinitate* For the votive mass of the Trinity, probably composed and assigned to Sunday by Alcuin, see *Sacr.Greg.*, nos. 1806–10, and Barré and Deshusses, 'A la recherche'. Specimens in contemporary sacramentaries of Anglo-Saxon origin or provenance include *Leofr.Miss.*, p. 176, *Miss.NMin.*, p. 207, *Miss.RJum.*, p. 241, *Miss.StAug.*, pp. 131–2, and *Winch.Sacr.*, nos. 1507, 1536 and 1565.

[51] *de quacumque necessitate euenerit* As part of a tendency to downplay the royalism of the *Concordia* (see above, pp. 43–9), Ælfric has dropped the intention *pro rege* from the daily matutinal mass (cf. *RC* 25: 'pro rege uel quacumque inminente necessitate'). Ælfric's silence on the point is all the more striking, since the votive *missa cotidiana pro rege* (see *Sacr.Greg.{Supplementum Anianense}*, nos. 1270–2) remained a fixture in late Anglo-Saxon sacramentaries: e.g., *Leofr.Miss.*, pp. 179–80, *Miss.RJum.*, p. 249, *Miss.-StAug.*, p. 141, and *Winch.Sacr.*, nos. 1526, 1554 and 1588. See also Roper, pp. 38–9.

IV *The daily horarium* a Kalendis Octobris, *resumed (LME 11–12)*

LME 11   Votive masses of the day, Friday and Saturday; cf. *RC* 31

[52] *de sancta cruce . . . de sancta Maria* These votive masses (*Sacr.Greg.*, nos. 1835–40 and 1841–6), associated with Alcuin's circle in the eighth century (Barré and Deshusses, 'A la recherche'), came to be assigned to Friday and Saturday early in the ninth century on the Continent. They are, not surprisingly, a fixture in late Anglo-Saxon sacramentaries, although the date of their introduction into the English church remains disputed: specimens survive in *Corp.41*, p. 102 (incomplete), *Leofr.Miss.*, p. 178, *Miss.NMin.*, pp. 212–13 (incomplete), *Miss.RJum.*, pp. 244–6 (with two Saturday masses for the Virgin), and *Miss.StAug.*, pp. 135–7. Curiously, *Winch.Sacr.* has the votive mass of the Virgin (nos. 1508, 1537 and 1567) but not that of the Holy Cross, and resembles the Sacramentary of Fulda in this regard (Barré and Deshusses, 'A la recherche', p. 24; cf. Davril's introduction to *Winch.Sacr.*, pp. 19–20). On the votive

Commentary

masses among the Anglo-Saxons, see also Clayton, *The Cult of the Virgin Mary*, pp. 62–3. Roper (pp. 42–3 and 208 (Table 2:6)) claims that the *Concordia* is innovative in designating these specifically as the *principal* masses on these days.

LME 12   Special antiphons after Lauds and Vespers; cf. *RC* 21, 34 and 42

[53] *de sancta cruce . . . et de sancto cuius reliquie ibi habentur*   Again Ælfric has brought together points scattered in the source (*RC* 21 and 34), but neither the *Concordia* nor the *LME* describes in detail these special votive antiphons. The basic elements of each were probably an antiphon, versicle and collect; examples of Marian suffrages from the tenth-century 'Durham Collectar' (Durham, Cathedral Library, A. iv. 19) are printed by Clayton, *The Cult of the Virgin Mary*, pp. 63–5. Tolhurst (pp. 101–2 and 121) identifies as a further development of this devotion a full set of Offices of the Virgin (followed by a set for, among others, the Holy Cross) found in the miscellany London, BL, Cotton Tiberius A. iii (Christ Church, Canterbury, s. xi^{med}). The form and later development of these special votive antiphons are fully discussed by Roper, pp. 139–44. Unfortunately Ælfric does not identify the saint whose relics are kept ('cuius reliquie habentur') at Eynsham, and no other source supplies this detail. This is just one of a number of points at which Ælfric declines to adapt his text to local circumstances, retaining instead the blank formula of the source; cf. commentary to *LME* 25 (at n. 98) and 68 (at n. 313), below.

[54] *usque Aduentum Domini*   These votive antiphons after Lauds and Vespers were omitted during Advent (likewise at *RC* 42), but resumed thereafter.

[55] *Vigilia quoque pro defunctis*, etc.   This point is relevant not to the votive antiphons, but only to the mention of Vespers itself. Vigils of the Dead, a devotional Office of one to three Nocturns, was said after Vespers during the summer period (until 1 November); the Office of the Dead also included Lauds and Vespers (see Tolhurst, pp. 107–13; T. Symons, 'Monastic Observance in the Tenth Century: I. The Offices of All Saints and of the Dead', *DR* 50 (1932), 449–64 and 51 (1933), 137–52; Roper, pp. 58–64 and 215 (Table 3:4); and K. Ottosen, *The Responsories and Versicles of the Latin Office of the Dead* (Aarhus, 1993)). The point has apparently found its way into the *LME* here under the influence of *RC* 34, where the votive antiphons are prescribed separately, each in the context of a much fuller description of the liturgical hour it follows. Ælfric's habit of extracting and regrouping provisions found scattered in the source occasionally produces this kind of non sequitur; cf. comments above at nn. 17 and 37.

V *The full winter horarium* (LME *13–15*)

LME 13   The winter *ordo hymnorum*; cf. *RC* 39

[56] *A Calendis Nouembris*, etc.   Building on the autumnal or transitional order instituted *a Kalendis Octobris* (see *LME* 2), additional changes from 1 November mark the transition to the full winter horarium.

Commentary

⁵⁷ *dominica uespera*   I.e., first Vespers of Sunday. Sundays (and major feasts) have two Offices of Vespers, one on the preceding Saturday evening (first Vespers) and another on Sunday itself (second Vespers). The outline of hymns that follows respects an organization commonly used in medieval hymnal manuscripts, beginning with the *ordinarium de tempore* (regular Sundays and weekdays) then advancing through the *proprium de tempore* (hymns proper to seasons and some feasts in the Temporale); see Milfull, p. 24.

⁵⁸ *canatur hymnus*, etc.   This section contains some of Ælfric's most substantial and important additions to the *Concordia*; for an evaluation of the liturgical evidence, see Symons, 'Sources', pp. 151–4. In *LME* 13 Ælfric describes the hymns of the winter period (1 November through Passiontide); the hymns of Paschaltide and the summer period will be taken up later at *LME* 50 and 54. Though Ælfric provides only incipits of hymns, his expanded outline of the monastic hymnal serves as an important witness to the 'Winchester–Worcester type' of the so-called New Hymnal, as classified in Helmut Gneuss's important study (*Hymnar*, pp. 70–4 and 119–20; see esp. Tabelle II, pp. 60–8). The New Hymnal appears not to have reached England until the 'Benedictine revival' of the mid-tenth century, during which the variety of continental influences within the movement produced different forms of the hymnal at Winchester (spreading thence to Worcester) and Christ Church, Canterbury. According to Gneuss, the New Hymnal itself originated in the early ninth century in Frankish territory, possibly under the aegis of reforms associated with Benedict of Aniane. On this theory see, in addition to *Hymnar*, ch. 3, Gneuss's 'Latin Hymns in Medieval England', pp. 411–12; for a slight modification of Gneuss's hypothesis, see D. A. Bullough, with A. Harting-Corrêa, 'Texts, Chant, and the Chapel of Louis the Pious', rev. and repr. in *Carolingian Renewal*, pp. 241–71.

No definitive, critical edition of the medieval Latin hymns exists. Hallinger's apparatus to the *Concordia* and *LME* provide only references to J. Mearns's inventory, *Early Latin Hymnaries: An Index of Hymns in Hymnaries before 1100* (Cambridge, 1913). Anglo-Saxonists, however, are now well served by Milfull's *Hymns of the Anglo-Saxon Church*, which includes not only an edition of the hymnal with Old English gloss in Durham, Cathedral Library B. iii. 32, 1r–43r, collated against all other surviving Anglo-Saxon hymnals (including the prose versions of the *Expositio hymnorum* extant in two manuscripts), but also editions of most other hymns in use in Anglo-Saxon England but not contained in the 'Durham Hymnal' (her nos. 134–62). After her critical edition of each hymn, Milfull includes a literal prose translation of the Latin, notes on liturgical use, bibliographical references and further textual and interpretative commentary. In the present discussion of hymns that Ælfric lists in *LME* 13, then again in *LME* 50 and 54, the reader is referred to editions in *AH*, then to Milfull (cited by numbers assigned in her edition, which in turn follow the numbering of items in the New Hymnal used in Gneuss's *Hymnar*, pp. 60–8).

⁵⁹ 'O lux beata' . . . 'Christe qui lux es' . . . 'Primo dierum' . . . 'Aeterne rerum' . . . 'Lucis creator'   *AH* LI, 38, 21 and 24; L, 11; and LI, 34; Milfull, nos. 1, 12, 3, 4 and 13. *RC* 39 stipulates the Sunday hymns 'O lux beata' (first Vespers), 'Christe qui lux es' (Compline), 'Primo dierum' (Nocturns) and 'Aeterne rerum' (Lauds), followed by only

Commentary

vague references to the ferial and proper hymns. On the allocation of these hymns to the winter season, see Milfull, p. 24.

60 *'Iam lucis orto sidere'* . . . *'Nunc sancte nobis Spiritus'* . . . *'Rector potens'* . . . *'Rerum Deus'* AH LI, 40 and L, 19–20; Milfull, nos. 7–10. The hymns at the little hours were invariable throughout the year, save in Lent (see below, n. 70). They are not mentioned in the *Concordia*.

61 *'Conditor alme siderum'* . . . *'Verbum supernum'* . . . *'Vox clara'* AH LI, 46 and 48; Milfull, nos. 32–4.

62 *'Christe redemptor omnium'* . . . *'A Patre unigenitus'* . . . *'A solis ortus cardine'* usque *'Hostis Herodes'* AH LI, 49; XXVII, 66; and L, 58; Milfull, nos. 36, 46 and 44. According to Gneuss (*Hymnar*, pp. 119–20) and Milfull (p. 193) 'Christe redemptor' is the expected choice for monastic first Vespers of Christmas. But in his employment of the latter two hymns Ælfric departs not just from Winchester–Worcester usage but from every extant Anglo-Saxon monastic hymnal (see the following note). The assignment of 'A Patre unigenitus' to Nocturns appears to be unique to the *LME*. Winchester usage seems normally to have assigned this hymn to Nocturns of Epiphany; hymnals of the 'Canterbury type' also used it at Epiphany, though not at Nocturns (Milfull, p. 221). In the Canterbury hymnal, 'A solis ortus cardine' was sung at Nocturns of Epiphany, but in Winchester–Worcester usage this hymn was ordinarily assigned to Lauds of Candlemas (2 February) – and indeed Ælfric will re-use the hymn on that occasion as well (see below, n. 65). Of witnesses nearly contemporary with the *LME*, only the secular Office hymnal preserved in *Leofr.Coll*. assigns 'A solis ortus' to Christmas, though to first Vespers and not, as Ælfric, to Lauds (Milfull, p. 215). Vespers of Christmas is the position that became standard in England in the later Middle Ages (*Hymnar*, p. 119). Ælfric's reference 'usque "Hostis Herodes"' simply indicates that the hymn 'A solis ortus' is in fact the first seven stanzas of a longer abecedarian poem by Caelius Sedulius (*fl*. 450). Stanzas 8 (beginning 'Hostis Herodes impie') through 13 were taken as a separate hymn, assigned by the *LME* and extant hymnals to Epiphany (see below, n. 64).

63 *quia 'Veni redemptor' et 'Audi redemptor' non uidentur sapientibus honeste esse compositos* Winchester usage and the secular *Leofr.Coll*. assign 'Veni redemptor' to Christmas Nocturns; its assignation in books of the Canterbury group cannot be determined (Milfull, p. 202 (no. 39)). Apart from Ælfric's teaching here, monastic usage unanimously assigns 'Audi redemptor' to Lauds of Christmas, while the secular *Leofr.Coll*. appears to have divided the hymn over Nocturns and Lauds on the Octave of Christmas (1 January) rather than on Christmas itself (Milfull, p. 199 (no. 38)). Though Ælfric's departure from the norm – his rejection of 'Veni redemptor' (an authentic Ambrosian hymn) and 'Audi redemptor' from the Offices of Christmas – is quite clear, his reasons for doing so are not. He does not identify the *sapientes* whose judgement he is citing, and the phrase *honeste . . . compositos* is ambiguous. This cryptic statement in the *LME* has never been satisfactorily explained. Symons ('Sources', p. 153, n. 1) relays a suggestion that Ælfric might have flinched at the fourth (originally fifth) stanza of 'Veni redemptor': 'Procedens [*var.* -at] de thalamo suo, / pudoris aula regia, / gemine gigas substantiæ, / alacris ut currat uiam' (Milfull, no. 39,

Commentary

lines 13–16; she translates (p. 202) 'who comes out of his wedding chamber, out of the royal court of modesty, as a giant of twofold nature in order to run his race joyfully'). The reference to Christ as *gigas* is supported by an allegorical reading of Ps. XVIII.6: 'He hath set his tabernacle in the sun: and he, as a bridegroom coming out of his bride chamber, hath rejoiced as a giant to run the way.' But to scrupulous minds the metaphor might also raise the spectre of the evil race of giants who lived before the flood (Gen. VI.4–7). Ambrose's reference to a 'giant of twofold nature' looks to both the psalm verse and Genesis but ignores the inappropriate context of the latter, concentrating instead on the statement that the antediluvian giants were the offspring of 'the sons of God' and 'the daughters of men' (Gen. VI.4) – hence Ambrose's allegorical play on *gemina substantia* (see *Early Latin Hymns, with Introduction and Notes*, ed. A. S. Walpole (Cambridge, 1922), p. 54, n. 19). In any case, the exegetical, literary and popular associations of 'giants' often contaminated one another in early medieval tradition, not least among Anglo-Saxon authors and the sources known to them; see P. J. Frankis, 'The Thematic Significance of *enta geweorc* and Related Imagery in The Wanderer', *ASE* 2 (1973), 253–69, at pp. 258–9.

Against this suggestion offered by Symons, one might imagine Ælfric scrupling about 'giants' in a homiletic context *coram populo*, but the *LME* is written for an audience that should catch the echo of Ps. XVIII. And even if the speculation in Symons's note is correct, it does not account for Ælfric's rejection of the other hymn, 'Audi redemptor'. As I have translated the key phrase of his criticism ('to the experts . . . do not seem worthily composed'), the comment implies that certain authorities whom Ælfric respects have found technical faults in these hymns. Ambrose was certainly the first master of the four-line iambic dimeter hymn stanza, but his 'Veni redemptor' employs a relatively (though not absolutely) high number of metrical variations which, although allowable in quantitative metre, might have seemed clumsy to those who did not understand the verse form, or might have made some lines of the hymn difficult to sing in the same measure as the others. In the verse about the *gigas* quoted above, for example, in the first foot an anapest (*geminae*) is substituted for the iamb (or its more common alternative, the spondee); in his *De arte metrica*, Bede even cites this line as an example of variation in iambic tetrameter (*De arte metrica et De schematibus et tropis*, ed. C. B. Kendall, with M. H. King, in *Bedae Venerabilis Opera, Pars VI: Opera Didascalica 1*, CCSL 123A (Turnhout, 1975), 136, lines 19–23). Moreover, Ambrose has already used this fairly uncommon effect just two lines previously, in the first line of the same stanza (*thalamo*, third foot). The anonymous and presumably later hymn 'Audi redemptor', on the other hand, is metrically troubled and reads smoothly neither as quantitative nor as accentual verse (though its basis is 'rhythmical Ambrosian hymn verse (4 × 8pp)' according to Milfull, p. 199). Most noticeably, the first feet of the first and third lines of stanza four clash with the prevailing rhythm of the hymn: 'Genitum deum ex deo / miramur in hoc corpore, / hominem deo similem, / mysterium mirabile' (Milfull, no. 38, lines 13–16). While sung performance might level word accents normally used when reading, the first and third lines do tend towards falling rhythm in their first two feet, while a rising rhythm is the norm everywhere else. On the transition from quantitative to accentual

Commentary

verse in hymns, of which the present stanza seems a stark example, see D. Norberg, *Les Vers latins iambiques et trochaïques au Moyen Age et leurs répliques rythmiques*, Filologiskt arkiv 35 (Stockholm, 1988), 17–41. Clearly Ælfric had no prejudice against accentual hymns as such; he prescribes perfect specimens of the type for, among others, the daily Offices of Terce through None in Lent (see below, n. 70). His rejection of 'Veni redemptor' and 'Audi redemptor' may simply reflect an informed awareness of their metrical idiosyncrasies. In any case, 'A solis ortus' did eventually replace the latter at Christmas, and further study may yet provide an explanation for this change and so shed further light on what Ælfric means by *non honeste compositos*.

64 *'Hostis Herodes impie'* . . . *'A Patre unigenitus'* . . . *'Iesus refulsit omnium'* AH L, 58; XXVII, 66; and LI, 51; Milfull, nos. 45, 46 and 43. Unanimously assigned to Epiphany, there is nevertheless much disagreement between the Winchester–Worcester and Canterbury types over which of these hymns goes with which Office. The Canterbury hymnal assigns 'Hostis Herodes' to Lauds and 'Iesus refulsit' to Vespers; it assigns 'A Patre unigenitus' to no definite Office. The Winchester–Worcester hymnal, which Ælfric appears to follow, assigns 'Hostis Herodes' to Vespers, 'A Patre unigenitus' to Nocturns and 'Iesus refulsit' to Lauds (Milfull, pp. 212, 219 and 221).

65 *'Quod chorus uatum'* . . . *'Quem terra'* . . . *'A solis ortus'* AH L, 206, 86 and 58; Milfull, nos. 47, 65₁ and 44. These are the only proper hymns from the Sanctorale included by Ælfric. His usage represents the Winchester–Worcester hymnal, which agrees with the Canterbury type only in the assignment of 'Quod chorus uatum' to Vespers; for 'Quem terra' and 'A solis ortus' in the Canterbury hymnal, cf. Milfull, pp. 268 and 215.

66 *'Alleluia dulce carmen'* . . . *'Alleluia piis edite laudibus'* . . . *'Almum sidereæ iam patrie decus'* AH LI, 52 and XXVII, 74–5; Milfull, nos. 48–50. The latter two (for Nocturns and Lauds) are actually two divisions of a single hymn (Milfull, p. 228). The Winchester–Worcester and Canterbury traditions agree here.

67 *'Audi benigne conditor'* . . . *'Clarum decus ieiunii'* . . . *'Iesu quadragenarie'* AH LI, 53 and 57–8; Milfull, nos. 55, 58 and 57. The Winchester–Worcester hymnal assigns these hymns to Vespers, Nocturns and Lauds, respectively, on weekdays in Lent. Their precise distribution in the Canterbury hymnal is uncertain; see Milfull, pp. 240, 248 and 246, respectively, and *Hymnar*, p. 240.

68 *per quattuor ebdomadas continue* That is, from the Sunday after Ash Wednesday until Passion Sunday (two Sundays before Easter).

69 *'Vexilla regis'* . . . *'Arbor decora'* . . . *'Auctor salutis'* AH L, 74 and LI, 70; Milfull, nos. 67₁, 67₂ and 68. The poem *Vexilla regis* by Venantius Fortunatus (*fl.* 575) was divided into two separate four-stanza hymns for Vespers and Nocturns from Passion Sunday until Maundy Thursday. This distribution was a feature of the Winchester–Worcester hymnal, and perhaps in the Canterbury hymnal and the secular *Leofr.Coll.* too; see Milfull, p. 275, and *Hymnar*, note to p. 351. Likewise 'Auctor salutis' was probably sung at Lauds in both the Winchester–Worcester and Canterbury traditions (Milfull, p. 280).

70 *'Dei fide qua uiuimus'* . . . *'Meridie orandum est'* . . . *'Perfecto trino numero'* AH LI, 64–5 and 16; Milfull, nos. 51–3. These seasonal hymns for the little hours on Lenten ferias are one exception to the general rule imposed at *LME* 13 (see comments above, at

Commentary

n. 60). They occur thus placed in hymnals of both the Winchester–Worcester and Canterbury traditions, the only difference being that the former used these seasonal hymns only on the weekdays of Lent, while the latter used them on Sundays as well (Milfull, pp. 232 and 234–5). The ferial hymn for Prime, 'Iam lucis orto sidere', would remain unchanged through the year, including Lent.

LME 14   Fire in winter; cf. RC 40

71 *in domo*   This provision refers to the periods designated for *lectio* and work. The source speaks of a 'locus aptus fratribus' and uses the term *domus* three times (*RC* 40; cf. trans. *RC* (Symons) 29, p. 26: 'a suitable room shall be set aside for the brethren . . . the special room of which we have spoken . . . the aforesaid building'). The *domus* must have been an all-purpose building and shelter that served the same function as the cloister and was distinct from the other buildings mentioned, e.g., the church, refectory, dormitory, Chapter house and *auditorium*; see Spurrell, 'Architectural Interest', pp. 163–4.

LME 15   The *potus* after None; cf. RC 43

72 *festiuitate sancti Martini*   11 November.
73 *non bibant fratres*   Ælfric does not use the technical term *potus* for the refreshment (cf. *RC* 43: 'non sequitur potus'). This drink was allowed on Sundays and major feasts, as well as on ferias of the summer period (until 14 September); see *RC* (Symons) 30, p. 27, n. 3.

VI Proper customs: Advent through Candlemas (LME 16–25)

LME 16   Advent; cf. RC 44

74 *non canant 'Gloria in excelsis Deo'*   The provision applies to mass, not the Office. Though not found in the *Concordia*, this instruction was very likely taken for granted in Æthelwold's customary. The provision does occur in *DEC* 1, where it may reflect the influence of Amalarius, *Lib.off.* III.xl.9–10, which is quoted in *IBA* 1.
75 *nec . . . mittant pinguedinem*   Clarified by *RC* 44: 'pinguedo interdicitur, scilicet lardi' and translation at *RC* (Symons) 30, p. 27 and n. 6.

LME 17   Chapter, Christmas Eve; cf. RC 45

76 *recitetur in capitulo*   The martyrology reading at Chapter always announces the celebrations to be observed on the *following* day – in the present instance Christmas Day. On the use of the martyrology in monastic Chapter, see the introduction to *Das altenglische Martyrologium*, ed. G. Kotzor, 2 vols., Bayerische Akademie der

Commentary

Wissenschaften, philosophisch-historische Klasse, Abhandlungen, Neue Folge 88/1–2 (Munich, 1980) I, 235*–239*.

[77] *propter . . . descendit* This atypically florid passage is a verbatim quotation from *RC* 45.

LME 18   The Offices of Christmas; cf. *RC* 46

[78] *antiphone . . . de ipsa completione temporis* The phrase 'fullness of time' (from *RC* 46) refers to the theme of the antiphons for Christmas Vespers. As Hallinger's apparatus to the *Concordia* notes (following *RC* (Symons) p. 28, n. 3), ancient antiphoners present diverse series of antiphons, but the series preserved in *Worc.Ant.*, pp. 26–7, seems to fit the theme well. These are: 'Rex pacificus', 'Scitote', 'Completi sunt' and 'Ecce completa sunt' (*CAO* II, series 17b and 18).

[79] *in quarto responsorio* Because Christmas should be a feast of twelve lessons and twelve responsories (i.e., its Night Office has three Nocturns with four lessons and four responsories each), it is not certain whether the instruction applies to the fourth responsory in each of the three Nocturns or only in the third. The source (*RC* 46), here quoted verbatim, does not clarify the point.

[80] *post euuangelium* That is, the gospel of the day, read after the last responsory of the final Nocturn on Sundays and feasts of twelve lessons. Though Ælfric does not mention it, the gospel would be preceded by the hymn 'Te Deum laudamus', as is made clear at *RC* 46.

[81] *missa de nocte* A third proper mass *in nocte* was added on Christmas, to be celebrated between Nocturns and Lauds (*RC* 46 also indicates that all the bells shall be rung before this mass). The rubrics of the sacramentary assigned the next mass to dawn (*LME* 18 'in lucis crepusculo'), hence the extraordinary celebration (in effect) of a matutinal mass before Prime on this day; see Hughes, § 117.

LME 19   Special confession at Chapter; cf. *RC* 47

[82] *'Misereatur'* Incipit of the formula for general absolution: 'Misereatur uestri omnipotens Deus, et dimissis peccatis uestris, perducat uos ad uitam aeternam' ('May Almighty God have mercy on you and, forgiving your sins, lead you to everlasting life'). The brothers addressing the abbot in turn would substitue singular *tui . . . tuis . . . te* in the same formula. Note that this ceremony is not the same as the usual confession of faults in Chapter (described at *RC* 26, but not by Ælfric).

LME 20   Further instructions, Christmas Day; cf. *RC* 48

[83] *ornati ad tertiam* In other words, the ministers of the principal mass would not have time to vest between Terce and mass, and they must not slip away to do so during the Office itself.

[84] *'Tecum principium' et reliquae* Probably the same series found in the thirteenth-century

Commentary

Worc.Ant. for second Vespers: 'Tecum principium', 'Redemptionem', 'Exortum est' and 'Apud Dominum' (*CAO* II, series 19d); see *RC* (Symons), p. 29, n. 10, and Hallinger's apparatus to *RC* 48, 99.16.

LME 21   Feasts during the Octave of Christmas; cf. *RC* 49

[85] *Reliquis uero . . . competentibus*   Ælfric (following *RC* 49) means the three days immediately after Christmas, i.e., the feasts of St Stephen (26 December), St John the Evangelist (27 December) and the Holy Innocents (28 December). Vespers of these important feasts had proper antiphons (see, e.g., *CAO* II, series 20c, 21d and 22d) but, as Ælfric indicates, retained the psalmody of second Vespers of Christmas (Pss. CIX–CXI and CXXIX); see Tolhurst, p. 154; Hughes, §§ 427–8. In his supplement on the readings and responsories for the Night Office, Ælfric will refer to the Octaves of these days; see *LME* 77 and accompanying commentary.

LME 22   The Octave of Christmas: further customs; cf. *RC* 50; *Lib.off.* I.xli.2

[86] *ad nocturnam . . . pulsentur*   Almost verbatim from *RC* 50, but omitting the source's claim that this is a specifically English custom ('sicut in usum huius patriae indigenae tenent'); discussed by Symons, 'Sources', pp. 145–6. Only later (at *LME* 58) will Ælfric allude to the native character of this custom. Note that here he retains the phrase *uti ad missam* even though he earlier omitted the reference to bell-ringing at the *missa in nocte* (see above, n. 81).

[87] *Cerei . . . deportetur*   As at *RC* 50, the festal trappings (candles, incense and the ringing of the bells) are retained during the last three days of the Octave even though the Night Office reverts to its ferial form, implied by the absence of the gospel reading and hymn 'Te Deum' after the last Nocturn (see Symons, 'Sources', p. 145). The co-ordination of these practices is clearer in the *Concordia*, and *LME* 22 obscures their syntactic correlation ('licet . . . tamen'). The change by someone (not necessarily Ælfric) of concessive *tamen* to co-ordinating *etiam* urges that the *licet*-clause be construed with the preceding direction about bell-ringing, and that 'Cerei etiam . . .' begin a new sentence, even though reference to the 'Te Deum' and gospel natually belongs with the bells and incense, while the aforementioned bell-ringing takes place on some but not all feasts of twelve lessons.

[88] *non canitur 'Gloria in excelsis Deo' . . . necem crudelem*   Probably from Amalarius, *Lib.off.* I.xli.2:

> Praetitulatur in antiphonario sic: '"Gloria in excelsis Deo" non cantatur, nec alleluia, sed quasi in tristitia deducitur dies ille.' Compositor officii praesentis coniungi nos uult animis deuotarum feminarum, quae in morte innocentum doluerunt et planxerunt. Sicut separat nos ab actu malorum Iudaeorum in caena Domini siue in parascheue siue in sabbato amittendo oscula siue cetera sueta, ita coniungit in praesenti festiuitate dolori deuotarum feminarum. Causa earum tristitiae amittimus: 'Gloria in excelsis Deo' et alleluia.

On Ælfric's knowledge and use of the *Liber officialis*, see the introduction, above,

Commentary

pp. 59–68. In *R1(Sa)*, the version of the *Retractatio prima* closest to Ælfric's lost exemplar of Amalarius's work, the section on the Holy Innocents follows that on Christmas, as in the liturgical calendar (and unlike in other copies of the *R1* or in Amalarius's original). Ælfric had already treated the relevant gospel pericope (Matt. II.13–18) in *CH* I.v (ed. Thorpe I, 76–90), and some of the adaptations in the present Amalarian passage appear indebted to Ælfric's reminiscence of the biblical and exegetical tradition (e.g., *matrum* replacing *feminarum*; cf. Matt. II.18 and Jer. XXXI.15). On the homiletic sources, see Cross, 'Ælfric – Mainly on Memory', p. 139, and now J. Hill, 'Ælfric's Homily on the Holy Innocents: the Sources Reviewed', in *Alfred the Wise: Studies in Honour of Janet Bately on the Occasion of her Sixty-Fifth Birthday*, ed. J. Roberts and J. L. Nelson, with M. Godden (Cambridge, 1997), pp. 89–98. Ælfric's suppression of Amalarius's *compositor officii* rids the text of a cumbersome reference and allows amplification of the liturgy as a direct moral and typological response to biblical events; see above, pp. 67–8, and also commentary to *LME* 24 (at n. 93), 25 (at n. 103), 26 (at n. 106), 32 (at n. 168), 33 (at n. 171), 39 (at n. 204) and 43 (at n. 219).

LME 23 Resumption of the regular winter horarium; cf. *RC* 53 and 51

89 *Ab Octauis . . . agatur obedientia* These provisions mark the end of the festal customs described in *LME* 20–2 (Christmas and its Octave). Work (*obedientia*) is now resumed, while the festal 'Gloria in excelsis' is dropped from the mass and the bells are no longer rung at Nocturns, mass and Vespers. Ælfric's decision to insert the customs of *RC* 53 (the ferial order *post Octauas Domini*) before those of *RC* 51 (ferial psalms and antiphons at Vespers) allows a more orderly progression of topics than in the source. One of the two manuscripts of the *Concordia* (Cotton Tiberius A. iii) also states that during the period after the Octave of Christmas, and then again from the second day in the Octave of Epiphany, the matutinal mass shall be celebrated after Prime. But this contradicts the order laid down in *RC* 24–5 and *LME* 2, and neither Ælfric nor the other manuscript of the source (Cotton Faustina B. iii) includes such a provision; see *RC* (Kornexl), pp. 264–5 (commentary to line 733).

90 *cum antiphona . . . psalmi feriales* The manuscript reads singular *antiphona* (unabbreviated). Although the singing of the four psalms under a single antiphon was not unknown (Tolhurst, p. 153; Harper, *Forms and Orders*, p. 101), the more common form of monastic Vespers had one antiphon per psalm. Symons accordingly expands *antiph* at *RC* (Ti) 51, corresponding to the present instance in *LME* 23, as *antiphonis*; see *RC* (Symons) 32, p. 30, and likewise *RC* (Kornexl) 32.728. The Old English glossator in *RC* (Ti) may have taken the abbreviated Latin form as singular, but the ending of his *mid antefnan* could also represent a reduction of dative plural -*um*; see *RC* (Kornexl), p. 264 (commentary to line 728). The ambiguous Old English gloss does not rule out the possibility that singular *antiphona* was the intended reading of *LME* 23, and possibly a textual variant transmitted in Ælfric's exemplar of the *Concordia*.

Commentary

LME 24   Epiphany; cf. *RC* 52; *Lib.off.* IV.xxxiii.1 and IV.xliv.1

⁹¹ *non teneatur ieiunium*   Fasting was otherwise a normal requirement on the vigils of major feasts; see *ODCC*, *s.v.* 'vigil'.

⁹² *psalmos . . . eadem sollempnitate*   In other words, at first Vespers the psalmody shall be that of the day in the week, but with antiphons proper to Epiphany (e.g., *CAO* II, series 24c).

⁹³ *In Epiphania . . . interficere*   Adapted from Amalarius, *Lib.off.* IV.xxxiii.1:

> Unum amittimus in teophania ex his quae caelebramus in natiuitate Domini, id est inuitatorium . . . Igitur quia uoluit [*scil.* compositor officii] in isto distinguere nostram bonam inuitationem, qua inuitantur et excitantur fideles ad Deum deprecandum, ab inuitatione Herodis, qui propterea congregauit scribas et principes Iudaeorum, ut sciret ubi Christus nasceretur, quem cogitabat interficere, inuitatorium praesentis officii amisit.

In *R1(Sa)* this section, like that on the Holy Innocents, occurs in its calendrically correct place but is otherwise the same as in other copies of *R1*. Ælfric appears to have restored the Vulgate reading *sacerdotum* (Matt. II.4) for Amalarius's *Iudaeorum*. The influence of scripture may also explain the added prepositional phrase *ab eis* (cf. Matt. II.4: 'sciscitabatur *ab eis* ubi Christus nasceretur'), also found at *IBA* 4. Ælfric's tendency to 'correct' Amalarius's paraphrases with the actual words of scripture emerges as a consistent principle in his adaptations from the *Liber officialis*. On Ælfric's 'biblicizing' urge in other contexts, see Cross, 'The Literate Anglo-Saxon', pp. 89–93. Note also the omission, once again, of Amalarius's *compositor officii*, so that the present liturgy more easily seems the monks' immediate response to events of Epiphany, and not merely the contrivance of some anonymous human agent; cf. commentary to *LME* 22 (at n. 88), 25 (at n. 103), 26 (at n. 106), 32 (at n. 168), 33 (at n. 171), 39 (at n. 204) and 43 (at n. 219).

⁹⁴ *Ad nocturnas . . . 'Fluminis impetus laetificat'*   Adapted from Amalarius, *Lib.off.* IV.xliv.1:

> Solent musitare cantores de psalmo 'Deus noster refugium', quare praepostero ordine ponatur in tertio periocha. De qua re ita dicimus, sequentes ordinem euangelii: prius uenerunt magi adorare Dominum, quam baptizatus esset. Magi . . . uenerunt primo adorare Dominum, et postea baptizatus est ipse. Et apostoli atque ipsi baptizauerunt, quorum officium perspicue dilucidatur, et praecipue in antiphona 'Fluminis impetus', quae cantatur in tertia nocturna.

Amalarius's discussion here pertains to the Night Office for Epiphany, but in its secular form – i.e., a service of nine lessons (three Nocturns, each with three psalms, three antiphons and three readings). He argues that two of the nine antiphons, because they recall events in the life of Christ, should follow the sequence of those events as found in the gospels. According to the Roman Office and the numerical order of the psalter, Ps. XCIV (normally the invitatory, but this was omitted on Epiphany; see above, n. 93) and its antiphon ('Venite adoremus eum, quia ipse est Dominus Deus noster') should occupy the seventh place – i.e., the first antiphon and psalm of the third Nocturn, while Ps. XLV ('Deus noster refugium') and its antiphon ('Fluminis impetus laetificat, Alleluia, ciuitatem Dei, Alleluia') should fall second in the first

Commentary

Nocturn. The change proposed by Amalarius shifts Ps. XLV to seventh place and Ps. XCIV to sixth, because the antiphon of the latter ('Venite adoremus') recalls the adoration of the Magi, while that of the former ('Fluminis impetus') suggests Christ's baptism, as well as the baptisms performed in the apostolic era. Amalarius treats this point more fully, and with some variation, in his later work, the *Liber de ordine antiphonarii* XXI.2, 6 and 14 (*AEOLO* III, 57–9, and table, p. 165).

Amalarius compiled his own antiphoner after his journey to Rome (831) and to Corbie. Though this work does not survive, the arrangement *praepostero ordine* here described does occur in three of the secular Office antiphoners collated in *CAO* I, series 24b (the Compiègne, Gallicanus and Monza antiphoners). Amalarius's practice appears to rest on ancient (though probably not Roman) authorities. Ælfric's matter-of-fact citation of Amalarius on this point suggests that the *LME* is vindicating a practice already familiar in English reformed monastic circles rather than attempting to introduce a new custom. The form of the secular Office assumed by Amalarius, however, need not have replaced the monastic one at Epiphany, as was usual on other important occasions in the liturgical year – i.e., during the Triduum and the Octave of Easter, and at Nocturns of Pentecost (thus *LME* 34, 45, 46, 47–8 and 52, all prescribed by the *Concordia*; see Hallinger's apparatus to *RC* 61 and Tolhurst, pp. 206–7). Instead, Ælfric's antiphoner very likely tailored the arrangement *praepostero ordine* to a monastic Office of twelve lessons: Pss. XCIV and XLV and their antiphons could still occupy the sixth and seventh places, respectively, but as the end of the first Nocturn and beginning of the second (see *CAO* II, series 24b). *Worc.Ant.*, however, does not record the antiphons *praepostero ordine*, although their written order could, perhaps, have been altered in actual performance.

A monastic rather than secular version of *praepostero ordine* would also account for other of Ælfric's omissions from *Lib.off.* IV.xliv.1 (quoted above). Because the third Nocturn of the monastic Office consists of three canticles sung under a single antiphon, Amalarius's references to 'tertio periocha' and 'tertia nocturna' would be inappropriate; Ælfric prunes them away, and so must dispense with Amalarius's other arguments wherever these depend on the singing of 'Fluminis impetus' in the *third* Nocturn and 'Venite adoremus eum' in the second, as at *Lib.off.* IV.xliv.2:

Satis apertum est . . . nouum testamentum recoli in tertia nocturna, praecedentibus duabus nocturnis, quae habent in se memoriam sanctorum patrum qui fuerunt in ueteri testamento repleti Spiritu Sancto, siue de circumcisis, siue de gentilibus. Sequitur tertia nocturna cum antiphonis quae habent alleluia solito more, et perspicue demonstrant nouum testamentum, et baptismi sacramenta recolunt.

(Cf. Amalarius, *Liber de ordine de antiphonarii* XXI.7–12). Without the linking reference to the third Nocturn as the New Testament, Ælfric has also dropped the complicating mention of the apostles' celebration of baptism from *Lib.off.* I.xliv.1.

LME 25   Customs for Candlemas; cf. *RC* 54; *Lib.off.* IV.xxxiii.18

[95] *In Purificatione*, etc.   Elaborate customs grew up around this feast (2 February), also known as Candlemas, commemorating Mary's ritual Purification and the Presentation

Commentary

of Jesus in the Temple forty days after his birth. While most medieval *ordines* for the day agree in their main points (a procession, blessing and distribution of candles, proper antiphons), there can be significant differences in detail. Not surprisingly, Ælfric's provisions for the ceremonies follow those of *RC* 54, which differ from continental usages in some important respects (Symons, 'Sources', pp. 154–5). Special customs of Candlemas are also mentioned in Ælfric's homily for the same occasion (*CH* I.ix, ed. Thorpe I, 134–50, at p. 150), as well as in his second Old English pastoral letter to Archbishop Wulfstan (Brief III.178).

96 *audito signo ad tertiam* As at *LME* 2, Ælfric means the summoning bell before this Office. Terce itself will not actually take place until after the procession and blessing of candles.

97 *si aura sic permiserit* The placement of the phrase (adapted from *RC* 54) suggests a misunderstanding of its meaning in the source, where the condition seems to refer *only* to the wearing of albs. Ælfric's rewritten version implies that the holding of the procession itself is contingent on good weather (see also below, at n. 159).

98 *sancti cui . . . dedicata est* Ælfric's adherence to the source (*RC* 54) here, and the similar instructions for the Ash Wednesday and Palm Sunday processions (at *LME* 29 and 32, respectively), suggest that a procession to some other church actually did take place. One might imagine a simple procession to a side chapel within the monastic church (Spurrell, 'Architectural Interest', p. 167), although in that case the qualifying 'si aura sic permiserit' makes little sense (but see preceding note). If Ælfric's customary was written specifically for the monks at Eynsham, why did he not customize the document in such particulars as naming the church, chapel or altar to which the monks would process? That he did not suggests either a very mechanical method of using a source or, perhaps, his foreknowledge that the text would be read and used beyond the walls of Eynsham. Cf. the blank formulas similarly taken over at *LME* 12 (see above, n. 53) and 68 (see below, n. 313).

99 *reuertentes uero . . . cantando* Neither Ælfric nor the source specifies which antiphons are to be sung or prayers to be said (cf. *RC* 54), and contemporary witnesses vary: see *RC* (Symons), p. 31, nn. 3–4; Hallinger, apparatus to *RC* 54, 101.8; also contemporary *ordines* in *Cant.Ben.*, pp. 80–4, *Miss.NMin.*, pp. 69–72, and *Miss.RJum.*, pp. 158–60 (incomplete).

100 '*Responsum accepit Symeon*' *AMS*, no. 29b (from Luke II.26).

101 '*Erudi quaesumus Domine*' *Sacr.Greg.*, no. 123. The saying of this collect *ad ostium* appears to be peculiar to the *Concordia* and Ælfric (Symons, 'Sources', pp. 154–5); cf. *Cant.Ben.*, p. 84, and *Miss.NMin.*, p. 71, where 'Erudi' comes after the monks' entry into the church.

102 '*Cum inducerent*' *cum dominica oratione* For the text of this chant (either an antiphon or the verse of the responsory 'Responsum'), see *Cant.Ben.*, p. 84, and the ultimate source, Luke II.27. *Miss.NMin.* (p. 71) also adds a 'Kyrie' and further antiphons to the Virgin.

103 *hoc significante . . . lux mundi* Adapted from Amalarius, *Lib.off.* IV.xxxiii.18 (significant variants from *R1* are given in square brackets; on the significance of this recension, see above, pp. 62–5): '[Oportet nos *R1*] cereos accensos manibus

Commentary

portare in ypopanti, quod est in praesentatione sui unumquemque [sanctum significat *R1*] habere opera sua, in quibus clarus et lucidus appareat in coetu sanctorum angelorum . . .' Ælfric here explains the significance of the candles distributed to the community – and to the congregation, if one were present in the Eynsham church. Note Ælfric's typical substitution of the more common Latin name *Purificatio* for Amalarius's Greek *Ypopanti* [*sic*]; cf. the similar preference for *Epiphania* over *Theophania* in *LME* 24. The purpose clause (*ut . . . appareat*) effectively disposes of an awkward mixed construction (*quod est . . . significat*) with its dependent noun clause – a corruption apparently common to *R1* manuscripts and so probably in Ælfric's exemplar.

The subtle alteration of Amalarius's meaning also deserves attention. If the burning lights do represent the individual saints resplendent in their good deeds, the original reading *in praesentatione sui* would be preferable to Ælfric's *in Presentatione Domini, qui est lux mundi*, which does not carry the symbolism through to its natural conclusion. The monks do, after all, 'present' their candles to the celebrant before the offertory, yet Ælfric turns away from this obvious and immediate sign of the individual Christian's self-presentation (at death or in the Last Judgement), and towards an abstract reference to the Presentation of Christ as 'the light of the world' (cf. John VIII.12 or IX.5). Prompts for this interpolation are not far to seek: the day's gospel and at least one of the processional antiphons quote the familiar words of Simeon, who calls the infant Jesus 'lumen ad reuelationem gentium' (Luke II.32). Whatever inspired the alteration, Ælfric's paraphrase quietly blends the moral and allegorical significance of the candles, which consequently represent both Christ and the believer. The fusion of these two levels of meaning is also explicit in the antiphons, prayers and readings for Candelmas (e.g., in the mass collect: '. . . ut, sicut unigenitus Filius tuus hodierna die . . . in templo est praesentatus, ita nos facias purificatis tibi mentibus praesentari'). Ælfric may intend here as elsewhere to blur, for hortatory purposes, the distinction between present liturgical acts and the biblical events they commemorate; cf. commentary to *LME* 22 (at n. 88), 24 (at n. 93), 26 (at n. 106), 32 (at n. 168), 33 (at n. 171), 39 (at n. 204) and 43 (at n. 219).

The substituted phrase *qui est lux mundi* also recalls the short passage that concludes Ælfric's Old English homily for the same feast. In a brief pendant to the exposition of the gospel of the day, he explains the custom of the Candlemas procession, and adds, 'þeah ðe sume men singan ne cunnon, hi beron þeah-hwæðere þæt leoht on heora handum, forðy on ðissum dæge wæs þæt soðe leoht Crist geboren to þam temple, se ðe us alysde fram þystrum, and us gebrincð to þam ecan leohte, se ðe leofað and rixað a butan ende. Amen' (*CH* I.ix, ed. Thorpe I, 150, emphasis added). Earlier in the homily Simeon's prophecy and the Johannine phrase *lux mundi* are also explicitly linked: 'Symeon cwæð þa-gyt, "He is leoht to onwrigenysse ðeoda, and wuldor þinum folce Israhel." Ealle ðas word spræc se Symeon be ðam cilde to þam heofenlican Fæder, þe hine to mannum sende. *He is soð leoht þe todræfde þa þeostra ðises lifes, swa swa he sylf cwæð on his godspelle,* "Ic eom leoht ealles middangeardes, se ðe me fyligð, ne cymð he na on þystrum, ac he hæfð lifes leoht"' (*CH* I.ix, ed. Thorpe I, 144). The reference to John VIII.12 in the latter instance probably reflects the influence of one of Ælfric's

Commentary

sources, Haymo of Auxerre's homily on the Circumcision. The Old English homily for the Purification, though written approximately sixteen years earlier (according to Clemoes, 'Chronology', p. 243) may help explain Ælfric's departure from the text of the *Liber officialis* for *LME* 25. The conflation of ideas in the latter suggests a reminiscence of or conscious resort to the homily. The elaborations do not, however, appear in Ælfric's treatment of this liturgy for the second Old English pastoral letter to Wulfstan (Brief III.178).

VII Proper Customs: Septuagesima through Palm Sunday (LME 26–32)

LME 26   Septuagesima; cf. *Lib.off.* I.i.16–17, 6, 5, 19 and 1; *RC* 55–6

[104] *In Septuagessima*, etc.   Just as the season of Lent had evolved from a tendency to anticipate the celebration of Easter with a special period of mortification and penance, Lent itself gradually became the object of anticipation, so that the sixth and seventh centuries witnessed the development of a formally observed 'pre-Lent'. The latest and furthest extension was Septuagesima, actually a 'season' beginning on 'Septuagesima Sunday' three weeks before the first Sunday of Lent and lasting seventy days (thus ending on Saturday in Easter week); on these anticipatory developments of the liturgical calendar, see Vogel, *Medieval Liturgy*, pp. 309–11, with Tables at 404–6. The scant mention of Septuagesima or the two subsequent Sundays, Sexagesima and Quinquagesima, in the *Regularis concordia* (see *RC* 55–6) must have seemed a deficiency to Ælfric, for he borrowed extensively from the *Liber officialis* to fill out his discussion of the pre-Lenten period. Ælfric's treatment of Amalarian material at *LME* 26 bears close resemblance to his use of the same source in the Old English homily for Septuagesima Sunday (*CH* II.v, ed. Godden, pp. 41–51). Whether the homily was published in 992 or 994 × 995 – the respective dates for the second series given by Clemoes ('Chronology', p. 244) and Godden (*CH* II, pp. xci–xciii) – the Old English adaptation of the passage must predate the *LME* by about a decade, perhaps longer. When treating Septuagesima for the *LME*, Ælfric probably returned directly to the Latin source rather than to his Old English version. If he did consult the latter, he unaccountably vitiated those improvements he had introduced in the homily, such as the re-ordering of liturgical incipits and the generally greater cogency of the 'spiritual warfare' metaphor (see below, n. 107). Even if he did not resort to the homily, the Old English analogues nevertheless reveal much about how Ælfric interpreted his source. His earlier remarks on Candlemas (*LME* 25), with their interpolated reference to Christ as *lux mundi*, have also demonstrated the possibility that the interpretive context or arrangement of material in an earlier homily might exercise considerable influence when the subject was taken up again.

Some minor differences between *CH* II.v and *LME* 26 are also to be expected. Most noticeably, the Septuagesima homily incorporates numerous explanations of obscure or technical points for its non-specialist audience (e.g., 'Septuagesima is

Commentary

hundseofontigfeald getel'; 'Alleluia is ebreisc word. þæt is on leden Laudate dominum').

105 *cantica caelestia*, etc. Adapted from Amalarius, *Lib.off*. I.i.16 and 17:

> Quapropter alleluia in illo tempore non cantatur apud nos et dulcissimus ymnus angelorum 'Gloria in excelsis Deo', sed tractus pro alleluia . . . Alleluia et 'Gloria in excelsis Deo' cantica caelestia sunt.

Cf. *CH* II.v, lines 234–7 and 278–9 (ed. Godden, pp. 49 and 51):

> We willað eow secgan be ðyssere andweardan tide. hwi seo halige gelaðung forlæt on godes cyrcan Alleluian. and Gloria in excelsis deo fram ðisum andwerdum dæge oð þa halgan eastertide . . . Alleluia is swa we cwædon heofonlic sang.

Ælfric begins with the practical direction that the celebratory 'Alleluia' and 'Gloria in excelsis Deo' be dropped from the mass in this season. His explanation – that these *cantica caelestia* do not belong in a penitential season – lacks the support of Amalarius's fuller argument (based on Ps. CXXXVI.4) that the exiled and enslaved Israelites cannot sing the songs of the Lord in a foreign land. *LME* 26 departs from both the source and *CH* II.v, however, by inserting the mention of *cantica caelestia* in the introductory sentence. The severity of Ælfric's abridgement has obscured the logic behind this and other instances of re-organization for *LME* 26, but the more expansive Old English version reveals how he must have understood the progression of Amalarius's ideas. The church's self-imposed humiliation and preparation for *bellum spiritale* actually consist of giving up the *cantica caelestia* rather than of fasts or other penitential practices that Amalarius associates with soldierly exercise of 'warfare' (cf. *Lib.off*. I.i.18–19). Though Amalarius will later speak of suppressing the 'uocem gaudii et laetitiae, uocem sponsi et sponsae' (*Lib.off*. I.i.5–6, from Jer. XXV.10; see below, n. 106), he will not directly equate these with the 'heavenly songs' of 'Alleluia' and 'Gloria in excelsis', mention of which he postpones to a later part of the chapter (I.i.16–17). In *R1* manuscripts, however, the redactor has omitted the intervening material, with the resulting enjambment of these ideas: 'Omittamus cum eis uocem gaudii et laetitiae, uocem sponsi et sponsae [*here much omitted material*] quapropter alleluia in illo tempore non cantatur apud nos, et dulcissimus hymnus "Gloria in excelsis Deo"' (I.i.6/I.i.16). Evidence of this sort strongly supports that Ælfric knew the *Liber officialis* in the form of the *R1*. The corresponding material in *R1(Sa)* does not differ significantly from the standard *R1*.

106 *Et humiliamur . . . sponsi et sponse* Adapted from Amalarius, *Lib.off*. I.i.6 and 5:

> (6) Fors dictator septuagesimae nouit per Christi gratiam nobis peccata dimissa; septuaginta annos mutauit, quia in aliquibus criminibus communicamus priori populo, septuaginta diebus, et quod illi inuiti sustinuerunt, quia serui erant, nos uoluntarie pro peccatis nostris sustineamus, quia liberi sumus; omittamus cum eis uocem gaudii et laetitiae, uocem sponsi et sponsae.
>
> (5) Quanto tempore in captiuitate fuerit [*scil*. populus Israel], Hieremias manifestat dicens: 'Perdam ex eis uocem gaudii et laetitiae, uocem sponsi et uocem sponsae, uocem molae et lumen lucernae, et erit uniuersa terra eius in solitudine et in stupore, et seruient omnes gentes istae regi Babilonis septuaginta annis . . .'

Commentary

Cf. *CH* II.v, lines 246–51 and 253–5 (ed. Godden, p. 50):

... þæt israhela folc for heora mandædum. and forgægednyssum wurdon gehergode. and hundseofontig geara on babiloniscum þeowdome buton blisse and myrhðe wunodon. Nu hylt godes gelaðung þis hundseofontigfealde getel sylfwilles for hire gyltum. swa swa se ealda israhel neadunge heold on hæftnunge ... Se witega hieremias witegode þe ðære israhela ðeode. þæt hi sceoldon on ðam hundseofontig geara fæce geswican. blisse stemne and fægnunge. brydguman stemne. and bryde.

To judge from the shared emphases of the two treatments, most significant to Ælfric was the equation of the Babylonian captivity with the church's observance of a special penitential season, a correspondence to which he draws his audience's attention through carefully balanced antitheses ('sponte ... inuitus' / 'sylfwilles ... neadunge'). The verbal antithesis neatly underscores a typological one by celebrating the church's exalted status as the new Israel even while acknowledging its common lot with the old ('pro peccatis nostris' / 'for hire gyltum'). For unknown reasons, both Latin and Old English versions also reverse the progression of ideas in *Lib.off.* I.i.5 and 6. Ælfric may have felt that the long quotation from Jeremiah (XXV.10–11; cf. VII.34) at *Lib.off.* I.i.5 was unnecessary since Amalarius's subsequent commentary (I.i.6) repeats the crucial references to the 'uox gaudii et laetitiae'. In any case, the conclusion ('sine uoce', etc.) returns to and emphasizes the point of the preceding sentence, the dismissal of the celebratory 'Alleluia' and 'Gloria in excelsis Deo'. Once again Ælfric represents the liturgical act as a response unmediated by Amalarius's intrusive pseudo-historical agent (here the 'dictator septuagesimae' of *Lib.off.* I.i.6); cf. commentary to *LME* 22 (at n. 88), 24 (at n. 93), 25 (at n. 103), 32 (at n. 168), 33 (at n. 171), 39 (at n. 204) and 43 (at n. 219).

[107] *Ergo officia ipsa ... 'Omnis ... se abstinet'* Adapted from Amalarius, *Lib.off.* I.i.19:

Constitutione officii sui ipsud ieiunium ... intimauit [*scil.* praeceptor officii] in prima oratione missae dicens: 'Vt qui iuste pro peccatis nostris affligimur'. Hic enim afflictionem sonat. In introitu dicit: 'Circumdederunt me gemitus mortis, dolores inferni circumdederunt me' ... Propter hos dolores non possumus laetari et securi esse, sed praeparare debemus nos ad bellum, ut apostolus: 'Omnis autem, inquit, qui in agone contendit, ab omnibus se abstinet.'

Cf. *CH* II.v, lines 258–69 (ed. Godden, p. 50):

... for ðan þe us gedafenað þæt we sylfwilles fram ðisum andwerdan dæge mid sumere stiðnysse to ðam gastlicum gefeohte us sylfe gegearcian. swa swa seo cyrclice þenung us manað to heofunge. and to ure synna bereowsunge. Ærest on ðære mæssan officio we singað 'Circumdederunt me gemitus mortis'. Deaþes geomerunga me beeodon. and helle sarnyssa me beeodon. and ic on minre gedrefednysse drihten clypode. and he of his halgan temple mine stemne gehyrde. Eft on ðære mæssan collectan we cweðað. 'Qui iuste pro peccatis nostris affligimur'. þæt is. we ðe rihtlice for urum synnum sind geswencte. Eac se apostol on ðam pistole cwæð. Ælc ðæra þe on gecampe winð. forhæfð hine sylfne fram eallum ðingum.

In the fuller context of source, the notion of spiritual warfare is prefaced by a discussion of fasting, and it is this physical 'affliction' that is to be understood when Amalarius quotes the collect for Septuagesima Sunday: 'Preces populi tui ... exaudi:

Commentary

ut qui iuste pro peccatis nostris *affligimur*, pro tui nominis gloria misericorditer liberemur' (*Sacr.Greg.*, no. 144, emphasis added). Though nothing in this prayer specifically admonishes the faithful to prepare for spiritual battle, the *LME* links the quotation to Amalarius's other two – from the introit (*AMS*, no. 34, from Ps. XVII.5) and epistle (I Cor. IX.24–X.4) – as though all three patently support the theme. In both of Ælfric's versions (but not in the source), mention of 'spiritual warfare' precedes the incipits, but the homily makes much more effective use of Amalarius's quotations from the mass propers and even re-arranges the Latin incipits in their correct liturgical order (introit–collect–epistle). The resulting progression emphasizes the grief of repentance as a strict but necessary measure if the Christian is to wage spiritual combat successfully ('mid sumere stiðnysse to ðam gastlicum gefeohte us sylfe gegearcian'). The concept of *stiðnys* ('strictness' or 'rigour'), thus subtly introduced, provides a helpful transition between the challenges of soldierly and penitential discipline. By comparison, the abridgement at *LME* 26 has sundered Amalarius's point from the necessary supporting argument.

[108] *Nam Septuagessima . . . sabbati finitur*   Adapted from Amalarius, *Lib.off*. I.i.1:

Septuagesima computatur secundum titulationem [traditionem *R1*] sacramentorii et antiphonarii nouem ebdomadibus ante pascha Domini et finitur post pascha Domini in septima sabbati. Die dominica habet initium et in sabbati finem.

Cf. *CH* II.v, lines 243–5 (ed. Godden, pp. 49–50): 'Seo tid onginð on ðisum sunnandæge. nigon wucon ær eastron. and geendað on ðam Sæternesdæge þære easterlican wucan.' Here and frequently in the *LME*, the conjunction *nam* has so little causal force that it can be virtually ignored or allowed only a vague co-ordinative function (cf. below, n. 296). Here Ælfric explains, in words very close to Amalarius's own, the computation of the season according to the church's calendar. Although this material comes at the head of Amalarius's chapter in the *Liber officialis* (and in *R1*), Ælfric has postponed it to the end of his discussion in the *LME* (though not in the homily). That an appeal 'secundum disputationem Amalarii' should be substituted for 'secundum [traditionem] sacramentorii et antiphonarii' perhaps bears witness to Amalarius's considerable prestige, or to Ælfric's scholarly habit of citing immediate sources.

[109] *Consuetudo dicit . . . pinguedinem*, etc.   As usual, the introductory tag indicates a return to the *Concordia* following interpolation from another source. *RC* 55 requires the monks to approach the Lenten fast in stages, first by giving up fats, then, from Quinquagesima, milk and eggs (and foods made from these). See also *LME* 28.

[110] *dimissa 'Alleluia'. . . canendi sunt*   St Benedict had stated that 'Alleluia' should suffice as the antiphon for the six psalms of the second Nocturn in the ferial Night Office (*RSB*, c. IX.9). *RC* 56 indicates only that in Lent there shall be three antiphons *de psalmis* – i.e., one per two psalms. Ælfric is more specific, providing the incipit of each antiphon for each day of the week; this significant addition to the source is comparable to his expansive treatment of the hymnal at *LME* 13 and 50; see discussion above, pp. 35–6.

[111] 'Vt non delinquam . . . Sana Domine . . . Eructauit cor . . .' *CAO* II, series 27a and 38a (from Pss. XXXVIII.2, XL.5 and XLIV.2, respectively).

Commentary

¹¹² *'Auertit Dominus . . . Intende in me . . . Iuste iudicate . . .' CAO* II, series 28a and 39a (from Pss. LII.7, LIV.3 and LVII.2, respectively).

¹¹³ *'Quaerite Dominum . . . Domine Deus . . . Quam bonus . . .' CAO* II, series 29a and 40 (from Pss. LXVIII.33, LXIX.2 and LXXII.1, respectively).

¹¹⁴ *'Exultate Deo . . . Tu solus altissimus . . . Benedixisti Domine. . .' CAO* II, series 30a and 41b (from Pss. LXXX.2, LXXXII.19 and LXXXIV.2, respectively).

¹¹⁵ *'Cantate Domino. . . Quia mirabilia fecit . . . Iubilate Deo . . .' CAO* II, series 31b and 42a (from Pss. XCV.2, XCVII.1 and XCVII.4, respectively).

¹¹⁶ *'Visita nos . . . De necessitatibus . . . Confitebor Domino . . .' CAO* II, series 32a and 43a (from Pss. CV.4, CVI.6 and CVIII.30, respectively).

LME 27   Sexagesima; cf. *Lib.off.* I.ii.1

¹¹⁷ *In Sexagesima*, etc. That is, the Sunday after Septuagesima Sunday (see above, n. 104). Apart from the last phrase (*similiter . . . diei*), *LME* 27 is an almost verbatim quotation from Amalarius, *Lib.off.* I.ii.1. The only striking departure is readily explained as a variant in Ælfric's exemplar: all of the *R1* manuscripts, including *R1(Sa)*, have the incorrect *Sexagesima* for *Septuagesima*.

¹¹⁸ *'Deus qui conspicis . . . subsistimus'*   In the Hadrianum (*Sacr.Greg.*, nos. 628 and 748) and all extant Anglo-Saxon sacramentaries, the collect quoted by Amalarius is assigned not to Sexagesima but to the feasts of Sixtus (6 August) and Martin (11 November). Hallinger's apparatus to *LME* 27 (p. 163.27–8) suggests that the confusion is with the collect for the second Sunday in Lent, beginning 'Deus qui conspicis omni nos uirtute destitui' (*Sacr.Greg.*, no. 202). Amalarius's sacramentary may have erroneously alloted either collect to Sexagesima, but it is perhaps easier to believe that similar incipits led him to misremember the correct prayer: 'Deus qui conspicis quia ex nulla nostra actione confidimus, concede propitius ut contra aduersa omnia doctoris gentium protectione muniamur' (*Sacr.Greg.*, no. 147). The normal distribution of all three of these prayers in *Sacr.Greg.* is reflected in *Corp.41, Leofr.Miss., Miss.NMin., Miss.RJum., Miss.StAug.* and *Winch.Sacr.*, so the case is strong that Ælfric has taken over an erroneous detail from his source. Note, however, that the correct incipit, lacking the necessary reference to *uirtus*, would not have advanced Amalarius's theme ('in nobis non est uirtus soluendi').

LME 28   Quinquagesima; cf. *Lib.off.* I.iii.1; *RC* 55

¹¹⁹ *Quinquagesima*, etc. That is, the Sunday before Ash Wednesday and the formal beginning of Lent. Again, Ælfric has lifted this entire section from Amalarius.

¹²⁰ *propius*   Nocent emends to *proprius* following Hanssens's edition, although *propius* is an authentic *R1* variant and so was probably the reading of Ælfric's exemplar. The reading in *R1(Sa)*, *propitius*, may represent a subsequent correction.

¹²¹ *Modo*   Manuscripts of *R1* leave Amalarius's original *iam* unchanged, and there is reason to suspect that the substitution of *modo* is Ælfric's. In the *Grammar* he defines *modo* as 'nuða oððe hwiltidum', whereas '*iam* eallunga oððe nu getacnað þreo tida,

Commentary

forðgewitene and andwerde and towearde' (*Ælfrics Grammatik und Glossar: Text und Varianten*, ed. J. Zupitza (Berlin, 1880), p. 235, lines 13–14, and p. 241, lines 18–19). If Ælfric took the primary meaning of *modo* to be *nuða*, in Old English an emphatic marker of present time as opposed to past (see Mitchell, *Old English Syntax*, § 2569), he may have preferred it therefore to the possibly ambiguous *iam* which can refer to the past, present and future. Notably, Ælfric's first gloss of *iam* is not a temporal marker at all (*eallunga* 'altogether'). Compare a similar use of *modo* in c. 17 of Ælfric's abbreviation of Wulfstan of Winchester's *Vita S. Æthelwoldi*: cf. Wulfstan's 'nunc autem consuete Burh appellatur' (c. 24) and Ælfric's 'modo consuete Burh nominatur' (*Life of St Æthelwold*, ed. Lapidge and Winterbottom, pp. 40 and 76, respectively).

122 *'Esto mihi . . . refugii'* The introit for Quinquagesima Sunday, AMS, no. 36a (from Ps.(Romanum) XXX.3).

123 *abstinere . . . de ouis fiunt* Cf. *RC* 55: 'a Quinquagesima uero quadragesimalem teneant abstinentiam more solito'. This restriction, combined with that from *pinguedo* observed since Septuagesima (*LME* 26), marks the beginning of full Lenten abstinence; see *RC* (Symons), p. 32, n. 1.

LME 29   Ash Wednesday; cf. *RC* 57

124 *Consuetudo: Quarta feria . . . nona decantata*, etc. The source for this passage (*RC* 57) actually begins with a general instruction about the processions on all Wednesdays and Fridays in Lent (until Maundy Thursday) and from the Octave of Pentecost until 1 October. Ælfric postpones this information until after his description of Ash Wednesday, which is very close to the *ordo* set down in the *Concordia*. Ælfric and the *Concordia* agree in placing these ceremonies after None, although in other customaries the procession and imposition of ashes commonly take place after Sext (Symons, 'Sources', p. 155).

125 *quia legimus . . . prime preuaricationis* Source(s) unknown, but there is an analogue in Ælfric's Old English sermon for Ash Wednesday: 'We rædað on bocum ægðer ge on ðære ealdan æ, ge on þære niwan, þæt þa menn þe heora synna be-hreowsodon, þæt hi mid axum hi sylfe bestreowodon, and mid hæran hi gescryddon to lice. Nu do we þis lytle on ures lenctenes anginne, þæt we streowiað axan uppan ure heafda to geswutelunge þæt we sculon ure synna behreowsian, on ure lencten-licum fæstene' (*LS* XII, ed. Skeat I, 262–4, lines 33–40). It may not be necessary to posit an immediate source for either passage, since the link between sin, mortality and the sign of the ashes was widely re-inforced by both scripture and the liturgy (e.g., Gen. III.19).

126 *'Exaudi nos Domine'* AMS, no. 37a; for outlines of the Roman and Sarum rites for Ash Wednesday, see the chart by Hughes, § 915.

127 *cum psalmo* Specified at *RC* 57 as Ps. LXVIII.

128 *'Deus misereatur nostri', collecta* Ps. LXVI. The *Concordia* includes *preces* between the psalm and collect; *DEC* 5 further specifies, 'Preces: "Peccauimus Domine; Adiuua nos".'

Commentary

[129] *reliquas antiphonas decantando* Not specified by Ælfric or the *Concordia*, but *DEC* 5 includes 'Antiphonas "Iuxta uestibulum" et "Imutemur [*sic*] habitu"' (see *RC* (Symons), p. 32, n. 9, and *AMS*, no. 37a).

[130] *ecclesiam quo eunt*, etc. Again Ælfric retains an instruction to process to some other church but does not specify the name or location; see above, n. 98.

[131] *et dominicam orationem, flexis genibus* This phrase or an equivalent is absent from the *Concordia*. My translation associates kneeling with the Lord's Prayer only, not with the saint's antiphon, but Ælfric's original is ambiguous.

[132] *'Ad te leuaui oculos meos'* Ps. CXXII.

[133] *usque ad Exaltationem sanctae crucis* That is, until 14 September, but cf. *RC* 57 ('usque ad kalendas octobris'), as well as *DEC* (O) 5 ('usque ad Kalendas Nouembris') and *DEC* (R) 5 ('ad Calendas Octobris'). This extraordinary disagreement must owe something to the fact that important changes to the horarium were already associated with each of these dates. The Office was divided into its winter and summer periods by Easter and 1 October (or 1 November for hymns, placement of Vigils of the Dead, etc.), while the distribution of meals and *lectio* changed three times per year (at Lent, Easter and 14 September (= Exaltation of the Holy Cross)); see *RC* (Symons), pp. xli and xxxiii–xxxv.

[134] *semper discalciatis pedibus* Not in the *Concordia* (see *RC* (Symons), p. 32, n. 5). In the Latin it is not clear whether the instruction applies whenever the procession takes place or only in the latter of the two designated periods (i.e., from the Octave of Pentecost to 14 September). Given the penitential character of these processions, the phrase 'discalciatis pedibus' probably applies to both the Lenten and summer periods; the analogues cited in Hallinger's apparatus to *LME* 29, 165.1 support this interpretation.

[135] *'Exsurge Domine'* Same as *AMS*, no. 201a.

LME 30 Lent; cf. *Lib.off*. I.iv.1 + *Lect.discr.long*. II.1; *RC* 59

[136] *Amalarius: In Quadragesima*, etc. Almost verbatim from *Lib.off*. I.iv.1. The *LME* reading *quia* for correct *quem* probably stems from an abbreviation incorrectly expanded. *Quia* is not an attested *R1* variant.

[137] *'Inuocauit me et ego exaudiam eum'* *AMS*, no. 40a, the mass introit for the first Sunday in Lent (from Ps.(Romanum) XC.15).

[138] *'Tempore accepto . . . adiuui te'* II Cor. VI.2, from the epistle reading at mass (II Cor. VI.1–10).

[139] *angeli Domini custodiunt nos* From the gradual, *AMS*, no. 40a. (from Ps. XC.11).

[140] *scuto ueritatis circumdati sumus* From the tract, *AMS*, no. 40a (from Ps. XC.5).

[141] *'Vade retro Satanas'* Matt. IV.10, from the gospel of the day (Matt. IV.1–11, Jesus's temptation in the desert). Ælfric has slightly altered the quotation as given in the *Liber officialis*, 'Vade, Satana' (or 'Vade, Satanas' in *R1(Sa)*) to the common Old Latin variant 'Vade retro Satanas'. Ælfric's preference for the reading *uade retro* over simple *uade* finds confirmation in his Old English homily for the first Sunday in Lent. There, in Ælfric's comments on Christ's rebuke, three manuscripts of the homily include a Latin annotation:

Commentary

Quidam dicunt non dixisse saluatorem Satanę 'uade retro' sed tantum 'uade'. Sed tamen in rectioribus et uetustioribus exemplaribus habetur 'uade retro Satanas', sicut interpretatio ipsius nominis declarat. Nam diabolus 'deorsum ruens' interpretatur. Apostolo igitur Petro dicitur a Christo 'uade retro me', id est 'sequere me'. Diabolo non dicitur 'uade retro me' sed 'uade retro', sicut iam diximus, et sic scripsit beatus Hieronymus in una epistola.

The three manuscripts containing this interpolation are CCCC 198, and Cambridge, University Library Ii. 4. 6 and Gg. 3. 28. The last of these (from which the above quotation is transcribed) is probably a copy of a collection produced under Ælfric's own supervision (see Sisam, *Studies*, pp. 165–71). It is very likely that the above Latin comment is the work of Ælfric himself – perhaps a marginal note that became incorporated into the text of the homily. On this note and others like it, see the introduction to *CH* II, ed. Godden, p. lxxxiii. On Ælfric's willingness elsewhere to adopt non-Vulgate readings, see R. Marsden, 'Ælfric as Translator: the Old English Prose *Genesis*', *Anglia* 109 (1991), 319–58, at p. 333. The alteration of the biblical verse at *LME* 30 also shows Ælfric again correcting what he may have perceived as a misquotation of scripture by his source (cf. the example of *sacerdotum* above, at n. 93).

142 *reliquie et cruces occultantur*, etc.   Cf. *Lib.off.* I.i.23 and the widespread *R1* interpolation (Hanssens's *Lect.discr.long.* II.1):

> Eadem quoque ratione nos dicimus quod melius est non adorare crucem istis diebus quibus ante passionem ieiunauit Christus . . . Sed si quis uoluerit, faciat, et nos soli non facimus, quia absurdum putamus illam adorare, dum alleluia relinquimus, et, ut nouum sit nobis in die eius passionis, cum de loco occulto ostensa sit nobis. Et iterum, ecce in quadragesimo reliquiae atque cruces occultantur. Et uelamen inter sancta sanctorum et populum ponitur. Igitur si quis sapiens fuerit, in mente prouidebit si iustum sibi sit cruces adorare, dum occultantur. Et si adorauerit, in die passionis eius opus ei non erit nobiscum crucem adorare.

While Bateson (*Excerpta ex institutionibus*, p. 182, n. 4) was correct to claim that this passage does not come from the authentic *Liber officialis*, she could not have known about the post-Amalarian interpolations found only in *R1* manuscripts. The anonymous compiler of that recension has inserted this teaching about the veneration of crosses and relics between the chapters on Septuagesima and Sexagesima, rather than at a more obvious place, the beginning of Lent (although the choice does make sense in view of his argument based on the presence of 'Alleluia', which is absent from Septuagesima onwards; cf. *LME* 26). In appropriating this passage, Ælfric has moved it to a more functional place among the customs proper to the forty days of Lent. Otherwise he follows the wording of the source closely, although he clarifies the interpolator's argument by re-ordering certain phrases so that the instruction (the veiling of holy objects) precedes the justification (the omission of 'Alleluia').

143 *aliquid nobis augendum*, etc.   This custom closely follows the Lenten devotions at *RC* 59, which in turn echoes *RSB*, c. XLIX.5. Notably, Ælfric's Lenten customs omit all reference to the wearing of chasubles by the priest, deacon and subdeacon at mass in Lent and on Ember Days (cf. *RC* 58). The *Concordia* goes into some detail on the point, dictating that the subdeacon shall remove his chasuble when he reads the epistle and that the deacon shall wear his folded over his left shoulder when he reads the gospel.

Commentary

[144] *duos psalmos prostrati . . . peroremus deuoti* Verbatim from *RC* 59. The devotion imposed by Ælfric and the *Concordia* was in part a response to Benedict's admonition in *RSB*, c. XLIX, that monks should assume some extra spiritual obligation in Lent. These extra psalms, or *psalmi prostrati*, were a commonly prescribed devotion in early medieval monastic customaries (Symons, 'Sources', p. 276), and the *Concordia* and *LME* agree in their descriptions of the custom. At the end of every Office except Nocturns, the monks shall prostrate themselves and say two psalms, specified as one from the seven penitential (Pss. VI, XXXI, XXXVII, L, CI, CXXIX and CXLII) and one from the fifteen gradual psalms (Pss. CXIX–CXXXIII), followed by the 'Kyrie', Lord's Prayer, the *preces pro peccatis* and a collect. The devotion is discussed in detail by Tolhurst, pp. 93–101.

[145] *'Domine ne in furore tuo' et 'Ad Dominum'* Pss. VI and CXIX.

[146] *preces pro peccatis* Printed by Tolhurst, p. 99, beginning '(V.) Adiuua nos deus salutaris noster et propter gloriam nominis tui domine libera nos. (R.) Et propicius [*sic*] esto peccatis nostris propter nomen tuum', followed by thirteen further versicle-response petitions (though the form might be shortened; see Tolhurst, p. 95).

[147] *'Beati quorum', 'Leuaui'* Pss. XXXI and CXX.

[148] *'Domine ne in furore tuo' (ii) et 'Letatus sum'* Pss. XXXVII and CXXI.

[149] *'Miserere mei Deus' et 'Ad te leuaui oculos meos'* Pss. L and CXXII.

[150] *'Domine exaudi' et 'Nisi quia Dominus'* Pss. CI and CXXIII.

[151] *'De profundis', 'Qui confidunt'* Pss. CXXIX and CXXIV.

[152] *'Domine exaudi' (ii) et 'In conuertendo'* Pss. CXLII and CXXV.

[153] *offerat . . . ad missam maiorem* This exact provision does not occur in the source. An earlier passage in the *Concordia* (*RC* 25), omitted by Ælfric, directs that on Monday the right side of the choir shall present the offerings at the matutinal mass, the left at the principal mass, and that this order will reverse on Tuesday, and so alternate through the rest of the week.

[154] *Sabbato . . . radent se fratres* The source, *RC* 59, confirms that the Saturday before the fourth Sunday in Lent is intended, although the terms 'media(na)' and (as here) 'mediante Quadragessima' anciently referred to the fifth (later 'Passion') Sunday; see Vogel, *Medieval Liturgy*, p. 309.

LME 31   Passion Sunday; cf. *Lib.off.* IV.xx.1–3 and 5

[155] *Amalarius: Dies Passionis Domini*, etc.   From Amalarius, *Lib.off.* IV.xx.1–3 and 5. Ælfric's first sentence is quoted verbatim, but the rest of his passage is a significant adaptation:

(1) Dies passionis Domini computantur duabus ebdomadibus ante pascha Domini. Neque enim ab re est, quod in duabus ebdomadibus recolitur eius passio, quoniam in duobus temporibus huius mundi scribitur et informatur idem [eadem *R1*] passio . . .

(2) In illis diebus amittimus per xi dies in solis responsoriis gloriam sanctae trinitatis, quoniam per humilitatem ueniendum est ad passionem Christi. Passio et persecutio humiliant, quantum ad praesens cernitur, massam quae ex Adam sumpta est. Hanc imitationem humilitatis designant

Commentary

turbae quae obuiam uenerunt Domino die palmarum ad descensum montis Oliueti. Ymnus scilicet 'Gloria Patri et Filio, et Spiritui sancto' gloriam sanctae trinitatis recolit.

(3) Quoniam una est persona filii Dei et filii hominis, qui pati uenerat, conformat se sancta ecclesia capiti suo et de glorificatione eius reticet [reticetur *R1*], usque dum exaltetur per triumphum uictoriae.

(5) Ab illo die quando amittimus 'Gloria Patri', duae ebdomadae sunt, hoc est quattuordecim dies usque in pascha Domini. Dies paschae iam de tertia ebdomada est, in qua restauratur omnis amissa glorificatio. In tertio tempore legis gratiae omnia beneficia redduntur ecclesiae, quae expectauerunt patres nostri, qui tenebantur in claustris inferni, tempore naturalis legis et tempore legis litterae.

Amalarius's chief point is the omission of the 'Gloria Patri' at the end of the responsories in the Night Office, justified by Christ's suppression of his own divinity during the last two weeks of his earthly life. The arguments seem confusing, not least because Amalarius unaccountably separates the interpretation of the two weeks of Passiontide as the the two ages of this world, *ante legem* and *sub lege*, from the analogous interpretation of Paschaltide as the age *sub gratia* (*Lib.off.* IV.xx.1 and 5, quoted above). Ælfric joins the ideas of these two separate passages and declines to speculate on the theological implications of omitting the 'Gloria Patri'.

156 *omittimus inuitatorium*, etc. At first glance, Ælfric appears to have supplemented Amalarius in the detail 'omittimus inuitatorium et in responsoriis "Gloriam" sanctae Trinitatis' (cf. *Lib.off.* IV.xx.2, quoted in the preceding note). I have not emended the text, but as it stands the point is problematic. It not only opposes the teaching of the source but creates an internal contradiction in the *LME*. The invitatory psalm (Ps. XCIV) was commonly omitted on Epiphany (see *LME* 24) and during the last three days of Holy Week. When discussing the special customs of the Triduum, Ælfric will even note 'Inuitatorium non canimus' (*LME* 33) – a superfluous instruction if the monks omitted this element of Nocturns from Passion Sunday onwards. If the manuscript is correct here, Ælfric's instruction to give up the invitatory from Passion Sunday preserves a notable local variation of liturgical practice. More likely, however, is an error of haplography at some stage in the copying of this sentence, which may have originally read 'omittimus *in inuitatorio*' or '*in inuitatoriis*'. Ælfric's original instructions may therefore have been to omit the 'Gloria Patri' at the end of the invitatory and at the end of the responsories from Passion Sunday until the Triduum. Then, on the last three days of Holy Week, the 'Gloria Patri' would be dropped from all parts of the mass and Office. This hypothesis sets right a contradiction in the *LME* and brings Ælfric into agreement with the common practice of the early medieval church. Although *ordines* do not always refer to the invitatory specifically (nor does Amalarius mention it at *Lib.off.* IV.xx.2), the 'Gloria patri' was regularly dropped after it as well as after the responsories in Passiontide; for specific mentions, see *OR XXVIII.*2 and *XXXI.*2; see also the thirteenth-century commentary by Gulielmus Durandus, the *Rationale diuinorum officiorum* VI.lxiv.4 (211v): 'Et est aduertendum, quod tacetur [*scil.* 'Gloria Patri'] in introitibus et responsoriis, quia illa sunt de passione, *et in Venite exultemus Domino* [i.e., Ps. XCIV, the invitatory]. In psalmis vero et hymnis, non' (emphasis added). Amalarius himself elsewhere (*Lib.off.* IV.xxxvii.7)

Commentary

refers to the dropping of the invitatory 'in diebus passionis Domini', but the immediate qualification 'quando Iudaei congregabantur ad pessima consilia de nece Domini' (i.e., Wednesday of Holy Week, by traditional reckoning; see *Lib.off.* I.xi.2) indicates that the *dies passionis* there meant are the Triduum, not the entire two weeks of Passiontide.

A minor liturgical notice also occurs in Ælfric's Old English homily for Passion Sunday: 'Þeos tid fram ðisum andwerdan dæge oð ða halgan eastertide is gecweden cristes ðrowungtid . . . On ðisum dagum we forlætað on urum repsum Gloria patri. for geomerunge þære halgan ðrowunge. buton sum healic freolstid him on besceote' (*CH* II.xiii, ed. Godden, p. 127, lines 1–2 and 8–10). Unlike the Old English homily for Septuagesima, this passage does not reflect the influence of the *Liber officialis*, nor does it deal with the liturgy in any detailed way. On the other hand, the Old English makes a point of mentioning that in Passiontide the 'Gloria patri' is dropped after the responsories (OE *repsas*), but says nothing about omitting the invitatory.

LME 32   Palm Sunday; cf. *RC* 60; *Lib.off.* I.x.1 + *Lect.discr.long.* II.3–4 and 6

[157] *dum matutinalis missa canitur*, etc.   Ælfric's description of the Palm Sunday rituals follows that of *RC* 60 closely, and once again these two depart from continental practice in a number of details; see *RC* (Symons), p. 35, n. 2; Symons, 'Sources', p. 155–6; Hallinger, apparatus to *RC* 60, 106.2–3. Hughes (§ 917) provides comparative outlines of the fully developed Roman and Sarum versions, and a broader conspectus of medieval and early modern sources is provided by Schmidt, pp. 694–704.

[158] *ubi palme benedicendae sunt*   The awkward use of *ubi* (? for *quo*) hints of either a careless abridgement or a subsequent textual corruption (cf. *RC* 60: 'ad aecclesiam ubi palmae sunt'). This provision, similar to those given for Candlemas and Ash Wednesday, takes for granted the presence of some neighbouring church or chapel (cf. above, nn. 98 and 130). At this point the source again mentions an antiphon and collect in honour of the saint to whom the processional church is dedicated (*RC* 60), though it is not clear that Ælfric's *oratio processionis* corresponds to this (see n. 160, below).

[159] *si aura permiserit*   Here Ælfric takes the phrase as the source intends, i.e., with reference to the wearing of albs (cf. *RC* 60: 'omnes, si fieri potest et aura permiserit, albis induti'). He seems to have misunderstood the same phrase at its earlier occurrence in the Candlemas *ordo* (see comment at n. 97, above).

[160] *finita oratione processionis*   Cf. *RC* 60: 'Finita oratione [*scil.* in honour of the saint]'. From here on both the *Concordia* and the *LME* give only the roughest outline of what was assuredly a complex order of prayers, readings and chants. The most complete Anglo-Saxon witness from Ælfric's time may be the *ordo* copied in s. xi[1] at Christ Church, Canterbury, as part of *Cant.Ben.* (pp. 22–8). Ælfric briefly refers to the ceremonies of Palm Sunday in *CH* I.xiv (ed. Thorpe I, 218) and again in the second Old English pastoral letter to Wulfstan (Brief III.181).

[161] '*Turba multa . . . post eum abiit*'   The prefatory gospel reading, John XII.12–19.

Commentary

¹⁶² *benedictio palmarum*   For the form, see, e.g., *Cant.Ben.*, pp. 23–5.

¹⁶³ *'Pueri Hebreorum'*   The first of a widely used series of processional antiphons; see, e.g., *Cant.Ben.*, p. 25.

¹⁶⁴ *Transacta processione*, etc.   Ælfric skips over the return to the main church and the singing of the *antiphonae maiores* mentioned, but not specified, at *RC* 60. Cf. *Cant.Ben.*, pp. 25–6, where these are given in full: (1) 'Ante sex dies', (2) 'Cum audisset', (3) 'Occurrunt turbe' and (4) 'Ceperunt omnes'.

¹⁶⁵ *'Gloria laus' cum uersibus . . . sicut mos est*   For the text of the famous hymn, attributed to Theodulf of Orléans (d. *c.* 821), see *AH* L, 160–3. The *pueri* have returned to the church ahead of the procession in order to begin the hymn from within (*deintus*). The refrain, beginning 'Gloria laus et honor tibi sit', was sung by all between the verses, which were sung by the cantor; see the arrangement at *Cant.Ben.*, pp. 27–8, and *RC* (Symons), p. 35, n. 6.

¹⁶⁶ *'Ingrediente Domino'*   See *Cant.Ben.*, p. 28.

¹⁶⁷ *sicut supra dictum est*   That is, as described in the *ordo* for Candlemas, wherein Terce also comes between the procession and mass (*LME* 25).

¹⁶⁸ *in memoriam illius rei*, etc.   Adapted from Amalarius, *Lib.off.* I.x.1:

> [Dies palmarum dicitur, id est uictoriarum. *R1*] Eadem die Dominus de Bethania descendit Hierusalem, quando obuiam uenit ei turba, ut Iohannes narrat: 'In crastinum autem turba multa, quae uenerat ad diem festum, cum audisset quia uenit Iesus Hierusolimam, acceperunt ramos palmarum, et praecesserunt [processerunt *R1*] obuiam ei, et clamauerunt: 'Osanna, benedictus qui uenit in nomine Domini, rex Israhel.' In memoriam illius rei nos per ecclesias nostras solemus portare ramos et clamare: 'Osanna'.

Ælfric preserves the Vulgate (and *R1*) reading *processerunt*   For once, however, Amalarius's commentary does not intrude an anonymous human 'author of the liturgy', so his resulting first-person plural statement ('nos per ecclesias . . .') suits the kind of dramatic emphasis Ælfric has elsewhere had to introduce through revision; cf. commentary to *LME* 22 (at n. 88), 24 (at n. 93), 25 (at n. 103), 26 (at n. 106), 33 (at n. 171), 39 (at n. 204) and 43 (at n. 219).

¹⁶⁹ *triumphalem uictoriam Christi*   Note the variant beginning of the source passage preserved in *R1* manuscripts ('palmarum . . . id est uictoriarum', quoted in the preceding note). The sentence may lie behind Ælfric's closing reference to Christ's 'triumphalem uictoriam', but the idea is an exegetical commonplace. Ælfric discusses the symbolism of the palms without recourse to Amalarius in his Old English homily for this same occasion:

> Nu sceole we healdan urne palm, oðþæt se sangere onginne ðone offrung-sang, and geoffrian þonne Gode ðone palm, for ðære getacnunge. Palm getacnað syge. Sygefæst wæs Crist þaþa he ðone micclan deofol oferwann, and us generede; and we sceolon beon eac sygefæste þurh Godes mihte, swa þæt we ure undeawas, and ealle leahtras, and ðone deofol oferwinnan, and us mid godum weorcum geglencgan, and on ende ures lifes betæcan Gode ðone palm, þæt is, ure sige, and ðancian him georne, þæt we, ðurh his fultum, deoful oferwunnon, þæt he us beswican ne mihte. (*CH* I.xiv, ed. Thorpe I, 218)

In the second Old English pastoral letter to Archbishop Wulfstan, Ælfric merely

Commentary

notes that the practice has a symbolic meaning, but refers the reader to (his own?) previous discussions of the subject (Brief III.181–2).

170 *Eadem die ad Passionem*, etc. Seemingly a conflation of a notable *R1* variant (Hanssens's *Lect.discr.long.* II.3–6, quoted here) and phrases from *RC* 60:

> Eadem die ad passionem Domini diaconus dicat: 'Dominus uobiscum,' et respondent omnes: 'Et cum spiritu tuo'; sed cum dicit 'Passio Domini' et reliqua, nullus respondeat 'Gloria tibi Domine' . . . Et ad illam passionem [*scil.* in feria quarta] diaconus dicat: 'Dominus uobiscum,' et respondent omnes: 'Et cum spiritu tuo,' sed cum dicit 'Passio Domini' et reliqua, nullus respondeat 'Gloria tibi Domine' . . . Ad illam passionem [*scil.* in feria sexta] diaconus non dicat: 'Dominus uobiscum,' sed: 'Passio Domini' et reliqua, nullo respondente: 'Gloria tibi Domine.'

A gospel account of Christ's Passion was read on Palm Sunday, Wednesday of Holy Week and Good Friday. The formulaic dialogue introducing and concluding these readings differs slightly from that during the rest of the year. Here Ælfric's sources pose a complex problem, for he appears to have drawn phrases from both *RC* 60 and the *Retractatio prima*. The evidence of *DEC* 6 further complicates the picture, for it agrees almost verbatim with the *LME* in its instruction for the Passion reading on Palm Sunday, but for those of the following Wednesday and Good Friday, where Ælfric has separate, successive instructions, the *DEC* follows the *Concordia*. In excluding the *DEC* from Ælfric's canon, Clemoes explained this partial correspondence between the *LME* and *DEC* as a result of their common descent from 'a version of the *Regularis Concordia* slightly different from any now extant' ('Supplement to the Introduction', *Hirtenbriefe*, ed. Fehr, p. cxlvi, n. 94). If so, then this 'variant version' of the *Concordia*, underlying both the *LME* and the *DEC*, already contained an interpolation from *R1*. It seems, therefore, that the *Liber officialis* was being used by someone to supplement the *Concordia* even before Ælfric's writing of the *LME*. Yet Ælfric himself takes credit for introducing Amalarian material into Æthelwold's customary (see *LME* 1), and the present instance is not the only case of close textual correspondence between the *LME* and *DEC*. The case for and against Ælfric's influence, direct or indirect, on the *DEC* is re-examined in Jones, 'Two Composite Texts'.

VIII Proper customs: the triduum sacrum *(LME 33–45)*

LME 33 Nocturns, Tenebrae and the special 'Kyrie'-responsory; cf. variant *Lib.off.* in *R1(Sa)*, pp. 18–21; *RC* 61 and 62

171 *In Cena Domini*, etc. From this point, through the discussion of the Easter Vigil, Ælfric's exemplar of the *Liber officialis* must have departed significantly from other *R1* manuscripts, resembling instead the variant of that recension now preserved in Salisbury, Cathedral Library, 154 (Salisbury, s. xi[ex]). Despite some general similarities to the common Amalarian and *R1* teaching (cf. *Lib.off.* IV.xxi.4–6), in its details

Commentary

LME 33 unambiguously follows *R1(Sa)*, pp. 18–19, which, unlike Amalarius's treatise, takes the form of a dialogue:

> Scito a te quaeri cur prohibeas more solito 'Domine labia mea aperies' siue 'Deus in adiutorium meum' et 'Gloriam' sequentem dicere?
> Audi, scrutator, intende consuetudini tuae et disce ab ea utrum oporteat nec ne. Qui solet tecum dicere hoc quod putasti, nisi fallor, princeps congregationis. Princeps enim nostrae congregationis in hac nocte traditus est . . . Non habemus nostrum episcopum de quo dicit apostolus: 'Conuersi estis nunc ad pastorem et episcopum animarum uestrarum' [I Peter II.25]. Ipse enim dicit: 'Traditus sum et non egrediebar' [Ps. LXXXVII.9]. Quia non egreditur ad discipulos, non est qui dicat: 'Deus in adiutorium meum'. Scriptum est: 'Recessit pastor noster, fons aquae uiuae' [cf. Jer. II.13?]. Inuitatorium non canimus quia dispersae sunt oues et non est pastor qui congreget [cf. Isa. XIII.14 and Jer. XLIX.5]. Pastor de se monstrat tubam canere prophetalem, '<Percutiam inquiens> [percutiens inquies *MS*] pastorem et dispergentur oues gregis' [Matt. XXVI.31 or Mark XIV.27; cf. Zach. XIII.7].
> Preceptor mi, cur precipis a Cena Domini ut nec in psalmis nec in ullo loco 'Gloria' dicatur usque in Pascha?
> Cur inquam? Cui habes dicere gloriam? Filio Dei? Quem solemus glorificare inter iniquos deputatum esse uidemus [cf. Luke XXII.37] . . .
> Didascale mi, dic mathiti: quis est qui benedictionem petat aut dicat 'Tu autem Domine, miserere nobis'?
> Comprehenso pastore grex omnis fugam iniit, 'discipuli omnes relicto eo fugerunt' [Matt. XXVI.56].

During the last three days of Holy Week, the liturgy underwent a dramatic change, reaching a climax in the Great Vigil of Easter. Further customs were dropped from the daily horarium in order to create a solemn and austere atmosphere. In addition to the 'Alleluia' and 'Gloria in excelsis' (omitted at mass since Septuagesima) and the 'Gloria Patri' at the end of the invitatory and responsories (omitted in the Night Office since Passion Sunday), the invitatory itself was now dropped, and all the Offices lost their opening dialogues 'Deus in adiutorium meum intende' and/or 'Domine labia mea aperies', as well as the 'Gloria Patri' at the end of the individual psalms.

The author of this passage in *R1(Sa)* may have derived from Amalarius's original his focus on some liturgical implications of Christ's absence following his arrest. Whatever its sources, the resulting text of *R1(Sa)* is much more consistent in this emphasis than the corresponding passages at *Lib.off.* IV.xxi.4–6. Ælfric's extensive verbatim use of the source, which is little more than a tissue of biblical quotations, also recalls his own preference for scriptural wording and justifications evidenced elsewhere in the *LME* (see above, nn. 93 and 141). Ælfric may also have appreciated the way this passage presents the Triduum as a virtual recapitulation of events surrounding Christ's Passion; on this pattern cf. commentary to *LME* 22 (at n. 88), 24 (at n. 93), 25 (at n. 103), 26 (at n. 106), 32 (at n. 168), 39 (at n. 204) and 43 (at n. 219).

This conception of the liturgy as a kind of (anti-)typological response to historical events was facilitated by the associative habits of mind developed by 'spiritual' biblical exegesis. If Ælfric's reading of the liturgy belongs to this broader context, his 'spiritual' understanding of liturgical acts may nevertheless have had at least one

185

Commentary

practical effect. In both the First and Second Series of *Catholic Homilies*, a brief notice, apparently by Ælfric himself, follows the homily for Palm Sunday, declaring flatly that 'ecclesiastical customs' (*circlice ðeawas*) forbid the delivery of a sermon on any of the last three days of Holy Week, which days are accordingly termed *swigdagas* 'silent days'; see *CH* I.xiv (ed. Thorpe I, 218) and *CH* II.xiv (ed. Godden, p. 149, line 357). The rare Old English term *swigdagas* has captured the attention of philologists and liturgical scholars who have debated the exact nature of the 'circlice ðeawas' mentioned, as well as the evidence that Ælfric's dictate, if widely known, was widely ignored by eleventh-century compilers of Latin and vernacular homiliaries. In the margins of two manuscripts, an eleventh-century annotator – very likely St Wulfstan's chancellor and biographer, Coleman – has even left a record of vehement objection to Ælfric's no-preaching rule (see Ker, 'Old English Notes Signed "Coleman"', p. 27).

Ælfric's idiosyncratic position and the term *swigdagas* may reflect the impact of the monastic liturgy, which was characterized during the Triduum by its austere silences and omissions (J. Hill, 'Ælfric's "Silent Days"', in *Sources and Relations*, ed. Collins *et al.*, pp. 118–31, at 123–5). Liturgical commentaries such as Amalarius's offered the means for applying to the preacher's office the idea that already justified the omission of the opening versicles, invitatory, 'Gloria Patri' and other parts of the Office – namely, the idea that the *pastor* is absent (Frank, 'A Note', p. 183). Ælfric's quotations of *R1(Sa)* at *LME* 33 prove his familiarity with this commentary tradition. What cannot be determined precisely is whether or not he would also have associated preaching (not normally part of the Night Office) with the 'officia principis congregationis' that are to be silenced. Some commentators on the liturgy did so explicitly (see Frank, 'A Note', pp. 181 and 184–5), and Ælfric may have made a similar connection. It is far from clear what the occasions for preaching within a monastery were. In the earlier Anglo-Saxon period, preaching appears to have been a common pastoral function of religious communities; see A. Thacker, 'Monks, Preaching and Pastoral Care in Early Anglo-Saxon England', in *Pastoral Care*, ed. Blair and Sharpe, pp. 137–70. For the reform period, the question has been examined, and different conclusions reached, by Gatch, *Preaching and Theology*, and M. Clayton, 'Homiliaries and Preaching in Anglo-Saxon England', *Peritia* 4 (1985), 207–42. The *Regularis concordia* allows for an extra-liturgical exposition of the gospel on feast days, delivered by the abbot in Chapter (*RC* 26). Opportunities are also documented, of course, in the monastic cathedrals (St Wulfstan and Coleman of Worcester come immediately to mind) but are conceivable also in smaller, non-episcopal monastic churches, especially where these undertook parochial functions (cf. Ælfric's instructions on the baptism of infants, *LME* 46 and n. 230). Whatever the occasion, the abbot and prior would be the only members of the community likely to bear the responsibility of preaching, and the term *princeps congregationis* would suit either of them. Given the teaching, moreover, of *RSB*, cc. II.2 and LXIII.13, that the abbot stands *uice Christi*, the logic of associating the literal silence of the preacher with the figurative 'absence' of Christ, who is *pastor* and *episcopus* (I Peter II.25, quoted in *R1(Sa)*), becomes easier to understand.

172 '*Domine labia mea . . . Deus in adiutorium . . .*' The opening dialogues of versicles and responses for Nocturns (from Pss. L.17 and LXIX.2).

Commentary

[173] *benedictionem* ... *'Tu autem Domine'* The lessons at Nocturns were preceded by a blessing, administered by the presider to the reader, and concluded with a formula (*admonitio*) 'Tu autem Domine, miserere nostri'; on variations of the latter, see also *LME* 79.

[174] *'discipuli . . . fugerunt'* Matt. XXVI.56; cf. Mark XIV.50.

[175] *candelas . . . extinguimus*, etc. The *Concordia* only implies the observance of Tenebrae (*RC* 61): 'peracto quicquid ad cantilenam illius noctis pertinet euangeliique antiphona finita *nihilque iam cereorum luminis remanente*' (emphasis added). On the form and development of the ritual, see MacGregor, *Fire and Light*, pp. 16–132; also Hughes, § 906, Hardison, *Christian Rite*, pp. 118–19, and Andrieu, Introduction to *OR XXVI* (III, 313–20).

[176] *propter discessum ueri solis . . . sepulchro uelatur* Ælfric's treatment of the symbolism of Tenebrae resembles the Amalarian matter in other *R1* manuscripts (drawn from *Lib.off*. IV.xxii.1) only very generally. His reliance on a variant version like that in *R1(Sa)*, pp. 20–1, is manifest:

> Dic, frater mi, quem imitaris quando hunc numerum [*scil*. extinctionum] tenes?
>
> Quem, frater, nisi solum [*sic*] illum qui .xxiiii. horis diem complet, unde ait Salomon: 'Oritur sol et occidit et ad locum suum reuertitur, ut iterum oriatur' [Eccl. I.5]? Ipse sol qui ad lucem mortalibus datus est ortu suo et occasu cotidie interitum mundi demonstrat . . . Omnibus notum est diem atque noctem uolui in .xxiiii. horis.
>
> Quid, frater, pertinet causa de qua agimus ut extinguantur candelae?
>
> Dicam, frater, si Deus permiserit. Candelae tipum gerunt solis. Absentia solis facta utimus candelis pro sole absente. Sol namque tipum gestat saluatoris, de quo scriptum est: 'Timentibus nomen eius orietur sol iustitiae' [cf. Mal. IV.2]. Occubuit sol iustitiae. Sol creatura non potest uidere creatorem suum pendentem in ligno . . . Vt reor, animaduertis extinctionem candelarum nostram per orbem monstrare luctum.
>
> Cur, mi adelfe, quoniam sol iustitiae semel occubuit, nobis agere per tres noctes precipis?
>
> Aspice, frater, si dicat tibi euangelium a sexta hora tenebras factas usque ad oram [*sic*] nonam; quod spatium, nisi fallor, .iii. noctes per tres horas significatas sanciunt . . . Et iterum teneto per tres noctes extinctionem candelarum quia et tuus sol triduo sepulchro uelatur.

The anonymous compiler has adopted the controlling metaphor of Christ the 'Sun' whose arrest and execution (metaphorically his 'setting') are dramatically symbolized in the act of extinguishing twenty-four candles. The title 'sun of righteousness' comes from the book of Malachi (IV.2), while the evangelists record a darkening of the sun at Christ's death on the cross (Luke XXIII.44–5; also Matt. XXVII.45 and Mark XV.33). Linkage of the darkness at the crucifixion to the title 'sun of righteousness' occurs in expositions of Ps. CIII.19, 'sol cognouit occasum suum' (see, e.g., Caesarius of Arles, *Sermones, editio altera*, ed. G. Morin, CCSL 103 (Turnhout, 1953) I, Ps. CIII, pars 3, also Augustine, *Enarrationes in psalmos*, ed. E. Dekkers and J. Fraipont, CCSL 40 (Turnhout, 1956) III, Ps. CIII, sermo 3, pars 22). While the tradition here represented by *R1(Sa)* and the *LME* has surprisingly little in common with Amalarius's abridged teaching in the standard *R1* version, it has abundant parallels in other medieval liturgical commentaries; cf. the tenth-century *Liber de diuinis officiis* of pseudo-Alcuin, c. XVIII (PL 101, 1209): 'Tenebrae

Commentary

luminum ideo exstinctione figurantur, quia tunc uera lux mundi occubuit, et tenebrae totum mundum operuerunt'; likewise Durandus, *Rationale diuinorum officiorum* VI.lxxii.15 and 17.

The sources of the passage in *R1(Sa)* are, again, largely biblical, but the possibility deserves mention that the anonymous compiler may have had access to authentic Amalarian material not included in the *Retractatio prima*. Both major editions of the *Liber officialis* issued prior to Amalarius's journey to Rome in 831 had included a much richer treatment of the service of Tenebrae, showing more similarities to the passage quoted above than does the printed text of *Lib.off.* IV.xxii.1. Amalarius drastically revised and 'Romanized' his earlier teaching for the third edition, however, which in turn served as the basis for *R1*. The earlier, unrevised readings from the first and second editions are printed in a separate appendix by Hanssens (*AEOLO* II, 545–60, at p. 552):

(1) Quod lumen ecclesiae extinguitur in his noctibus, uidetur nobis aptari ipsi soli iustitiae, qui extinctus est et sepultus tribus diebus et tribus noctibus. . . Sol qui praesentem mundum inluminat, per diem et noctem uiginti quattuor horis perlustrat orbem suum . . . (2) Igitur per singulas noctes memoratarum feriarum uiginti quattuor lumina accenduntur; et quia ipse sol significat *solem nostrum*, qui occubuit uespere passionis, per lumen quod nos possumus accendere et extinguere instar ortus solis et occasus, demonstramus ortum et occubitum *ueri solis* aliquo modo. Inluminatur nostra ecclesia uiginti quattuor luminibus, et per singula cantica, in quibus nobis oportebat exultare, decidimus mestitia, quia *uerus sol noster* occubuit, et sic quasi per singulas horas defectus solis augetur usque ad plenam extinctionem. Hoc enim fit ter, quia *triduo* recolitur sepultura Domini. (*Lect.discr.long.* I.21.1–2, emphasis added)

Certain details in *R1(Sa)* and Ælfric are closer to Amalarius's prior treatment of this subject than to the revised form found in the third edition (and hence the *R1*): predominant is the image of Christ 'the Sun', who is extinguished and buried in the tomb for three days. The earlier form of the *Liber officialis*, like *R1(Sa)*, also emphasizes the number of hours in each day, rather than the total of the three days.

177 *finita ultima antiphona in euuangelio* That is, at the conclusion of the canticle 'Benedictus' (Luke I.68–79) and its proper antiphon. The term *euangelium* is commonly used for both the 'Benedictus' at Lauds and the 'Magnificat' (Luke I.46–55) at Vespers.

178 *duos pueros . . . 'Christus . . . usque ad mortem'* On the sources of this custom, see *RC* (Symons), p. 36, n. 6. Ælfric's instructions for this special choral devotion are essentially those of *RC* 61, although he substitutes the directions 'in australi / boreali porticu' for 'in dextera / sinistra parte'. Like Ælfric, the fragmentary Old English translation of the *Concordia* in CCCC 201 similarly uses 'to þan suðportice . . . on þam norðportice' ('Ein weiteres Bruchstück', ed. Zupitza, p. 6, lines 45–7). The *Concordia* also implies that *pueri* shall sing all the non-choral parts, while Ælfric assigns the third part ('Domine miserere nobis') to two monks. In the *LME* this custom is not optional, as it is in the *Concordia*, where mention of the elaborated chant is prefaced by a verbose apology, whose first-person verbs may express Æthelwold's own reservations (see *RC* (Kornexl), pp. xlvii–xlviii). In the *Concordia* the description of this special 'Kyrie' also introduces an allegorical justification for its

Commentary

inclusion after Tenebrae: 'ut tenebrarum terror, qui tripertitum mundum dominica passione timore perculit insolito, ac apostolicae predicationis consolatio, quae uniuersum mundum Christum patri usque ad mortem pro generis humani salute oboedientem reuelauerat, manifestissime designetur'. It is peculiar that Ælfric imports so much allegorical exposition from Amalarius yet seems to have omitted what little of it was already present in the *Concordia* (but see *LME* 53 and commentary below, at n. 271).

DEC 7 (manuscript O only) provides a slightly different and more detailed set of instructions for the special 'Kyrie': in each of the three repetitions, the two boys at the west end of the church sing these verses: (1) 'Qui passurus aduenisti propter nos: miserere nobis'; (2) 'Qui prophetice promisisti, Ero mors tua, O mors: Domine miserere nobis'; and (3) 'Vita in ligno moritur; infernus ex morsu expoliatur: Domine miserere nobis.' This fuller form in *DEC* (O) includes all but one of the verses recorded for a similar ritual inserted in two of Hesbert's monastic antiphoners after Lauds of Holy Saturday (see *CAO* II, no. 74c). The entire rite, similar in detail to *DEC* 7 (O), is also found on p. 562 of CCCC 422 ('The Red Book of Darley', Winchester, s. xi^{med}).

[179] *Et si ... redeant requiem* Verbatim from *RC* 62, which nevertheless allows that those who so desire may remain awake and silent as an act of 'spiritual discipline' (*spirituali exercitio*).

LME 34   Triduum customs, various; cf. *RC* 63, 64, 76 and 72

[180] *tabulam* Not mentioned at *RC* 63, but frequently elsewhere in the source. Symons (*RC* (Symons) p. 20, n. 11) defines this device as a 'wooden instrument used to give the signal for manual labour . . . for the Maundy . . . and in connection with deaths' (see, respectively, *RC* 32, 53 and 83; 35; 99, 102 and 103). Ælfric uses the term only here and at *LME* 69 (announcing the death of a monk from another monastery). The present instance, however, falls outside of the occasions when, according to Symons, the *tabula* was used. Evidently it was also struck during the Triduum to summon the monks to worship, since the bells were not to be rung during this time: see *Lib.off.* IV.xxi.7; cf. ON *dymbildagar* 'wooden-clapper days' as an equivalent for the Triduum (discussed by Frank, 'A Note', pp. 180–1).

[181] *more canonico*, etc. Ælfric and his source (*RC* 63) take for granted the custom of substituting the secular for the monastic Office during the last three days of Holy Week and on Easter itself. Ælfric refers to the secular *cursus* in terms borrowed from the source: *more canonico* as here and at *LME* 34, 45, 46 and 47; or, less obviously equivalent, 'secundum auctoritatem beati Gregorii papae' – referring to Gregory the Great's supposed authorship of the secular Office antiphoner (*LME* 47). Prime begins directly (i.e., without the usual opening dialogue) with its psalmody, Ps. LIII ('Deus in nomine tuo') and the first two secular subdivisions of Ps. CXVIII (i.e., verses 1–16 and 17–32). Ælfric does not provide details for the rest of this and the remaining hours, except to note (in the next sentence) that they too shall be said 'more canonico'. The secular disposition of the psalms is given in greater detail in the source (*RC* 63).

Commentary

On the use of the secular Office in this period, see Tolhurst, pp. 212–16; on the origins of this custom and its transmission to the *LME* via the *Concordia*, see Symons, 'Sources', pp. 15–21.

[182] *'Deus in nomine tuo'* Ps. LIII.

[183] *'Beati inmaculati' usque 'Legem pone'* The first two divisions of Ps. CXVIII according to the secular *cursus*: 'Beati immaculati' (verses 1–16) and 'Retribue' (verses 17–32), with 'Legem pone' (verse 33) marking the beginning of the third division. In the monastic Office, the divisions of Ps. CXVIII are only half as long and differently distributed (i.e., verses 1–8, 9–16 and so on).

[184] *psallant psalterium . . . agant prostrati* Verbatim from *RC* 64.

[185] *omnes horas . . . exceptis nocturnis* Distilled from the description of the secular *cursus* at *RC* 63 and 76; cf. Briefe I.127–8 and III.26–7. In addition to the substitution of the secular forms, the Office is marked by the increased use of silent and private recitation (except for the service of Tenebrae).

[186] *nudipedalia usquequo crux adoretur* For this provision Ælfric skips ahead in the source to *RC* 72. The ceremonial Adoration of the Cross on Good Friday is described at *LME* 43, below.

LME 35   The washing of the altars; cf. *RC* 65; variant *Lib.off.* in *R1(Sa)*, p. 22

[187] *Facto . . . donec lauetur* Dependent on *RC* 65, with some rewording.

[188] *intellegimus lauationem . . . erga fratrem suum* The same teaching is found verbatim in *R1(Sa)*, p. 22. The compiler of that text may, in turn, have based his comments on *Lib.off.* I.xii.36 and 39, the latter part of which was not, however, included as part of the original *R1*.

LME 36   Paupers' mass and maundy; cf. *RC* 66

[189] *missa pauperibus ante ad hoc collectis* A later provision (*LME* 62), also taken over from the *Concordia*, implies that a number of the poor were regularly fed and sheltered by the monks.

[190] *uirorum tantum* The explicit restriction to men only (for which I have found no analogues) interrupts an otherwise close quotation of *RC* 66.

LME 37   The new fire; cf. variant *Lib.off.* in *R1(Sa)*, p. 22

[191] *in illa massa fragili . . . ignis requiratur* Not found in the standard texts of the *Liber officialis* or *R1*, but verbatim in *R1(Sa)*, p. 22, where it occurs as part of a lengthy theological treatment of this topic, the finer points of which are lost in Ælfric's abridgement. The equation of the new fire with the rekindling of the Holy Spirit in the human heart is much clearer in the full context of *R1(Sa)*, which also explains that the fire is rekindled on each of the three days to symbolize that the Spirit is sent and 'extinguished' three times: bestowed first on the patriarchs, it was lost in Egypt;

Commentary

it was given next through the law, which came to an end in Christ; poured out, finally, on Pentecost, it will grow cold in the last days (here Matt. XXIV.12 is quoted). For this material I find no close parallels – in particular for the striking use of Dan. II.34, 'de monte sine manibus' – in other medieval liturgical commentaries. *RC* 67 calls for the kindling of a fire on each of the three days of the Triduum, but is not otherwise close. The nearest approximation of the ritual in Amalarius's writings is his description of the kindling and extinguishing of the fire on Good Friday at Rome (*Lib.off.* IV.xxii.2), which is actually a different ceremony altogether. Several of the *Ordines romani* require that at the church entrance a new fire be struck from a rock on each of the three days, and in some minor respects the wording of *R1(Sa)* and the *LME* agrees more closely with these *ordines* than with the *Regularis concordia*. See, e.g.: *OR XXVI*.3–5 and 14, *OR XXVIII*.25–7, *OR XXIX*.14–16, *OR L*.xxv.11 (= *PRG* XCIX.215); also pseudo-Alcuin, *Liber de diuinis officiis*, c. XVI–XVII [*sic*] (PL 101, 1205). All of these analogues agree with the *LME* in using forms of the phrase *ignis de lapide* as against *ignis de silice* of *RC* 67. Other expositors commenting on a similar ritual (the kindling of a new fire at the beginning of the Easter Vigil) equate the rock with Christ and the spark or resulting fire with the Holy Spirit: see Durandus, *Rationale diuinorum officiorum* VI.lxxx.1: '[ignis] nouus de lapide percusso cum calibe . . . debet elici . . . de lapide, id est de Christo, qui est lapis angularis, qui uerbere crucis percussus Spiritum sanctum nobis effudit . . . nouus ignis elicitur, dum per eius passionem uel resurrectionem Spiritus sanctus effunditur' (fol. 232v); also Iohannes Beleth, *Summa de ecclesiasticis officiis*, c. CVII (c) (ed. Douteil II, 198). This ceremony would take place only on Holy Saturday, however, not on the first two days of the Triduum – though Durandus later acknowledges (*Rationale* VI.lxxx.2) that in some churches a new fire is kindled on each of the three days of the Triduum. On the widely varying forms of ceremony attending the new fire, see MacGregor, *Fire and Light*, pp. 135–247.

192 *imago serpentis . . . accendantur luminaria ex ea* Following his source, Ælfric does not impose this ritual as a mandatory practice (*RC* 67: 'si ita placuerit'). For analogues, see Symons, 'Sources', pp. 25–6, and Hallinger's apparatus to *RC* 67, 112.9. Unlike the *Concordia*, the *LME* does not specify that on each day a monk of progressively higher rank shall carry the candle (the *aedituus* on Thursday, *decanus* on Friday and *praepositus* on Saturday). Reference to the *harundo serpentina* occurs in a great many medieval sources; see MacGregor, *Fire and Light*, pp. 259–66.

LME 38   Principal mass and stripping of the altars on Maundy Thursday; cf. *RC* 68; variant *Lib.off.* in *R1(Sa)*, pp. 21–2

193 *non dicatur 'Dominus uobiscum' ad missam*, etc.   During the Triduum the liturgical greeting 'Dominus uobiscum' and the kiss of peace are dropped from the mass; cf. Brief III.34–5. Suppression of large portions of the Office has already been noted at *LME* 33. For the Chrism Mass here mentioned, as well as for a further allegorical justification for omitting the kiss of peace, see *LME* 39 and commentary.

Commentary

[194] *altaria exspoliamus . . . uestimentis suis*, etc.   Not from the original *Liber officialis* or *R1*, but found almost verbatim in *R1(Sa)*, pp. 21–2:

> Age, frater, dic: cur precipis altaria expoliare a uespere quintae feriae usque mane sabbati?
> Dominus enim tuus expoliatus est uestimento suo et tu quaeris gloriari in uestimento? Nuda sunt eo tempore in quibus solemus Deo oblationes offerre quoniam expoliatus est ille per quem acceptabilis fit Deo oblatio nostra. De illo enim scriptum est: 'Tunc milites presidis suscipientes Iesum in pretorio congregauerunt ad eum uniuersam cohortem, et exuentes eum' [Matt. XXVII.27–8].

This interpretation may have been prompted by the liturgy itself, especially if, by this date, the verse 'Diuiserunt sibi uestimenta mea et super uestem meam miserunt sortem' (Ps. XXI.19) was the antiphon chanted with Ps. XXI ('Deus Deus meus') during the *denudatio* ceremony (see Schmidt, p. 777, whose earliest source, however, is the *Missale Lateranense* of *c*. 1230; cf. Hughes, § 923). These typological associations will figure prominently again at a second 'stripping' during the reading of the Passion gospel on Good Friday (see below, n. 217). The custom of stripping the altars is briefly mentioned in the second Old English pastoral letter to Wulfstan (Brief III.29).

[195] *Nuda sint altaria . . . oblatio nostra*   Verbatim as in *R1(Sa)*, quoted in the previous note. The term *oblatio* and the phrase *fieri acceptabilis* appropriately echo the offertory prayers of the mass. The phrase *eo tempore* ('at that time') must refer not only to the time after Vespers but to the whole period from the *denudatio* until the Great Vigil. In effect, no mass could take place on a 'naked' altar. The Mass of the Presanctified on Good Friday (see *LME* 44) was a special case, since it did not actually involve confection of the eucharist.

LME 39   The Chrism Mass; cf. variant *Lib.off.* in *R1(Sa)*, pp. 22–7

[196] *crisma ab episcopo sacrandum est*, etc.   The description of an episcopal rite is, strictly speaking, out of place in a customary for any house other than a monastic cathedral, and even there the more obvious place for such instructions would be the pontifical (Hughes, § 921). Ælfric's inclusion of this material probably reflects a scholarly interest in the rite itself and in the unusual exposition provided by his exemplar of the *Retractatio prima*. While a monk at the Old Minster Ælfric would have witnessed the Chrism Mass annually, yet in both *LME* 39 and the comparable portions of the pastoral letters (Briefe 3.1–9 and 20–2; III.1–9 and 37; cf. 2a.ix–x) he gives only a general outline of the constituent ceremonies. His typical dependence on the wording of the pseudo-Amalarian material in *R1(Sa)* warrants the suspicion, moreover, that *LME* 39 reflects its immediate written source more than Ælfric's memory of the actual rite performed at Winchester. The bare provisions of *LME* 39 are that (i) three oils shall be blessed: the oil of the sick, the chrism and the oil of catechumens (the third oil is not named explicitly in the *LME* but identified in the source, and further as *oleum sanctum* / *halig ele* at Briefe 3.4–5 and III.2 and 5); (ii) the chrism shall contain oil mixed with balsam; (iii) the bishop shall bless the oil of the sick before he communicates, and the two remaining oils after he communicates but before

Commentary

communion is given to the people; (iv) the first and third blessings shall be performed inaudibly, the second out loud; finally, (v) some act of special reverence is made to the vessels containing the newly blessed oils. These features represent the version of the rite largely standard in Romano-Frankish sources by this date; on its development in the *Ordines romani*, the sacramentaries and the Romano-German Pontifical, see the excellent survey by Maier, *Die Feier der Missa chrismatis*, ch. 1, §§ 1–2. Much of the late Anglo-Saxon evidence, however, belongs to a different tradition. The comparable *ordines* in *Pont.Egb.*, pp. 128–30, *Pont.Lan.*, pp. 81–2, and *Ben.ARob.*, pp. 13–15, all derive from a seventh-century Roman *ordo* for Holy Thursday. See A. Chavasse, 'A Rome, le jeudi-saint, au VIIe siècle, d'après un vieil ordo', *Revue d'histoire ecclésiastique* 50 (1955), 21–35; also Banting's introduction to *Pont.Egb.*, pp. xxvi–xxix, and Maier, *Die Feier der Missa chrismatis*, pp. 66–75. The allegorical teaching blended with the instructions in Ælfric's source, *R1(Sa)*, pp. 22–7, is highly unusual and bears little resemblance to the equivalent parts of the authentic *Liber officialis* (I.xii.2–31 – only a fraction of which was, in any case, included in *R1*). The remarkable extent of the additions here in *R1(Sa)* bespeaks its compiler's judgement that the standard *R1* did not do the Chrism Mass justice. Ælfric adapts only a small part of the entire teaching in *R1(Sa)*, which includes extensive commentary on many details of the ceremony.

197 *quia eo die . . . discipulis contradidit*   Verbatim as in *R1(Sa)*, p. 23. The reference to the institution of the sacraments occurs in much the same form at Briefe 3.2 and 2a.viii, though these use the phrase *charismata noui testamenti* for the plainer *sacramenta ecclesiae* of the *LME*. The institution of the eucharist on this day is an obvious tradition; less clear is the justification for associating the blessing of the oils with the same occasion. On this point, *R1(Sa)* is just as obscure as Ælfric. One medieval tradition claimed that anointing with oil was implicit in Christ's 'baptismal' act of washing the disciples' feet (Maier, *Die Feier der Missa chrismatis*, p. 144), while another associated the blessing of the oils with the anointing of Jesus's feet 'ante biduum Paschae' by Mary of Bethany: see, e.g., Isidore, *De ecclesiasticis officiis* I.xxix.2 (ed. C. M. Lawson, CCSL 113 (Turnhout, 1989), 32); Hrabanus Maurus, *De clericorum institutione* II.36 (PL 107, 347); and pseudo-Alcuin, *Liber de diuinis officiis*, c. XVI–XVII [*sic*] (PL 101, 1205).

198 *primum uas . . . gratiam curationum*   A fusion of two separate sentences lifted almost verbatim from the variant *Lib.off.*, as in *R1(Sa)*, p. 23. The argument of this passage is not entirely clear in the source, and Ælfric's abridgement makes it harder still. The first vessel is associated with the Old Testament, the latter two with the New. The identity of the *antiqui patres* is less ambiguous in *R1(Sa)*: 'Vt Heliseus quoniam [*?for* quondam] Naaman Sirum a lepra mundauit [cf. IV Reg. V.1–14] et filium uiduae resuscitauit [cf. III Reg. XVII.2–24], et cetera.'

199 *quia Christus solus . . . Passionis bibit*   Almost verbatim from the variant *Lib.off.*, as in *R1(Sa)*, p. 24: 'Solus episcopus communicat antequam benedicantur duo commemorata uascula. Solus enim Christus suum corpus optulit [*sic*] Deo Patri et accepit calicem, id est Passionem . . .'

200 *et postea . . . crismatis et olei sui*   Ælfric continues to follow the source as preserved in

Commentary

R1(Sa), p. 24. The sentence returns to the introductory emphasis on associating the blessing of oils with the institution of the eucharist (see above, n. 197).

201 *'misericordia . . . obuiauerunt'* Ps. LXXXIV.11; the echo is part of a larger reliance on the source; cf. *R1(Sa)*, p. 23: 'Et ideo non solum oleum inuenitur in chrismate, sed et balsamum, quoniam lex, quamuis per gratiam Dei esset, tamen in umbra erat, quamuis misericordia Dei in illis [*sic*] esset, ueritatem tamen in Christo expectabat. In Christo enim nouo homine balsamum et oleum mixtum est quia "misericordia et ueritas" in Christo "sibi obuiauerunt".' I find no parallels for the striking use of this psalm verse in any other medieval commentaries on the rite.

202 *Media uero . . . 'Non nosmetipsos . . . sed Iesum Christum'* Adapted with slight alterations from the source; cf. *R1(Sa)*, p. 24: 'et medium [*scil*. uasculum], id est mediator, excelsa uoce quoniam unum hominem tantum predicamus, de quo dicit Paulus: "Non nosmet ipsos predicamus sed Iesum Christum" [II Cor. IV.5].'

203 *Et seruent . . . sanctificare sacrificium* That is, they shall preserve consecrated bread sufficient for communion at the Mass of the Presanctified on Good Friday. The instruction is commonplace, but Ælfric probably inserted the point here under the influence of his source; cf. *R1(Sa)*, p. 27: 'Quod postea precipitur seruare de sancta usque in crastinum ideo fecit quia sequenti die non canimus specialem orationem "Te igitur" in qua continetur consecratio panis et uini ut fiat corpus et sanguis.' Cf. the parallel at Brief III.37.

204 *osculum . . . tradidit Christum* Adapted from Amalarius, *Lib.off.* I.xiii.18:

Similiter et a pacis osculo in istis diebus nos abstinemus, non quod pacis osculum malum sit, ubi ex caritate uera profertur, sed ut demonstretur quam iniuriam passus sit Christus a suo proditore, ut et nos uitemus eandem iniuriam in fratribus. Quod dico, tale est: locutione et opere debemus subditis monstrare uitandum esse malum Iudae.

The ceremonial kiss of peace was not exchanged during the Triduum, except between the bishop and his attending priests at the Chrism Mass (thus *LME* 38, from *RC* 68). In the source (including *R1* and *R1(Sa)*) the equation with Judas's kiss occurs in Amalarius's treatment of the Good Friday liturgy, though Ælfric inserts it at the end of his Chrism Mass *ordo*. He had already encountered similar teaching in the source-passage for *LME* 33, where the variant *Lib.off.* had discouraged all manner of liturgical greeting during the Triduum; cf. *R1(Sa)*, p. 19: 'Aut numquid uis more proditoris Iudae hac in nocte salutare tuum pastorem, et ille tibi dicat, "Osculo filium hominis tradis?" [Luke XXII.48], et audias poeticum, "Quid socium simulas et amica fraude salutas?" [Sedulius, *Carmen paschale* V.66]?' (this replacing in *R1(Sa)* the teaching of *Lib.off.* IV.xxi.6). Ælfric's paraphrase of this instruction agrees in essence with the source, including its first-person exhortation that heightens the sense of participation in the gospel narrative; cf. commentary to *LME* 22 (at n. 88), 24 (at n. 93), 25 (at n. 103), 26 (at n. 106), 32 (at n. 168), 33 (at n. 171) and 43 (at n. 219). The omission of the peace is also mentioned in the second Old English pastoral to Wulfstan (*Hirtenbriefe*, ed. Fehr, Brief III.35).

Commentary

LME 40 Maundy Thursday, continued; cf. RC 69

205 *mixtum* The drink normally taken only by the servers and reader in refectory; see *RC* (Symons), p. xxxvi. Both Ælfric and the *Concordia* grant this drink to all the brothers on Maundy Thursday.

206 *suum peragat mandatum* This is not the brothers' daily foot-washing or that of the poor (*LME* 41 and 36, respectively), but a special observance apparently unique to the *Concordia* and *LME*; see *RC* (Symons), p. 40, n. 2.

LME 41 Maundy Thursday, continued; cf. RC 70

207 *ad refectionem pergant* Ælfric hardly ever mentions the monks' meals, although it is reasonable to assume an arrangement comparable to that found in the *Concordia*, which allows one meal in the evening throughout Lent; see *RC* (Symons), p. xxxv.

LME 42 Maundy Thursday, continued; cf. RC 71

208 *signo collationis* The *collatio*, an additional service of reading, took place before Compline. The name derives from *RSB*, c. XLII.3: 'et legat unus collationes uel uitas patrum aut certe aliud, quod aedificet audientes'. Ælfric mentions the service only here (prompted by *RC* 71), but the term is also used at *RC* 36 and 76.

209 *'Ante diem festum'* John XIII.1ff., only as far as verse 15, according to *RC* (Symons), p. 41, n. 1. The reading is continued in the refectory after *collatio*, as both the *Concordia* and *LME* indicate.

210 *caritatem* In the *Concordia* the term *caritas* in this limited sense is used for the ritual, including a drink, after the regular Saturday maundy (*RC* 35); see *RC* (Symons), pp. xxxvi–xxxvii and 23, n. 2; also *RC* (Kornexl), pp. 238–9 (commentary to line 550) and p. 298 (commentary to lines 1006–10). Even though Ælfric uses the term here for the drink on Maundy Thursday without the authority of his source, the teaching is the same; cf. *RC* 71: 'abbas propinando circumeat fratres cum singulis potibus'.

LME 43 Good Friday; cf. *Lib.off.* I.xiii.1 and 3; RC 73 (also perhaps *Lib.off.* I.i.16 and I.xiii.12); variant *Lib.off.* in *R1(Sa)*, pp. 28–30; *Lib.off.* I.xiv.1 + *Lect.discr.long.* II.8

211 *Amalarius . . . operari* Adapted from Amalarius, *Lib.off.* I.xiii.1: 'Parascheue, ut Beda [ut Beda *om. R1*], praeparatio interpretatur. Quo nomine Iudaei qui inter Grecos conuersabantur, sextam sabbati, quae nunc a nobis sexta feria uocatur, appellabant, quod eo uidelicet die quae in sabbato fuerint necessaria praepararent . . .' The ultimate source of the quotation is Bede's *Expositio in Lucam* for verse XXIII.54 (*Bedae Venerabilis Opera, Pars II: Opera Exegetica 3*, ed. D. Hurst, CCSL 120 (Turnhout,

Commentary

1960), 409). The inclusion of this brief passage is consistent with Ælfric's pedagogical concern to clarify technical terminology, here the Greek *paraskeuē*, as well as the historical circumstance of the Jewish prohibition of work on the Sabbath. The manuscript reading *que est Parasceue*, which leaves the subject of the sentence (*Feria sexta*) without a main verb, has required minor emendation (see the textual apparatus). Such awkwardness may hint at a scribal error or corruption in the exemplar, although Ælfric's own method of mixing abridgement and paraphrase could sometimes lead to syntactic slips of this kind.

212 '*In tribulatione sua mane*' Hosea VI.1–6. Amalarius's original text reverses the order of this reading and the following one from Exodus (see below, n. 214). Ælfric's series of lessons and tracts conforms to a standard arrangement (as in Brief III.39; cf. *Miss.RJum.*, p. 88). On the evidence of some *R1* manuscripts, including the version *R1(Sa)*, it is clear that Amalarius's original (and obsolete) arrangement was commonly adapted to the 'Gregorian' standard. It may be supposed, then, that Ælfric's exemplar of the *Liber officialis* did not require correction on this point, and that his citation of the readings, tracts and collects in *LME* 43 follows the *R1* and not *RC* 73. Ælfric's reliance on the former is also confirmed by the introductory phrase about the abbot's taking his seat, which echoes an interpolation ('primitus sedente pontifice') common to *R1* manuscripts (and likewise *R1(Sa)*, p.28).

213 '*Domine audiui*' . . . '*Deus a quo et Iudas*' AMS, no. 78a, and *Sacr.Greg.*, no. 328.

214 '*Dixit Dominus ad Moysen et Aaron*', *in qua agnus . . . immolatur* Verbatim from Amalarius, *Lib.off.* I.xiii.3; the reading is Exodus XII.1–11.

215 '*Eripe me Domine*' AMS, no. 78a.

216 *tractus a trahendo . . . 'emisit spiritum'* Perhaps influenced by *Lib.off.* I.xiii.12 ('Dein sequitur passio. In ea uelut ipsum Christum in cruce uidemus'), plus a phrase from a wholly different context at I.i.16 ('A trahendo dicitur tractus'), but the similarities are admittedly not very close. At this point *R1(Sa)* follows the other *R1* manuscripts and does not offer any closer parallel. The final words *emisit spiritum* echo Matt. XXVII.50, though Matthew's was not the version of the Passion read on Good Friday.

217 *in modum furantis . . . sortem mittentes* This ritual and the phrase *in modum / modo furantis* occur commonly in *ordines*, including *RC* 73. Ælfric's added reference to the soldiers' division of Christ's garments and the echo of Ps. XXI.19 (also quoted in the Passion reading at John XIX.24) hearken back to his comments on the stripping of the altars after Vespers on Maundy Thursday (*LME* 38; see above, n. 194). The association of this Good Friday ritual, too, with the division of Christ's garments mentioned at Maundy Thursday is not found in the standard *Lib.off.* or *R1*, but occurs prominently in *R1(Sa)*, pp. 28–9:

> Vt prediximus ista expoliatio altaris aut apostolorum desolationem significat aut sui corporis expoliationem. Et bene bis leguntur duae expoliationes altaris quia bis redemptor noster expoliatus est, dicente euangelio: 'Et exuentes eum . . . [full quotation of Matt. XXVII.28].' Haec iterata indutio uestimentorum significat iteratum cooperimentum altaris usque dum in eo euangelium iacet. Ablato inde euangelio aufertur et eius cooperimentum sicut et hic scriptum est de uestimentis saluatoris nostri: 'Postquam autem crucifixerunt eum diuiserunt uestimenta eius sortem mittentes', et cetera [Matt. XXVII.35; cf. Ps. XXI.19].

Commentary

It is easy to see how the significance of these two 'strippings' could be conflated, and their shared associations are commonplace in treatises other than the authentic *Liber officialis*: e.g., pseudo-Alcuin, *Liber de diuinis officiis*, c. XVIII (PL 101, 1209); Durandus, *Rationale diuinorum officiorum* VI.lxxvii.10. Interestingly, a similar linkage occurs in the partial translation of the *Concordia* preserved in CCCC 201: 'þonne mon ræde "Partiti sunt uestimenta mea", þa twegen diaconas, þe standað on twa healfe þæs altares, toteon þæt getreagode hrægl, þe up on þam altare ligð under þære Cristes bec, *on þæt gemet, þe þæs hælendes reaf todæled wæs*' ('Ein weiteres Bruchstück', ed. Zupitza, p. 16, lines 222–6, emphasis added).

218 *orationes sollempnes . . . orauit in cruce* The *orationes solemnes* are a long series of intercessions and collects for various intentions; the precise form is specified in neither the *LME* nor the *Concordia*, but see *Sacr.Greg.*, nos. 338–55; also *Corp.41*, pp. 90–1, *Leofr.Miss.*, pp. 95–6, *Miss.RJum.*, pp. 88–90, *Miss.StAug.*, pp. 37–9, and *Winch.Sacr.*, nos. 374–91. Ælfric appears to be following *RC* 73 closely. The reference to Jesus's praying on the Cross probably refers to Luke XXIII.34, quoted at *Lib.off.* I.xiii.15, included as part of the *R1*.

219 *Illi enim inridentes . . . pro eis orando* The absence of a genuflection at the prayer *pro perfidis Iudeis* is commonplace in *ordines* for this day (e.g. *OR XXIV*.3; *XXVII*.39; *OR XXVIII*.3; *OR XXIX*.33; *OR XXXI*.41 and *PRG* XCIX.310). Surprisingly, the instruction not to genuflect at the prayer for the Jews is absent from *RC* 73, although it has been inserted at the appropriate place among the excerpts constituting *DEC* 8. Ælfric's justifying argument is closest to *R1(Sa)*, p. 31, which is a slight adaptation of *Lib.off.* I.xiii.17. The variant version in *R1(Sa)* reads:

Per omnes orationes genuflexionem facimus, ut per hunc habitum corporis mentis humilitatem ostendamus, excepto quando oramus pro perfidis Iudaeis. Fugiamus eorum consensum qui Dominum irrident. Illi irridentes genua ponebant in terra, sicut scriptum est: 'Et genu flexo ante eum illudebant dicentes "Aue rex Iudeorum"' [Matt. XXVII.29].

That Amalarius's account of this practice gained a certain currency is attested by its inclusion in some of the most widely read liturgical commentaries: e.g., pseudo-Alcuin, *Liber de diuinis officiis*, c. XVIII (PL 101, 1210); Durandus, *Rationale diuinorum officiorum* VI.lxxvii.13; and Beleth, *Summa de ecclesiasticis officiis*, c. XCVIII.1. No commentator appears to have raised the objection that, according to three of the evangelists, it was the soldiers of the Roman garrison at Jerusalem rather than the Jews who mockingly knelt before Jesus and hailed him as 'King of the Jews' (Matt. XXVII.27–9, Mark XV.16–9, John XIX.2–3; cf. Luke XXII.63–5). The version in *R1(Sa)* has altered Amalarius's original teaching only slightly – most noticeably by 'improving' his scriptural allusions (cf. *LME* 33 and above, n. 171) and by inserting the first-person exhortation 'Fugiamus eorum consensum' etc. The present tense makes the admonition both timeless (to shun those who mock the Lord on any occasion) and urgently present (to avoid being, in the scheme of sacred history, an anti-type of those who crucified Christ). The result continues a pattern of emphasis that Ælfric deliberately incorporated into his customary, viz., to bridge the historical distance between the monks' Holy Week liturgy and the original events of Christ's

Commentary

Passion; cf. also commentary to *LME* 22 (at n. 88), 24 (at n. 93), 25 (at n. 103), 26 (at n. 106), 32 (at n. 168) and 33 (at n. 171) and 39 (at n. 204).

[220] *deportetur crux . . . per ordinem salutent*   Perhaps from Amalarius, *Lib.off.* I.xiv.1, with the interpolated *R1* ending (Hanssens's *Lect.discr.long.* II.8): 'Post hoc monet libellus memoratus ut praeparetur crux ante altare, quam salutant et osculantur omnes [presbiteri, diaconi et ceteri per ordinem *R1*].' Compared to the *Regularis concordia*, the *LME* provides only scanty instructions for the Adoration of the Cross on Good Friday. Cf. *RC* 73–4, which prescribes a lengthy adoration and gives a detailed account of the proper chants and prayers, which may then be followed by an elaborate ceremony of the 'burial' of the cross (*depositio crucis*); see also Brief III.43–9, which confirms Ælfric's familiarity with the entire ritual described in the *Concordia*. The simplified ceremony of the *LME* may have better suited Eynsham, with its small numbers and, perhaps, limited ranks of higher clergy. Where the adoration service in the *Regularis concordia* assumes the presence of deacons, subdeacons, acolytes and a *schola cantorum*, Ælfric refers only to 'cantors' who both carry the cross and sing the appointed chants, which by this time had perhaps found their way into the gradual and so did not need to be given here in full. For the sources of these rites and secondary literature, see the extensive apparatus to the CCM edition (7.3, 116–18) and Hardison, *Christian Rite*, pp. 137–8; see also L. Gjerløw, *Adoratio Crucis: the Regularis Concordia and the Decreta Lanfranci: Manuscript Studies in the Early Medieval Church of Norway* (Oslo, 1961).

LME 44   The Mass of the Presanctified; cf. *RC* 75; variant *Lib.off.* in *R1(Sa)*, pp. 31–4; significant analogues at Briefe I.122–6 and III.50–4

[221] *ponat diaconus corporale . . . mixto uino non consecrato*   These two minor details are not included at *RC* 75, but Brief I.122 refers to both the corporal and the mixed wine; Brief III.50 refers to the corporal and the wine, but omits the addition of water. On the complex interrelations here among the *Concordia*, the *LME* and the pastorals, see above, pp. 25–6.

[222] *Corpus Christi solummodo . . . per corpus et sanguinem eius*   Ælfric's enigmatic teaching is illuminated by its source, the variant *Lib.off.*, as in *R1(Sa)*, pp. 31–4. Ælfric has excised his quotation from a long, complex discussion that cannot be quoted in full here. Its major point, however, is to justify the presence of both bread and wine at the Good Friday Mass of the Presanctified, even though only the bread, preserved from the previous day, serves as the consecrated element. According to the argument, wine symbolizes the animating soul that must be present in order for the bread to be the living, not the dead, Body of Christ. Many incidental details of this ceremony are addressed during the course of discussion, but the rhetorical climax is the summation at *R1(Sa)*, p. 33, which Ælfric quotes with minor adaptations:

Vivit uero et non uidebit mortem [cf. Ps. LXXXVIII.49], unde cotidie laetamur in spe. Si non credidissemus eum uere mortuum esse, corpus eius non dimissemus sine sanguine eius [referring to the reservation of the bread alone]; et si non crederemus eius ueram resurrectionem non item

Commentary

presentaremus uinum et aquam ut haberemus sacramenta uiuentis hominis in nobis per corpus et sanguinem eius.

The sources of this remarkable teaching are unknown. During the course of his career, Amalarius substantially altered his own teaching about the reservation of the sacrament for the Mass of the Presanctified, but none of his known versions is close to that in *R1(Sa)*; see *Lib.off.* I.xii.34 and cf. I.xv.1 and Hanssens's *Lect.discr.long.* I.3. There are some inconclusive similarities between *R1(Sa)* and one of Ælfric's well-known sources, the *Liber de corpore et sanguine domini* of Paschasius Radbertus, c. XIX (PL 120, 1327–9).

223 *in his . . . oportet* That is, Maundy Thursday, Good Friday and Holy Saturday, known as the *triduum sacrum*. *RC* 75 directs that all shall communicate but makes no general statement about the whole Triduum. Ælfric's wording instead reflects the variant *Lib.off.* in *R1(Sa)*, p. 34, 'Quod in his tribus festis diebus communicare oporteat . . .' The source-passage emphasizes the need for the faithful to be united to Christ's suffering body ('in tribulatione positum . . . Et quanto magis conpatimur, tanto magis Christi corpori adunamur').

LME 45   Good Friday: Vespers and afterwards; cf. RC 76

224 *more canonico* See above, at n. 181.
225 *'Confitebor tibi Domine', 'Domine probasti me', 'Eripe me Domine', 'Domine clamaui', 'Voce mea'*: Pss CXXXVII–CXLI, i.e., the usual five psalms for secular Vespers of Friday. Ælfric is more explicit than *RC* 76 ('Vespertinum officium canat unusquisque priuatim in loco suo'), where use of the secular *cursus* must be inferred from the practice laid down earlier (at *RC* 63) for Maundy Thursday.

IX Easter: the Great Vigil through the Octave (LME 46–8)

LME 46   The Great Vigil; cf. RC 77; Lib.off. I.xviii.1 and perhaps 5; I.xxvii.1–2 and 30; variant *Lib.off.* in *R1(Sa)*, pp. 54–5; *Lib.off.* I.xxxi.8

226 *sanctificet diaconus . . . nouo igne benedicto* Except for its two brief Amalarian references, Ælfric's treatment of the complex rituals of the Easter Vigil is a succinct paraphrase of provisions at *RC* 77. The reference to the 'new fire that has been blessed' reminds us that, according to *LME* 37 (from *RC* 67), the blessing of a new fire has taken place on each of the three evenings of the Triduum. The ceremony of blessing the Paschal candle, including the long chant 'Exultet iam angelica turba caelorum' (mentioned explicitly at *RC* 77), was largely standardized by this time, although the various components might be scattered over several books (sacramentary, pontifical, gradual, etc.); see the conspectus by Schmidt, pp. 809–26, and *Sacr.Greg.(Supplementum Anianense)*, nos. 1021–3. The 'Exultet' is copied out in full in *Leofr.Miss.*,

Commentary

pp. 96–7, and *Miss.RJum.*, pp. 90–2; for the blessing of the fire see, e.g., *Pont.Egb.*, pp. 3 and 136; *Claud.Pont.I*, pp. 67–8; *Cant.Ben.*, pp. 44–5.

227 *qui cereus . . . cognoscitur esse* Adapted from Amalarius, *Lib.off.* I.xviii.1 (perhaps with an echo of I.xviii.5): 'Vt diximus, cera humanitatem Christi designat . . . Iste cereus, qui praefigurat humanitatem Christi, inluminatus benedicitur, quia humanitas Christi, postquam assumpta est a diuinitate, semper fuit inluminata . . .' Only Amalarius's equation of the Paschal candle with Christ's humanity is found in *R1* and *R1(Sa)*. Thus the added reference to Jesus as the 'light of the world' (cf. John VIII.12, IX.5 and XII.46) would appear to be Ælfric's own; cf. his similar adapation of Amalarius's teaching about Candlemas (*LME* 25; see above, n. 103). The verb *praefigurat* is used imprecisely; my translation 'stands for' reflects the probable meaning (to judge from Amalarius's equivalent *designat*).

228 *constitutionem sancti Gregorii papae* Hall ('Some Liturgical Notes', pp. 301–2) argues that the 'Gregorian arrangement' of readings simply indicates a commonly used set of four Old Testament lections: 'In principio creauit' (Gen. I.1–II.2), 'Factum est in uigilia' (Exodus XIV.24–XV.1), 'Apprehenden septem mulieres' (Isa. IV.1–6) and 'Haec est hereditas' (Isa. LIV.17–LV.11); for this series see *Sacr.Greg.*, nos. 362–7, and Schmidt, pp. 827–37. These are the readings specified at *RC* 77 (see Symons, 'Sources', pp. 30–1), as well as at *DEC* 9 and the anonymous Old English *ordo* preserved in CCCC 190 (printed as 'Anhang I' in *Hirtenbriefe*, ed. Fehr, pp. 228–30); at Ælfric's Brief III.58 only the incipit of the first reading is given. This same system of readings, together with the usual tracts (see *AMS*, no. 79a) and collects may be seen in *Miss.RJum.*, pp. 92–3. Hall cites as a further witness *Miss.StAug.* (pp. 39–40), although its value as evidence is complicated by marginal corrections ('Some Liturgical Notes', p. 303, n. 25). Note that this 'Gregorian' series is not used in *Leofr.Miss.*, pp. 97–8, or in *Winch.Sacr.*, nos. 393–407, where we find instead the twelve-lesson scheme that would become standard in the 'Modern Roman' liturgy. The arrangement of four readings survived in the Sarum rite, albeit with a different fourth lection (Deut. XXXI.22–30) than in the earlier 'Gregorian' system; see Hughes, § 929, and the very convenient summary by Remley, *Old English Biblical Verse*, pp. 78–87. Hall's explanation is convincing, especially with the fuller information of the *Concordia* to support it. The possibility remains, however, that the phrase *secundum constitutionem sancti Gregorii papae* may mean nothing more than 'in the sacramentary' – just as elsewhere 'secundum auctoritatem beati Gregorii papae' (*LME* 47) means simply 'according to the [secular] Office antiphoner'.

229 *septene letaniae*, etc. A litany of the saints in which every petition was repeated seven times (and likewise, also in *LME* 46, *quinae*, 'five times', and *ternae*, 'three times') is a well-attested custom in processions to and from the font in the Vigils of Easter and Pentecost (cf. *LME* 51). On this form of prayer, see *Anglo-Saxon Litanies of the Saints*, ed. Lapidge, pp. 36 and 46–8, with the example at pp. 233–4 (no. XXXI).

230 *Infantes . . . pontifex ferebat* Adapted from Amalarius, *Lib.off.* I.xxvii.1–2 and I.xxvii.30:

Syluester papa constituit ut a presbytero ungeretur neofytus in cerebro . . . Beda dicit in tractatu super Actus apostolorum: 'Nam presbyteris, siue extra episcopum seu praesente episcopo, cum

200

Commentary

baptizant, chrismate baptizatos ungere licet, sed quod ab episcopo fuerit consecratum; non tamen frontem ex eodem oleo signare, quod solis debetur episcopis, cum tradunt Spiritum paraclitum baptizatis' . . . Ipsa crux [*scil.* the sign of the cross traced in oil on the forehead of the newly confirmed] nullo in loco melius figitur, quam in eo ubi summus pontifex laminam auream, in qua sculptum erat nomen Dei ineffabile, figebat.

This teaching was included in both *R1* and *R1(Sa)*, but only in the latter (pp. 51–3) was it moved to a place close to other material relevant to the Easter Vigil. Amalarius took a keen interest in the rites of Christian initiation and devoted several lengthy chapters to these ceremonies, but the adult catechumenate must have been as increasingly rare in his day as it apparently was in Anglo-Saxon England; see S. Foot, '"By Water in the Spirit": the Administration of Baptism in Early Anglo-Saxon England', in *Pastoral Care*, ed. Blair and Sharpe, pp. 171–92, at 186–90. In other contexts, Ælfric takes infant baptism for granted (see *CH* II.iii, ed. Godden, p. 26, lines 257–61). Similarly, in *R1(Sa)* Amalarius's original emphasis has been qualified by additions and adaptations that acknowledge the norm of infant rather than adult baptism. In fact, from all the Amalarian teachings pertinent to baptism, Ælfric includes only this practical direction that priests should anoint the newly baptized on the top of the head (*in cerebro*) rather than on the forehead (*in fronte*). (The latter anointing is proper only to the rite of confirmation, an episcopal rather than presbyteral function.) This provision implies that infants were baptized at the Easter Vigil by a priest or priests of the Eynsham community (although *LME* 39 cautions that not all of the rituals Ælfric mentions necessarily took place at Eynsham; see above, n. 196). The same instruction occurs at Briefe 3.6 and III.6, though neither of these includes the justifying reference to the *lamina aurea* (from *Lib.off.* I.xxvii.30), an allusion to a vestment worn by the high priest of the Temple (see Exodus XXVIII.36–8).

231 *Cereus . . . sapientium uirginum* Amalarius mentions the candles of the neophytes at the Easter Vigil (e.g., *Lib.off.* I.xxvi.5) but offers no interpretation similar to the one given here. Ælfric's treatment depends on a lengthy interpolation in the variant *Liber officialis*, equivalent to *R1(Sa)*, pp. 54–5, beginning 'Postquam autem uestitur infans uestimentis suis, dabitur ei lampas in manu. Iste [*sic*] lampas coadunatur lampadibus sapientium uirginum, sicut dicitur in euangelio secundum Matheum [*sic*].' The association with the parable of the wise and foolish virgins (Matt XXV.1 13) probably derives, in turn, from the formula 'Accipe lampadem', found in some sacramentaries, recited at the presentation of a candle to the newly baptized. See *Sacr.Greg.*, no. 120*, *Winch.Sacr.*, no. 437, and *Miss.RJum.*, pp. 99–100. The development of this theme in *R1(Sa)* includes extensive moral and anagogical comment on the parable based on Gregory's *XL Homiliae in Euangelia*, no. XII (PL 76, 1118–23).

232 *'Accendite' ter* *RC* 77 does not stipulate 'three times', although this information could have been contained in the gradual. The qualifying *ter* has also been added at *DEC* 9. On the *magister scholae*, see commentary to *LME* 2 (at n. 13), above.

233 *Sequitur collecta . . . euuangelium* The collect and epistle indicated by incipit at *RC* 77 are 'Deus qui hanc sacratissimam noctem' (*Sacr.Greg.*, no. 377) and 'Si consurrexistis'

Commentary

(Col. III.1–4). The gospel reading is not specified. Symons (*RC* (Symons), p. 48, n. 11) infers from *DEC* 9 that the lection was 'Cum transisset sabbatum' (Mark XVI.1–7), but this part of the *DEC* is an interpolation from *Lib.off.* I.xxxi.8, where the reference to Mark's gospel should probably be read as a proof text for the accompanying interpretation (see following note) rather than a citation of the gospel actually read at the Vigil. From the later liturgy (both Roman and Sarum rites) we would expect the reading from Mark at the principal mass of Easter Day and the version from Matthew (XXVIII.1–7) to be read at the Vigil; this arrangement is found in *Leofr.Miss.*, p. 98. *Lib.off.* I.viii.31 does appear to claim that Mark was read at the Vigil, although Hanssens suggests that Amalarius has simply erred (*AEOLO* II, 160, note to lines 37–40). For the gradual 'Alleluia: Confitemini' and the tract 'Laudate', see *AMS*, no. 79b.

234 *non portantur cerei . . . ad imitationem mulierum quae aromata detulerunt* The basic instruction is found at *RC* 77 ('Ante euangelium non portantur luminaria in ipsa nocte sed incensum tantum'), but the justification looks to Amalarius, *Lib.off.* I.xxxi.8: 'Vt opinor, propter mulierum imitationem dicit romanus libellus non portari hac nocte ante euangelium aliud nisi timiama . . . Hoc tantummodo obtulerunt mulieres.' Ælfric's wording reflects the influence of both the *Liber officialis* and the *Concordia*; cf. the strikingly similar treatment of these sources at *DEC* 9. Though Ælfric tends to shun unusual vocabulary, he may have justified the retention of *timiama* (Gr. *thymiama*) by its appearance in the Vulgate (Exodus XXV.6). His added phrase *quae aromata detulerunt* clarifies the context as the visitation of Jesus's tomb by the holy women on Sunday morning (Matt. XXVIII, Mark XVI, Luke XXIV and John XX). This context needs no explanation in the source itself, since just prior to *Lib.off.* I.xxxi.8 (noted above) Amalarius has quoted Mark XVI.1: 'Euangelium narrat secundum Marcum modum conuentus feminarum et dicit: "Cum transisset sabbatum, Maria Magdalene et Maria Iacobi et Salome emerunt aromata, ut uenientes ungerent Iesum."' Ælfric's *aromata* may come from this earlier passage in *Lib.off.*, or directly from scripture (in addition to Mark XVI.1, see Luke XXIII.56 and XXIV.1).

235 *non cantatur . . . nec communio* The *LME*'s instruction comes verbatim from *RC* 77 and is also reflected at Briefe I.130 and III.60. After the word *communio*, *RC* (Ti) adds *et pacem non dare nisi qui communicent*, a phrase not found in *RC* (Fa), the *DEC* or the *LME*. The uniquely attested phrase appears to be a late and clumsy addition to the original text of the *Concordia*, on which see *RC* (Kornexl), pp. 320–2 (commentary to lines 1196–7). Yet, as noted above (pp. 24–5), there may be a hint of this teaching about the *pax* preserved at Brief III.60: 'Ac ge ne sculon singan offerendan on þæm dæge ne agnus dei ne communia *ne gan to pacem*' (emphasis added). On the inclusion or omission of these items in a variety of early sources, see Schmidt, pp. 868–71 (Conspectus XVI, items 16 and 23–6).

236 *'Laudate Dominum omnes gentes'* Ps. CXVI; see also Briefe III.62 ('þone sceortan sealm') and I.131.

237 *'Vespere autem sabbati' . . . una compleat oratione* Verbatim from *RC* 77; cf. Briefe I.131–2 and III.62–3. For the 'Magnificat' antiphon 'Vespere autem sabbati', see *CAO* II, no. 75b.

Commentary

238 *ad mandatum . . . more canonicorum* From *RC* 77, after which point in the source Ælfric omits a short, general statement about the use of the secular Office at all the hours on Easter (*RC* 78: 'Septem canonicae horae a monachis in aecclesia dei more canonicorum propter autoritatem [*sic*] beati Gregorii papae sedis apostolicae, quam ipse in antiphonario dictauit, celebrandaae [*sic*] sunt').

LME 47 Easter Nocturns; cf. *RC* 79

239 *'Domine labia mea aperies' semel, 'Deus in adiutorium meum intende'* Pss. L.17 and LXIX.2, the opening versicles of Nocturns. In the monastic Office 'Domine labia mea aperies' (with the response, 'Et os meum adnuntiabit laudem tuam') is normally said three times.

240 *secundum auctoritatem beati Gregorii papae* The reference to Gregory is borrowed from a previous, more general statement in the *Concordia* that Ælfric omitted in his transition from the Vigil to Nocturns (quoted above, n. 238). The appeal to Gregorian practice, and indeed most of the detailed provisions that follow in *LME* 47–8, simply re-inforce the point that the secular Office replaced the monastic one on this solemn occasion (and through the whole of Easter week). The repetition of this basic teaching is understandable, since monks would not necessarily be familiar with the forms of the secular Office even if their books contained the proper numbers and sequences of antiphons, readings and the rest (cf. above, p. 9, n. 29). The Night Office of Easter consisted of only one secular (festal) Nocturn, hence the mention of only three antiphons, psalms, readings and responsories; see Hughes, §§ 406 and 826.

241 *incipiat prior hymnum*, etc. Throughout the *Concordia* the term *prior* is used for 'abbot', a practice that Ælfric adopts on occasion; see *RC* (Symons), pp. xxx and 17, n. 1; also *RC* (Kornexl), p. 206 (commentary to line 306). Notably absent here is the *Visitatio sepulchri* or so-called *Quem quaeritis*-play that the *Concordia* states shall immediately follow the third responsory, before the conclusion of Nocturns with the 'Te Deum'; cf. *RC* 79.

242 *uersum uerbotenus 'Surrexit Dominus'* This use of *uerbotenus* is odd. The words are lifted verbatim from *RC* 79, where Symons (*RC*, p. 50, n. 6) translates the phrase 'straight through' – i.e., the priest shall read both the versicle, 'Surrexit Dominus de sepulchro', and the response, 'Qui pro nobis pependit in ligno.' Kornexl suggests, however, that the adverb may have little semantic weight (meaning simply 'wortgetreu, [wort]wörtlich'), since the gratuitous formation of adverbs in *-tenus* is a hallmark of 'hermeneutic' Latinity; see *RC* (Kornexl), p. 330 (commentary to line 1260).

243 *'Dominus regnauit', quia 'Deus misereatur nostri' debet sequi 'Deus Deus meus' more canonicorum* Monastic Lauds of Sunday would normally include: Pss. LXVI and L (both invariable), CXVII and LXII (both proper to Sunday), and CXLVIII–CL (all three invariable and counted as one psalm). Here again Ælfric thinks it necessary to spell out the meaning of *more canonicorum*: i.e., Ps. XCII ('Dominus regnauit') was sung first at secular Lauds on Sundays and feasts. Furthermore, in the secular *cursus* Ps. LXVI ('Deus misereatur nostri'), ordinarily the first psalm at monastic Lauds, was

203

Commentary

sung immediately after Ps. LXII ('Deus Deus meus ad te de luce uigilo'), both under a single antiphon. Ælfric (following *RC* 79) is simply saying that Lauds shall begin with Ps. XCII and that Ps. LXVI, though retained, comes later in the Office, where it follows a psalm (LXII) that it would, in monastic usage, ordinarily precede. Ps. XCII ('Dominus regnauit') will also be sung first at Lauds on Sundays in Advent and on Septuagesima Sunday, according to a later remark at *LME* 75, although the mention does not seem to imply substitution of the full secular Office on those occasions (see commentary below, at n. 357).

244 *non canimus de omnibus sanctis nec ymnos*   Cf. *RC* 79, which excludes the Offices of All Saints during the Octave of Easter but makes no explicit mention of the hymns. The omission of hymns is probably to be understood, however, under the rubric *more canonicorum*, since hymns were only a late addition to the secular Office (s. ix in Francia); see S. Bäumer, *Geschichte des Breviers* (Freiburg, 1895; French trans. as *Histoire du bréviaire* by R. Biron, Paris, 1905) I, 366; also Milfull, p. 5.

LME 48   Easter Day: Prime through Vespers; cf. *RC* 80

245 '*Deus in nomine tuo*' . . . *precibus et collecta*   That is, secular Prime: Pss. LIII ('Deus in nomine tuo'), CXVII ('Confitemini Domino quoniam bonus'), CXVIII.1–16 ('Beati immaculati'), CXVIII.17–32 ('Retribue seruo tuo') and the so-called Athanasian Creed ('Quicumque uult'), all sung with 'Alleluia' instead of antiphons. Some variation of the text 'Haec dies' (based on Ps. CXVII.24) was sung in place of certain items at all the hours during the Easter Octave (see *OR* L.xxxiii.17). Here at *LME* 48 Ælfric calls it a *uersus*, which may mean the short versicle and response just before the *preces*; the usual capitulum and *responsorium breue* are omitted entirely. For the *preces* series 'Viuet anima mea' and 'Erraui' (Ps. CXVIII.175–6), followed by the Apostles' Creed (*simbolum*) and further *preces*, see Tolhurst, pp. 31–6. Note the absence during the Octave of the usual litany after Prime (see *LME* 2 and commentary above, at n. 10).

246 '*Legem pone*', '*Memor esto*', '*Bonitatem*'   Ps. CXVIII.33–48, 49–64 and 65–80, i.e., the divisions of Ps. CXVIII for secular Prime on Sunday.

247 *gradalem* '*Haec dies*' . . . *sine capitulo et sine uersu*   The gradual chant from the mass of the day (*AMS*, no. 80) takes the place of the usual capitulum and versicle; see *RC* (Symons) 53, p. 51, n. 13; also Hughes, § 912.

248 '*Defecit*', '*Quomodo dilexi*', '*Iniquos*'   Ps. CXVIII.81–96, 97–112 and 113–28.

249 '*Mirabilia*', '*Clamaui*', '*Principes*'   Ps. CXVIII.129–44, 145–60 and 161–76.

250 '*Dixit Dominus*', '*Confitebor*', '*Beatus uir*'   Pss. CIX–CXI. On the special form of Easter Vespers, see Tolhurst, pp. 226–30, and Hughes, § 430.

251 *sequentia*   Several items from the mass made a special appearance at Vespers through the Easter Octave (see Hughes, § 912; Harper, *Forms and Orders*, p. 151), including some form of the gradual 'Haec dies' (also used at the little hours; see above, nn. 245 and 247) and the 'Alleluia'. Given this pattern, the present *sequentia* (from *RC* 80) has been understood to mean a 'sequence hymn' from the Easter mass, perhaps 'Fulgens praeclara' (*AH* LIII, 62) or 'Victimae paschali' (*AH* LIV, 12), as suggested at *RC*

Commentary

(Symons), p. 51, n. 18. It should be noted, however, that *DEC* (R) 10 offers the variant reading 'Alleluia cum uersu sequente'.

252 *eant ad fontem* The procession to the font, mentioned with similar brevity at *RC* 80, is the vestige of an ancient Roman ceremony for the newly baptized; see *OR* XXVII.74; Hardison, *Christian Rite*, pp. 173–5; Hughes, § 912.

253 *'Laudate pueri Dominum' . . . 'In exitu Israel' cum antiphona et collecta* Pss. CXII and CXIII. *RC* 80 does not mention that an antiphon accompanies the second psalm; cf. *DEC* 10, which gives as antiphons 'Sedit angelus' for Ps. CXII and 'Christus resurgens' for CXIII (see *CAO* II, series 147c 'Ad processionem').

254 *'Cum inuocarem', 'In te Domine speraui', 'Qui habitat', 'Ecce nunc'* Pss. IV, XXX, XC and CXXXIII, the usual four for secular Compline. *RC* 80 does not specify the psalmody but indicates 'more peragatur canonicorum'.

255 *'Nunc dimittis' . . . uersus 'In pace in idipsum' . . . preces cum collecta et benedictione* RC 80 notes the canticle 'Nunc dimittis' (Luke II.29–32) and unspecified *preces*. Ælfric's fuller instructions accord with the outline inferred by Tolhurst, pp. 175–6; for the *preces* series beginning 'In pace in idipsum' (Ps. IV.9), see *ibid.*, pp. 37–9.

256 *iste ordo* Referring not just to Compline, but to the structure and psalmody of the secular Office at all the hours.

X *The summer horarium from the Octave of Easter to Pentecost* (LME 49–57)

LME 49   Resumption of the monastic *cursus*; cf. *RC* 81 and 85

257 *ordo iam regularis pleniter inchoetur* After being replaced by the secular Office during the Triduum and Octave of Easter, the monastic Office (including the hymns) returns, together with the devotional Offices of All Saints (cf. *LME* 47). This is in effect the beginning of the summer horarium, and *RC* 81–4 includes a short summary of the order of Offices and how they differ from those during the winter. Ælfric can omit some of this material (*RC* 83) because he has already mentioned the main difference of the summer order in an aside at *LME* 5 (i.e., the daily order of Prime + matutinal mass + Chapter + Terce instead of the winter arrangement Prime + Terce + matutinal mass + Chapter). Other portions he omits because his own teaching will depart from that of the *Concordia*. For *RC* 81 (the number of readings and responsories in the summer Night Office), cf. *LME* 80 and commentary; for *RC* 82 (the summer interval between Nocturns and Lauds), cf. *LME* 57; for *RC* 84 (silence and the *auditorium*), cf. *LME* 60. Ælfric also omits the apparently misplaced short chapter in the *Concordia* on the duties of the officer known as the *circa* (*RC* 86–7), on which see *RC* (Kornexl), p. cxliv.

258 *De omnibus sanctis . . . octauas Pentecosten* The psalms at the Offices of All Saints are all said under a single antiphon through Pentecost week, but the Offices of the Dead and the *psalmi familiares* will resume, according to *RC* 85, only after the Octave of Pentecost.

Commentary

259 *Et omnes sinaxes . . . praedictum tempus*   The use of 'Alleluia' in the Office and at mass during the fifty days after Easter is not discussed in the *Concordia*; Ælfric's usage is close to the tradition of *OR L*.xxxiii.18.

260 *genuflexionem non facimus nec letanias canimus*   RC 85 better explains this provision in terms of its practical consequences, namely that Vigils of the Dead, the *psalmi familiares* and the litany before daily mass shall be omitted, since an unspecified *ordo ecclesiasticus* prohibits kneeling during Paschaltide.

LME 50   The Sunday hymnal: Easter through Pentecost (not in *RC*)

261 '*Ad cenam Agni prouidi*' . . . '*Iesu nostra redemptio*' . . . '*Aurora lucis rutilat*'   See *AH* LI, 87, 95 and 89; Milfull, nos. 70–2. Winchester–Worcester and Canterbury traditions agree in their usage. On these types, see commentary to *LME* 13 above, at n. 58.

262 '*Hymnum canamus gloriae*' . . . '*Optatus uotis omnium*' . . . '*Aeterne rex altissime*'   *AH* L, 103; LI, 92 and 94; Milfull, nos. 73 (*var*. 'Hymnum canamus Domino') and 74–5. Winchester–Worcester and Canterbury traditions agree in their usage.

263 '*Iam Christus astra ascenderat*' . . . '*Veni creator Spiritus*' . . . '*Beata nobis gaudia*'   *AH* LI, 98; L, 193; LI, 97; Milfull, nos. 79–81 (= one hymn) and 76–7. In hymnals of the Canterbury type, 'Iam Christus astra' is divided into three parts and distributed over Terce, Sext and None; see Milfull, pp. 312, 314 and 316.

LME 51   The Vigil of Pentecost; cf. *RC* 88

264 *In uigilia Pentecosten*   In addition to the instructions here given by Ælfric, the *Concordia* indicates that 'Gloria in excelsis Deo' shall be sung at mass and provides the collect, epistle, 'Alleluia' and tract incipits (*RC* 88).

265 *prima lectio . . . sicut in missali habentur*   RC 88 provides a full list of the lessons, chants and collects, as does an anonymous Old English *ordo* preserved only in CCCC 190 (printed as 'Anhang II' by Fehr, *Hirtenbriefe*, pp. 232–3). In both of these texts, however, there is evidence of confusion about the proper order, exacerbated perhaps by copying errors. The order should be (from *Sacr.Greg.*, nos. 507–14, and *AMS*, no. 79a–b; see also *OR L*.xxxix.3–12):

1   lesson: 'Temptauit Deus Abraham' (Gen. XXII.1–19)
    tract: 'Cantemus Domino' (*AMS*, no. 79a)
    collect: 'Deus qui in Abrahae' (*Sacr.Greg.*, no. 508)

2   lesson: 'Scripsit Moyses canticum' (Deut. XXXI.22–30)
    tract: 'Attende caelum' (*AMS*, no. 79a–b)
    collect: 'Deus qui nobis per prophetarum' (*Sacr.Greg.*, no. 510)

3   lesson: 'Apprehendent' (Isa. IV.1–6)
    tract: 'Vinea facta est' (*AMS*, no. 79b)
    collect: 'Deus qui nos ad celebrandum' (*Sacr.Greg.*, no. 512)

Commentary

4   lesson: 'Audi Israel' (Bar. III.9–38)
tract: 'Sicut ceruus' (*AMS*, no. 79b)
collect: 'Omnipotens sempiterne Deus' (*Sacr.Greg.*, no. 516)

(Note: in the Hadrianum the prayer immediately following the fourth reading and tract is 'Deus incommutabilis uirtus' (*Sacr.Greg.*, no. 514), while 'Omnipotens sempiterne' follows in a group headed 'Aliae orationes' (nos. 516–19)).

In *RC* (Fa) and in the Old English *ordo* (as well as in *Miss.RJum.*, p. 116) the tracts 'Attende caelum' and 'Vinea facta est' are transposed. The Tiberius manuscript of the *Concordia* is defective at this point, but also carries the trace of confusion by giving 'Vinea caelum' [*sic*] as the incipit of the second tract; on the profound disorder here, see *RC* (Symons), p. 57, n. 1, and the lengthy discussion at *RC* (Kornexl), pp. 353–6 (commentary to lines 1406–14). Of all texts influenced by the *Concordia*, only *DEC* 11 preserves the correct order of readings, chants and prayers. Among versions apparently uninfluenced by the *Concordia*, the correct order is also found in *Miss.NMin.*, pp. 11–12, but with the fourth collect 'Concede quaesumus' (*Sacr.Greg.*, no. 515); *Winch.Sacr.*, nos. 588–93, includes all the correct components even though the rubrics lend the impression that the collects precede their associated readings. The arrangement in Ælfric's own sacramentary cannot be determined from the *LME*. It would be surprising, however, if he had tolerated so faulty an order as in the *Concordia*, which effectively puts 'a chant from Isaiah ["Vinea facta est"] into the mouth of Moses' (quotation from Hohler, 'Some Service-Books', p. 72). Though Amalarius need not have been Ælfric's source, the tracts 'Attende caelum' and 'Vinea facta est' are correctly placed and discussed in the *Liber officialis* (cf. *RC* (Symons), p. 57, n. 1) and in a portion that was included in *R1*.

266 *letanias . . . canimus* On the sevenfold-fivefold-threefold litany of the saints in the procession *ad fontes*, see *RC* 88; cf. the same direction previously at *LME* 46 (Easter Vigil; see above, n. 229).

267 *cum responsorio et ymno more solito* The *responsorium breue* and hymn were omitted from Vespers of Holy Saturday, which followed a shortened form of the secular Office and was largely absorbed into the Great Vigil; here (first Vespers of Pentecost) the Office seems to be the full monastic form.

LME 52 Pentecost, continued; cf. *RC* 89–90

268 *tribus psalmis . . . ut in antiphonario titulatur* That is, the shortened Office of a single secular (festal) Nocturn, as at Easter (cf. *LME* 47); taken almost verbatim from *RC* 89.

269 *Ceteris uero horis . . . regularis ordo teneatur* Likewise verbatim from *RC* 89. Here again, as at *LME* 49, *regularis ordo* means the monastic Office. Unlike the Octave of Easter, that of Pentecost calls for the substitution of the monastic by the abbreviated secular Office only at Nocturns (see preceding note). Ælfric will eventually clarify that the shortened form of Nocturns shall be retained through the Octave of Pentecost (*LME* 72; see below, n. 339).

270 *exceptis ieiuniorum diebus* That is, the Ember Days (Wednesday, Friday and Saturday) that fall in Pentecost week (see below, n. 291). Cf. *RC* 90, which states, in addition to

Commentary

this custom, that during the Octave 'Alleluia' shall be sung in place of the gradual at mass and that Vespers of All Saints shall be said (i.e., in full, with an antiphon to each psalm – not under a single antiphon, as from the Octave of Easter; cf. *RC* 85 and corresponding provisions at *LME* 49).

LME 53   The Octave of Pentecost and Trinity Sunday; cf. *RC* 90

271 *non repetatur officium . . . aduentum Spiritus sancti*   The manuscript reads '.vi.^{tem} diebus', which I have taken as a confusion of *septem* rather than *sex* (but cf. the viable equivalent at *LME* 48, 'sex *reliquis* diebus', i.e., the week exclusive of Sunday). Contrary to usual practice, the mass of the principal feast – here designated by the opening words of its introit, 'Spiritus Domini repleuit orbem terrarum, Alleluia', etc. (*AMS*, no. 106) – is not repeated on the following Sunday, which is instead made a special feast of the Trinity. Ælfric probably owes this detail to *RC* 90, although, surprisingly, he rejects the source's figurative explanation for the practice ('rursus in octauis Pentecostes dominica non repetitur *Spiritus domini*, eo quod septem tantum colamus dona spiritus sancti'; cf. a similar rejection at *LME* 33, commentary at n. 178). The omission is all the stranger since the commonplace equation of a seven-day 'Octave' of Pentecost with the sevenfold gifts of the Holy Spirit also occurs at *Lib.off.* I.xxxix.1 ('Quia enim Spiritus Sancti septiformis est gratia, iure sollempnitas aduentus eius per septem dies laude hymnorum debita simul et missarum celebratione colitur'). As noted by Förster ('Über die Quellen', p. 49), Amalarius is the likely source for a similar comment in Ælfric's Old English homily for Pentecost, 'We wurðiað þæs Halgan Gastes tocyme mid lofsangum seofon dagas, forðan ðe he onbryrt ure mod mid seofonfealdre gife . . .' (*CH* I.xxii, ed. Thorpe I, 326). An almost identical statement occurs in his later homily, roughly contemporary with the *LME*, for the Octave of Pentecost (*Supplementary Collection*, ed. Pope I, 418, lines 66–8). Although the *Concordia* and *Liber officialis* present in essence the same teaching, Ælfric's wording in the Pentecost homily (First Series) clearly follows Amalarius; note the parallels: *tocyme*/*aduentus*; *seofonfeald giefu*/*septiformis gratia* (rather than the *septem dona* of *RC* 90); *mid lofsangum*/*laude hymnorum*. Ælfric treats the seven gifts of the Spirit on a number of occasions, but only in the Pentecost homily does he associate them with a seven-day 'Octave' of Pentecost. The departure from the *Concordia* at *LME* 53 is therefore also a departure from Ælfric's own earlier, Amalarian-inspired treatment of the subject.

272 *de sancta Trinitate*   On the displacement of the Octave-Sunday of Pentecost by a special feast of the Trinity, see Hallinger's apparatus to *RC* 90, 136.1, and Hughes § 107, n. 16. The observance of Trinity Sunday was widespread in the early Middle Ages but not universally imposed until 1334; see *ODCC*, *s.v.* 'Trinity Sunday', and for variation in early medieval observances, Bernold of Constance, *Micrologus de ecclesiasticis obseruationibus*, c. LX (PL 151, 979–1022, at 1019–20). Ælfric's mention of this feast comes almost verbatim from the *Concordia*. My translation follows Symons's example in supplying an understood subject of *agatur*, but Kornexl argues that *illa ebdomada* is the nominative subject rather than a temporal ablative phrase; see *RC*

Commentary

(Symons) 59, p. 58; cf. *RC* (Kornexl), p. 361 (commentary to lines 1441–2). On Trinity Sunday elsewhere in the *LME* and Ælfric's works, see comment below, at n. 341).

LME 54   The Sunday hymnal after Pentecost; cf. *RC* 91

273 *In tota estate*   In other words, the *ordinarium de tempore* for the summer period, from the Octave of Pentecost until 1 November. The special hymns for Easter through Pentecost have already been given at *LME* 50, those for the winter period at *LME* 13.

274 *'Deus creator omnium'* . . . *'Nocte surgentes'* . . . *'Ecce iam noctis'* . . . *'Lucis creator'* . . . *'Te lucis ante terminum'*   See *AH* L, 13; LI, 26, 31, 34 and 42; Milfull, nos. 2, 5, 6, 13 and 11. Note that the hymn for Sunday (second) Vespers is the same as in the winter period ('Lucis creator'; cf. *LME* 13). Winchester–Worcester and Canterbury traditions agree in their usage.

275 *tria cantica . . . sicut in hymnario habentur*   These are the canticles sung in place of psalms in the third Nocturn of Vigils on feasts of twelve lessons. The *Concordia* does not mention the canticles, but their use was established by *RSB*, c. XI.6, and would have been taken for granted. They are often found copied as an appendix to hymnal manuscripts (thus Ælfric's remark, 'sicut in hymnario habentur'). On the order and grouping of these 'monastic canticles' in Anglo-Saxon manuscripts, see M. Korhammer, *Die monastischen Cantica im Mittelalter und ihre altenglischen Interlinearversionen*, TUEP 6 (Munich, 1976), pp. 10–25, especially the table at 14–15; also Tolhurst, pp. 182–4.

LME 55   Occurrences and the ranking of feasts (not in *RC*)

276 *Si Natiuitas sancti Iohannis baptiste . . . uolumus tenere*   The feast of the Nativity of John the Baptist (24 June) took precedence over that of his martyrdom (or Decollation, 29 August); see Ortenberg, *The English Church*, pp. 205–6. This and the following sentences of *LME* 55 discuss the priority of Offices when important feast days and Sundays coincide or, in technical parlance, 'occur'; see Hughes, § 114, and, for analogues in other customaries, Hallinger's apparatus to *LME* 55, 177.9. Feasts were ranked according to their ability to supplant the dominical liturgies in whole or in part, although *LME* 55 presupposes nothing so complex as the system of terms and categories familiar in the later medieval and Tridentine liturgy (see Harper, *Forms and Orders*, pp. 53–4). Ælfric's guidelines in this section cover only a few important days. For a tentative reconstruction of the saints' days observed in Ælfric's calendar, see M. Lapidge, 'Ælfric's *Sanctorale*', in *Holy Men and Holy Women*, ed. Szarmach, pp. 115–29.

277 *Adsumptione et Natiuitate sanctae Mariae*   15 August and 8 September, respectively; see Clayton, *The Cult of the Virgin Mary*, pp. 52–62.

278 *festiuitate sancti Michaelis*   29 September; see Ortenberg, *The English Church*, pp. 108–13.

Commentary

279 *festiuitate omnium sanctorum*   1 November.

280 *si plenam habent hystoriam . . . de dominica*   The term *historia* ('history'), originally used of the Old Testament lections at the Night Office, came to include readings from the lives of the saints, as well as the responsories which were usually drawn from these readings. On occasion (though not in the *LME*) 'history' could be synonymous with the entire service of Vigils; see Hughes, § 202. The term *sedes* in this sentence ('primam sedem et tertiam') refers to the individual Nocturns.

LME 56   Litanies before mass and the 'subdiaconal' fast; cf. *RC* 85 and 33

281 *letanie canende sunt*   The resumption of the litany before the principal mass on ferias is implied by *RC* 85. This litany (not to be confused with the one said after Prime – cf. *LME* 2 and commentary above, at n. 10) is introduced at *RC* 33, although the present instance (*LME* 56) is Ælfric's first mention of it; see *Anglo-Saxon Litanies of the Saints*, ed. Lapidge, p. 44.

282 *ieiuni id faciant*   Holding the paten at mass was traditionally a duty of the subdeacon, who also frequently assumed the lector's job of reading the epistle (Amalarius's complaint about this practice at *Lib.off.* II.xi.4 suggests that it was already widespread in the ninth century). Ælfric seems to delegate these tasks to two different participants and does not specify their clerical rank(s). The *Concordia* makes no comparable mention of these activities or of any fast enjoined on those who perform them, but a partial analogue is found in the pastoral letters to Wulfstan, at Brief 3.70 ('Et qui aliquid gustauerit aut edendo aut bibendo non præsumat legere nec epistolam nec euangelium, quia qui facit deum inhonorat et se ipsum condempnat') and the Old English version of the same at Brief III.96. Fehr's source apparatus (at Brief 3.70) refers to two provisions in the penitentials of Egbert and Theodore, but these pertain only to the general fast required of all communicants, not to any special observance by those performing the subdeacon's duties. One closer source may derive from a remark about the subdiaconate in Isidore's *De ecclesiasticis officiis* II.x, repeated among the decrees of the 816 Council of Aachen as *capitulum* VI. The Aachen legislation was an intermediate source for much of the Isidorean material in the excerpts *De septem gradibus ecclesiasticis* attributed to Ælfric and preserved in a copy of his florilegium (Boulogne-sur-Mer, Bibliothèque Municipale, 63, fols. 1–34; on the sources of the *De septem gradibus*, see *The Copenhagen Wulfstan Collection*, ed. Cross and Tunberg, p. 16). Of subdeacons the Boulogne excerpts say (abridging the Aachen text), 'Isti [*scil.* subdiaconi] uasa corporis et sanguinis Iesu Christi diaconis ad altare offerunt. Quibus propheta dicente iubetur "Mundamini, qui fertis uasa Domini" [Isa. LII.11]' (22v; the transcription by Fehr, *Hirtenbriefe*, p. 257, is incomplete). The quoted biblical command 'Mundamini' does not distinguish spiritual from physical purity. But here the compiler of the Boulogne excerpts has carefully excised an intervening sentence which included the phrase 'casti et continentes sint ab uxoribus', and so has concealed that the capitular (and Isidorean) context understands Isaiah's charge 'Mundamini' primarily in terms of sexual abstinence. The Boulogne abridgement has thereby voided the assumption that subdeacons (still considered a minor order at this date)

Commentary

might have wives. By re-interpreting *as a fast* what was originally a call for sexual purity among subdeacons (or those who, though not of that grade, perform their liturgical functions), Ælfric avoids altogether the possibility of married ministers serving at the altar. Whether or not Ælfric compiled the Boulogne excerpts, he certainly knew and used them, and the present detail of *LME* 56 may represent a further application of their implicit point.

LME 57   The summer interval; cf. RC 82

283 *interuallum estiuis noctibus*   Ælfric departs from both the intermediate (*RC* 82) and the ultimate source (*RSB*, c. VIII.4) by doing away with a custom ill-suited to northern latitudes and, moreover, virtually impossible to reconcile with the accretion of devotional Offices between Vigils and Lauds since St Benedict's time.

284 *Beneuentanis*   The region of Benevento (southern Italy) boasts the site of Monte Cassino, where St Benedict first organized a religious community governed by his celebrated *Rule*.

285 *laudes quas de omnibus sanctis canimus*   Ælfric does not mention Lauds of the Dead, but these likely followed Lauds of All Saints, according to the order given at *RC* 21.

XI Additional summer and miscellaneous customs (LME 58–64)

LME 58   The ringing of bells; cf. RC 18, 50 and perhaps 34

286 *sonari primum signum . . . ad orationem*   The provision for Nocturns is clear at *RC* 18, while the continuous ringing of the bell for Vespers is absent, or only vaguely implied, at *RC* 34. In the *Concordia* there are three separate bells before Nocturns and two before Vespers.

287 *Mos etiam apud nos . . . ante uesperam*   Ælfric has already referred to this custom – but not its putatively English character – when describing the Octave of Christmas (*LME* 22). It was in that earlier context that the source praised as a venerable Anglo-Saxon custom the ringing of the bells at Nocturns, the principal mass and Vespers on important feasts (*RC* 50; see interpretation by Symons, 'Sources', pp. 144–6). Days 'when no work is done' ('ab opere cessatur') would include Sundays, feasts of twelve lessons and ferias within the Octaves of Christmas and Easter.

LME 59   The repetition of liturgies in the time after Pentecost (not in RC)

288 *Si defuiant nobis officia aestate*, etc.   Depending on the date of Easter, there could be as few as twenty-three or as many as twenty-eight Sundays after Pentecost. If Easter were early, the sacramentary might not contain enough masses for all the Sundays until the beginning of Advent. Ælfric does not specify which masses are to be repeated or in what order, but he apparently does not envision the solution, later

Commentary

standard, of transferring to this period those masses that had not been used in the season after Epiphany.

289 *'Dicit Dominus: Ego cogito cogitationes pacis'* In other words, this mass shall be said only on the last Sunday after Pentecost; the identification refers, as usual, to the opening words of the introit (based on Jer. XXIX.11–12 and 14), for which see *AMS*, no. 198.

LME 60   The *auditorium*; cf. *RC* 84

290 *auditorium habendum in monasterio* The corresponding provision in the source (*RC* 84) pertains more generally to the keeping of silence after Vespers until Chapter of the following day and during periods for *lectio*. While allowing speech in the *auditorium* for exceptional reasons, the *Concordia* stresses that it shall not be a place for idle chatter ('fabulis aut otiosis . . . loquelis'). See *RC* (Symons), p. 55, nn. 2–3; *RC* (Kornexl), pp. 340–1 (commentary to line 1351); also Spurrell, 'Architectural Interest', p. 165.

LME 61   Ember Days; cf. *RC* 93

291 *Quattuor Temporibus ieiuniorum* Also known as Ember Days, these days of fasting and abstinence were observed on Wednesday, Friday and Saturday in the week after the feast of Saint Lucy (13 December), the week after the first Sunday of Lent, the week after Pentecost Sunday and the week after the feast of the Exaltation of the Holy Cross (14 September); see *ODCC*, *s.v.* 'Ember Days'. The Anglo-Saxon custom differed from continental practice, according to which the spring and summer fasts were also observed on fixed days rather than times dependent on the date of Easter. Ælfric and his source favour the native custom: 'abstinentia . . . cum magna custodiatur diligentia, excepto dum in Pentecosten ebdomada euenerit' (*RC* 93; cf. the prior reference to Ember Days in the week after Pentecost, at *LME* 52, based on *RC* 90; see above, n. 270). Ælfric and his contemporaries were certainly aware that their custom differed from that of the Continent. The anonymous Latin sermon *De ieiunio quattuor temporum*, appended to the *DEC* in CCCC 190 and included in four other manuscripts associated with Wulfstan's 'commonplace book', endorses the rival practice of observing the spring and summer Ember Days in the first week of March and the second week of June; see Cross, 'A Newly-Identified Manuscript', pp. 65–6 (item 3) and 73–6 (edition). Further evidence of the conflict between the two systems has been detected in the Old English poem 'The Seasons for Fasting'; see Sisam, *Studies*, pp. 48–9 and 55–6.

292 *'Flectamus genua'* Between the readings and collects on Ember Days the priest would say 'Oremus', then the deacon would instruct the people to kneel by singing 'Flectamus genua' and to rise at the end of the prayer by 'Leuate'. The practice was ancient and widespread; see Hughes, § 519.

293 *eadem abstinentia quae in Quadragessima fit* The details of the Lenten fast are given at

Commentary

LME 26 and 28, both derived from *RC* 55. In the present general statement about the Ember Days, Ælfric omits the detail from *RC* 93 that the fast shall be less rigourous 'dum in Pentecosten ebdomada euenerit'.

LME 62   The daily maundy of the poor; cf. *RC* 94 and perhaps 95

[294] *regula sancta satis monet*   For the brothers' maundy on Saturdays, see *RSB*, c. XXXV.7–9, and *RC* 35.

[295] *qui in monasterio iugiter pascuntur*   Both Ælfric and his source (*RC* 94, here quoted almost verbatim) take for granted that every monastery will be engaged in this kind of charity.

[296] *nam de susceptione hospitum regula docet*   The actual relation of this phrase to the preceding topic (the paupers' maundy) is questionable. Ælfric often uses *nam* with little or no causal force (cf. above, n. 108). The present clause – which might appear to conflate hospitality towards guests (ref. to *RSB*, c. LIII) and charity towards the poor – is probably better viewed as another instance of overly severe abridgement and 'splicing' (this time of *RC* 95, which immediately follows the description of the paupers' maundy).

LME 63   Lay dominion prohibited; cf. *RC* 10

[297] *nullus laicorum habeat dominium*, etc.   One of only two provisions in the *LME* clearly adapted from the proem of the *Concordia* (*RC* 10); for the other, see *LME* 64 and below, nn. 299–300.

[298] *ad munimen loci, non ad tirannidem*   The same phrase occurs in the Eynsham 'foundation charter' (S 911), the relevant portion of which recurs verbatim in a charter (of doubtful authenticity) issued in the name of King Edgar to Æthelwold's foundation at Thorney (see above, p. 45 and n. 11). All of these instances recall, moreover, *RC* 10, where royal custody is limited 'ad sacri loci munimen' but without any qualifying reference to 'tyranny'. It is plausible although not certain that the *Concordia* witnesses the original phrase, of which the Thorney and Eynsham charters present an elaboration; the exact relationship between the latter texts and the *LME* is also unknown, though I think it more likely that the *LME* is quoting S 911 than vice versa. The reference to 'tyranny' may be purely formulaic, but it does coincide suggestively with the declining ideal of royal-monastic partnership. As discussed in the introduction, a more cautious attitude toward royal dominion likely prevailed *c.* 1000 than in the 960s and 970s, and the immediate circumstances of Eynsham's foundation (and Ælfric's promotion) may have included Æthelmær's fall from King Æthelred's favour (see above, pp. 12–15). In the context of Ælfric's seeming efforts to tone down the pervasive royalism of the *Regularis concordia*, the added mention of 'tyranny', relegated to this inconspicuous place in his customary, may be heard as a quiet but sincere note of criticism (see above, 44–5).

Commentary

LME 64   Dining with seculars prohibited; cf. *RC* 13, 95 and perhaps 10

299 *Nec quispiam . . . excepto rege et filiis eius*   *LME* 64 is a composite of teachings from the *Concordia* about dining with laymen or even, it seems, secular clergy. The special allowance for the king and his sons may rest on *RC* 10: 'Potentibus uero, non causa conuiuandi sed pro monasterii utilitate atque defensione . . . obuiandi intra infraue monasterium licentiam habeant.'

300 *aut abbas seu fratres . . . temerario ausu adire presumant*   Ælfric combines two prohibitions occuring separately in the *Concordia*, beginning with *RC* 95 ('ut uidelicet in monasterio degens extra refectorium nec ipse abbas nec fratrum quispiam nisi causa infirmitatis manducet uel bibat'), then drawing a phrase from the proem at *RC* 13 ('Secularium uero conuiuia . . . nullo modo ausu temerario nec praelati nec subiecti adire praesumant').

XII Duties pertaining to the final illness and death of a monk (LME 65–9)

LME 65   When a monk is sick; cf. *RC* 98

301 *Cum quislibet frater infirmatur*   The following customs, including the form of the death announcement or *breue* (*LME* 68) and the prayer *pro defuncto fratre* (*LME* 69), are closely modelled, often verbatim, on the *Concordia*. Most of the practices here mentioned are widely attested in other contemporary sources; for analogues, see Hallinger's apparatus to *RC* 98–103.

302 *indicetur hoc abbati*   Cf. *RC* 98, which indicates that the sick monk shall be assigned a 'keeper' (*custos*), who shall make the former's condition known to the whole community (*conuentus*).

303 *ad uisitandum infirmum*   Liturgical *ordines* for this visitation and anointing survive in several Anglo-Saxon manuscripts. Of particular interest are versions in Oxford, Bodleian Library, Laud misc. 482, and CCCC 422, both of which contain extensive Old English rubrics. These bilingual *ordines* are printed by B. Fehr, 'Altenglische Ritualtexte für Krankenbesuch, heilige Ölung und Begräbnis', in *Texte und Forschungen zur englischen Kulturgeschichte: Festgabe für Felix Liebermann*, ed. M. Förster and K. Wildhagen (Halle, 1921), pp. 20–67. See also *Miss.RJum.*, pp. 287–95, and partial instructions in *Winch.Sacr.*, prior to no. 1778.

304 *consequente letania*   See *Anglo-Saxon Litanies of the Saints*, ed. Lapidge, pp. 44–5, with references to texts printed in his edition.

LME 66   The death and burial of a monk; cf. *RC* 99

305 *commendationem anime: 'Subuenite sancti Dei'*   The text is preserved as part of the long *ordo in agenda mortuorum* in *Leofr.Miss.*, p. 198, and in *Miss.RJum.*, p. 297.

Commentary

[306] *si ita ratio dictauerit*   A difficult phrase lifted verbatim from *RC* 99, loosely translated 'if such be the rule' at *RC* (Symons) 66, p. 65. My rendering 'if resources permit' may be overtranslation, but the literal meaning ('if reason dictates') and the context urge an interpretation of *ratio* as 'practical consideration' or 'good sense'. In other words, Ælfric (following his source) allows the community to weigh circumstances and determine whether or not this custom – which entails the loss of what could be a valuable liturgical vestment – is 'reasonable' in every instance.

[307] *missam celebrent pro anima eius*   That is, the matutinal mass; this reference anticipates the fuller provisions that will follow in *LME* 67.

LME 67   Special observances in the month following a monk's burial; cf. *RC* 100

[308] *dominica oratione et collecta*   The Lord's Prayer and collect are not mentioned but probably understood at *RC* 100. The 'seven psalms' are the penitential psalms (see above, n. 10).

[309] *unum ex supradictis . . . psalmum*   That is, one of the seven penitential psalms, which were, additionally, already to be chanted after Prime (see above, n. 10) and in the *trina oratio* before Nocturns (see above, n. 15).

[310] *uigilia pleniter agatur*   That is, the form with three Nocturns and a total of nine lessons, as opposed to the shorter form that will be said from the eighth up to the thirtieth day.

[311] *triginta missas . . . celebret, et alii fratres in psalmodiis . . . adiuuent*   The directive to priests implies the celebration of 'private masses' (cf. above, at n. 46). The task assigned to the brothers departs from the source (*RC* 100), which enjoins extra psalmody only on deacons (an entire psalter) and subdeacons (fifty psalms). Because of the ambiguous referent of the phrase *in quantum ualent*, the latter part of Ælfric's sentence might also be construed 'to assist [his soul] by reciting as much psalmody as they can'.

[312] *notetur in anniuersariis*   In the *Concordia* enrolment in the list of annual remembrance is explicitly noted among confraternal obligations (see *RC* 102 – the basis, in other respects, for *LME* 69) and not, as here, in the context of a death in one's own house; on this and other apparent departures from the source, see comments below, at nn. 315–17. The anniversaries would have been read at daily Chapter (Tolhurst, p. 54). Extant Anglo-Saxon *libri uitae* and necrologies are now collected and provided with extensive commentary by J. Gerchow, *Die Gedenküberlieferung der Angelsachsen mit einem Kataloge der libri vitae und Necrologien*, Arbeiten zur Frühmittelalterforschung 20 (Berlin, 1988).

LME 68   The *breue*; cf. *RC* 101

[313] *monasterii (illius)*   Once more Ælfric has declined to tailor a general formula for the use of his own house, repeating verbatim the text provided at *RC* 101. Cf. commentary above to *LME* 12 (at n. 53) and 25 (at n. 98).

Commentary

LME 69 Confraternal obligations; a prayer; cf. RC 102

[314] *monasterio noto* The term *notus* is used of a monastery in confraternity; cf. *RC* 102: 'noto ac familiari'.

[315] *quindecim graduum psalmos* A significant departure from *RC* 102 ('septem penitentiae prostrati in oratorio modulentur psalmos'), although neither this nor any of the apparent innovations in this section (see below, nn. 316–17) was necessarily introduced by Ælfric.

[316] *prima die, septima, tricessima* The source (*RC* 102) includes the *third* day as well, although its absence in the *LME* may be the result of a copyist's omission. Even if the departure is not accidental, Ælfric's role in altering the source is again uncertain.

[317] *Oratio pro defuncto fratre* In the *LME* the relation of this prayer to the preceding material is unclear: is it to be said for any dead brother, or for one within or one outside the confraternal fold? There is no ambiguity in the source (*RC* 102), where the prayer is clearly attached to the seven penitential psalms chanted for a dead brother in confraternity. The apparent displacement of this prayer and of the instruction about the anniversaries (*LME* 67; see above, n. 312), as well as the substitution of the gradual for the penitential psalms (see above, n. 315), suggest that Ælfric's exemplar offered a slightly different version of the end of the source. In her discussion of the closing segments of the *Concordia* as preserved in Cotton Tiberius A. iii, Kornexl favours this possibility; see *RC* (Kornexl), p. 384 (commentary to line 1651). On the sources and analogues of the prayer 'Satisfaciat', see Hallinger's apparatus to *RC* 102, 145.5.

[318] *Mariae . . . Benedicti . . . omniumque sanctorum tuorum* In her edition (*Excerpta ex institutionibus*, p. 193, n. 2) Bateson concludes that Ælfric's omission of St Peter, who is included in the *Concordia*'s version of this prayer, indicates a dedication of Eynsham to St Mary, St Benedict and All Saints. In the Eynsham 'foundation charter' (S 911), however, the dedication implied is to St Saviour and All Saints only: 'monasterio . . . in honore sancti saluatoris, omniumque sanctorum suorum, iure dedicato' (*EC* I, 20). Here Bateson must have relied instead on the words of Æthelmær's Old English appendix to the same charter: 'ic an þysse are Gode. ⁊ sancte Marian. ⁊ eallon his halgon. ⁊ sancte Benedicte into Egnesham' (*ibid.* I, 24), but this statement need not refer specifically to the dedication. A. Binns's survey of dedications notes only that to St Saviour and All Saints (*Dedications of Monastic Houses in England and Wales, 1066–1216* (Woodbridge, 1989), p. 72), but Gordon follows Bateson and Æthelmær's Old English statement (*Eynsham Abbey*, p. 28). Against the inference of Bateson and Gordon, however, is Ælfric's consistent refusal elsewhere to customize his text to the degree of specifying dedications for Eynsham's processional chapels and side altars, or of naming the saint(s) whose relics are interred there; cf. commentary to *LME* 12 (at n. 53), 25 (at n. 98) and 68 (at n. 313). One might reasonably question why Ælfric would bother to customize the present quite incidental liturgical formula and no other. That Peter's name was simply missing from the prayer in Ælfric's exemplar remains a possibility, supported perhaps by the *Concordia* in Cotton Faustina B. iii, where the main scribe also omitted Peter (though the name was later inserted

Commentary

above the line by a second hand; see *RC* (Kornexl), p. cxi and n. 61, with Abbildung V, p. cclxxvi).

[319] *Finiunt consuetudines*   Assuming that *LME* 70–80, still to come, were present from the beginning and not a later supplement, the words 'Finiunt consuetudines' may be read as the author's signal only that he has reached the end of that portion of the text based on his main source, Æthelwold's *liber consuetudinum* (or *Regularis concordia*). This interpretation accords with the typical use of the word *consuetudo* throughout the *LME* to signify a return to Æthelwold's text after some digression based on other sources. Ælfric includes no provisions from the 'extra' material found at the end of the Tiberius manuscript of the *Concordia*: see *RC* (Ti) 103, on prayers for those who 'ualde necessarii sunt siue in spiritualibus siue corporalibus' – i.e., patrons, rulers, important clergy; and *RC* (Ti) 104, an exemption of monasteries from payment of the heriot. These sections may or may not have been in Ælfric's exemplar, and Kornexl is doubtless right to hold that the words *finiunt consuetudines* alone cannot decide the issue; see *RC* (Kornexl), p. 384 (commentary to line 1684), responding to *RC* (Symons), p. 67, n. 9, where Ælfric's *finiunt* is taken as confirmation that the final items included in the Tiberius manuscript were not part of the 'original' *Concordia*.

XIII Readings and responsories for the Night Office (LME 70–80)

LME 70   Preface; Septuagesima through the Triduum

[320] *consuetudinem in qua hucusque conuersati sumus*   Although the system of Office readings and responsories that underlies *LME* 70–80 cannot be recovered in all of its details, M. McC. Gatch has shown that this neglected part of the text preserves evidence vital for any study of the Anglo-Saxon monastic Office and, more narrowly, for study of Ælfric's long-term translation programme. A number of Ælfric's biblical translations and non-homiletic reading pieces were intended, Gatch claims, as 'summaries of the readings of the Office histories for Lent and the summer', perhaps requested specifically by the pious laymen Æthelweard and Æthelmær in their effort to approximate, in an abbreviated, vernacular form, the monks' yearly cycle of prayer and reading ('The Office', pp. 352–62, quotation at 362). This portion of Ælfric's customary draws on no single identifiable source. The broader liturgical tradition underlying it, however, was first discussed by Hall, 'Some Liturgical Notes'. Hall demonstrates that this *ordo lectionum* – which he calls an 'appendix' to the *LME* – agrees in the main with the arrangement described in *Ordo romanus XIII A*, although it is occasionally closer to other versions of that *ordo* (i.e., XIII B–D, representing ninth- to twelfth-century northern European adaptations of the same basic plan). *OR XIII A* is held to emanate from the Roman church of St John Lateran and represent the practice of the first half of the eighth century. Andrieu (*Les Ordines romani* II, 477–8) hesitates to name a more specific origin than Rome itself, but the association of *OR XIII* with the Lateran has become commonplace in subsequent scholarship (e.g., Vogel, *Medieval Liturgy*, p. 167; Martimort, *Lectures liturgiques*, pp. 72 and 80;

Commentary

Gatch, 'The Office', p. 353). Given its likely origins in the non-monastic liturgy of the Lateran Basilica, the structure of the Office implied in *OR XIII A* was occasionally unsuited to the monastic form of Nocturns, and Ælfric's tendency to follow closely the wording of his source without adequate adaptation (see above, pp. 68–70) compounds the interpretative challenges in this section (see commentary to *LME* 71 (at n. 337), 76 (at n. 358) and 77 (at n. 363), below).

While the similarities noted by Hall confirm the general tradition reflected in *LME* 70–80, *OR XIII A* could have supplied only part of the information in Ælfric's 'appendix'. Ælfric – or a prior redactor of the *ordo* he happens to be using – also supplements the order of readings by adding the incipits of twenty-one responsories (each the first of a whole series) associated with the various lections. Among witnesses collated by Andrieu for his edition of *OR XIII A*, this type of augmented *ordo* is scarce, represented by one manuscript, E (Douai 857, s. xi[1]), as well as by a unique twelfth-century St Gall manuscript of *OR XIII D*. Ælfric's 'appendix' includes a larger number of responsories than either of these (Hall, 'Some Liturgical Notes', p. 298). The addition of responsory incipits to a basic *ordo lectionum* was a natural step, since these two elements of the Night Office are so closely related (being usually drawn from the same source). The concord between readings and responsories was an important concern of medieval liturgists, including Amalarius in his *Liber de ordine antiphonarii* (*AEOLO* III, 19–109).

This 'appendix' to the *LME* is an extraordinarily rare survival among Anglo-Saxon liturgical sources, even though its provisions give only a basic outline of practice. Office antiphoners and lectionaries must have been available in every Anglo-Saxon monastery, but so little evidence of either type of book survives that Ælfric's plan is difficult to check against contemporary sources. In the rare instances that these are available (chiefly from the mid-eleventh-century Worcester 'Portiforium' of St Wulfstan), they are cited extensively below. Otherwise, although the following notes refer to the comparative tables in Hesbert's *Corpus antiphonalium officii*, it must be stressed that precise agreement of content, much less of order, between Ælfric's antiphoner and Hesbert's sources cannot be demonstrated beyond the first responsory of the series (and not even the accompanying verse of that; see below, n. 322). Though they are not cited throughout, also useful for comparative study of the Night Office are the tabular appendices to Hanssens's edition of Amalarius's *Liber de ordine antiphonarii* (*AEOLO* III, 110–224) and the detailed outline of readings and responsories compiled from mostly Cluniac sources of s. x–xii, published as Appendix IX.1 ('Die Lektionenordnung im Jahreskreis') of CCM 7.4, 37–84. A basic survey of the uses of biblical lections in the Anglo-Saxon Office is also provided by Remley, *Old English Biblical Verse*, pp. 67–78.

321 *in mediam Quadragessimam* That is, up to the fourth Sunday of Lent. *OR XIII A*.1 directs that the entire Heptateuch shall be read in the period from Septuagesima to Passion Sunday (the fifth Sunday of Lent); see below, at n. 324.

322 *una die tantum hystoriam 'Alleluia dum praesens est'* Witnesses to this set of responsories are printed in *CAO* II, series 52a. Here and throughout the 'appendix', Ælfric gives only the incipit of the first responsory of the first Nocturn as a cue to the

Commentary

full texts and their verses, which would be found, with musical notation, in the antiphoner. Usually the series of responsories would contain at least twelve – the number needed for Nocturns of Sunday – though arrangements vary enormously. The Sunday texts would be divided and distributed over subsequent ferias for as many weeks as the accompanying readings or season lasted, although the exact distribution is often impossible to discern from early medieval sources (for representative later arrangements, see Hughes, §§ 419–22 with figs. 4.7–8). The responsories for Septuagesima Sunday (beginning with 'Alleluia dum praesens est'; cf. Wisdom IV.2) are a notable exception, however, since the 'Alleluia' could not be sung after that Sunday until its re-appearance at Easter (see *LME* 26 and commentary above, at nn. 104–6 and 110). On the present use of *historia* in the restricted sense of 'responsory' only, compare *LME* 55 and commentary above, at n. 280. Unless otherwise noted, all further citations of entire series of responsories refer to monastic sources, arranged by Hesbert in parallel columns in *CAO* II. For the full text of a responsory and its verse(s), the reader must consult Hesbert's *CAO* IV, where the complete texts and their verses are edited, in alphabetical order, from monastic and secular sources. Antiphons are similarly edited in *CAO* III.

323 *responsoria de psalmis*, '*Quam magna multitudo*' *et cetera*   For 'Quam magna multitudo' see *CAO* II, series 27a and 139a 'De psalmis'. Of Hesbert's monastic sources, the antiphoner of St Maur-les-Fossés (s. xi–xii) and that of Saint-Denis (s. xii) place 'Quam magna multitudo' (from Ps. XXX.20) as the first responsory of the first Nocturn on Monday following Septuagesima Sunday. For a thorough inventory and comparative study of the responsories *de psalmis*, see R. Le Roux, 'Étude de l'office dominical et férial: les répons "de psalmis" pour les matines de l'Épiphanie à la Septuagésime selon les cursus romain et monastique', *Études grégoriennes* 6 (1963), 39–148.

324 *Exodum* . . . '*Locutus est Dominus ad Moysen*'   By Ælfric's arrangement only the first two books of the Heptateuch are read from Septuagesima to Passion Sunday, within which period Exodus is allotted only one week. The assignment of Exodus to mid-Lent Sunday in many sources – contrary to the scheme of *OR XIII A* – has been interpreted as a symptom of how early medieval accretions to the Office forced a curtailment of the readings at Nocturns (Gatch, 'The Office', p. 355). For the responsory series 'Locutus est Dominus', see *CAO* II, series 64a.

325 *Hieremiam prophetam*   That is, the book of Jeremiah only; Lamentations will be taken up during the Triduum.

326 '*Isti sunt dies*' . . . '*In die qua inuocaui te*'   *CAO* II, series 66b and 68b. The first responsory only ('Isti sunt dies') of the former series would not be used again over the succeeding days (see following note).

327 *Sed hoc ipsum* . . . *nisi a dominica die*   The quotation ('Quarta decima die', etc.) comes from the text of the responsory: 'Isti sunt dies quos obseruare debetis temporibus suis: Quartadecima die ad uesperum Pascha Domini est, et in quintadecima solemnitatem celebrabitis altissimo Domino' (*CAO* IV, no. 7013; the accompanying verse varies by source). The chant text is based in part on Lev. XXIII.5–6 and Num. XXVIII.16–17.

Commentary

328 *de Lamentatione . . . tractatus sancti Augustini . . . de apostolo*, etc. That is, Lamentations, Augustine's *Enarratio* of Ps. LXIII, and I Cor. XI.23 ff., all as in *OR XIII A*.3; see also Hughes, § 416. The detailed description of readings for the Triduum was not part of the original *OR XIII A*, but a later interpolation (*Les Ordines romani*, ed. Andrieu II, 477). Anglo-Saxon copies of this *ordo* preserved in manuscripts of Wulfstan's 'commonplace book' (CCCC 190 and Rouen 1382), however, do not contain the expanded outline for the Triduum, making Ælfric's witness all the more valuable. A single extant leaf (now Columbia, University of Missouri Library, Fragmenta Manuscripta 1) of what may be an Anglo-Saxon Office lectionary contains passages from the Triduum lessons from Lamentations; see L. E. Voigts, 'A Fragment of an Anglo-Saxon Liturgical Manuscript at the University of Missouri', *ASE* 17 (1988), 83–92.

329 '*Festinemus ingredi in illam requiem*'   Heb. IV.11 ff.

330 *in tertia sede . . . sicut in toto anno facimus*   The *tractus euangelii* is ordinarily a patristic homily on the gospel pericope. On the usual distribution of readings from scripture, sermons and homilies in the individual nocturns, see Gatch, 'The Office', p. 353, n. 43. When the Night Office consisted of three nocturns, the lections of the first were usually taken from scripture, those of the second from patristic sermons specific to the day or season, and those of the third from a patristic homily on the gospel of the day. On Sundays after Epiphany and Pentecost, however, the sermons were usually omitted from the second nocturn, which was then given over to a continuation of the biblical readings. There were, however, many exceptions and occasional modifications to this scheme; see Hughes, §§ 415–17. It is now commonly recognized that the homiliary, a book containing the *homeliae* and some *sermones* read at the Night Office, provided Ælfric a valuable anthology of Latin sources for his Old English compositions; see C. Smetana, 'Ælfric and the Early Medieval Homiliary', *Traditio* 15 (1959), 163–204; idem, 'Ælfric and the Homiliary of Haymo of Halberstadt', *Traditio* 17 (1961), 457–69.

LME 71   Easter through Ascension

331 *tres lectiones . . . ipsius festiuitatis*   At *LME* 47 Ælfric has already mentioned the Easter Night Office of a single Nocturn with three lessons. *LME* 71 confirms that, in accordance with common practice (though not specified in *OR XIII A*), this shortened form of the Office was said through the entire Octave of Easter and that the three readings were drawn not from scripture but from homilies on the gospel (on this arrangement, see Hughes, § 417). *OR XIII A*.6 states only that 'in pascha ponunt' the book of Acts, the seven canonical epistles and the Apocalypse until the conclusion of the Octave of Pentecost. The duration of each reading is not specified.

332 '*Angelus Domini*' . . . '*Maria Magdalene*'   *CAO* II, series 75c and 76b. The latter is assigned to Easter Monday in most of Hesbert's sources.

333 *epistolis canonicis*   That is, James, I–II Peter, I–III John and Jude, collectively known as the 'canonical' epistles in the west and the 'catholic' epistles in the east (see Andrieu's note to *OR XIII A*.6). Hall's paraphrase of Ælfric on this point ('Some

Commentary

Liturgical Notes', p. 299) might give the incorrect impression that the seven canonical epistles were read *during* Easter week rather than in the following one. The trouble lies in the variable meanings of 'Octave' both in Latin and English. Ælfric uses *in octauis* to mean: (a) 'on [the day of] the Octave', i.e., the eighth day (inclusive) from the feast itself; (b) 'during or through those eight days; or, (c) as here at *LME* 71, 'from the Octave' [i.e., on eighth day and thereafter]. Hughes (§ 103) discusses the preferred terminology, which ideally would distinguish the prepositions *in, ab* or *infra* and inflect the noun 'Octave' accordingly.

334 *dominica post octauas . . . Ascensionem Domini*   In other words, from the Sunday fourteen days after Easter until the Thursday of Ascension. *OR XIII A* does not mention the feast of the Ascension.

335 *'Ego sicut uitis'*   *CAO* II, series 82^{9}b and 88. Among Hesbert's sources this responsory occurs in the first position in the first Nocturn only in one manuscript (Rheinau antiphoner, s. xiii). Elsewhere this history is variously called 'De auctoritate' or 'De Apocalypsi'.

336 *'Narrabo nomen tuum'*   *CAO* II, series 85 and 89; none of Hesbert's sources provides 'Narrabo' as the first responsory in the first Nocturn.

337 *tres lectiones de capite Actuum . . . sermones de eadem festiuitate*   *OR XIII A* names Acts only as the first book read 'in Pascha'. Ælfric appears to be following a tradition closer to *OR XIII B*.26, which prescribes three readings from Acts (I.1–14, I.15–26 and II.41–6) followed by 'homilies pertaining to the same day'. The provision of *OR XIII B*.26 suggests a secular festal Office of nine lessons (i.e., three readings from Acts in the first Nocturn, then three from the church fathers in each of the second and third Nocturns). To adapt the same provision for monastic use, an additional reading from scripture or the homiliary would have to fill out the first Nocturn, bringing the total of its lessons to four. See, for example, the adapted Night Office for Christmas and Epiphany in Cluniac customaries of s. x–xii, cited below at nn. 358 and 363; for Ascension, however, these same sources require all twelve readings to be from homilies on the gospel of the day (CCM 7.4, 57). It is unlikely that Ælfric's failure to include such a modification signals the replacement of the expected Office of twelve lessons on Ascension by a secular form with nine (cf. Hughes, § 826 with fig. 8.3). The lingering ambiguity recalls, however, that Ælfric's verbatim reliance on sources can lead to the appearance of idiosyncratic usage at Eynsham (for another disturbing example, see commentary to *LME* 27 above, at n. 118). In the present instance Ælfric has probably simply adopted the wording of his source (some version of a secular *ordo* similar to *OR XIII B*.26) without due attention to the change of format, which demands a fourth reading from Acts or some other book.

338 *'Post Passionem Domini'*   Very likely an error for 'Post Passionem suam', unanimously attested by Hesbert's sources at *CAO* II, series 93a. There is a responsory beginning 'Post Passionem Domini' assigned to the feast of St Denys (9 October; see *CAO* II, series 114b). The confusion, whether Ælfric's or a later scribe's, likely arose from the similarity of the incipits. The mistake could hardly be made otherwise, since the full text of 'Post Passionem suam' is self-evidently proper to the Ascension (see *CAO* IV, no. 7403). The same error occurs in one version of the eleventh-century customs

Commentary

known as the *Cluniacenses antiquiores, Redactio Nonantulana* § 46 (see CCM 7.2, 104). *Worc.Ant.* (p. 147) has the correct text 'Post Passionem suam'.

LME 72 Pentecost until the first Sunday of August

339 *tres lectiones de tractibus euuangeliorum* Apparently the shortened Office of a single Nocturn with three lessons, as through the Octave of Easter (see above, n. 331). This form was already specified for the Night Office of Pentecost itself, and here Ælfric implies its extension through the entire week; cf. *LME* 52 and commentary above, at n. 268. The use of patristic readings rather than scripture during this week is commended by *OR XIII* D.7–8. On the short form of Nocturns through the Octave of Pentecost, see also *OR* L.xl.3 and Amalarius, *Lib.off.* IV.xxvii.21–2.

340 *'Dum complerentur'* *CAO* II, series 95b.

341 *In octauis . . . de sancta Trinitate* Ælfric has already referred to this feast once at *LME* 53 (see above, n. 272). In the present sentence, *in octauis* must mean 'on the day of the Octave [of Pentecost]' and imply the week following as well. Although later the feast would be restricted to the Sunday, Ælfric unambiguously states that it has an Octave; see also his Old English homily for the Octave of Pentecost: 'and nu todæg we heriað þa halgan Þrynysse mid urum ðeowdome, and on ðyssere wucan oð Sunnanæfen we singað be þam' (*Supplementary Collection*, ed. Pope I, 418, lines 73–5). The postponement of the histories 'De Regum' until the following Sunday also indicates observance of an Octave (see below, n. 343), as does the arrangement of Offices in *Port.Wulst.* (II, 48–59), where Nocturns of Trinity Sunday include readings from an unidentified source and the responsory series beginning 'Benedicat nos Deus' (*CAO* II, series 43^2a, 97a, 120^3b and 127^3a). In accordance with Benedict's *Rule* (c. X.2), *Port.Wulst.* gives only one lesson and responsory for ferias during the Octave of the Trinity, since with these days the summer horarium begins, with its curtailed Night Office. At *LME* 80, however, Ælfric will recommend the continuance of three readings and responsories on ferias throughout the summer (see commentary below, at n. 368).

342 *post octabas . . . ponimus Regum* The observance of Trinity Sunday and its Octave means that readings from Kings cannot begin until the second Sunday after Pentecost; see the preceding note.

343 *'Deus omnium'* *CAO* II, series 97^2 and 129b 'De historia regum'; cf. the lections and responsories 'De libro Regum' at *Port.Wulst.* II, 40–41.

LME 73 Saints' days

344 *alia congruentia . . . sumimus* Hall speculates ('Some Liturgical Notes', p. 300, n. 13) that *LME* 73 may reflect the influence of antiphonary rubrics or of an *ordo antiphonarum*, where such directions are common (cf. Ælfric's statement at *LME* 55 on the distribution of propers on occurrent saints' days). Antiphons, lections and responsories of the *commune sanctorum* according to mid-eleventh century Worcester usage are preserved in *Port.Wulst.* II, 25–38.

Commentary

LME 74 August to Advent

345 *ponimus Salomonem* Like most medieval *ordines lectionum*, Ælfric's does not specify which of the wisdom books shall be read or in what order. For the later Office, Hughes (§ 416 and n. 33) notes that the *historia sapientiae* is drawn from Ecclesiastes only, while earlier medieval sources admit one, some or all of the four wisdom books (Proverbs, Ecclesiastes, Wisdom and Ecclesiasticus (Sirach)). *OR XIII B.9* specifies all of these plus the Song of Songs. The lections given in *Port.Wulst*. II, 42 (under the erroneous title 'De Iudit') begin with Proverbs.

346 *'In principio'* *CAO* II, series 102^{11} and 130a; cf. *Port.Wulst*. II, 42, where 'In principio' falls in third position in the first Nocturn.

347 *Iob duobus ebdomadibus* Ælfric is closer to *OR XIII D*.11 (and 29), which specifies Job 'usque in medium septembris', than to the *A*-version, which says only that Job, Tobit, Judith, Esther and Esdras shall be read between 1 September and 1 October. Gatch ('The Office', p. 359) has called attention to the supporting evidence of *CH* II.xxx: 'Mine gebroðra. We rædað nu æt godes ðenungum be ðan eadigan were Iob' (ed. Godden, p. 260, lines 1–2; in CUL, Gg. 3. 28, the piece bears the rubric *Dominica .i. in mense Septembri. Quando legitur Iob*). Lections from Job are given at *Port.Wulst*. II, 43.

348 *'Si bona'* *CAO* II, series 108^3a and 131a; *Port. Wulst*. II, 43–4; see also the series (missing its beginning) in the margin of *Corp.41*, manuscript p. 475 (noted by Grant's inventory at *Corp.41*, p. 106), where there are five responsories from Job, of which the first (presumably not the first of the series when it was complete) is 'Induta est' with the verse 'Dies mei'.

349 *legimus Tobiam* In limiting Tobit to the third week the *LME* is more explicit than analogous texts, including *OR XIII D*, which assigns Tobit, Judith and Esther as a group to the latter two weeks of September. For the lections, see *Port.Wulst*. II, 44–5.

350 *'Peto Domine'* The manuscript's abbreviation 'Peto đ' is expanded 'Peto domin*um*' in the CCM edition, but cf. *CAO* II, series 109^2 and 132b 'De Tobie', and *Port.Wulst*. II, 44–5; see also *Corp.41*, manuscript p. 475 (noted by Grant, *Corp.41*, p. 106), for six responsory and verse incipits headed 'Incipit responsoria de Tobi ad medium Septembris usque in dominica mensis Octobris', of which the first is 'Peto Domine', with the verse 'Omnia iudicia' written out in full and neumed.

351 *'Tribulationes'* *CAO* II, series 109^3 and 134 'De Iudith', although in only one of Hesbert's monastic sources does 'Tribulationes' occur as the first responsory of the first Nocturn. In *Port.Wulst*. II, 45, it appears as the seventh responsory of the group 'De Tobi [*sic*]'; see also *Corp.41*, manuscript pp. 475–6 (noted by Grant, *Corp.41*, p. 106) under the rubric 'Responsoria de Iudith', followed by a series of only three, beginning 'Adonai Domine' with the verse 'Benedicite'.

352 *'Adaperiat'* *CAO* II, series 137a–b and 113^2a 'De historia Machabeorum'; lections and responsories are given at *Port.Wulst*. II, 46; responsories only in *Corp.41*, manuscript p. 476 (noted by Grant, *Corp.41*, p. 106) under the rubric 'Incipit responsoria dominica .i. mensis October [*sic*] usque in dominica .i. mensis Nouember [*sic*]', followed by a series of nine, beginning 'Adaperiat Dominus' with the verse 'Exaudiat Dominus'.

Commentary

353 *minores prophetas*   Twelve books in all: Hosea, Joel, Amos, Obadiah, Jonah, Micah, Nahum, Habakkuk, Zephaniah, Haggai, Zechariah and Malachi.

354 *'Vidi Dominum'*   *CAO* II, series 138a–b and 115² 'De prophetis'; *Port.Wulst.* II, 47; see also the incomplete series in *Corp.41*, manuscript pp. 476–7 (noted by Grant, *Corp.41*, p. 106) under the rubric 'Incipit responsoria de minoribus prophetis ad dominica .i. mensis Nouembris usque medium Aduentum', followed by only two, beginning 'Vidi Dominum' with the verse 'Seraphim'.

LME 75   Advent

355 *legimus Isaiam*   The different versions of *OR XIII* unanimously assign Isaiah to this season. The *LME* is also unambiguous but difficult to reconcile with a statement at the beginning of the Old English homily for the first Sunday of Advent, wherein Ælfric refers to readings from the 'prophets' (plural) through the liturgies of the season: 'Nu stent se gewuna on Godes gelaðunge, þæt ealle Godes ðeowan on cyrclicum ðenungum, ægðer ge on halgum rædingum ge on gedremum lofsangum, ðæra witegena gyddunga singallice on þyssere tide reccað. Þa witegan, þurh Godes Gast, witegodon Cristes to-cyme ðurh menniscnysse, and be ðam manega bec setton, ða ðe we nu oferrædað æt Godes ðeowdome ætforan his gebyrd-tide' (*CH* I.xxxix, ed. Thorpe I, 600). In liturgical contexts *lofsang* commonly means 'hymn', although here it might refer loosely to the responsories at Nocturns (normally OE *repsas*). The statement in the homily suggests confusion or conflation of the readings for Advent (Isaiah) with those for November (Ezechiel, Daniel and the twelve minor prophets), although in some Cluniac customaries Isaiah *and* the twelve minor prophets are assigned to ferias in the season of Advent (see CCM 7.4, 37).

356 *'Aspiciens'*   *CAO* II, series 1a.

357 *'Dominus regnauit'* . . . *Septuagessima sola*   This comment is more relevant to diurnal customs for Advent and Septuagesima (*LME* 16 and 26) than to the present 'appendix' on Nocturns, and its inclusion here seems an afterthought or a trace of Ælfric's cutting-and-splicing method of abridging sources. The unspoken rationale for the custom is the close association in the secular Office between Ps. XCII ('Dominus regnauit') and Sundays or feasts (see, e.g., Amalarius's *Lib.off.* IV.x.6 and IV.xvii.5–7; similarly his *Liber de ordine antiphonarii* V.5). At Lauds on certain Sundays in the calendar, however, the monastic Office also made use of this triumphal psalm, though not always in the same way. Ælfric's only prior mention of a special use of Ps. XCII occurs in his description of Lauds of Easter Sunday (*LME* 47, adapted from *RC* 79), but there the inclusion results *de facto* from the wholesale substitution of the secular for the monastic Office – i.e., Ps. XCII always replaces Ps. L ('Miserere mei') as the first for Sunday Lauds in the secular *cursus* (see above, n. 243). Here *LME* 75 notes a similar use of Ps. XCII on Sundays in Advent and on Septuagesima Sunday, meaning that on these occasions Ps. XCII takes the place of Ps. L (the second psalm sung daily at monastic Lauds), even though the Office does not otherwise follow the secular form, as it would on Easter. Tolhurst's remarks (p. 196), however, seem to conflate the use of Ps. XCII on Advent Sundays and Septuagesima Sunday

Commentary

(within the otherwise monastic Office) with its use in Easter (within the secular Office). Hallinger's note to *LME* 75, 183.16 mentions no analogues in other monastic customaries, but a pseudo-Amalarian commentary on the differences between the Roman and Benedictine Offices – possibly written by the celebrated Adémar of Chabannes (d. *c.* 1034) – does take special note of the distinctive monastic use of Ps. XCII on Advent Sundays and Septuagesima Sunday; see *De regula sancti Benedicti praecipui abbatis*, cc. XVI, XXXVI and XLIII (*AEOLO* III, 276, 282 and 284).

LME 76   Christmas

358 *'Primo tempore alleuiata est'* . . . *'Consolamini'* . . . *'Consurge, consurge, induere'*   Isa. IX.1–X.4, XL.1–XLI.20 and LII.1–15. These are the incipits given in all versions of *OR XIII* (terminations supplied from *OR XIII B*.14). Once again Ælfric's adherence to the wording of his source (ultimately dependent on *OR XIII A*.13) gives the impression of an Office of nine lessons. Other monastic customaries adapt the provision so that the readings from Isaiah are followed by a fourth to complete the first Nocturn. Some Cluniac sources, for example, add as a fourth reading either the pseudo-Augustinian sermon beginning 'Omnes scripturae' or Proverbs VIII.12 ff.; see *CCM* 7.4, 38, and cf. commentary to *LME* 71 (at n. 337), above, and 77 (at n. 363), below. On Christmas some medieval sources would also admit an Office of a single (festal) secular Nocturn, as at Easter and Pentecost (Harper, *Forms and Orders*, p. 150), but Ælfric's added mention of *sermones patrum*, in addition to the three lessons from Isaiah, indicates more than a single Nocturn here.

359 *'Hodie nobis'*   *CAO* II, series 19b.

LME 77   From Christmas through the Octave of Epiphany

360 *de ipsa festiuitate Natiuitatis Domini*   For readings and responsories, see *LME* 76 and commentary above, at nn. 358–9.

361 *sermones congruentes* . . . *responsoria de Natiuitate Domini canimus*   The responsories are those of Christmas, but the *sermones* are proper to the Octave, also the feast of the Circumcision (1 January). *OR XIII A*.17, *B*.18 and *D*.16 indicate that the readings on the Octave may either be those of Christmas or proper to the Circumcision. The use of scriptural lessons, if any, on this feast is not clear.

362 *de ipsis legimus et canimus*   That is, repetition of the propers for these saints on 2–4 January; cf. *LME* 21 above (with commentary at n. 85), which requires Vespers antiphons proper to these saints' days with the psalms as of Christmas (second) Vespers. As Hall observes ('Some Liturgical Notes', p. 300), it is odd that Ælfric refers to the Octaves of these feasts but not to the feasts themselves. *OR XIII A*.14–16 assigns readings from Acts to the feast of St Stephen and from the Apocalypse to the feasts of St John and the Holy Innocents; *OR XIII B*.15–17 is even more specific, namely: Acts VI.1–VIII.8 (Stephen), Rev. I.1–IV.11 (John) and Rev. V.1–XI.19 (Holy Innocents). For the responsory series on these days, see *CAO* II, series 20a–b, 21b–c and 22b–c.

Commentary

363 *'Omnes sitientes'* . . . *'Surge inluminare'* . . . *'Gaudens gaudebo in Domino'* Isa. LV.1–13, LX.1–22 and LXI.10–LXIV.4 (terminations supplied from *OR XIII* B.19). For the accompanying responsories, see *CAO* II, series 24b–c. Again the mention of only three scriptural lessons (ultimately reflecting *OR XIII* A.18) suggests the imperfect adaptation of a secular source; cf. commentary to *LME* 71 (at n. 337) and 76 (at n. 358). One solution, attested in Cluny-influenced sources (see CCM 7.4, 42), was to keep these readings but divide the first into Isa. LV.1–5 and 6–13, yielding the expected total of four in the first Nocturn.

364 *epistolas Pauli uel tractus psalmorum* This conforms to *OR XIII* A.20: 'praeter has festiuitates [thus, in the period from Christmas to the Octave of Epiphany] . . . ponunt apostolum uel decadas psalmorum sancti Agustini [*sic*] usque in septuagesima'. The corresponding series of lections in *Port.Wulst.* II, 38–9, bearing the rubric 'Dominicis diebus', begins with Rom. XII.1 but also includes lessons from some non-Pauline epistles, viz., two readings from I John and one from I Peter. According to *LME* 71 and *OR XIII* A.6 these readings and all others drawn from the seven canonical epistles belong to the second week after Easter. The *decadae* mentioned are probably sequential readings from Augustine's *Enarrationes in psalmos*; see Hallinger's note to *LME* 77, 184.12–13, and Martimort, *Lectures liturgiques*, p. 80.

365 *'Domine ne in ira tua'* *CAO* II, series 26b–c and 139a 'De psalmis'; also *Port.Wulst.* II, 38–9.

LME 78 The continuation of readings in the refectory

366 *legimus in refectorio quicquid de ea in ecclesia omittimus* This solution was widely adopted as supplementary devotions and votive Offices effectively limited the time available for Nocturns. Just how much of the Bible would have to be read in the refectory may be surmised from Ælfric's outline for the period of Septuagesima through Lent (*LME* 70): of the entire Heptateuch he assigns only Genesis and Exodus to the seven weeks from Septuagesima to Passion Sunday. Since he does not make allowance for Leviticus, Numbers, Deuteronomy, Joshua and Judges (or Ruth, often grouped with these) at any other time in the year, it seems reasonable that these books, if read at all, were also taken up in Lent – in compliance with the general scheme of *OR XIII* – but in the refectory rather than in church (Gatch, 'The Office', p. 355). The burden of finishing the historical books (see *LME* 72–4) would be alleviated somewhat by Ælfric's unusual insistence that on ferias in the summer period the monks read three lessons (as in winter) instead of the single one required by Benedict; on this notable departure from contemporary practice, see *LME* 80 and below, n. 368.

LME 79 Formulas for terminating the readings

367 *'Haec dicit Dominus'* . . . *'Tu autem Domine, miserere nostri'* These formulas, recited at the conclusion of each lesson, are standard; see Hughes, § 415.

Commentary

LME 80   Lessons on summer ferias; repetition of Sunday masses

368 *ut tres lectiones . . . iam preteritis annis tenuimus*   The provision stands out as atypical and even surprising, given Ælfric's acknowledgement at *LME* 57 that the hours of darkness during an English summer are not sufficient to accommodate the interval between Nocturns and Lauds prescribed by the *Rule* (see above, n. 283). On ferias in summer, to complete three readings and still begin Lauds at first light (*RSB*, c. VIII.4: 'incipiente luce'), the Eynsham monks would have to rise even earlier for the Night Office. The supererogatory nature of this custom runs counter to Ælfric's tendency to simplify some rituals prescribed in his sources (see Gatch, 'The Office', pp. 355–6, and 'Old English Literature and the Liturgy', p. 242). From another perspective, however, the insistence on three readings in the summer accords well with Ælfric's reputation for rigour in certain matters, even by the standards of his own fellow reformers (see above, p. 43). Ælfric's tone suggests that the practice, if not his own invention, was at least quite dear to him, though no available evidence indicates that three readings in summer were the custom at Æthelwold's Old Minster (cf. *Life of St Æthelwold*, ed. Lapidge and Winterbottom, pp. lxvii–lxxvii).

Ælfric's phrase *iam preteritis annis tenuimus* presents difficulties of interpretation that bear directly on the origins of this provision and on the dating of the whole customary. Gatch renders the sentence (p. 356, n. 49) '. . . that we maintained three lections with as many responsories the whole summer at Nocturns as in winter in past years'. The syntax is a little strange: *ut* + indicative here seems equivalent to a noun clause, not unlike OE *þæt* + indicative. But the implications of the clause, construed with *iam preteritis annis*, are clear enough: the *LME* – or at least this final section of it – was written two or more years after Ælfric became head of the community he is now addressing. In dating the *LME* close to the refounding of Eynsham (*c*. 1005), opinion has perhaps placed too much weight on the comparatively vague phrase *nuper rogatu Æþelmæri* in the preface (*LME* 1); see above, pp. 10–11.

369 *et quod missas dominicas . . . ut saltem ter celebrentur*   The words *et quod* here continue the earlier construction begun with *Volo . . . uos scire . . . ualde gratum mihi fore, quod . . .* The mass of each Sunday would normally be repeated daily through the following week, except on feast days with their own propers. Ferias in Lent had long since acquired proper masses of their own, however, so that repetition of Sunday masses was effectively suspended (see Hughes, § 517). *LME* 80 marks an exception to this arrangement by encouraging a limited repetition of Sunday masses even in Lent. In his commentary to *LME* 80, 185.6–9, Hallinger adduces one analogue from the Cluny-derived *Consuetudines Vallumbrosanae* (ed. CCM 7.2, 315–79) wherein Sunday masses *per annum* are also limited to two repetitions, but these are fixed on Tuesday and Thursday.

370 *similiter omnes dominicas missas . . . ne uilescere uideantur*   To construe the last sentence as it stands in the manuscript takes some effort. The case of *omnes dominicas missas* may be explained by an extension of the earlier verb *repetitis*, or, as I have supplied, a subjunctive *repetatis*. The subject of the clause *ut . . . ter celebrentur* is accordingly understood as *dominicae missae*. The qualifying phrase *si festiuitates intercurrunt* is also

227

Commentary

difficult, since *intercurrere* may take an accusative object, and one is left uncertain whether *festiuitates* is the subject or object of *intercurrant*. The present translation assumes the former, though the latter is at least possible (the subject would then again be *dominicae missae*, understood). The translation of *tantummodo* as 'as many as' instead of the more usual 'only' seems necessary to avoid a contradiction. Otherwise Ælfric now seems concerned to *limit* the repetitions to three, even though he has just implied that this is the minimum (cf. *saltem* in the previous sentence), not maximum, desired. Ælfric's Latin is seldom so obscure as in this passage, and the high concentration of interpretative cruces in the last sentence may indicate a corrupted text. Even so, I understand his general meaning to be that Sunday masses throughout the year, even in Lent, shall be repeated at least as the matutinal mass on the following Monday and Tuesday.

APPENDIX

Concordance of section divisions in the *Regularis concordia*

This book has most often cited the Symons–Spath edition of the *Regularis concordia* in the CCM (1984), although at present the most widely available text may still be Thomas Symons's edition and translation of 1953. Because the CCM and Symons (1953) use different section divisions, and because the most recent edition by Lucia Kornexl (1993) follows the latter, I include the following table of correspondences to facilitate comparison of the editions of Symons and Kornexl with texts in the CCM.

RC (CCM) section	=	*RC* (Symons) and *RC* (Kornexl) section
1–10		1–10 (*pari passu*)
11–13		11
14		12
15–19		14–18 (*pari passu*)
20–2		19
23–5		20
26–7		21–2 (*pari passu*)
28–9		23
30–1		24
32–4		25
35		26
36–8		27
39		28
40–2		29
43–4		30
45–9		31
50–3		32
54		33
55–8		34

Appendix

59–60	35–6 (*pari passu*)
61 (to p. 109.17)	37
61 (from p. 109.17)–62	38
63	39
64–6	40
67–8	41
69–71	42
72–3 (to p. 116.4)	43
73 (from p. 116.5)	44–5
74	46
75–6	47
77	48–9
78–9 (to p. 124.8)	50
79 (from p. 124.8 to 126.7)	51
79 (from p. 126.7)	52
80	53
81–2	54
83	55
84–5	56
86–7	57
88	58
89–90	59
91–2	60
93–5	61–3 (*pari passu*)
96–7	64
98–9 (to p. 141.21)	65
99 (from p. 142.1)	66
100–1	67
102–3	68
104	69

Bibliography

Andrieu, M., ed., *Les Ordines romani du haut moyen âge*, 5 vols., Spicilegium Sacrum Lovaniense, Études et Documents 11, 23–4 and 28–9 (Louvain, 1931–61)

Bannister, H. M., 'Note on MS Hatton 113', in *Early Worcester MSS*, ed. Turner, pp. lx–lxii

Banting, H. M. J., ed., *Two Anglo-Saxon Pontificals (the Egbert and Sidney Sussex Pontificals)*, HBS 104 (London, 1989)

Barker, K., ed., *The Cerne Abbey Millennium Lectures* (Cerne Abbas, 1988)

Barré, R. and J. Deshusses, 'A la recherche du Missel d'Alcuin', *Ephemerides Liturgicae* 82 (1968), 1–44

Barrow, J., 'The Community of Worcester, 961–c. 1100', in *St Oswald*, ed. Brooks and Cubitt, pp. 84–99

Bateson, M., 'Rules for Monks and Secular Canons after the Revival under King Edgar', *EHR* 9 (1894), 690–708

'A Worcester Cathedral Book of Ecclesiastical Collections, Made c. 1000 A.D.', *EHR* 10 (1895), 712–31

Bateson, M., ed., *Excerpta ex institutionibus monasticis Æthelwoldi episcopi Wintoniensis compilata in usum fratrum Egneshamnensium per Ælfricum abbatem*, in *Compotus Rolls of the Obedientiaries of St. Swithun's Priory, Winchester*, ed. G. W. Kitchin (London, 1892), pp. 171–98 (Appendix VII)

Benedictine Monks of Solesmes, ed., *Antiphonaire monastique, xiiie siècle, codex F.160 de la Bibliothèque de la cathédrale de Worcester* [facsimile], Paléographie musicale ser. 1, no. 12 (Tournai, 1922)

Bethurum, D., 'Archbishop Wulfstan's Commonplace Book', *PMLA* 57 (1942), 916–29

Bethurum, D., ed., *The Homilies of Wulfstan* (Oxford, 1957)

Bishop, T. A. M., *English Caroline Minuscule* (Oxford, 1971)

Blair, J., *Anglo-Saxon Oxfordshire* (Oxford, 1994)

Blair, J. and R. Sharpe, ed., *Pastoral Care Before the Parish* (Leicester, 1992)

Bibliography

Breck, E., ed., 'Fragment of Ælfric's Translation of Æthelwold's De Consuetudine Monachorum and its Relation to Other MSS. Critically Edited from the MS. Cotton. Tib. A.iii in the British Museum' (dissertation, Univ. of Leipzig, 1887)

Brehe, S. K., 'Reassembling the *First Worcester Fragment*', *Speculum* 65 (1990), 521–36

Brooks, N. and C. Cubitt, ed., *St Oswald: Life and Influence* (London, 1996)

Bullough, D. A., *Carolingian Renewal: Sources and Heritage* (Manchester, 1991)

Cabaniss, A., *Amalarius of Metz* (Amsterdam, 1954)

Campbell, A., ed., *Chronicon Æthelweardi: The Chronicle of Æthelweard* (London, 1962)

Campbell, J., 'England *c.* 991', in *The Battle of Maldon: Fiction and Fact*, ed. J. Cooper (London, 1993), pp. 1–17

Campbell, J., ed., *The Anglo-Saxons* (London, 1982)

Clayton, M., *The Cult of the Virgin Mary in Anglo-Saxon England*, CSASE 2 (Cambridge, 1990)

Clemoes, P., 'Ælfric', in *Continuations and Beginnings: Studies in Old English Literature*, ed. E. G. Stanley (London, 1966), pp. 176–209

'The Chronology of Ælfric's Works', in *The Anglo-Saxons: Studies in Some Aspects of their History and Culture Presented to Bruce Dickins*, ed. P. Clemoes (London, 1959), pp. 212–47

'The Old English Benedictine Office, Corpus Christi College, Cambridge, MS. 190, and the Relations between Ælfric and Wulfstan: a Reconsideration', *Anglia* 78 (1960), 265–83

Clemoes, P. and K. Hughes, ed., *England Before the Conquest: Studies in Primary Sources Presented to Dorothy Whitelock* (Cambridge, 1971)

Collins, M., J. Price and A. Hamer, ed., *Sources and Relations: Studies in Honour of J. E. Cross, Leeds Studies in English*, n.s. 16 (1985)

Cross, F. L. and E. A. Livingstone, ed., *The Oxford Dictionary of the Christian Church*, 3rd ed. (Oxford, 1997)

Cross, J. E., 'Ælfric – Mainly on Memory and Creative Method in Two *Catholic Homilies*', *Studia Neophilologica* 41 (1969), 135–55

'The Literate Anglo-Saxon – on Sources and Disseminations', *Proceedings of the British Academy* 58 (1972), 67–100

'A Newly-Identified Manuscript of Wulfstan's "Commonplace Book", Rouen, Bibliothèque Municipale, MS 1382 (U.109), fols. 173r–198v', *Journal of Medieval Latin* 2 (1992), 63–83

Cross, J. E. and J. Morrish Tunberg, ed., *The Copenhagen Wulfstan Collection: Copenhagen Kongelige Bibliotek Gl. Kgl. Sam. 1595*, EEMF 25 (Copenhagen, 1993)

Bibliography

Darlington, R. R., ed., *The Vita Wulfstani of William of Malmesbury*, Camden Society 40 (London, 1928)

Davril, A., ed., *The Winchcombe Sacramentary (Orléans, Bibliothèque municipale 127 {105})*, HBS 109 (London, 1995)

Deshusses, J., ed., *Le Sacramentaire grégorien, ses principales formes d'après les plus anciens manuscrits*, 2 vols., Spicilegium Friburgense 16 and 24 (Fribourg, 1971–9)

Dewick, E. S. and W. H. Frere, ed., *The Leofric Collectar*, 2 vols., HBS 45 and 56 (London, 1914–21)

Dietrich, E., 'Abt Ælfrik: zur Literaturgeschichte der angelsächsischen Kirche', *Zeitschrift für die historische Theologie* 25 (1855), 487–594, and 26 (1856), 163–256

Doble, G. H., ed., *Pontificale Lanaletense (Bibliothèque de la Ville de Rouen A.27 Cat. 368)*, HBS 74 (London, 1937)

Douteil, H., ed., *Iohannis Beleth Summa de ecclesiasticis officiis*, 2 vols, CCCM 41 and 41A (Turnhout, 1976)

Dreves, G. M., C. Blume and H. M. Bannister, ed., *Analecta hymnica medii aeui*, 55 vols. (Leipzig, 1886–1922)

Dubois, M.-M., *Ælfric: Sermonnaire, docteur et grammairien: Contribution a l'étude de la vie et de l'action bénédictines en Angleterre au xe siècle* (Paris, 1943)

Dumville, D. N., *English Caroline Script and Monastic History: Studies in Benedictinism, A.D. 950–1030*, SASH 6 (Woodbridge, 1993)

'The English Element in Tenth-Century Breton Book-Production', in *Britons and Anglo Saxons in the Early Middle Ages* (Aldershot, 1993), Essay XIV, pp. 1–13

Liturgy and the Ecclesiastical History of Late Anglo-Saxon England: Four Studies, SASH 5 (Woodbridge, 1992)

Durandus, G., *Rationale diuinorum officiorum a Gulielmo Durando, Mimatensi episcopo, I.V.D. clariss. concinnatum atque nunc recens utilissimis adnotationibus illustratum* (Venice, 1599)

Fehr, B., 'Das Benediktiner-Offizium und die Beziehungen zwischen Ælfric und Wulfstan', *Englische Studien* 46 (1912–13), 337–46

Fehr, B., ed., *Die Hirtenbriefe Ælfrics in altenglischer und lateinischer Fassung*, BaP 9 (Hamburg, 1914; repr. with a supplement to the introduction by P. Clemoes: Darmstadt, 1966)

Flower, R., 'The Script of the Exeter Book', in *The Exeter Book of Old English Poetry* [facsimile], ed. R. W. Chambers, M. Förster and R. Flower (Exeter, 1933), pp. 83–90

Förster, M., 'Über die Quellen von Ælfrics exegetischen Homiliae Catholicae', *Anglia* 16 (1884), 1–61

Frank, R., 'A Note on Old English *Swidagas* "Silent Days"', in *Studies in Honour of René Derolez*, ed. A. M. Simon-Vandenbergen (Ghent, 1987), pp. 180–9

Gameson, R., 'Book Production and Decoration at Worcester in the Tenth and Eleventh Centuries', in *St Oswald*, ed. Brooks and Cubitt, pp. 194–243

Garmonsway, G. N., ed., *Ælfric's Colloquy*, 2nd ed. (London, 1947)

Gatch, M. McC., 'The Office in Late Anglo-Saxon Monasticism', in *Learning and Literature*, ed. Lapidge and Gneuss, pp. 341–62

'Old English Literature and the Liturgy: Problems and Potential', *ASE* 6 (1977), 237–47

Preaching and Theology in Anglo-Saxon England: Ælfric and Wulfstan (Toronto, 1977)

Gneuss, H., *Hymnar und Hymnen im englischen Mittelalter: Studien zur Überlieferung, Glossierung und Übersetzung lateinischer Hymnen in England*, Buchreihe der Anglia 12 (Tübingen, 1968)

'Latin Hymns in Medieval England: Future Research', in *Chaucer and Middle English Studies in Honour of Rossell Hope Robbins*, ed. B. Rowland (London, 1974), pp. 407–24

'Liturgical Books in Anglo-Saxon England and their Old English Terminology', in *Learning and Literature*, ed. Lapidge and Gneuss, pp. 91–141

Godden, M. R., ed. *Ælfric's Catholic Homilies: The Second Series. Text*, EETS s.s. 5 (London, 1979)

Godden, M. R., with D. Gray and T. Hoad, ed., *From Anglo-Saxon to Early Middle English: Studies Presented to E. G. Stanley* (Oxford, 1994)

Gordon, E., *Eynsham Abbey, 1005–1228: A Small Window into a Large Room* (Chichester, 1990)

Gransden, A., 'Traditionalism and Continuity during the Last Century of Anglo-Saxon Monasticism', *Journal of Ecclesiastical History* 40 (1989), 159–207

Grant, R. J. S., ed., *Cambridge, Corpus Christi College 41: The Loricas and the Missal*, Costerus Essays in English and American Language and Literature, n.s. 17 (Amsterdam, 1979)

Gretsch, M., *Die Regula Sancti Benedicti in England und ihre altenglische Übersetzung*, TUEP 2 (Munich, 1973)

Hall, J., ed., *Selections from Early Middle English, 1130–1250*, 2 vols. (Oxford, 1920)

Hall, J. R., 'Some Liturgical Notes on Ælfric's *Letter to the Monks at Eynsham*', *DR* 93 (1975), 297–303

Hallinger, K., ed., *Consuetudines Cluniacensium antiquiores cum redactionibus deriuatis*, CCM 7.2 (Siegburg, 1983)

Consuetudinum saeculi x/xi/xii monumenta: Introductiones, CCM 7.1 (Siegburg, 1984)

Consuetudinum saeculi x/xi/xii monumenta non-Cluniacensia, CCM 7.3 (Siegburg, 1984)

Hallinger, K. with C. Elvert, ed., *Clauis uoluminum CCM VII/1–3*, CCM 7.4 (Siegburg, 1986)

Hanslik, R., ed., *Benedicti regula*, 2nd ed., Corpus Scriptorum Ecclesiasticorum Latinorum 75 (Vienna, 1977)

Hanssens, I. M., ed., *Amalarii episcopi opera liturgica omnia*, 3 vols., Studi e Testi 138–40 (Rome, 1948–50)

Hanssens, J. M., 'Le texte du "Liber officialis" d'Amalaire', *Ephemerides Liturgicae* 47 (1933), 113–25, 225–48, 313–28, 413–24 and 493–505; 48 (1934), 66–79, 223–32 and 549–69; 49 (1935), 413–35

Hardison, O. B., Jr., *Christian Rite and Christian Drama in the Middle Ages: Essays in the Origin and Early History of Modern Drama* (Baltimore and London, 1965)

Harper, J., *The Forms and Orders of Western Liturgy from the Tenth to the Eighteenth Century: A Historical Introduction and Guide for Students and Musicians* (Oxford, 1991)

Hesbert, R.-J., ed., *Antiphonale missarum sextuplex . . . d'après le graduel de Monza et les antiphonaires de Rheinau, de Mont Blandin, de Compiègne, de Corbie, et de Senlis* (Brussels, 1935)

Corpus antiphonalium officii, 6 vols., Rerum Ecclesiasticarum Documenta, Series Maior, Fontes 7–12 (Rome, 1963–79)

Hicks, C., ed., *England in the Eleventh Century: Proceedings of the 1990 Harlaxton Symposium*, Harlaxton Medieval Studies 2 (Stamford, 1992)

Hill, J., 'Monastic Reform and the Secular Church: Ælfric's Pastoral Letters in Context', in *England in the Eleventh Century*, ed. Hicks, pp. 103–17

'Reform and Resistance: Preaching Styles in Late Anglo-Saxon England', in *De l'Homélie au sermon: Histoire de la prédication médiévale*, ed. J. Hamesse and X. Hermand (Louvain, 1993), pp. 15–46

'The "Regularis Concordia" and its Latin and Old English Reflexes', *Revue Bénédictine* 101 (1991), 299–315

Hohler, C. E., 'Some Service-Books of the Later Saxon Church', in *Tenth-Century Studies*, ed. Parsons, pp. 60–83

Hughes, A., *Medieval Manuscripts for the Mass and Office: A Guide to their Organization and Terminology* (Toronto, 1982)

Hughes, A., ed., *The Portiforium of St Wulstan*, 2 vols., HBS 89 and 90 (London, 1958–60)

Hurt, J., *Ælfric*, Twayne's English Authors Series 131 (New York, 1972)

Irvine, S., ed., *Old English Homilies from MS Bodley 343*, EETS o.s. 302 (Oxford, 1993)

Bibliography

James, M. R., *A Descriptive Catalogue of the Manuscripts in the Library of Corpus Christi College, Cambridge*, 2 vols. (Cambridge, 1909–12)

John, E., 'The King and the Monks in the Tenth-Century Reformation', in *Orbis Britanniae and Other Studies*, SEEH 4 (Leicester, 1966), 154–80

'The Return of the Vikings', in *The Anglo-Saxons*, ed. Campbell, pp. 192–213

Jones, C. A., 'Ælfric's *Letter to the Monks of Eynsham*: a Study of the Text and its Sources' (unpubl. PhD dissertation, Univ. of Toronto, 1995)

'*Meatim sed et rustica*: Ælfric of Eynsham as a Medieval Latin Author' (forthcoming)

'Two Composite Texts from Archbishop Wulfstan's 'Commonplace Book': the *De ecclesiastica consuetudine* and the *Institutio beati Amalarii de ecclesiasticis officiis*', *ASE* 27 (1998), 233–71

Ker, N. R., *Books, Collectors and Libraries: Studies in the Medieval Heritage*, ed. A. G. Watson (London and Ronceverte, WV, 1985)

Catalogue of Manuscripts Containing Anglo-Saxon (Oxford, 1957)

'Old English Notes Signed "Coleman"', *Medium Ævum* 18 (1949), 29–31; repr. in his *Books, Collectors and Libraries*, pp. 27–30

Keynes, S., 'Cnut's Earls', in *The Reign of Cnut: King of England, Denmark and Norway*, ed. A. Rumble (London, 1994), pp. 43–88

The Diplomas of King Æthelred 'the Unready', 978–1016: A Study in their Use as Historical Evidence, Cambridge Studies in Medieval Life and Thought, 3rd ser., 13 (Cambridge, 1980)

Knowles, D., *The Monastic Order in England: A History of its Development from the Times of St Dunstan to the Fourth Lateran Council, 940–1216*, 2nd ed. (Cambridge, 1963)

Kornexl, L., ed., *Die Regularis Concordia und ihre altenglische Interlinearversion*, TUEP 17 (Munich, 1993)

'The *Regularis Concordia* and its Old English Gloss', *ASE* 24 (1995), 95–130

Lapidge, M., 'Æthelwold as Scholar and Teacher', in *Bishop Æthelwold*, ed. Yorke, pp. 89–117; repr. in his *Anglo-Latin Literature, 900–1066*, pp. 183–211, with addenda, p. 482

Anglo-Latin Literature, 900–1066 (London and Rio Grande, OH, 1993)

Lapidge, M., ed., *Anglo-Saxon Litanies of the Saints*, HBS 106 (London, 1991)

Lapidge, M. and H. Gneuss, ed., *Learning and Literature in Anglo-Saxon England: Studies Presented to Peter Clemoes on the Occasion of his Sixty-Fifth Birthday* (Cambridge, 1985)

Lapidge, M. and M. Winterbottom, ed. and trans., *Wulfstan of Winchester: The Life of St Æthelwold* (Oxford, 1991)

Logeman, W. S., ed., 'De Consuetudine Monachorum', *Anglia* 13 (1891), 365–454, and 14 (1893), 20–40

Bibliography

MacGregor, A. J., *Fire and Light in the Western Triduum: Their Use at Tenebrae and at the Paschal Vigil*, Alcuin Club Collection 71 (Collegeville, MN, 1992)

McIntyre, E., 'Early-Twelfth-Century Worcester Cathedral Priory with Special Reference to the Manuscripts Written There' (unpubl. DPhil thesis, Oxford Univ., 1978)

Maier, P., *Die Feier der Missa chrismatis: die Reform der Ölweihen des Pontificale Romanum vor dem Hintergrund der Ritusgeschichte*, Studien zur Pastoralliturgie 7 (Regensburg, 1990)

Martimort, A. G., *Les Lectures liturgiques et leurs livres*, Typologie des sources du moyen âge occidental 64 (Turnhout, 1992)

Mason, E., *St Wulfstan of Worcester, c. 1008–1095* (Oxford, 1990)

'St Oswald and St Wulfstan', in *St Oswald*, ed. Brooks and Cubitt, pp. 269–84

Milfull, I. B., ed., *The Hymns of the Anglo-Saxon Church: A Study and Edition of the 'Durham Hymnal'*, CSASE 17 (Cambridge, 1996)

Mitchell, B., *Old English Syntax*, 2 vols. (Oxford, 1985)

Mores, E.-R., *De Ælfrico, Dorobernensi archiepiscopo, commentarius: ex autographo in bibliotheca Thomæ Astlei, arm. asservato* (London, 1789)

Nocent, H., ed., *Aelfrici abbatis epistula ad monachos Egneshamnenses directa*, in *Consuetudinum saeculi x/xi/xii monumenta non-Cluniacensia*, ed. Hallinger, CCM 7.3, 155–85

Ortenberg, V., *The English Church and the Continent in the Tenth and Eleventh Centuries: Cultural, Spiritual, and Artistic Exchanges* (Oxford, 1992)

Parsons, D., ed., *Tenth-Century Studies: Essays in Commemoration of the Millennium of the Council of Winchester and Regularis Concordia* (London and Chichester, 1975)

Pfaff, R. W., ed., *The Liturgical Books of Anglo-Saxon England*, Old English Newsletter Subsidia 23 (Kalamazoo, MI, 1995)

Pope, J. C., ed., *Homilies of Ælfric: A Supplementary Collection*, 2 vols., EETS o.s. 259–60 (London, 1967–8)

Remley, P. G., *Old English Biblical Verse: Studies in Genesis, Exodus and Daniel*, CSASE 16 (Cambridge, 1996)

Robertson, A. J., ed., *Anglo-Saxon Charters* (Cambridge, 1939)

Robinson, J. A., *The Times of Saint Dunstan* (Oxford, 1923)

Roper, S. E., *Medieval English Benedictine Liturgy: Studies in the Formation, Structure, and Content of the Monastic Votive Office, c. 950–1540* (New York and London, 1993)

Rule, M., ed., *The Missal of St Augustine's Abbey, Canterbury* (Cambridge, 1896)

Salter, H. E., ed., *The Cartulary of the Abbey of Eynsham*, 2 vols., Oxford Historical Society 49 and 51 (Oxford, 1907–8)

Bibliography

Sauer, H., 'Die Exkommunikationsriten aus Wulfstans Handbuch und Liebermanns Gesetze', in *Bright is the Ring of Words: Festschrift für Horst Weinstock zum 65. Geburtstag*, ed. C. Pollner, H. Rohlfing and F.-R. Hausmann (Bonn, 1996)

'Zur Überlieferung und Anlage von Erzbischof Wulfstans "Handbuch"', *Deutsches Archiv für Erforschung des Mittelalters* 36 (1980), 341–84

Sauer, H., ed., *Theodulfi Capitula in England: die altenglischen Übersetzungen, zusammen mit dem lateinischen Text*, TUEP 8 (Munich, 1978)

Sawyer, P. H., ed., *Anglo-Saxon Charters: An Annotated List and Bibliography*, Royal Historical Society Guides and Handbooks 8 (London, 1968)

Schmidt, H. A. P., *Hebdomada Sancta*, 2 vols. (Rome, 1956–7)

Sisam, K., *Studies in the History of Old English Literature* (Oxford, 1953)

Skeat, W. W., ed. and trans., *Ælfric's Lives of Saints*, 4 vols., EETS o.s. 76, 82, 94 and 114 (London, 1881–1900; repr. as two volumes, 1966)

Spurrell, M., 'The Architectural Interest of the *Regularis Concordia*', *ASE* 21 (1992), 161–76

Squibb, G. D., 'The Foundation of Cerne Abbey', *Notes and Queries for Somerset and Dorset* 31 (1984), 373–6, repr. in *The Cerne Abbey Millennium Lectures*, ed. Barker, pp. 11–14

Stafford, P., *Unification and Conquest: A Political and Social History of England in the Tenth and Eleventh Centuries* (London, 1989)

Strayer, J. R., ed., *Dictionary of the Middle Ages*, 13 vols. (New York, 1982–9)

Symons, T., 'Sources of the Regularis Concordia', *DR* 59 (1941), 14–36, 143–70 and 264–89

Symons, T., ed. and trans., *Regularis concordia Anglicae nationis monachorum sanctimonialiumque: the Monastic Agreement of the Monks and Nuns of the English Nation* (London, 1953)

Symons, T. and S. Spath, with M. Wegener and K. Hallinger, ed., *Regularis concordia Anglicae nationis*, in *Consuetudinum saeculi x/xi/xii monumenta non-Cluniacensia*, ed. Hallinger, CCM 7.3, 61–147

Szarmach, P. E., ed., *Holy Men and Holy Women: Old English Prose Saints' Lives and their Contexts* (Albany, NY, 1996)

Thorpe, B., ed., *The Homilies of the Anglo-Saxon Church: The First Part Containing the Sermones Catholici or Homilies of Ælfric*, 2 vols. (London, 1844–6)

Tolhurst, J. B. L., *Introduction to the English Monastic Breviaries*, vol. VI of *idem*, ed., *The Monastic Breviary of Hyde Abbey, Winchester*, 6 vols., HBS 69–71, 76, 78 and 80 (London, 1932–42)

Tupper, F., Jr., 'History and Texts of the Benedictine Reform of the Tenth Century', *Modern Language Notes* 8 (1893), cols. 334–67

Turner, C. H., *Early Worcester MSS: Fragments of Four Books and a Charter of the Eighth Century Belonging to Worcester Cathedral* (Oxford, 1916)

Bibliography

Turner, D. H., ed., *The Claudius Pontificals (from Cotton MS. Claudius A.iii in the British Museum)*, HBS 97 (London, 1971)

The Missal of the New Minster, Winchester (Le Havre, Bibliothèque Municipale, MS 330), HBS 93 (London, 1962)

Ure, J. M., ed., *The Benedictine Office: An Old English Text*, Edinburgh University Publications in Language and Literature 11 (Edinburgh, 1957)

Vogel, C., *Medieval Liturgy: An Introduction to the Sources*, English trans. and rev. of his *Introduction aux sources de l'histoire du culte chrétien au moyen âge* (Spoleto, 1981) by W. G. Storey and N. K. Rasmussen (Washington, DC, 1986)

Vogel, C. and R. Elze, ed., *Le Pontifical romano-germanique du dixième siècle*, 3 vols., Studi e Testi 226–7 and 269 (Rome, 1963–72)

Warren, F. E., ed., *The Leofric Missal* (Oxford, 1883)

Webber, T., *Scribes and Scholars at Salisbury Cathedral, c. 1075–c. 1125* (Oxford, 1992)

White, C. L., *Ælfric: A New Study of his Life and Writings*, Yale Studies in English 2 (New Haven, 1892; repr. with supplementary bibliography by M. R. Godden: Hamden, CT, 1974)

Whitelock, D., 'Archbishop Wulfstan, Homilist and Statesman', *Transactions of the Royal Historical Society*, 4th. ser., 24 (1942), 25–45

'Wulfstan at York', in *Franciplegius: Medieval and Linguistic Studies in Honor of Francis Peabody Magoun, Jr.*, ed. J. B. Bessinger and R. P. Creed (New York, 1965), pp. 214–31

Whitelock, D, ed., *Anglo-Saxon Wills* (Cambridge, 1930)

Sermo Lupi ad Anglos, 3rd ed. (London, 1963)

Whitelock, D., M. Brett and C. N. L. Brooke, ed., *Councils and Synods, with Other Documents Relating to the English Church, Vol. I: A.D. 871–1204: Part I: 871–1066* (Oxford, 1981)

Whitelock, D., with D. C. Douglas and S. I. Tucker, ed. and trans., *The Anglo-Saxon Chronicle: A Revised Translation* (London, 1961)

Wilcox, J., ed., *Ælfric's Prefaces*, Durham Medieval Texts 9 (Durham, 1994)

Wilson, H. A., ed., *The Missal of Robert of Jumièges*, HBS 11 (London, 1896)

The Benedictional of Archbishop Robert, HBS 24 (London, 1903)

Woolley, R. M., ed., *The Canterbury Benedictional (British Museum, Harl. MS. 2892)*, HBS 51 (London, 1917)

Wormald, P., 'Æthelwold and his Continental Counterparts: Contact, Comparison, Contrast', in *Bishop Æthelwold*, ed. Yorke, pp. 13–42

Yorke, B., 'Æthelmær: the Foundation of the Abbey at Cerne and the Politics of the Tenth Century', in *The Cerne Abbey Millennium Lectures*, ed. Barker, pp. 15–26

Bibliography

Yorke, B., ed., *Bishop Æthelwold: His Career and Influence* (Woodbridge, 1988)

Zupitza, J., ed., 'Ein weiteres Bruchstück der Regularis Concordia in altenglischer Sprache', *Archiv* 84 (1890), 1–24

Index of liturgical *formae*

The list below includes only incipits cited in the edition proper (but here given in normalized spelling). The number after the incipit refers to the relevant section(s) of the *LME* rather than to page numbers. Accompanying most references is a symbol in parentheses, indicating the type of text: (A) = antiphon; (C) = collect; (Cant) = canticle; (D) = introductory or concluding dialogue; (E) = epistle or any reading at mass other than the gospel; (G) = gospel reading; (Gr) = gradual response or 'Alleluia'; (H) = hymn; (I) = introit; (L) = reading at Nocturns; (P) = prayer or *preces*; (Ps.) = psalm; (R) = responsory; (T) = tract; (V) = versicle or *uersus*. A few obvious items are not classified (*Kyrie*, *Pater noster*, *Gloria in excelsis Deo*, etc.). The following abbreviations are also used (but ignored for the purposes of alphabetization): C = Christe, Cs = Christus, D = Domine, Dm = Deum, Dni = Domini, Dno = Domino, Dns = Dominus, Ds = Deus, I = Iesu, Is = Iesus, qs = quaesumus, Sps = Spiritus.

Accendite 46
Adaperiat (R) 74
Ad cenam Agni (H) 50
Ad Dmn (Ps. CXIX) 30
Ad te leuaui oculos (Ps. CXXII) 4, 29, 30
Aeterne rerum (H) 13
Aeterne rex altissime (H) 50
Agnus Dei 38, 46
Alleluia 22, 26(x2), 46, 48(x4), 49(x3)
Alleluia Confitemini (Gr) 46
Alleluia dulce carmen (H) 13
Alleluia dum praesens est (R) 70
Alleluia piis edite laudibus (H) 13
Almum sidereae (H) 13
Angelus Dni (R) 71
Ante diem festum (G) 42
A Patre unigenitus (H) 13(x2)
Arbor decora (H) 13

A solis ortus (H) 13(x2)
Aspiciens (R) 75
Auctor salutis (H) 13
Audi benigne conditor (H) 13
Audi redemptor (H) 13
Aurora lucis rutilat (H) 50
Auertit Dns captiuitatem (A) 26

Beata nobis gaudia (H) 50
Beati immaculati (Ps. CXVIII.1–32) 34, 48
Beati quorum (Ps. XXXI) 4, 30
Beatus uir [qui timet] (Ps. CXI) 48
Benedixisti D [terram] (Ps. LXXXIV) 4
Benedixisti D terram (A) 26
Bonitatem (Ps. CXVIII.65–80) 48

Cantate Dno (A) 26

Index of liturgical formae

C qui lux es (H) 13
C redemptor (H) 13
Cs factus est obediens (A) 33
Circumdederunt (I) 26
Clamaui (Ps. CXVIII.145–60) 48
Clarum decus ieiunii (H) 13
Conditor alme siderum (H) 13
Confitebor Dno (A) 26
Confitebor [tibi D] (Ps. CX) 48
Confitebor tibi D (Ps. CXXXVII) 45
Confitemini Dno quoniam (Ps. CXVII) 48(x2)
Consolamini (L) 76
Consurge consurge induere (L) 76
Credidi propter (Ps. CXV) 6
Cum inducerent (A) 25
Cum inuocarem (Ps. IV) 48

De necessitatibus (A) 26
De profundis (Ps. CXXIX) 4, 6, 30
Defecit (Ps. CXVIII.81–96) 48
Dei fide qua uiuimus (H) 13
Ds a quo et Iudas (C) 43
Ds creator omnium (H) 54
Ds Ds meus [ad te] (Ps. LXII) 47
Ds in adiutorium (Ps. LXIX) 4
Ds in adiutorium (D) 33, 47(x2)
Ds in nomine tuo (Ps. LIII) 34, 48
Ds misereatur (Ps. LXVI) 4, 29, 47
Ds noster refugium (Ps. XLV) 24
Ds omnium (R) 72
Ds qui conspicis (C) 27
Ds qui in Abrahae (C) 51
Dicit Dns: Ego cogito (I) 59
Dilexi quoniam (Ps. CXIV) 6
Dixit Dns (Ps. CIX) 48
Dixit Dns ad Moysen (E) 43
D audiui (T) 43
D clamaui (Ps. CXL) 45
D Ds in adiutorium (A) 26
D exaudi (Ps. CI) 4, 30
D exaudi (Ps. CXLII) 4, 30
D labia mea (D) 33, 47
D ne in furore (Ps. VI) 4, 6, 30
D ne in furore (Ps. XXXVII) 4, 30

D ne in ira tua (R) 77
D probasti me (Ps. CXXXVIII) 45
Dns regnauit [decorem] (Ps. XCII) 47, 75
Dns uobiscum (D) 32, 38
Dum complerentur (R) 72

Ecce iam noctis (H) 54
Ecce nunc (Ps. CXXXIII) 48
Ego autem accepi (L) 70
Ego sicut uitis (R) 71
Eripe me D (Ps. CXXXIX) 45
Eripe me Dne (T) 43
Erraui (P) 48
Eructauit cor meum (A) 26
Erudi qs D (C) 25
Esto mihi in Dm (I) 28
Exaudi Ds orationem (Ps. LXIII) 70
Exaudi nos D (A) 29
Exaudiat te Dns (Ps. XIX) 4 (x2)
Exsurge D (A) 29
Exultate Deo (A) 26

Festinemus ingredi (L) 70
Flectamus genua (D) 61
Fluminis impetus (A) 24

Gaudens gaudebo (L) 77
Gloria in excelsis Deo 16, 22, 23, 26, 46(x2), 52
Gloria laus (H) 32
Gloria [Patri] 29(x2), 31, 33(x2), 47(x2)

Haec dicit Dns Ds exercituum (D) 79
Haec dies (Gr) 48(x2)
Haec dies (V) 48
Hodie nobis (R) 76
Hostis Herodes (H) 13(x2)
Hymnum canamus gloriae (H) 50

Iam Cs astra (H) 50
Iam lucis orto (H) 13
I nostra redemptio (H) 50
I quadragenariae (H) 13
In conuertendo (Ps. CXXV) 30
In die qua inuocaui (R) 70

Index of liturgical formae

In exitu Israel (Ps. CXIII) 48
In pace in idipsum (V) 48
In principio (R) 74
In te D speraui (Ps. XXX) 48
In tribulatione sua (E) 43
Inclina D (Ps. LXXXV) 4
Ingrediente Dno (R) 32
Iniquos (Ps. CXVIII.113–28) 48
Intende in me (A) 26
Inuocauit me (I) 30
Is refulsit (H) 13
Isti sunt dies (R) 70(x2)
Iubilate Deo (A) 26
Iuste iudicate (A) 26

Kyrie [eleison] 29, 30, 33, 48(x2)

Laetatus sum (Ps. CXXI) 30
Laudate (T) 46
Laudate Dnm omnes gentes (Ps. CXVI, used as *communio*) 46
Laudate pueri (Ps. CXII) 48
Legem pone (Ps. CXVIII.33–48) 34, 48
Leuaui oculos (Ps. CXX) 4, 30
Locutus est Dns ad Moysen (R) 70
Lucis creator (H) 13, 54

Magnificat (Cant) 46
Maria Magdalene (R) 71
Memor esto (Ps. CXVIII.49–64) 48
Meridie orandum est (H) 13
Mirabilia (Ps. CXVIII.129–44) 48
Misereatur (P) 19(x2)
Miserere mei Ds [secundum] (Ps. L) 4, 30
Miserere mei Ds miserere (Ps. LVI) 4

Narrabo nomen tuum (R) 71
Nisi quia Dns (Ps. CXXIII) 30
Nocte surgentes (H) 54
Nunc dimittis (Cant) 48
Nunc sancte nobis Sps (H) 13

O lux beata (H) 13
Omnes sitientes (L) 77
Optatus uotis omnium (H) 50

Pater noster 29, 30, 44
Perfecto trino numero (H) 13
Peto D (R) 74
Post passionem Dni (R) 71
Primo dierum (H) 13
Primo tempore alleuiata est (L) 76
Principes (Ps. CXVIII.161–76) 48
Pueri Hebraeorum (A) 32

Quaerite Dmn (A) 26
Quam bonus Israel (A) 26
Quam magna multitudo (R) 70
Quem terra (H) 13
Qui confidunt (Ps. CXXIV) 30
Qui habitat (Ps. XC) 48
Qui regis Israel (Ps. LXXIX) 4
Quia mirabilia (A) 26
Quicumque uult 48
Quod chorus uatum (H) 13
Quomodo dilexi (Ps. CXVIII.97–112) 48

Rector potens (H) 13
Rerum Ds (H) 13
Responsum accepit Simeon (R) 25
Retribue (Ps. CXVIII.17–32) 48

Sana D (A) 26
Satisfaciat tibi D Ds noster (P) 69
Si bona (R) 74
Sps Dni (I) 53
Subuenite sancti Dei (P) 66
Surge illuminare (L) 77
Surrexit Dns (V) 47

Tecum principium (A) 20
Te Dm laudamus (H) 22, 47
Te lucis ante terminum (H) 54
Temptauit Ds Abraham (E) 51
Tribulationes (R) 74
Tu autem Dne [miserere nostri] (D) 33, 79
Turba multa (G) 32
Tu solus altissimus (A) 26

Vsquequo D (Ps. XII) 4
Vt non delinquam (A) 26

243

Index of liturgical formae

Veni creator Sps (H) 50
Veni redemptor (H) 13
Venite adoremus eum (A) 24
Verba mea (Ps. V) 6
Verbum supernum (H) 13
Vespere autem sabbati (A) 46

Vexilla regis (H) 13
Vidi Dnm (R) 74
Visita nos D (A) 26
Viuet anima mea (P) 48
Voce mea (Ps. CXLI) 45
Vox clara (H) 13

General index

Aachen, 816 Council of, 210
abbot, 15, 16, 19, 34n., 56, 57, 60n., 113, 117, 119, 121, 129, 131, 133, 135, 141, 143, 157, 186, 196, 203, 214; election of, 44–45n.; lay abbots, 48; *see also* Ælfric, abbacy of
Abingdon, 30n., 46
abstinence, 141; from fats, 117, 121, 164, 175, 177; from milk and eggs, 121, 175, 177; *see also* fasts, fasting
acolyte, 198
Adoration of the Cross: *see* Veneration of the Cross
Advent, 139, 159, 211; abstinence and omission of 'Gloria' in, 117, 164; hymns of, 33, 115, 151; Night Office in, 69, 147, 224; use of Ps. XCII in, 224–5
Ælfhere, ealdorman, 46n.
Ælfric, archbishop of Canterbury, 6n., 94–5
Ælfric Bata, 53n., 95
Ælfric of Eynsham:
   abbacy of, 4-12, 48, 93, 95, 97-8, 150, 227; *see also* Eynsham Abbey
   as a reformer, 20, 39-53, 68, 70, 85, 91, 151, 210–11, 213–14, 227
   as a critic of Æthelred II, 47–9, 213
   'biblicizing' tendency of: *see* biblical quotations, accuracy of
   date of birth, 1, 46n.
   Latinity of, 14n., 51–3, 176–7, 182, 196, 202, 227–8; *see also* LME, compositional method of
   works of:
   biblical translations, 5, 47n., 91, 217
   Colloquy, 1, 5, 53, 152
   De septem gradibus ecclesiasticis, 73, 210–11
   Ely privilege, 48n.
   Glossary, 53n., 90
   Grammar, 5, 52, 53n., 90, 151, 176–7

homilies: 4, 5, 27, 52, 65–7, 89–90; for Advent, 1st Sunday in, 69, 224; for Candlemas, 24, 170, 171–2; for Epiphany, 201; for Holy Innocents, 167; for Lent, 1st Sunday in, 178–9; for Palm Sunday, 24, 182-4, 185-6; for Passion Sunday, 182; for Pentecost, 65n., 208; for September, 1st Sunday in, 223; for Septuagesima, 65, 172–5, 182; for the Greater Litany, 65n.; for the Octave of Pentecost, 208, 222; for the 22nd Sunday after Pentecost, 49n.
Letter to the Monks of Eynsham: aim and scope of, 3-4, 9, 11, 15, 18, 49–51, 68–9, 83, 95–6, 97, 99–100, 111; compositional method of, 54–8, 68–70, 153, 156, 159, 176, 192, 196, 202, 221–2, 225–6 (*see also* reminiscence); confused with *Regularis concordia*, 92–7; date of, 5–12, 25n., 26, 98n., 99, 150, 227; lack of detail in, 68–9, 159, 170, 178, 182, 215, 216–17; liturgical significance of, 34–42, 100; manuscript of: *see* manuscripts, CCCC 265; organization of, 19, 27-34, 44, 77, 101, 104, 151–2; preface to, 4, 10, 19-20, 32, 37, 39, 53, 93, 94, 95, 96n., 111, 150–1, 227; problematic provisions in, 36, 40–1n., 69–70, 161–3, 176, 192, 201, 221–2, 224–6; reception of, medieval, 79–92; reception of, modern, 92–102; sources of, 19–68 *passim*, 150–228 *passim*; title of, 3–5, 92, 94–101
Letter to Sigeweard, 4n., 5
Letter to Sigefyrth, 4n.
Lives of Saints, 5, 27; of St Swithun, 47; *De oratione Moysi*, 47–8; Ash Wednesday, 177

Index

pastoral letters: 4, 5, 27, 69n., 80, 95n.; to
  Wulfsige (Brief I), 24–7, 33, 190, 198,
  202; to Wulfstan: (Brief 2a), 10, 192–3;
  (Brief 2), 25n., 73; (Brief II), 25n.; (Brief
  3), 25n., 73, 192–3, 201, 210; (Brief
  III), 24–7, 33, 88, 99–100, 170, 172,
  182, 183-4, 190, 191–2, 194, 198, 200,
  201, 202, 210
prefaces, 4n., 5, 52n., 53, 99, 150–1
Prognosticon futuri saeculi, epitome of, 52n.
Vita S. Æthelwoldi, 4n., 5, 52n., 58, 95n.,
  151, 177
'Wyrdwriteras', 49

Æthelmær, ealdorman ('se greata'), 6–16, 95n.,
  111; retirement to Eynsham, 13–15,
  48–9, 150, 213
Æthelred II, king, 6–7, 12–14, 45–9, 83, 150, 213
Æthelstan, king, 47n., 62n.
Æthelweard, ealdorman ('the Chronicler'), 6,
  9n., 12–13, 48, 52n., 150, 217
Æthelweard II, ealdorman, 8–10, 13
Æthelwine, ealdorman, 48
Æthelwold, bishop of Winchester, 3, 5, 9, 19,
  20, 22, 27, 30n., 34, 37n., 39, 40n., 42,
  43, 44, 45n., 46, 49, 51, 52, 53n., 55n.,
  82n., 85–7, 91, 93n., 94, 95n., 96, 97,
  99, 111, 150–1, 164, 188–9, 213, 227
'Agnus Dei', 25, 129, 135
Agobard, archbishop of Lyons, 61n.
alb, 119, 125, 131, 141, 170, 182
Alcuin, 60, 91n., 158
Aldhelm, 91
Alfred, king, 2, 47n.
'Alleluia', 30n., 119, 121, 123, 135, 137, 166,
  173–5, 179, 185, 204–5, 206, 208,
  218–19
All Saints, feast of, 139, 210; in dedication of
  Eynsham, 7, 216
All Saints, Office of, 28n., 135, 137, 204, 205;
  Lauds of, 117, 139, 211; Vespers of,
  208; *see also* antiphons
Amalarius of Metz, 39n., 96n., 102, 106, 111,
  119, 121, 125, 129, 131, 151, 169
  career of, 60–1, 169, 199
  works of:
    Eclogae de ordine romano, 74
    Liber de ordine antiphonarii, 61, 169, 218,
      224
    Liber officialis (or *De ecclesiasticis officiis*), 19,
      23n., 33, 35, 59–68, 74, 98n., 107, 111,
      208, 210, 222, 224; Ælfric's exemplar
      of, 62–5, 68, 166–7, 171, 196;
      allegorical method of, 65–8; dramatic
      potential exploited by Ælfric, 67–8,
      167, 168, 171, 174, 183, 185, 194,
      197–8; *Retractatio prima* of, 62–5; use as
      source for the *LME*, 59, 62-8, 151, 164,
      166–7, 168–9, 170–2, 172- 5, 176,
      178–9, 180–2, 183-4, 184–6, 187–8,
      190-4, 195-9, 200–2, 207; *see also*
      manuscripts, Salisbury, Cathedral
      Library, 154; *Institutio beati Amalarii de
      ecclesiasticis officiis*
ambo, 131
Ambrose, 157, 161–2
Anglo-Caroline minuscule, Style I, 86; Style IV,
  75–6, 83
Anglo-Saxon Chronicle, 6, 12–13, 14–15, 52n.
anniversaries, 143, 215, 216
anointing, 98n., 135, 141, 193, 200–1, 214
Anselm, archbishop of Canterbury, 84
'anti-monastic reaction', 45–6, 47–8, 83, 84n.
antiphoner, 30n., 35, 36n., 70, 107, 108, 139,
  145, 149, 165, 189, 200, 203, 218, 219,
  222
antiphons: at 'Benedictus', 127, 135, 188; at
  'Magnificat', 135, 137, 202; common of
  saints, 222; ferial, 119, 167; of All
  Saints, 137, 208; of Ash Wednesday,
  123, 178; of Candlemas, 119, 170–1; of
  Christmas, 117, 165–6; of Easter, 135,
  137, 203, 204, 205; of Epiphany, 119,
  168–9; of Maundy Thursday, 192; of
  Palm Sunday, 125, 183; of SS Stephen,
  John and the Holy Innocents, 117, 225;
  of Septuagesima through Lent, 30n., 35,
  121, 175–6; of Tenebrae, 127
antiphons, votive: of the BVM, 32, 115, 159; of
  the Holy Cross, 32, 115, 159; of an
  unnamed saint, 56, 115, 159
Apostles' Creed, 137, 204
apostles, feasts of, 139
Ascension, feast of, 145, 147, 221–2
Ash Wednesday, 121, 123, 163, 170, 176,
  177–8, 182
asperges, 37n., 113, 119, 125, 153, 155–6, 157
Athanasian Creed, 135, 204
auditorium, 38n., 141, 164, 205, 212
August, 147
Augustine of Hippo, 66, 113, 157; *Enarrationes
  in psalmos*, 145, 187, 220, 226

baptism, 40n., 73, 98n., 135, 169, 200–1; of
  Christ, 119, 168–9
Bateson, Mary, 4, 77–8, 94, 97–9, 100, 103,
  179, 216
Bede, the Venerable, 2, 3, 42, 51, 66, 85, 91,
  107, 157, 162, 195–6, 200
Beleth, Iohannes, 191, 197

246

Index

bells, 113; allegorical significance of, 63n.; at death of a monk, 143; at Nocturns, mass and Vespers on major feasts, 34n., 40n., 51, 119, 141, 165, 166, 167, 211; before mass, 40n.; first bell for Nocturns, 111, 141, 153; first bell for Terce, 28, 111, 113, 152, 170; first bell for Vespers, 141; not rung in Triduum, 189
Benedict of Aniane, 160
Benedict, St, 28, 41, 145, 211; in dedication of Eynsham, 216; *see also* Benedictine *Rule*
Benedictine Office, 152, 155
Benedictine reform (or revival): *see* reform, monastic
Benedictine *Rule*, 2, 3, 4, 10, 18, 21, 22n., 28, 29, 30, 37, 38, 42, 88n., 111, 113, 123, 139, 141, 150, 152, 155, 158, 175, 179–80, 186, 195, 209, 211, 213, 222, 227; Old English version of, 52, 86
benedictional, 107
Benedictional of Archbishop Robert: *see* manuscripts, Rouen, Bibliothèque Municipale, 369
'Benedictus', 127, 135, 188
Benevento, 139, 211
Bernold of Constance, 74, 208
biblical quotation, accuracy of, 66–7, 168, 178–9, 185, 197
Birinus, St, 86
bishop, 19, 25, 74, 83n., 91n., 129, 135, 192–3, 194, 200–1; bishops, monastic, 42, 85
blessing: in the Office, 113, 127, 137, 153, 187, 205; of candles, 119, 170; of palms, 125, 182–3; of ashes, 121, 123; of fire: *see* fire, new; of oils: *see* Chrism Mass
Bloet, Robert, bishop of Lincoln, 17
blood-letting, 115, 158
'booklet', in composite manuscripts, 21n., 76n.
books, liturgical, 30, 35, 36, 37, 106; *see also* antiphoner; benedictional; collectar; customary; gospel book; gradual (book); homiliary; lectionary; martyrology; missal; pontifical; psalter; sacramentary
Breck, Edward, 96–7, 98n., 99
breue, 34, 143, 214, 215–16
Brittany, 62, 63n.
burial, 143, 214–15; clothes for, 143
Bury-St-Edmunds, 86n.

Caesarius of Arles, 187
Candlemas, 24, 33, 56n., 57, 88, 117, 119, 169–72, 182, 183, 200; hymns of, 115, 161, 163

candles, 119, 131, 135, 141, 166, 201, 202; *see also* Candlemas; *harundo serpentina*; Paschal candle; Tenebrae
Canterbury: Christ Church Cathedral, 21, 75, 107, 108, 159, 182; St Augustine's Abbey, 108; *see also* Dunstan.; hymnal, Canterbury-type
Canterbury Benedictional: *see* manuscripts, London, BL, Harley 2892
canticles, 139, 205, 209; *see also* 'Benedictus'; 'Magnificat'; 'Nunc dimittis'
cantor, 40, 123, 125, 133, 135, 145, 152, 168, 198; *see also* choir master; *schola*
capitulum, 135, 137, 204
cathedrals, monastic, 20, 51, 83n., 186, 192; *see also* bishops, monastic; Canterbury, Christ Church Cathedral; Winchester, Old Minster; reform, monastic
Cernel Abbey, 5, 6–7, 12, 16n., 46, 48
Chapter, 28n., 29, 38, 54, 111, 113, 117, 127, 133, 155, 156, 164–5, 186, 205, 212, 215
Chapter mass: *see* mass, matutinal
Charlemagne, 60
charters: S 210, 8n.; S 658, 45n.; S 673, 45n.; S 745, 45n.; S 786, 45n.; S 788, 45n.; S 792, 14n., 45n., 213; S 812, 45n.; S 911 (Eynsham 'foundation charter'), 5–15, 45n., 98n., 99, 150, 213; S 1217, 7; S 1425, 16
chasubles, 41, 179
choir, 125, 127, 137, 143, 180, 188–9
choir master (*magister scholae*), 135, 152, 201; *see also* cantor
chrism, 73, 201; *see also* Chrism Mass
Chrism Mass, 36, 40–1n., 51, 74, 83n., 129, 131, 191, 192–4
circa, 41, 205
Christmas, 105, 164–6, 167; hymns of, 115, 161–3; masses of, 117, 165, 166; Night Office of, 117, 147, 149, 165, 225–6; Octave of, 117, 119, 149, 161, 166–7, 211, 225; special Chapter for, 117, 164–5; Vespers of, 117, 165; Vigil of, 117, 164–5
Circumcision, feast of, 172, 225; *see also* Christmas, Octave of
Claudius Pontifical I: *see* manuscripts, London, BL, Cotton Claudius A. iii
clergy, ranks of, 40, 73, 143, 191, 198, 210–11, 215; *see also* subdeacon, deacon, priest, bishop
clergy, secular, 8–9, 20, 25, 42, 82–3, 87–8, 100, 141, 214; *see also* Office, secular
cloister, 55n., 56, 113, 117, 125, 157, 164

247

Index

Cluny, influences of, 218, 221–2, 224, 226, 227
Cnut, king, 9–10n., 46n., 83
Coleman, 72n., 82n., 84n., 85, 87, 89, 186
collatio, 131, 195
collect: after burial, 143, 215; after Easter Vigil (Vespers), 202; after votive antiphon, 159; at Christmas Chapter, 117; at Day Offices of Easter, 135, 137; at processions, 119, 123, 125, 170; with *psalmi familiares*, 31, 38, 113, 154–5; with *psalmi prostrati*,180; with psalms after Chapter, 113, 156; with *trina oratio*, 30, 153
collect, at mass, 104, 121, 131, 133, 135, 139, 171, 174–5, 176, 196, 200, 201, 206–7
collectar, 86n., 107, 108
commendatio animae, 143, 145, 214
communion: frequency of, 32, 41, 113, 157; at the Easter Vigil, 24–5; during the Triduum, 133, 199; in the Chrism Mass, 131; for the sick, 141; *see also* mass; Mass of the Presanctified
communion chant, 25, 135, 202
Compline, 29, 30n., 31, 33n., 37, 113, 115, 123, 131, 135, 153, 154, 195, 205
confession: public at Chapter, 38n., 155; sacramental on Sundays, 32, 113, 157; special form at Chapter on Christmas, 117, 165
confraternal arrangements, 34, 41, 84, 143, 215, 216
cope, 56n., 57n., 119
corporal, 25, 133, 198
Cotton, Sir Robert, 94
Crediton, 108
Cross: principal mass of, 115, 158–9; votive antiphon of, 32, 115, 159; veiling of in Lent, 123, 179; *see also* Exaltation of the Cross, feast of; Veneration of the Cross
customary: definition and generic features of, 3–4, 18, 37, 68, 150; 'the customary' referring to the *Regularis concordia*, 19–20, 150–1, 158, 217
Cuthbert, St, 91

dalmatic, 131
deacon, 40, 41, 125, 131, 133, 179, 184, 198, 212, 215; *see also* clergy, ranks of
Dead, Office of, 28n., 38n., 205; Vigils of, 115, 143, 145, 159, 178, 206, 215; Lauds of, 159, 211; Vespers of, 159
Dead, prayers for, 31n., 32, 38n., 113, 143, 145, 153, 154, 156, 214–17; *see also* Dead, Office of

De consuetudine monachorum, 93, 96, 99; see also *Regularis concordia*
De ecclesiastica consuetudine, 23, 24–6, 33n., 63n., 87, 100, 107, 164, 177, 178, 184, 189, 197, 200, 201, 202, 205, 207, 212
depositio crucis, 40, 198
De regula S. Benedicti praecipui abbatis, 225
dominion, lay, 44–5, 48, 49, 141, 213
drink: *potus*, 117, 164; *mixtum*, 131, 195; *caritas*, 131, 195
Dunstan, archbishop of Canterbury, 20, 30n., 42, 85, 91, 151
Durandus, Gulielmus, 181–2, 188, 191, 197

Eadmer, 84n.
Eadnoth I, bishop of Dorchester, 17
Eadric Streona, ealdorman, 10n., 13
Eadui Basan, 75
Ealdred, bishop of Worcester, 75, 82–3
Easter, 32, 33, 38n., 69, 105, 121, 125, 139, 163, 178, 189, 202, 207, 211; Day Office of, 135, 137, 204–5, 224; Great Vigil of, 24, 39, 40n., 119, 133, 135, 139, 145, 185, 191, 192, 199-202, 207; Monday after, 117, 220; Night Office of, 40, 68, 135, 137, 145, 203–4, 207, 220, 225; Octave of, 33, 137, 145, 169, 203, 204, 205, 207, 208, 211, 220; Saturday after, 121; season of, 33n., 34, 35, 113, 156, 160, 205–6, 209, 221; seasonal hymns after, 35, 137, 160, 206, 209
Edgar, king, 7, 19, 20, 45-9, 50n., 84n., 93n., 111, 213
Edward the Elder, king, 62n.
Edward the Martyr, king, 45, 48, 83
Egbert Pontifical: see manuscripts, Paris, Bibliothèque Nationale, lat. 10575
Ely, 9, 48n., 86n., 88n.
Ember Days, 38n., 41, 60, 139, 141, 179, 207–8, 212–13
Epiphany, 119, 149, 168–9, 181; hymns of, 115, 161, 163; Octave of, 119, 149, 167, 226; Sundays after, 212, 220; Vigil of, 115, 119
Exaltation of the Cross, feast of, 38n., 41, 123, 164, 178, 212
Excerptiones Ecgberti, 73
excommunication, rite of, 74, 75
Exeter, 75, 107, 108
'Exultet', 199–200
Eynsham Abbey: Æthelmær's refoundation of, 5-9; Anglo-Norman refoundation, 16–17; cartulary of, 6n.; conditions at implied by the *LME*, 29–30, 35–6, 39–40, 68, 102, 152, 153, 198, 215;

248

Index

dedication of, 7, 68, 216–17; fourteenth-century customary of, 4n.; recent excavations of, 8; site of an earlier minster, 7–9; *see also* Ælfric, abbacy of; Æthelmær; Æthelweard II; charters, S 911

fasts, fasting, 41–2n., 119, 139, 168, 173, 174, 175, 210–11, 212–13; *see also* abstinence

fire, in winter, 55n., 115, 117, 164

fire, new, 64, 129, 190–1, 199

'First Worcester Fragment', 90–1

Fleury, 42n., 74

Florus of Lyons, 61n.

font, procession to: at Easter Vespers, 137, 205; at Easter Vigil, 135, 200; at the Vigil of Pentecost, 200, 207

foot washing: *see* maundy

genuflection: *see* kneeling

Ghent, 42n.

Glastonbury, 30n., 46, 108

'Gloria in excelsis Deo', 117, 119, 135, 139, 164, 166, 167, 173–4, 185, 206

'Gloria Patri', 123, 125, 127, 135, 180–2, 185–6

Good Friday, 33n., 65, 123, 125, 127, 131, 133, 145, 166, 184, 192, 194, 195–9; *see also* Mass of the Presanctified; Triduum; Veneration of the Cross

gospel: at *collatio*, 131, 195; at mass, 41n., 119, 123, 125, 133, 135, 167, 178, 179, 182, 202; at the Night Office, 117, 119, 165, 166; explanation of at Chapter, 186; Passion gospel, 125, 131, 133, 184, 192, 196

gospel book, 131, 133, 196–7

gradual (book), 39, 198, 199, 201

gradual chant, 123, 137, 178, 202, 204, 208

gradual psalms, 28n., 41, 143, 180, 216

Great Malvern, 84n.

Gregory I, pope, 66, 75n., 133, 135, 189, 200, 201, 203

Gregory IV, pope, 61

'Gregorian' readings, 39n., 133, 200

Gregorian Sacramentary, 158, 170, 174–5, 176, 196, 197, 199, 200, 201, 206–7

harundo serpentina, 129, 191

hermeneutic style, 51–3, 54n.; *see also* Ælfric, Latinity of

history (Office), 139, 210, 217, 218–19, 223

Holy Innocents, feast of, 33n., 117, 119, 166–7, 168; Octave of, 166, 225

Holy Saturday, 40, 65, 117, 127, 131, 133, 135, 145, 166, 199, 207; *see also* Triduum

Holy Week: Wednesday in, 125, 182, 184; *see also* Good Friday; Holy Saturday; Maundy Thursday; Palm Sunday; Triduum

homiliary, 88–90, 186, 220, 221

homilies: *see* Ælfric, works of; homiliary; lessons (at the Office)

Hrabanus Maurus, 73, 193

Hugh, bishop of Lincoln, 16

hymnal, 30n., 35, 107, 108, 139, 160, 209; Canterbury-type, 160–4, 206, 209; 'New Hymnal', 86, 160; Winchester-Worcester type, 86, 160–4, 206, 209; *see also* hymns

hymns, 30n., 33, 35, 36, 86, 105, 135, 139, 178, 204, 205, 207; in Paschaltide, 137, 206; in summer, 139, 209; in winter, 115, 159–64; on Palm Sunday, 183; peculiarities in Ælfric's hymnal, 161–3; *see also* 'Gloria in excelsis Deo'; sequence hymn; 'Te Deum'

incense, 119, 131, 135, 141, 166, 202

Institutio beati Amalarii de ecclesiasticis officiis, 63n., 107–8, 164, 168; see also Amalarius, *Liber officialis*

interval, summer, 38n., 139, 205, 211, 227

introit, 121, 123, 139, 141, 174–5, 177, 178, 208, 212

invitatory, 119, 125, 127, 135, 168, 181–2, 185–6

Isidore of Seville, 193, 210

Jerome, 66, 179

John the Baptist, St: Nativity, feast of, 139, 209; Decollation, feast of, 209

John the Evangelist, St: feast of, 149, 166; Octave of, 166, 225

John of Worcester, 80n.

Joscelyn, John, 92–4, 96, 99n.

Judoc, St, 62n., 86

'King Edgar's Establishment of the Monasteries', 19n., 52n.

kneeling, 56, 117, 133, 137, 141, 178, 197, 206, 212

'Kyrie eleison', 105, 123, 135, 137, 153, 170, 180; as special Triduum responsory, 127, 188–9

laity, 40, 88, 141, 153, 171, 214; *see also* dominion, lay

Lanfranc, *Monastic Constitutions* of, 3, 15

Lauds, 29, 31, 32, 33n., 37, 38n., 104, 113, 115, 117, 123, 127, 135, 139, 147, 154,

Index

Lauds (cont.)
  159, 165, 188, 203–4, 205, 211, 224–5, 227; see also All Saints, Office of; 'Benedictus'; Dead, Office of; hymns
law codes, 88; *IV Edgar*, 73n., 74, 76, 81
lectionary, 36n., 70, 107, 218, 220; see also gospel; lessons
Lent, 33n., 36, 41, 123, 125, 141, 172, 176, 178-80; 1st Sunday in, 123, 178–9, 212; 2nd Sunday in, 176; 4th Sunday in (*mediante*), 125, 145, 180, 218, 219; 5th Sunday in, 180 (see also Passion Sunday); hymns in, 115, 161, 163–4; meals in, 38n., 195 (see also fasts, fasting); Night Office in, 145, 217, 218–19, 226; repetition of Sunday masses in, 149, 227
Leofric Collectar: see manuscripts, London, BL, Harley 2961
Leofric Missal: see manuscripts, Oxford, Bodleian Library, Bodley 579
lessons:
  at mass: during Lent and on Ember Days, 41–2n., 179; Easter Vigil, 133, 135, 200–2; first Sunday in Lent, 123, 178; Good Friday, 131, 196; reader of the epistle to fast, 139, 210–11; Septuagesima Sunday, 121, 174–5; Vigil of Pentecost, 139, 206–7; see also gospel (at mass)
  at the Office: 19, 35, 36, 69, 127, 165, 166, 168, 203, 205, 210, 217-29 *passim*
  from homilies on the gospel, 135, 147, 220
  from saints' lives and passions, 139, 147, 149
  from scripture:
    Heptateuch, 218–19, 226
    Genesis, 145, 219, 226
    Exodus, 145, 219, 226
    Kings, Esdras, Tobit, Judith, Esther, Job: 147, 222
    'Solomon, books of', 147, 223
    Proverbs, Ecclesiastes, Song of Songs, Wisdom, Ecclesiasticus, 223
    Isaiah, 147, 149, 224, 225, 226
    Jeremiah, 145, 159, 219
    Lamentations, 145, 219, 220
    Ezechiel, 147, 149, 224
    Daniel, 147, 224
    minor prophets, 147, 224
    Maccabees, 147, 223
    Acts, 147, 220, 221, 225
    Pauline epistles, 145, 149, 220
    canonical epistles, 145, 220, 226
    Revelation, 145, 225
  from sermons, 147, 149, 220, 221, 222, 225
  readings continued in refectory, 149, 226
  three lessons retained on summer ferias, 41, 43, 149, 222, 226, 227
  see also Augustine of Hippo; gospel (at the Night Office); capitulum
litany, 86n., 137, 206; after Prime, 28n., 113, 152, 204; before principal mass, 139, 210; in procession to the font, 135, 139, 200, 207; in visitation of the sick, 141, 214
Lord's Prayer, 26, 113, 119, 123, 133, 135, 137, 143, 153, 170, 178, 180, 215
Louis the Pious, 60, 61
Lucy, St, feast of, 212

Magi, 119, 168
'Magnificat', 135, 137, 188, 202
manuscripts:
  Boulogne-sur-Mer
    Bibliothèque Municipale
      63: 210–11
      82: 63n.
  Cambridge
    Corpus Christi College
      41: 107, 158, 176, 197, 223–4
      146: 87n.
      178: 86n., 89
      190: 23n., 36n., 74n., 77, 80n., 87, 107, 200, 206, 212, 220
      192: 63n.
      198: 179
      201: 33n., 152, 197
      265: 19n., 63n., 71-91, 92–3, 94, 98n., 103; description of, 71-7; *LME* in, 71, 74, 76–7, 79-82, 87; marginal glosses to *LME* in, 92–3n.; scripts in, 74–7; Wulfstan's 'commonplace book', relation to, 71, 72–3, 76, 77–91
      270: 108, 158, 176, 197, 200
      391: 86n., 108, 218, 222–4, 226
      422: 189, 214
    Trinity College
      B. 11. 2 [241]: 62n., 63n.
    University Library
      Gg. 3. 28: 90n., 179, 223
      Ii. 4. 6: 179
  Columbia
    University of Missouri Library
      Fragmenta Manuscripta 1: 220
  Copenhagen
    Kongelige Bibliotek
      Gl. Kgl. Sam. 1595: 78–9

250

Index

Durham
Cathedral Library
A. iv. 19: 159
B. iii. 32: 160
Le Havre
Bibliothèque Municipale
330: 108, 158, 170, 176, 207
London
British Library
Cotton Claudius A. iii: 107, 200
Cotton Faustina B. iii: 21–2, 94, 167, 207, 216–17
Cotton Nero A. i: 77
Cotton Nero E. i: 81
Cotton Tiberius A. iii: 21–2, 93–4, 95, 98n., 99n., 159, 167, 207, 216, 217
Cotton Vespasian A. xiv: 78
Harley 2892: 107, 170, 182–3
Harley 2904: 87n.
Harley 2961: 108, 161, 163
Orléans
Bibliothèque Municipale
127 [105]: 108, 158, 176, 197, 200, 201, 207, 214
Oxford
Bodleian Library
Barlow 37: 74n., 78, 81
Bodley 579: 108, 158, 176, 197, 200, 202, 214
Bodley 718: 77
Hatton 113–14: 89
Hatton 115: 89n.
Junius 121: 78, 89n.
Laud misc. 482: 214
Christ Church
Eynsham Cart.: 6n.
Corpus Christi College
197: 86n.
Paris
Bibliothèque Nationale
lat. 3182: 77
lat. 10575: 108, 193, 200
nouv. acq. lat. 1983: 63n.
Rouen
Bibliothèque Municipale
274 [Y. 6]: 108, 158, 170, 176, 197, 200, 201, 214
368 [A. 27]: 108, 193
369 [Y. 7]: 107, 193
1382 [U. 109]: 36n., 87, 107, 220
Salisbury
Cathedral Library
154: 64–5, 67, 109, 166–7, 168, 173, 176, 178, 184–6, 187–8, 190-4

Worcester
Cathedral Library
F. 160: 108, 165–6, 169, 222
F. 174: 90
Martin, St, feast of, 117, 164, 176
martyrology, 30n., 38n., 117, 155, 164–5
Mary, the Blessed Virgin: Assumption, feast of, 139, 209; in dedication of Eynsham, 216; Nativity, feast of, 139, 209; principal mass of, 115, 158–9; Purification of, 119 (*see also* Candlemas); votive antiphon of, 32, 115, 159
mass:
insufficient number for Sundays after Pentecost, 141, 211
matutinal, 28n., 29n., 38n., 54n., 111, 113, 152–3, 155, 156, 157, 205; after Christmas and Epiphany, 167; for the Dead, 143, 215; for the king, 44, 158; for the sick, 141, 215; of Christmas, 117, 165; of ferias 32, 44, 115, 158; of Palm Sunday, 125, 182; of Sundays, 32, 115, 158; offerings at, 125, 180
not celebrated on Good Friday, 25, 131, 194
of the day: *see* mass, principal
of the poor, 129, 190
principal, 29n., 34n., 111, 113, 117, 131, 139, 141, 152–3, 156, 167, 210, 211; in Christmas Octave, 117, 119; lay presence at, 40, 153; of Candlemas, 119, 171; of Christmas, 117; of Easter Day, 204; of Fridays and Saturdays, 32, 115, 158–9; of Maundy Thursday, 129, 131, 191–2; offerings at, 125, 180; processions before, 41, 113, 122, 155–6, 178
private, 143, 157, 215
repetition of Sunday masses during the week, 41n., 149, 227–8
see also: 'Agnus Dei'; 'Alleluia'; Chrism Mass; collect (at mass); communion; communion chant; Easter, Great Vigil of; 'Gloria in excelsis Deo'; gospel (at mass); gradual chant; introit; lessons (at mass); Mass of the Presanctified; offertory; peace, kiss of; tract
Mass of the Presanctified, 25–6, 133, 192, 194, 198–9
maundy: of the monks, 131, 135, 141, 189, 195; of the poor, 129, 141, 190, 213
Maundy Thursday, 25n., 65, 74, 76, 123, 127, 129, 131, 133, 145, 163, 166, 177, 184–95 *passim*, 196, 199; *see also* Chrism Mass; Triduum

251

Index

meals, 28, 38, 131, 143, 178, 195; with whom and where allowed, 141, 214
Michael, St, feast of, 139, 209
missal, 108; *see also* sacramentary
Missal of Robert of Jumièges: *see* manuscripts, Rouen, Bibliothèque Municipale, 274
Missal of St Augustine's Abbey: *see* manuscripts, CCCC 270
Missal of the New Minster: *see* manuscripts, Le Havre, Bibliothèque Municipale, 330
Mores, Edward-Rowe, 94–5
morrow mass: *see* mass, matutinal

Nasmith, James, 94
Night Office, 10, 19, 28n., 29, 30n., 31, 33, 34n., 35, 36, 37, 38n., 40, 41, 43, 69, 102, 105, 113, 115, 117, 119, 127, 135, 137, 139, 141, 145, 147, 149, 151, 153, 165, 166, 167, 168, 175, 180–2, 184–9, 203–4, 205, 207–8, 209, 210, 211, 215, 217–28 *passim*; *see also* All Saints, Office of; Dead, Office of; hymns; lessons (at the Office); responsories
Nocturns: *see* Night Office
None, 29n., 38, 111, 113, 115, 117, 121, 123, 129, 131, 133, 137, 156, 163, 177, 206
November, 28, 32, 55, 115, 139, 147, 159, 160, 178, 209
'Nunc dimittis', 137, 205

occurrence, rules governing, 30n., 35, 115, 139, 209–10
'Octave', uses of term, 220–1, 222; *see also* individual feasts
October, 27, 41, 111, 147, 156, 159, 177, 178, 223
offertory, 25, 125, 135, 143, 180, 192
Office, Divine: 28, 29, 34, 37, 39n., 61, 69, 102, 106, 115, 117, 137, 164, 178, 186, 191, 203, 204, 205, 217
daily and seasonal divisions of:
feasts and Sundays, 28, 32, 38n., 113, 115, 117, 137, 139, 155–6, 157, 164, 203, 211
ferias: 28, 29, 38n., 41, 54n., 111, 113, 119, 139, 149, 151–3, 156, 164, 167, 211
summer period, 10, 28, 38, 41, 54n., 111, 113, 139, 149, 151, 153, 156, 159, 164, 178, 205, 209, 211, 217
winter period, 10, 28–9, 32–3, 55, 111, 113, 115, 149, 151, 153, 156, 167, 178, 205, 209; *see also* November; October; September
see also All Saints, Office of; antiphons;

Benedictine *Rule*; 'Benedictus'; canticles; capitulum; Chapter; collect; Compline; Dead, Office of; 'Gloria Patri'; gospel (at the Office); history (Office); hymns; interval, summer; invitatory; Lauds; lessons (at the Office); Lord's Prayer; 'Magnificat'; Night Office; None; Office, secular; *preces*; Prime; *responsorium breue*; responsories; Sext; 'Te Deum'; Terce; verse; versicle; Vespers
Office, secular, 9n., 66, 69–70, 87, 127, 133, 135, 152, 168–9, 189–90, 199, 200, 203–5, 207, 218, 221, 222, 224–5
oils, holy: *see* chrism; Chrism Mass
orationes solemnes, 133, 197–8
ordo, 33n., 54, 69, 70, 74, 76, 104, 170, 177, 181, 182, 193, 194, 196, 214, 217–18, 220, 222, 223
Ordines romani:
XIII, 69–70, 217–26 *passim*
XIII A, 36, 217–21, 225–6
XIII B, 217, 221, 223, 225, 226
XIII D, 217, 218, 222, 223, 225
XXIV, 197
XXVI, 191
XXVII, 197
XXVIII, 181, 191, 197
XXIX, 191, 197
XXXI, 181, 197
L, 191, 206, 222
Oswald, archbishop of York, 20, 30n., 42, 48, 82–3, 84n., 85, 87, 91

Palm Sunday, 24, 33n., 36, 125, 170, 182–4, 186
Parker, Matthew, 92–3
Paschal candle, 133, 199–200
Paschasius Radbertus, 199
Passion Sunday, 36, 145, 163, 180–2, 185, 219, 226
Passiontide, 33, 125, 145, 160, 180–2; hymns of, 115, 163
paten, 41–2n., 139, 210
peace, kiss of, 24–5, 113, 129, 131, 191, 194, 202
penitential psalms: after Prime, 28, 111, 152, 215; for a dead monk, 41, 143, 215, 216; within the *psalmi prostrati*, 180; within the *trina oratio*, 153; in visitation of the sick, 141
Pentecost, 34, 85n., 137, 147, 169, 191; Day Office of, 207; hymns of, 137, 206; Night Office of, 139, 207–8, 222, 225; Octave of, 38n., 60, 105, 113, 123, 137, 139, 147, 156, 177, 178, 205, 207,

252

Index

208–9, 212–13, 222; Sundays after, 211–12; Vigil of, 39, 139, 200, 206–7
Peter, St, 216–17
Peterborough Abbey, 88n.
pontifical, 33n., 107, 108, 192, 199; *see also* Romano-German Pontifical
Pontificale Lanaletense: *see* manuscripts, Rouen, Bibliothèque Municipale, 368
porch (*porticus*), 127, 188
Portiforium of St Wulfstan: see manuscripts, CCCC 391
preces, 31, 113, 117, 123, 127, 137, 153, 154, 177, 204, 205; *pro peccatis*, 123, 180
pre-Lent, 35–6, 172; *see also* Quinquagesima; Septuagesima; Sexagesima
Presentation, feast of: *see* Candlemas
priest, 41, 119, 125, 129, 135, 143, 179, 198, 200–1, 212; *see also* clergy, ranks of
Prime, 28n., 29, 30n., 32, 38, 111, 113, 115, 123, 127, 135, 137, 151–2, 153, 154, 155, 156, 157, 164, 165, 167, 189, 204, 205, 210, 215
prior, 54, 82, 83, 88, 113, 135, 155, 186; as term for abbot, 203
procession: at Candlemas, 119, 170; before principal mass on Sundays, 41, 113, 155–6; in visitation of the sick, 141; on Palm Sunday, 125, 182–3; on Wednesdays and Fridays in Lent and summer, 123, 177, 178; *see also* font, procession to
psalmi familiares, 30–1, 32, 38, 44, 113, 139, 153–5, 205, 206
psalmi prostrati, 123, 180
psalter, 29n., 37, 87, 108, 109, 127, 168, 190, 215
pseudo-Alcuin, 187–8, 191, 197
pueri, 28, 45n., 111, 125, 127, 152, 188; see also schola
Purification, feast of, 117, 119: *see* Candlemas

Quinquagesima, 36n., 66n., 121, 123, 172, 176–7

Ramsey Abbey, 30n., 48, 86n., 87
reading (*lectio*), 28, 38, 111, 117, 141, 152, 164, 178
refectory, 44, 117, 131, 133, 141, 149, 164, 195, 214, 226
reform, monastic, 9–10, 19-20, 36, 41–2, 42–51, 62, 70, 82–6, 91, 97, 100, 157, 160; Carolingian precedents for, 21, 22n., 49–50, 59, 66n.; 'English' character of, 28n., 34n., 42–3, 51, 166, 211; *see also* Ælfric, as reformer; bishops, monastic; cathedrals, monastic; *Regularis concordia*; uniformity, liturgical
'regular order' (= monastic Office), 137, 139, 207; *see also* Office, Divine
Regularis concordia: Ælfric's exemplar of, 21-7, 36–7, 57, 68, 167, 184, 216–17; allegorical exposition in, 188–9, 208; authorship of, 3, 19, 111, 151; 'epilogue' to, 34, 53, 54n., 217; Eynsham monks' familiarity with, 18, 30, 50, 111, 151, 153, 155; influence on charters, 14n.; Latin style of, 53–4, 55n., 97; manuscripts of, 21-6, 27, 34n., 36, 53, 54n., 56n., 93–4, 97n., 98, 167, 202, 207, 216–17; Old English translations of, 33n., 93–4, 95–7, 98–9n., 152, 197; organization of, 21, 27–8; political aspect of, 15, 34, 42–9, 153–4, 158, 213; proem to, 19, 34, 42–51, 53–4, 213–14; transmission of, 22, 27, 50, 68, 83; use as source for the *LME*, 19–58, 93, 96, 150–217 *passim*; *see also* customary
relics, 68, 115, 123, 159, 179
Remigius, bishop of Lincoln, 16–17
reminiscence, 66n., 67, 167, 171–2, 172–5, 200
responsorium breue, 139, 204, 207
responsories: 19, 35, 36, 166, 170, 205, 218–19; 'Gloria Patri' dropped after, 125, 180–2, 185; of Ascension, 147, 221–2; of Advent, 147; of August through November, 147, 223–4; of Christmas, 117, 147, 165; of Christmas Octave, 149; of Easter, 135, 145, 203, 220; of Easter Octave, 145, 220; of Epiphany, 149; of Epiphany Octave, 149, 226; of Passiontide, 145, 219; of Pentecost, 139, 147; of Pentecost Octave, 147, 222; of saints' days, 139, 147, 149, 222; of Septuagesima through Lent, 145, 218–19; of the Triduum, 127, 145, 220
Retractatio prima: *see* Amalarius, *Liber officialis*; manuscripts, Salisbury, Cathedral Library, 154
Rochester, 46
Roman Office: *see* Office, secular
Romano-German Pontifical, 74, 83n., 191, 193, 197
royalty, prayers for, 28n ; *see also* mass, matutinal; *psalmi familiares*

sacramentary, 30n., 33n., 39, 40, 86, 107, 108, 139, 165, 176, 193, 199, 200, 201, 206–7, 211; *see also* Gregorian Sacramentary; missal

253

Index

sacristan, 119, 127
St Albans Abbey, 16
St John Lateran, basilica of, 217-18
saints' days, 117, 147, 222; *see also individual saints*; occurrence
Samson, bishop of Worcester, 84n.
Samson Pontifical: *see* manuscripts, CCCC 146
schola, 141, 151, 152, 157; schola cantorum, 152, 198; *see also pueri*; choir master
Sedulius, Caelius, 161, 194
September, 147, 223; *see also* Exaltation of the Cross
Septuagesima, 33, 36n., 60, 65, 119, 121, 139, 149, 172-6, 179, 182; hymns of, 115, 163; Night Office lessons and responsories, 145, 218–19, 226; Night Office antiphons, 30n., 35, 121, 175–6; Septuagesima Sunday, 121, 147, 174–5, 185, 204, 219, 224–5
sequence hymn, 137, 204–5
sermons: *see* lessons (at the Office); homiliary; Ælfric, works of; Wulfstan of York, works of
Sexagesima, 36n., 66n., 121, 172, 176, 179
Sext, 28n., 111, 113, 115, 123, 129, 137, 153, 156, 177, 206
shaving, 40, 125, 180
shoes, 28n., 111, 127, 133, 143
sick: care for the, 34, 141, 143, 214; permitted to sit during the Office, 115; permitted to eat outside refectory, 141, 214
silence, rule of, 38, 205, 212
silent days (*swigdagas*), 185–6
Sixtus, St, 176
Stephen, St, feast of, 149, 166; Octave of, 166, 225
stole, 56n., 57n., 119, 121, 143, 215
Stow St Mary's, 17
stripping of altars, 129, 192, 196–7
subdeacon, 40, 41, 179, 198, 210–11, 215; *see also* clergy, ranks of
substrate, vernacular: *see* Ælfric, Latinity of
Swein Forkbeard, king, 14–15
Swithun, St, 86
Silvester I, pope, 200
Symons, Thomas, 100, 102, 104, 109

tabula, 54n., 127, 143, 189
'Te Deum', 119, 134, 165, 166, 203
Tenebrae, 127, 187–8, 190
Terce, 28n., 29, 30n., 111, 113, 115, 117, 119, 123, 125, 137, 152, 153, 155, 156, 157, 163, 165, 170, 183, 205, 206
Testimonie of Antiquitie, 93
Theodulf of Orléans, 73, 183

Thierry of Amorbach, 42n.
Thomas, archbishop of York, 85
Thorney Abbey, 14, 45, 213
thurible: *see* incense
tract, 131, 133, 178, 196, 200, 202, 206–7
'Tremulous Hand' of Worcester, 90
Triduum, 24, 36, 64, 65, 69, 88, 169, 181–2, 184–9 *passim*, 205, 220; *see also* Good Friday; Holy Saturday; Maundy Thursday
trina oratio, 28n., 29n., 30–1, 32, 111, 113, 153, 215
Trinity, Holy, 125; feast of (Trinity Sunday), 139, 147, 208–9; matutinal mass of, 115, 158; Octave of, 222

uniformity, liturgical, 49–51, 66, 151; *see also* reform, monastic

Venantius Fortunatus, 163
Veneration of the Cross, 38–9, 40, 123, 127, 133, 179, 190, 198
verse, 133, 135, 137, 170, 205, 218, 219, 223–4
versicle, 135, 137, 159, 180, 186, 203, 204
Vespers, 31, 32, 33, 34n., 37, 38, 113, 115, 117, 119, 123, 131, 133, 135, 137, 139, 141, 154, 159, 165, 166, 167, 168, 188, 192, 196, 199, 204, 207, 209, 211, 212, 225; first and second Vespers, 160; *see also* All Saints, Office of; Dead, Office of; hymns; 'Magnificat'
vesting: for mass, 117, 123, 165; for processions, 119, 125; removal of vestments, 131; *see also* burial, clothes for
vigil: *see individual feasts*
Vigils: *see* Night Office
Vikings, raids by, 47, 62
Visitatio sepulchri, 40, 68, 208

Wærferth, bishop of Worcester, 91n.
Wanley, Humphrey, 94, 96n.
washing, 40, 111, 117; of altars and church floor, 127, 190; of corpse, 143; *see also* maundy
Westbury-on-Trym, 30n., 84
Wilfrid of Ripon, 91
William of Malmesbury, 82n., 85
Winchcombe Sacramentary: *see* Orléans, Bibliothèque Municipale, 127
Winchester, 19, 20, 39, 46, 48, 86–7, 93n., 111, 192; Council of, 19n., 42n., 50; influence on Worcester, 85–7, 100; New Minster, 30n., 45n., 62n., 107, 108; Old Minster, 5, 30n., 36–7, 46, 86, 97, 151, 192, 227

254

Index

Worcester, 63n., 69n., 72–3, 75, 81n., 82–7, 88–91, 93, 107–8; Ælfric's reputation at, 88–91; conservatism of, 84–7, 91; Old English manuscripts copied at, 84, 88–91; preaching at, 88–90; scripts written at, 72, 74–5, 86; Winchester influence on, 85–7, 100
work, 28, 38, 119, 141, 164, 167, 189, 211
Wulfsige, bishop of Sherborne, 24, 25
Wulfstan II, archbishop of York, 2, 5, 10, 24, 25–6, 72–3, 77–82, 87–8, 91n., 95n., 99–100, 170, 172, 182, 183, 192, 194, 210; *Canons of Edgar*, 88n.; 'commonplace book' of, 23n., 63n., 69n., 71, 72–3, 77–82, 87, 212, 220; hand of, 78; liturgical interests of, 87–8; reputation at Worcester, 88; sermons of, 73, 81n., 87n.; styled 'abbot', 80, 88
Wulfstan II, bishop of Worcester, 72n., 82–91, 186; as a reformer, 82–7, 88–91; episcopacy of, 83–4, 88; priorate of, 82–3, 88; *see also* manuscripts, CCCC 391; Oxford, Bodleian Library, Hatton 113–14
Wulfstan of Winchester, 58, 177

York, 79n., 83, 88, 107